Contemplating
Edith Stein

Edith Stein during the summer vacation of 1926 in Breslau.
Photograph courtesy of Edith-Stein-Archiv, Karmel "Maria vom Frieden," Cologne.

Contemplating Edith Stein

edited by

JOYCE AVRECH BERKMAN

UNIVERSITY OF NOTRE DAME PRESS

Notre Dame, Indiana

Library of Congress Cataloging in-Publication Data

Contemplating Edith Stein / edited by Joyce Avrech Berkman.
   p. cm.
   Includes bibliographical references and index.
   ISBN 0-268-02188-0 (cloth : alk. paper)
   ISBN 0-268-02189-9 (pbk. : alk. paper)
   1. Stein, Edith, Saint, 1891–1942.   2. Christian philosophers—Germany—
Biography.   3. Carmelite Nuns—Germany—Biography.   4. Christian
martyrs—Germany—Biography.   I. Berkman, Joyce Avrech.
   BX4705.S814C66   2006
   193—dc22

                                    2005034403

∞ *This book is printed on acid-free paper.*

Dedicated with joy to my deep-hearted family,

admirably always ready to question,

and to the Queen Esthers and Saint Teresas of our world

Contents

$\mathcal{A}$cknowledgments

Edith Stein's analysis of the potential for a creative synergistic relationship between individual and community applies richly to my experience, individually and collaboratively, in editing and contributing essays to this volume. From the outset of my work on this book to its physical weight in your hands, a community of Stein scholars has shaped my thought and nourished my energy and morale.

In identifying those Stein scholars most responsible for this volume, my first debt is to an extraordinary woman and scholar no longer alive, though her spirit animates this entire work. Although my scholarship on Edith Stein began in 1991, the idea of editing a volume of essays did not form in my mind until 1992, after I met Sr. Mary Catharine Baseheart, SCN, who, until her death in 1994, directed the Edith Stein Center for Study and Research at Spalding University in Louisville, Kentucky. Sr. Mary Catharine, who subsequently invited me as keynote speaker for the Center's 1996 lecture series, urged that I take a first step toward writing a biography of Stein by editing a volume of essays on her. I sensed that Sr. Mary Catharine took particular glee in my being neither Catholic nor a philosopher and thus possibly able to bring new perspectives, those of the social and intellectual historian steeped in interdisciplinary methods, to Stein analysis. Her hope, too, was that my interdisciplinary orientation might extend knowledge of Stein beyond its usual restricted audience. She argued that Stein was captive to hagiographers and self-serving Catholic educators who focused on her spiritual journey at the expense of her philosophical contributions. Sr. Mary Catharine's own posthumously published work on Stein's philosophy, the first comprehensive English-language account of Stein's secular thought, testifies to her mission to introduce Stein's intellectual brilliance and range to a wide scholarly audience. Not only did Sr. Mary Catharine inspire my work, she provided me with critical sources, such as the then unpublished English translation of Stein's *Philosophy of Psychology and the Humanities* that she and another dedicated Stein scholar, Marianne Sawicki, were jointly translating.

Not long after my early conversations with Sr. Mary Catharine, I met another published Stein scholar, Linda Lopez McAlister, professor emerita of philosophy and women's studies at the University of South Florida. During a dinner conversation with Linda in 1998 I raised the idea of our collaborating on a volume of scholarly essays on Stein-as-philosopher for the English reading public. As it turned out, she, too, harbored the ambition of editing such a volume. We were both ardently committed to a historically grounded critical examination of Stein's complex life and diverse secular writings. Fervent feminists (Linda had already published an essay on Stein's feminism, her essay originally delivered as the lecture that inaugurated Spalding University's Edith Stein Center), we issued a call for papers in autumn 1998 that reflected our shared goals, seeking writing that recognized Stein's pioneering position as a modern Catholic feminist and as a woman in the historically male-dominated field of philosophy. To our regret and largely for reasons of health, Linda was unable to continue beyond 2001 as this volume's coeditor. I remain most grateful that at least for a brief and formative time I found a colleague with kindred vision and initiative when this volume was but a gleam in our eyes.

Many of this volume's scholars have provided essential intellectual and psychological support. Even a simple sentence in an e-mail of twinkling sympathy with the patience and mental stamina that editing a volume for publication entails hoisted me over a difficult barrier. I had the pleasure of conversing with five of the volume's authors at the American Philosophical Association Conference in New York City in late December 2000. Several of us presented papers on a Stein panel that Linda had organized. One of the panelists, Sarah Borden, was of significant help at critical junctures. Sarah Borden's thorough Stein bibliography alerted me to key primary and secondary sources, while her unpublished and published scholarship on Stein stimulated and clarified my thought. At a vital time, Sarah loaned me her personal copy of the German edition of Stein's autobiography. Since Linda was no longer available to translate German scholars' essays selected for this volume, Sarah located two translators for two of these essays, Jonathan Knutzen and Stephen Lake. Fr. John Sullivan, OCD, who was a member of the audience at the Stein panel and has contributed an essay to this volume, provided timely, cheerful help and facilitated my contact with two other dedicated Stein scholars: Steven Payne, Editor-in-Chief, ICS Publications, and Sr. Josephine Koeppel, OCD. Sr. Josephine, as American representative of Sr. Maria Amata Neyer, OCD, director of the Edith-Stein-Archive in Cologne, Germany, kindly authorized use of photographs for this volume that Steven Payne made available.

Although our Stein comradeship began several years before the conference, Anthony (Tony) Calcagno occupies a unique place in my heart among this volume's authors. Initially based on e-mail cameraderie, our friendship steadily deepened. When we arranged to meet in person, Tony and his father hosted me and my husband at their home in Toronto. Tony has become one of our most cherished friends. Multilingual and with extraordinary generosity, he translated two of the other German essays contained here as well as the one Italian essay. His command of the thought of major contemporary Continental philosophers and his invaluable scholarly writings on Husserl and Stein, important as these were in elevating me into new realms of understanding of Stein, hardly begin to suggest the magnitude of his help and support through the unflagging care and goodness he exercised in response to my stream of scholarly questions and publication concerns. In his spirited Italian, Tony would conclude a paragraph or e-mail with "Forza e Corragio," the very words I needed to embrace.

Profoundly meaningful for me in pursuing this project was my time in Rome from October 8 to 11, 1998, for Stein's canonization. I traveled there with Elizabeth Carr, Catholic chaplain at Smith College. Elizabeth has her own scholarly relationship to Stein and teaches courses on women saints, including Stein. In addition to the Stein conference held at the Teresianum, my stay in Rome included a meeting with Linda Lopez McAlister to reflect on current Stein scholarship and develop plans for the volume we were still at that time to coedit.

Moving beyond the community of Stein scholars included in this volume, I heartily thank Stein scholars whose work does not appear here, singling out two prominent scholars in particular: John Wilcox and Marianne Sawicki. Wilcox, succeeding Sr. Mary Catharine as director of the Stein Center at Spalding University, guided me in my later research visits at the center. Marianne Sawicki's published English translation of Stein's treatises and her illuminating scholarship on Stein are indispensable to a precise, indeed phenomenologically sound, understanding of Stein's philosophy. Susanne Batzdorff, Stein's niece, clarified several confusing matters for me. Sr. Maria Amata Neyer, OCD, whom I met at the Edith-Stein-Archiv of the Cologne Carmel several days before I joined the Fulbright German Studies Summer (2000) Seminar in Berlin, provided particular assistance. I owe my meeting with Sr. Maria Amata Neyer to a non-Stein scholar, Britta Zangen, who hosted me in Düsseldorf and drove me to a number of key Stein sites in Germany. The visit with Sr. Maria Amata Neyer, the tour with Britta, and the Fulbright German Studies Summer Seminar enriched my knowledge of Stein archival holdings and grounded my understanding of Stein geographically and historically. I had many invigorating conversations about Stein with another Fulbright scholar, Elizabeth Baer. During this same visit in Germany I met and launched a friendship with volume contributor Theresa Wobbe.

An array of friends, students, and colleagues contributed to research and editorial dimensions of this volume. Particularly notable among these were Tiziana Rota, who translated the Italian text on Stein's philosophy by Luciana Vigone; Professor Eva Reuschmann, who translated Stein's writings on the state; and

Professor Emeritus Alex Page, who translated letters by Stein, letters to me from German scholars, and scholarly German texts. The Guatemalan-American playwright/professor Arthur Giron spoke most helpfully with me about his play *Edith Stein* and shared with me his chapbook and research on Stein. U.S. colleagues in German studies, the University of Massachusetts/Amherst women's studies and history departments, and the Five College (Smith, Mt. Holyoke, Amherst, and Hampshire Colleges and the University of Massachusetts–Amherst) faculty seminars in German studies and history provided feedback on my essays and public presentations. One of my students, Jennifer Kim, undertook extensive bibliographical research. Many others sent me pertinent newspaper items, journal articles, and audiotapes and sustained my sense of purpose.

A timely indirect stepping-stone in the development of my work on this volume was the publication, facilitated by Professor Jane Marcus, of my essay in *Women's History Review* 6, 1 (Summer 1997), comparing Stein and Vera Brittain's approaches to issues of gender and national identity.

I relied on a number of computer whizzes, such as the University of Massachusetts/Amherst reference librarian Emily Silverman, Matthew Daube, and Mary McClintock. Mary deserves emphatic appreciation for her crucial role in making this volume possible. She assisted me not only in myriad computer matters but in my initial copyediting, in formatting the manuscript for submission, and, most signally, in providing gentle and astute counsel in handling editorial options. The title of her business, Better Me Than You, crystallizes her empathic response to an author's or editor's state of mind during later stages of a manuscript's completion

Editors Bruce Wilcox and Clark Dougan at the University of Massachusetts Press gave me excellent suggestions for shaping the entire volume. Though they were prepared to adopt the project, they judged that another press might better serve the volume and suggested that I ask Barbara Hanrahan, newly director at the University of Notre Dame Press, about her interest in the volume. Most happily, Barbara recognized the importance of our study and took the volume under her wing. I had the joy of meeting Barbara at an Organization of American Historians conference and found her in person, as she had been on the phone, in e-mail conversations, and through editorial suggestions, to be a sharp, meditative intellect, frank and firm in her views, with a deeply compassionate spirit. She, the anonymous external readers for the manuscript, and other editors at the University of Notre Dame Press served as this volume's midwives. Copyeditor Elisabeth Magnus valiantly and meticulously scrutinized the entire volume, leaping with consummate skill upon points of confusion, insufficient citation, and grammatical goofs.

Throughout the volume's entire gestation, my family provided incomparable support. Though I, like Stein, come from a Jewish heritage, my family members raised no eyebrow over my preoccupation with a Jew-turned-Catholic's life and work. My brother Norman arranged for my presentation on Stein at the Pacific Palisades, California, synagogue; my sister Gloria sent me relevant articles and discussed aspects of Stein's life at length with me; and my remarkable mother Lillian, in her late nineties, was both amused and curious about my work. They, my sons Zak and Jeremy, and their spouses Teri and Sheila buoyed me through rough times and celebrated with me at every major point of publication progress.

I cannot imagine this volume appearing without the brilliant, stalwart, and supremely loving support of my husband, Leonard Berkman. From the kindly acts of bringing cups of coffee to my desk and accompanying me to conferences to the exacting and sensitive task of critiquing each draft of each essay I wrote, Lenny kept me emotionally afloat and intellectually focused. An impatient person, I depended upon his unflappable trust in the eventual resolution of seemingly insurmountable problems. When a question of editorial diplomacy or an intellectual conundrum or the loss of communication with one of the contributors troubled my sleep, he awoke with me in the middle of the night, listened carefully, and offered thoughtful advice. As Lenny knows, my work on Stein is not over. I plan to write a comparative study of the impact of World War I on female intellectuals, focusing specifically on the experience and thought of Edith Stein, Vera Brittain, and Gertrude Stein (long a favorite and influential writer in his own work). I am exceedingly fortunate in looking forward to his passionate companionship throughout the forthcoming years.

Introduction

JOYCE AVRECH BERKMAN

On August 3, 1916, shortly after nearly a half-million German soldiers died at the Battle of the Somme and widespread hunger provoked women to loot markets and stage food riots in various parts of Germany, a contrastingly joyful feat entered the historical record: a young Jewess became the second woman in German history to receive a doctorate in philosophy. For Edith Stein's dazzling thesis and oral examinations, she earned summa cum laude honors. The triumph celebrated was memorable. When Stein and two of her friends arrived at the home of Edmund Husserl, her revered mentor and the renowned founder of phenomenology, Husserl's daughter crowned the new graduate with a "gorgeous wreath" of ivy and daisies. In stark counterpoint, Stein's walk home had to take place "in pitch darkness," a total blackout imposed in the face of a potential air raid, but she continued euphoric. Her landlady observed that Stein's usual serious countenance was now aglow.[1] Beyond the celebration itself, Stein was euphoric because Husserl, desperate for someone to organize, decipher, and transcribe his scattered shorthand manuscripts, had accepted with alacrity her proposal to serve as his assistant. She compared their mutual elation to that of "a young couple at the moment of their betrothal."[2] Such good fortune in the midst of war, she wrote with smiling tact to a soldier at the front, her philosopher friend Fritz Kaufmann, was admittedly "a bit troubling."[3] Although the soaring spirits of Stein's professional honeymoon were not to last long, this August 1916 was one of happiness beyond measure, and it marked the beginning of her prodigious philosophical career.

Today, at the outset of the twenty-first century, Stein the brilliant philosopher is not widely recognized. Rather, Stein the nun Sister Teresa Benedicta a Cruce, murdered at Auschwitz on August 9, 1942, and canonized by Pope John Paul II on October 11, 1998, stirs popular interest and debate. Before and after her canonization, journalists' and scholars' attention centered on her religious experience and writings. This multidisciplinary edition of essays eschews that belabored focus along with the tendency toward hagiographic interpretations of her life. Since Stein's canonization diverted public attention even further from her extraordinary intellectual contributions and her intriguing complex biography, this volume helps to redress the growing imbalance. Constituting the first anthology in English of serious scholarly meditations on Stein, these essays treat little-studied dimensions of Stein's life as well as her wide-ranging secular prose, long in need of rigorous analysis.

Stein's philosophical treatises broke new and fertile ground. She made bold, far-reaching inquiries into the phenomenon of empathy; the nature of personhood, causality, and motivation; the individual in relation to community, society, and state; women and gender; and educational theory and pedagogy. Her feminist essays, harbingers of Christian feminist thought in the late twentieth century, remain fresh and vital. Along with her biographical sketches, Stein's unfinished autobiography, *Aus dem Leben einer jüdische Familie (Life in a Jewish Family)*,[4] signals her stylistic versatility, her provocative insights into identity formation and individual behavior, and her unflagging commitment to human equality and freedom. Her treatise *Finite and Eternal Being (Endliches und ewiges Sein)* won critical acclaim for its synthesis of the theology of St. Thomas Aquinas with secular phenomenological philosophy. Her *Kreuzeswissenschaft: Studien über Johannes a Cruce (The Science of the Cross: Studies on St. John of the Cross)* offers penetrating analysis of its titular subject. Versed in more than five languages, Stein produced German translations of works by John Henry Cardinal Newman and St. Thomas Aquinas. Her copious, intellectually rich, and generous correspondence abounds in philosophical reflections and testifies to her sustained passion for truth seeking and to her fervent belief in multiple perspectives and dialogue. Throughout her adult years, she was a brilliant and beloved teacher and counselor within academic Catholic institutions and a lecturer in various European countries to Catholic teachers at educational congresses. Nonetheless, much of Stein's writing remained unpublished and untranslated for most of the twentieth century. It is highly significant that throughout the past and present decade, a host of hardworking and perceptive scholars have dedicated themselves to an impressive array of published editions of Stein's work in German, Italian, and English.

Clearly, Stein has left a vital legacy, the scope of which this volume begins to map. Her striking personality, trailblazing treatises, and commentary at philosophical conferences within and outside Germany influenced both her contemporaries (not only philosophers within and beyond the circle of her mentor Edmund Husserl but Husserl himself) and intellectuals today.

Contemplating Edith Stein explores this remarkable intellectual span. Its essays inquire into Stein's own personhood, her distinctive attributes, her identity development, key turning points and people in her life, her primary professional relationships, her political activism, and her myriad modes of self-representation, specifically her struggle, constantly shifting with her private and societal experience, to combine her selves as female, Jew, German, Catholic, and Carmelite nun. Historically embedding her life and work, these essays examine her as a creature as well as creator of her times, a person of intrepid mind, moral integrity, and originality, yet whose character, life choices, and scholarship reveal inevitable human limitations and flaws. From these essays at their most provocative, questions arise: How are we to understand those areas of Stein's confusion and discontinuity? In what ways did Stein express her self-perceptions and periodic reinvention of herself? Honest phenomenologist that she was, Stein sought to contemplate phenomena from as many views as possible and with as few preconceptions and prejudices as she could manage. This volume strives to follow her example.

These essays share a dual commitment to empathic *and* critical contemplation of Stein. They are in dialogue with each other. The reader will encounter in text and endnotes divergent, even conflicting, perspectives on Stein's writings and life. We hope that our volume's title characterizes not only Stein's mental and spiritual activity and that of each scholar here but also the activity of each reader of this volume

Of course, these essays' contemplation reflects their wrestling with a confluence of late-twentieth-century historical developments: the rise and diffusion of feminism and women's studies scholarship, with their focus on neglected women intellectuals and on women's experience and gender analysis; the spread of phenomenological concepts into fields of study outside their usual philosophical domain; postmodern inquiry into the complexities of personal identity; Jewish and Holocaust studies; and popular and professional historical fascination with twentieth-century Germany. Additionally, as suggested earlier, these essays take advantage of vigorous late-twentieth-century and ongoing editions and translations of Stein's writings. Until the 1980s, scholars without German fluency had only limited access to Stein's thought, a core reason for the dearth of published scholarship on Stein in English. As the "Review of the Literature" in this volume heralds, the systematic English translation of Stein's collected works began in 1986 under the auspices of the Institute for Carmelite Studies (ICS) in Washington, D.C. As of today, almost all of Stein's extant writings have been translated into English, most recently her magnum opus, *Finite and Eternal Being,* and *The Science of the Cross.* Not until 1990 did a repository for Stein documents in the United States become established. Sr. Mary Catharine Baseheart, SCN, Spalding University professor of philosophy, whose scholarship focused on Stein's work, launched the Edith Stein Center for Study and Research at the Spalding campus in Louisville, Kentucky. After Sr. Mary Catharine's death in 1994, John R. Wilcox, another of Spalding's professors of philosophy, took on the center's directorship.

Within Belgium and Germany, scholars have been engaged in serious study of Stein for much longer. Amazingly, the bulk of Stein's manuscripts escaped Nazi search and Allied bombing of the monastery in Echt, Holland, Stein's final residence. What followed was a remarkable relay race of Stein devotees. The initial postwar spur came from Fr. Herman L. van Breda, a Belgian Franciscan who had rescued Edmund Husserl's library and writings in 1938 and knew of Stein's work. In 1947, at van Breda's instigation, Avertanus Hennekes, the Dutch provincial of the discalced Carmelite order, arranged for Stein's papers to be preserved at the Husserl Archive in Louvain. Fr. Romaeus Leuven, OCD, in coordination with Dr. Lucy Gelber, already on the Husserl Archive staff, began the work of preparing Stein's manuscripts for publication. As our volume contributor Antonio Calcagno recounts in yet another of his carefully researched essays, in 1955 the contract between the Carmelites and the Husserl Archives was broken. With the blessing of Romaeus Leuven, OCD, Dr. Gelber dramatically took possession of all Stein's texts and housed these in her home, which became the Stein archive in Brussels, the Archivum Carmelitanum Edith Stein.[5] The original manuscripts moved yet again, back to the rebuilt Cologne Carmel, the monastery where Stein had spent most of her cloistered life. There Sr. Maria Amata Neyer, OCD, who had entered the Cologne Carmel in 1944, devoted herself to organizing and editing Edith Stein's manuscripts, letters, and papers and seeing them published. During the past decades, two publishing houses, Nauwelaerts in Louvain and subsequently Herder in Freiburg im Breisgau, Germany, published fourteen volumes of Edith Stein's work. These first appeared in 1950, though the majority of the volumes emerged several decades later. Currently, the Archivum Carmelitanum Edith Stein and the Edith Stein International Institute supervise the

Herder publication of a new set of twenty-four volumes, including revised and expanded editions of previous volumes as well as hitherto unavailable Stein writings. Two of the contributors to *Contemplating Edith Stein*, Hanna-Barbara Gerl-Falkovitz and Beate Beckmann-Zöller, together with Maria Amata Neyer, OCD, guide this magnificent enterprise. Simultaneously, another of the contributors to this volume, Angela Ales Bello, directs a comparably invaluable Italian translation of Edith Stein's work under the aegis of Città Nuova Publisher, Rome.

Contemplating Edith Stein is divided into three parts: Part One, on Stein's personality, self-perception, crucial personal and professional relationships, and major life turning points and decisions; Part Two, on her views on female identity, concerns with women's issues, and feminism; and Part Three, on her philosophical inquiry. Of course, all three parts are interrelated, and since the terrain of a number of these essays overlaps, my arrangement follows each essay's primary emphasis. As an aftermath to Parts One through Three, this volume contains a brief Stein Chronology and Sarah Borden's comprehensive, judicious, and useful "Review of the Literature in English on Edith Stein." Borden's bibliographical essay guides the reader to numerous sources cited in the various essays here as well as to pathways to further study and contemplation of Stein.

The sixteen essays in this volume were written during the past few years; eight have been previously published. Inevitably, given the rapid recent advance of Stein material in print, each essay's scholarship reflects the currents of thought and extent of Stein publications and translations at the time of each author's writing. Below, editorial commentary introduces each of this volume's three sections and underscores relevant historical context for the essays within that section.

These essays vary in tone and style, ranging from those accessible to readers with little knowledge of Stein to those that build upon the reader's greater (though not expert) familiarity with Stein's history and outlook. (Five essays appear here in translation, four from German, one from Italian.) All contributors to this volume are sensitive to the need to bring Stein's often complex philosophical concepts to the nonspecialist. This heterogeneity offers the reader more than a prismatic illumination of Stein; it highlights the breadth of scholarly engagement with her life and thought. Disciplines of author expertise represented in this volume include history, sociology, literature, German studies, religion, philosophy, and education. Not surprisingly, since Stein's writings cover so many fields of intellectual endeavor, the U.S. and European scholars here include not only a spectrum of higher education faculty and administrators but also a fiction writer and a priest. Whereas most scholarly essays and books on Stein have been written by Catholics for Catholics, the contributors to this polyphonic volume are Jews, Protestants, Catholics, and unbelievers. While this volume emphasizes Stein's secular, rather than spiritual and religious, writings, attention to Stein's religious development necessarily enters into various discussions. In fact, many contributors to this volume are deeply and positively engaged in study of Stein's religious development and writings.

Part One

Stein's complexity resists commonplace tendencies to theorize coherent selves. Constantly shaping and being shaped by a multitude of relationships to other human beings and historical events, her life offers ample evidence of the protean and dynamic nature of individual identity. Stein devoted much of her philosophical writing to meditations on the nature of personhood, focusing on how a person's self, as mediated through individual consciousness and as manifest in multiple kinds of self-representation, forms and changes. The essays in Part One explore from an array of angles Stein's experience, personality, self-consciousness, and self-representation.

Following my introductory essay addressed to readers unfamiliar with Edith Stein's life, particularly the evolution of her intellectual life and scholarship, Dana Greene's essay alerts readers to the hagiographic tendencies of most published biographies of Stein. Calling for rigorous and thorough scholarship, Greene sets forth solid criteria for a thoughtful critical biography. Appreciative of Stein's contradictions and conflicts, Greene exhorts Stein scholars to elucidate, not eliminate, these revelatory tensions.

Patricia Hampl's essay presents a riveting portrait of Stein's passion for greatness, her yearning for philosophical and religious truth and for service to humanity. As she carefully probes the paradox of Stein's efforts at self-sacrifice, the question of her martyrdom, and the issue of her canonization, Hampl's chief focus is the riddle of Stein's personality and legacy. She illuminates Stein's contemplative and mystic nature, her sense of redemptive sacrifice, and her telling moments of recourse to Latin. Unblinking, Hampl confronts problematic aspects of Stein's autobiography and the ambiguous evidence of her final days.

By contrast, Father John Sullivan, OCD, seeks to convey Stein's gaiety. Two dominant Stein traits form his essay's warp and woof: her sense of humor and her compassion. Favoring the cheerful strains of Stein's lighter side, Sullivan views her humor and compassion as an interweave central to her empathic imagination, philosophic discourse, and understanding of personhood.

A being who can be so merry, yet so serious, scientific, and mystical, so constantly reinventing herself, leads Scott Spector, like Hampl, to focus on Stein's riddle, reconfiguring that riddle to explore how Stein's "unruly" self-representations, particularly in her autobiography and in her photographic poses, contribute to her contested personality and historical significance. Spector discusses the ways Stein modulated the boundaries among Jews, Christians, and Germans, as well as among women and men, to promote easier identity passage across. As Spector argues, Stein simultaneously buttressed and subverted conventional and often bigoted notions of race, gender, and religion.

Theresa Wobbe's essay is sociologically framed. She directs her eye to Stein's female intellectual cohort and asks us to consider Stein's aspiring to be a philosopher and to hold a professorial position as consonant with the aims of Germany's first generation of college-educated women. Wobbe looks at Stein's decision to become a nun from the angle of feminist struggles to transform gender perceptions and roles within theological scholarship and religious communities.

The next two essays of Part One hone in on two significant phases of Stein's life. Angelika von Renteln targets Stein's years of personal crisis between the end of World War I (1918) and her conversion to Roman Catholicism (1922). Scholars offer numerous theories for Stein's conversion, but her correspondence and postwar treatises, as well as the writings of fellow phenomenologists Adolph Reinach and Hans Lipps, convince von Renteln that, without our discounting commonly cited influences, several underinvestigated developments in Stein's life were decisive, specifically her thwarted personal relationships with three magnetic individuals, the death of Adolph Reinach, and her experience of carefully organizing Reinach's notes after his death, particularly his notes about his conversion. Stein, von Renteln contends, ultimately resolved her personal and professional impasse and spiritual quandaries through community within the Catholic Church and the Dominican school at Speyer.

Hanna-Barbara Gerl-Falkovitz's essay treats a barely discussed absorbing feature of Stein's activity during the 1920s: Stein's motivations for translating John Henry Cardinal Newman's *Diary and Letters* and his *Idea of the University*. After her conversion, Stein was drawn to a particular kind of Catholic consciousness and community. Gerl-Falkovitz develops a fascinating story of Catholic intellectual interest in Newman before the 1920s, specifically around the initiatives of Stein's Jesuit mentor Erich Przywara. Detailing what she terms the "Przywara phenomenon" and its importance to the Catholic rejuvenation of the 1920s that served to catapult Newman's ascent, Gerl-Falkovitz links Stein to those Catholics who saw in Newman a way to reconcile science and religion, modern and traditional Catholic perspectives. Additionally, Gerl-Falkovitz elucidates Stein's affinities with Newman and her views on the challenges of translation.

As the concluding essay of Part One, my study of Stein's German-Jewishness looks at the entirety of her life, offering a historical analysis and interpretation of one of the most controversial and key elements of Stein's self-collage. It rejects a post-Holocaust lens in favor of interpreting Stein's choices, identity changes, and continuities within the historical circumstances of early-twentieth-century Germany. The essay pivots on changing political, social, national, religious, economic, and cultural realities that gave rise to and posed the dilemmas a German and Jewish woman such as Stein faced at successive moments of her life. It further ponders the shapeshifter interplay in Stein's hybrid ethnic, national, religious, and gender composite.

Part Two

From early adolescence Stein championed feminist beliefs and causes. Regrettably, much recent clerical attention to Stein sidesteps her feminist challenge to the political and religious institutions of her lifetime. The essays in this section examine Stein's philosophy of the female person and her commitment to sexual equality and justice.

A major source for Stein's feminist philosophy is her *Die Frau (Essays on Woman),* the focal work,[6] though not the lone primary reference, for the three essays of Part Two. A comprehensive analysis of Stein's feminism in relation to the thought of her feminist peers, as well as to a representative array of current feminist theories, remains to be written, but these three essays explore Stein's feminism with perceptive and critical insights.

Noting that the English translation of Stein's *Essays on Woman* evoked little interest among feminist theorists outside Catholic circles, Linda Lopez McAlister's essay presents a trenchant analysis of why this occurred and the importance of making Stein's thought more widely known. At the time that McAlister wrote this previously published essay, American and European feminists were struggling to sort through essentialist and antiessentialist theories of female identity. McAlister sets forth Stein's distinctive and nuanced essentialism, a feminism that was at the vanguard of its time and, though dated now in some respects, remains arresting.

Similarly, Rachel Feldhay Brenner's previously published essay hails Stein's feminism as a precursor of salient features of feminist thought of the 1970s and 1980s. Brenner situates Stein's feminist stance at once within the sociopolitical uproar of Stein's Germany and in late-twentieth-century feminist readings of Genesis. She sees Stein vacillate between her conviction of gender equality and the religious dogma of her time that subordinated women to men in public and marital domains. To scholars today, Stein's postconversion outlook appears to support the conventional "maternalist" version of feminism—that is, the claim that women's gender-specific preeminence as empathic caregivers and peace-makers amply warrants gender equality and justice. Nonetheless, as Brenner makes clear, Stein flagged the dangers of affirming a gender-specific female na-ture. Such belief, Stein held, downplays individuality, encourages women to be dependent and self-effacing, and devalues self-realization and the duty to pro-mote justice and societal health. Brenner discusses Stein's faith in the antidote of women's rigorous intellectual education.

For Lisa Dolling, Stein's insistence upon individual uniqueness grounds her feminist philosophy and underpins her feminist approach to education. Dol-ling, too, mines Stein's *Essays on Woman* for its approach to women's education, but her essay focuses on Stein as a liberal educational reformer. Tracing con-nections between Plotinus's and Stein's pedagogy, Dolling places Stein within liberal traditions of German and American educational theory, aligning Stein's ideals with those of the early-nineteenth-century liberal reformer Wilhelm von Humboldt and such twentieth-century philosophers as Martin Buber, Hans-Georg Gadamer, Mortimer Adler, and the feminists Nel Noddings and Martha Nussbaum.

Part Three

The four essays of Part Three address Stein's work as a philosopher. Antonio Calcagno opens this section with a singular and sharp analysis of a little known foundational preconversion treatise by Stein, not yet translated into English— her *Einführung in die Philosophie (Introduction to Philosophy)*. Begun in 1917, this treatise was among the few manuscripts that Stein, fleeing Nazi persecu-tion, took with her to the Carmelite convent at Echt in Holland. Calcagno's elu-cidation of *Introduction to Philosophy,* of other Stein texts, and of Husserl's writ-ings and correspondence arms his attack on the dominant scholarly view of Stein as mere student, assistant, and loyal follower of Husserl. Calcagno argues that Stein collaborated with Husserl as a peer, not hesitating to differ with him. Stein held ideas both consonant and highly dissonant with Husserl's; she wielded cru-cial influence on his widely read and acclaimed *Ideen (Ideas) II* and *III*. Be-yond his biographical, historical, and philosophical probe of Stein and Husserl's collaboration, Calcagno pursues Stein's singular concept of depth as the mysterious and ultimate ground of being, an idea that ties her metaphysical inquiry to her phenomenological constitution of personhood. Calcagno contends this to be a quintessential instance of Stein's originality and her freedom from Husserl's shadow.

Stein's position within the pantheon of philosophers is buttressed by Angela Ales Bello, who relates Stein's analysis of person to philosophers beyond and including Husserl, specifically Bergson, Conrad-Martius, Heidegger, and various ancient and medieval theorists. As her essay's historical context expands and enriches our sense of Stein's intellectual community, Bello confronts the difficult question of Stein's view of person as living: What does it mean for the "I" to be alive, finite, at once both free and under necessity? Bello charts Stein's phenomenological process for grasping the essence of things, her relation to idealism, and her idea of propulsive life force and its psychic activities.

Tackling Stein's view of person in her own distinctive way, Sarah Borden spotlights Stein's grasp of the elements that unite and differentiate all human beings. Drawing on a wide array of Stein's writings, especially her postconversion text *Finite and Eternal Being,* Borden balances the consistent and inconsistent features of Stein's analysis of individuality. Borden also dissects the elements in Stein's thought that compromise Stein's espousal of democracy and human equality.

In the final essay of Part Three, Beate Beckmann-Zöller investigates Stein's religious and moral philosophy, comparing Edith Stein with the philosopher Simone Weil (Stein's much-studied French contemporary, another woman of Jewish descent drawn to Catholicism). Beckmann asks what in their philosophical outlook enabled Stein but not Weil to convert. Raising issues of human freedom, goodness, and conscience, Beckmann argues that what divides the two philosophers are their dissimilar responses to the age-old conundrum of how to reconcile human freedom with God's presumed omnipotence and grace.

NOTES

1. Edith Stein, *Life in a Jewish Family, 1891–1916: Her Unfinished Autobiographical Account,* ed. Lucy Gelber and Romaeus Leuven, OCD, trans. Josephine Koeppel, OCD (Washington, DC: ICS Publications, 1986), 414. Originally published as *Aus dem Leben einer jüdischen Familie, Das Leben Edith Stein: Kindheit und Jugend,* vol. 7 of *Edith Steins Werke* (Louvain: Archivum Carmelitanum Edith Stein, E. Nauwelaerts, 1965). Published in a new edition as *Aus dem Leben einer jüdischen Familie und weitere autobiographische Beiträge,* ed. Maria Amata Neyer and Hanna-Barbara Gerl-Falkovitz, vol. 1 of *Edith Stein Gesamtausgabe* (Freiburg: Herder, 2002).
2. Stein, *Life in a Jewish Family,* 411.

3. Edith Stein to Fritz Kaufmann, August 16, 1916, in *Self-Portrait in Letters, 1916–1942*, ed. Lucy Gelber and Romaeus Leuven, OCD, trans. Josephine Koeppel, OCD (Washington, DC: ICS Publications, 1993), 1–2. Originally published as *Selbstbildnis in Briefen*, pt. 1, *1916–1934*, and pt. 2, *1934–1942*, vols. 8 and 9 of *Edith Steins Werke* (Druten: De Maas und Waler, 1976, 1977). This German edition has been recently re-edited and published in three volumes, vols. 2, 3, and 4 of a new critical edition of the complete writings of Edith Stein, *Edith Stein Gesamtausgabe* (Freiburg: Herder, 2000–2001), edited by Michael Linssen, OCD, in collaboration with Hanna-Barbara Gerl-Falkovitz.

4. Throughout this introduction, titles of Stein's writings first appear in juxtaposed German and English. Subsequently, the titles appear in English only. On occasion, when English translation cannot adequately convey Stein's intent, her term is kept in the original language. Generally, all German words appear in English.

5. Antonio Calcagno, book review of *Edith Stein: Edith Stein Gesamtausgabe* (Freiburg: Herder, 2000), *American Catholic Philosophical Quarterly* 76 (Summer 2002): 511–14. See, too, Sr. Maria Amata Neyer, "Geschichte des Edith-Stein-Archivs," *Edith Stein Jahrbuch* 4 (1998): 550–65, esp. 563.

6. According to recent research, "Challenges Facing Swiss Catholic Academic Women," chap. 8 of *Die Frau: Ihre Aufgabe nach Natur und Gnade*, ed. Lucy Gelber and Romaeus Leuven, OCD (Louvain: E. Nauwelaerts, 1959), was apparently written not by Stein but by the Swiss jurist Dr. Hilde Vérène Borsinger. This error in attribution was repeated in the English edition, *Essays on Woman*, ed. Lucy Gelber and Romaeus Leuven, OCD, trans. Freda Mary Oben (Washington, DC: ICS Publications, 1987). The new Herder edition, *Die Frau: Fragestellungen und Reflexionen*, ed. Sophie Binggeli and von Maria Amata Neyer, vol. 13 of *Edith Stein Gesamtausgabe* (Freiburg: Herder, 2000), excludes this chapter, but, happily for future German fluent scholars, it adds other Stein writings on women. Happily, too, the essays of Part Two do not rely on chap. 8.

Part One

"I Am Not a 'Cleverly-Designed Book'; I Am a Human Being with My Contradictions"

Who Is Edith Stein?

Chapter 1

The Intellectual Passion of Edith Stein
A Biographical Profile

JOYCE AVRECH BERKMAN

In her biographical sketch of St. Elizabeth of Thuringia, Edith Stein wrote, "Here is life whose outer facts are colorful and appealing enough to arouse fantasy, to awaken amazement and admiration. But that is not why we are concerned with it. We would like to pursue what lies behind the outer facts, to feel the beat of the heart that bore such a fate and did such things, to internalize the spirit that governed her."[1] What a paradox is Stein's desire "to pursue what lies behind the outer facts" of St. Elizabeth's life when Stein would shun pursuit of her own. Stein described herself to her friends and family as private in the extreme, from childhood retreating to her inner hidden world, where she brooded over what she heard and saw, confiding her feelings to no one.[2] We know tantalizingly little about her life's many key turning points. We have glimpses only of the impact of her father's death, the onset of puberty, her feelings about her own body and its sexuality, the men or women to whom she was romantically attracted, the bases of her adolescent atheism, the reasons she converted to Christianity and specifically Catholicism, and her reflections during her final days spent among deported and murdered Jews. Yet just as she sought to empathize enough with St. Elizabeth to penetrate her outward veil, know her true face, and feel her inner pulse, so do most Stein scholars eager to inhabit and comprehend Stein's spirit.

Until current postmodern biographers popularized the idea that a person's identity is a riotously shifting kaleidoscope, most biographers sought to detect unifying patterns or threads that shape an individual's life. Stein's biographers have emphasized different integrating elements. Most commonly they stress her lifelong search for truth. Some focus on her moral idealism, her zeal for goodness. Others point to her empathic and loving nature or to her longing for a psychological home, specifically an intellectual and spiritual community. In an eloquent short biography, the founder of the Edith Stein Archive at the Cologne Carmel, Maria Amata Neyer, OCD, highlights Stein's mission to serve humanity as her life's cardinal leitmotif.[3] At age twenty, Stein ruminated, "We are in the world to serve humanity. . . . This is best accomplished when doing that for which one has the requisite talents."[4] Neyer follows Stein through the various permutations of this goal—World War I nursing service, teaching in various institutions and settings, secular and religious scholarship, political advocacy to promote sexual and social justice and combat Nazism—ultimately concluding her biography with Stein's willingness to follow Jesus and die for the sake of all humanity.[5]

Neyer's is a most compelling thesis, convincing in many respects. The difficulty with her and most biographers' perspectives, however, is their muting of Stein's ambivalent desires, her clashing ideals and values, and, too, fundamental contradictions in Stein's life and thought. Crucially, as a Jew, a woman, and an unusually gifted and ambitious intellectual, she was a triple outsider who constantly strove to keep all the strands of her identity braided. Strands occasionally unraveled.[6] She suffered periods of deep, even suicidal, depression, chronic insomnia, and loss of appetite. Stein's drive to integrate her life led her to periodic self-invention with new identities, still newer strands of selfhood, and new chosen communities, which she hoped would create a snug braid, an integrated self. Is it any wonder that issues of personhood dominated her life's philosophical inquiry? Further, as with most mortals, Stein's feelings and behavior did not consistently conform to her ideals. In her biographical accounts of friends and family Stein mixed tenderness with tough realism, even mockery at times in her harsh details of their shortcomings. Stein struggled for a balance between objective and empathic description and between unbiased and sympathetic portraiture. This essay and those that follow struggle likewise.

This essay aims to provide a chronological overview of her life through the lens of her intellectual and philosophical education and evolution. Other essays in Part One of this volume explore captivating riddles of Stein's life, the aching tensions of Stein's identity transitions, her key personality traits and decisive personal relationships, issues in her religious development, and her mutable approaches to melding her Germanness and Jewishness. Since none of these essays will offer a basic biographical narrative of Stein's intellectual pursuits, priorities, and career as a philosopher, the present essay, while grappling with Stein's inner life, sets out to meet that need. Essays in *Part Three* of this volume investigate a number of Stein's philosophical texts, so I intend my ensuing remarks on Stein's works strictly to highlight the historical and biographical significance of her major publications.

On the most solemn of Jewish holidays, Yom Kippur, the Day of Atonement, October 12, 1891, Auguste née Courant Stein gave birth to Edith Stein, the youngest of her eleven children, four of whom had died in childhood.[7] The previous year Auguste and her husband Siegfried Stein, unable to make a success of their lumber business in Lublinitz and eager for their children to have the opportunity for secondary education while residing at home, moved to Breslau (now Wroclaw, Poland), the thriving economic and cultural capital of Silesia and Prussia's most tolerant and progressive city for Jewish families such as the Steins. The young Stein was the beloved pet of her family, whom she charmed with her shining gray eyes, dimpled chin, and petite frame. Although Stein grew up in the vibrant matrix of an extended family of many relatives, shortly before age two she suffered the tragic loss of her forty-eight-year-old father, who died of heat prostration during his walk on one of his lengthy forest inspection business trips.

Siegfried Stein's death had a decisive impact on Stein and her family. Widow Stein, devoutly Jewish and wearing black for the rest of her life, took the economic and emotional helm of the family with gusto and brilliance. Her indefatigable energy, business acumen, firm and kindly relations with her employees, readiness to deny herself comforts for the sake of the family, and insistence on frugal, simple family arrangements (because of limited bedrooms and beds, Stein slept with her mother until age six) gradually turned a precarious lumber firm into a prosperous enterprise. Its lumberyard even included a vegetable garden that was "a paradise for children" at play.[8] Effectively performing the conventional gender roles of both nurturant, self-denying mother and assertive, public-oriented father, Stein's mother exemplified the inspiring supermother of her day and became the wise counselor for her volatile immediate and extended family. Stein revered her mother's humor, wisdom, and love. She recalled that during her youth when she dreamed of an ideal home, "It was always one in which my mother lived with only Erna and me and in which she cared for us both."[9] (Erna, eighteen months Stein's senior, was the sibling to whom Stein was most attached.)

Auguste Stein instilled in her offspring the importance of will power and unflagging purpose, recurrently voicing her two favorite maxims: "'What one wants to do, one can do'" and "'As one strives, so will God help.'"[10] With few exceptions, Edith Stein's lifelong determination to pursue intellectual activity in the face of seeming insurmountable obstacles owed much to her mother's example and instruction in unyielding tenacity (as Edith Stein would proudly say, the "stone" of "Stein").[11]

Crucially, Auguste Stein stoked Stein's passion for learning. Despite her authoritarian personality and strict discipline, she encouraged her children's inquisitive and critical minds. Young Stein recalled her delight in the Passover seder, particularly the ritual of the youngest child raising essential questions about the holiday, such as why the first Passover night differed from other nights. From her early years Edith Stein learned the sacredness of curiosity and fine intellectual discriminations. Above all, Auguste Stein was resolute in providing her offspring with the finest education she could afford and fostering her children's educational achievements. If her schoolwork required the time, young Stein was excused from domestic chores. When, later, she was preparing for major examinations at the University of Göttingen, her mother sent her weekly a small care package consisting of homemade braided Jewish bread (challah), with goose liver and a slice of the Sunday roast.

For early-twentieth-century German Jews, education of daughters as well as sons was both a prized cultural and religious value and the single most important lever for social mobility. A disproportionate number of Jewish girls (as compared with non-Jewish German girls) entered higher education and the professions open to Jews and women.[12] The widowed Stein was painfully aware that a woman might find herself unable to rely on a traditional breadwinner. Although Auguste Stein did not interfere with her daughter's goal to become a philosopher and a teacher, her practical and ambitious mind occasionally spurred her to advise her daughter that "she would be pleased were I to study law."[13] Reminding her readers that women were not yet permitted to become lawyers, Edith Stein underscored that her mother wanted her to have "full freedom of choice."[14] Ultimately, Auguste Stein set educational independence as a higher priority than practical career considerations. As an undergraduate at the University of Breslau, Edith Stein weighed the pros and cons of various course choices with her mother. The elder Stein urged her, "Do whatever you consider right; you are the best judge of what you should do."[15]

The Stein offspring internalized their mother's concern for their educational success. Auguste Stein often welcomed her children to read to her. At about age six, the prodigy Stein read her Schiller's formidable drama *Maria Stuart*. Through innumerable stories, her elder sisters had whetted young Stein's desire for school and eased her transition there. Since her older sister Else was a teacher, Stein at age six declared that "I, too, wanted to be a teacher."[16] Even before Stein began Victoria School, she was determined to climb from the kindergarten class to elementary level. In 1897, at the request of two of Stein's sisters—Erna, recognized as an excellent student, and their older sister Else, fifteen years Stein's senior and a teacher at Victoria School—a flexible principal permitted young Stein to enter elementary school at midyear.

The premium placed on education was evident in the family's unflagging concern for and pride in each member's performance. Highly gifted Stein frequently assisted Erna in her essays and exam preparation. When any sibling and close friends faced a major examination, "the entire family shared in the ordeal. . . . By evening, Mother and nearly all our brothers and sisters had arrived to escort the victor on her triumphant way home from the battlefield."[17] Precocious and amply admired, young Stein "foresaw a brilliant future for myself."[18]

Describing herself as an "over zealous" pupil who leapt to answer questions and gobbled up new textbooks of literature and history, Stein believed she almost "felt more at home there [at school] than in our house."[19] By age fourteen and a half, Stein had completed Victoria School's nine grades with outstanding marks. She could choose to stay on another year, but by then school was no longer her home. Burnt out on academic studies, lacking close ties to teachers and classmates, troubled with the onset of puberty and unspecified ideological questions, she rejected her principal's and mother's advice, quit school, and traveled to Hamburg to assist Else with the birth of her second child. There she remained for ten months, learning domestic and child-raising skills. She also read extensively in her brother-in-law's medical texts. Both her sister and brother-in-law were atheists. "Deliberately and consciously," declares Stein, "I gave up praying here."[20] Stein had come to equate rational scientific and intellectual inquiry with religious skepticism.

From this period until her time at the University of Göttingen, Stein, except during the Yom Kippur fast and when she accompanied her mother to High Holy Days services, spurned religious practice and thought. Although esteeming her Jewishness, she never set forth the reasons for her abandonment of Judaism. Apart from a reference to her reading Spinoza, evidence of her familiarity with medieval and modern Jewish or Christian philosophy is lacking. Stein assumed that Jewish thought excluded concepts of an afterlife. Though personal immortality of the soul is not a universal article of Jewish faith, various religious texts endorse it. While generally knowledgeable about and affirming the Jewish holidays and rituals that her devout mother practiced, as a woman Stein was excluded from men's serious intellectual engagement with religious texts. Like many Jewish female intellectuals of her era, she felt alienated from the pervasive patriarchal and sexist features of contemporary liberal and orthodox Judaism.[21] Importantly, Jews in Breslau experienced much less anti-Semitism than elsewhere in Prussia. Aware of areas of anti-Semitic discrimination, such as the exclusion of Jews from teaching positions in most public schools, she nevertheless expected such prejudice to end in both law and Christian attitudes. Not having suffered anti-Semitic barriers to her intellectual progress until after World War I, Stein lacked the sense of an imperative to preserve and assert Judaism in a hostile environment.[22]

Following her return from Breslau in early 1907, Stein's appetite for intellectual study rapidly revived. Again with her mother's encouragement, Stein decided to prepare for the entrance examination to the upper level of the gymnasium undeterred by the gymnasium's principal declaring her goal "nearly unattainable."[23] She spent a half year of strenuous work with tutors in mathematics and Latin. Enjoying "the opportunity . . . to have my mental powers fully engaged in a task for which they were eminently suited,"[24] Stein recalled this period as among the first unalloyed happy times of her life. Of those taking the gymnasium exams, Stein alone passed for admission.

Stein's gymnasium curriculum epitomized educational ideals prized by middle-class Germans, especially German Jews.[25] These ideals were traditionally represented in the principles of *Wissenschaft* and *Bildung. Wissenschaft,* whose domain encompassed the combined study of humanities and sciences, cultivated the full blossoming of the human intellect, unimpeded rational inquiry, practical and theoretical understanding, respect for research, and the search for truth for its own sake. Although by the late nineteenth century the term had narrowed to scientific positivism, the broader definition of *Wissenschaft* survived. The complementary concept, *Bildung,* featured two cardinal educational goals. The first was intellectual achievement through command of classical thought, European literature and philosophy, and critical analysis and interpretation of honored texts, especially for their ethical and moral content. During Stein's gymnasium and college years, she read Greek and Roman classics; modern masterworks of fiction by such authors as Shakespeare, Turgenev, Dostoyevsky, and Ibsen; and philosophical treatises by Spinoza, Descartes, Montesquieu, Rousseau, Kant, Locke, Hume, John Stuart Mill, William James, Wilhelm Dilthey, and Henri Bergson. The second goal of *Bildung* involved aesthetic sophistication and refined manners. Although comprehensive academic excellence defined educational achievement, Auguste Stein, no more than most middle-class Germans, limited *Bildung* to classroom experience. Stein's family encouraged young Stein to play chess, dance, and write and enact skits, parodies, and playlets. Stein took particular pleasure at Purim in performing Queen Esther, a heroic figure Stein sought to emulate throughout her life. Her friends and family delighted in her fun-loving ways.[26] *Bildung* also embraced the classical premise that a healthy mind requires a healthy body. Stein's education included outdoor physical activity. All the more because young Stein was small, thin, and anemic, she avidly explored the countryside on long hikes and played tennis. She reveled in family summer excursions.

Stein painstakingly recounted her gymnasium experiences, flaunting moments when she had voiced her disagreement with ideas presented by teachers and classmates, boasting her ease and joy in writing essays, thrilling in high marks, relishing one teacher's comment that "a big gap" separated Stein from those below her.[27] After her stellar completion of gymnasium classes, Stein, now twenty, faced the hurdle of the *Abitur,* the comprehensive final examination required for students aspiring to attend a university. Late-nineteenth-century German feminist activism paved the way for women, as of 1908, to take this examination. Stein's magnificent performance on the written section exempted her from the orals. Although Stein's seemingly immodest presentation of her intellectual feats reflected a historically based family, cultural, even national ease of display, its expression by a woman was less typical, less conventionally approved. Stein's disregard of such a norm epitomized not only her mother's independence but her own disdain for gender constraints and her identification with her feminist peers, including her sister Erna. When Stein came of age in Breslau, the feminist movement was well established there. Stein readily joined the Prussian Society for Women's Right to Vote. With her sister Erna and friends then and later in college, she discussed extensively the issue of a double career and whether to sacrifice a public career for marriage. Stein insisted she would not sacrifice a profession for marriage. Not surprisingly, at her class's farewell party the "terse epigrams" about each graduate included one, oft-cited, for Stein:

> Let woman equal be with man,
> So loud this suffragette avers,
> In days to come we surely can
> See that a Cab'net Post is hers.[28]

Following her successful *Abitur* and a memorable visit with relatives in Berlin, Stein in April 1911 entered the University of Breslau. Her chosen fields of study were literature and philosophy. Enraptured with philosophical questioning, she took Spinoza's *Ethics* everywhere with her on vacation walks: "While others lolled around under the trees, I would search out a deer lookout, climb up to it, and then become absorbed, alternately, in deductions about the sole substance, and . . . in the view of sky, mountains, and woods."[29] Although her first priority was "acquiring knowledge," she would need to support herself eventually; she selected teaching as her career. For this she would have to pass state boards in German, history, and Latin. Stein was determined to take courses that suited her interests as well as those preparatory for the board exams. She was relieved to discover philosophy listed among subjects recently deemed qualifying. She enrolled in Richard Hönigswald's course in natural philosophy. Her interests soon extended to psychology. During her first university year, William Stern's psychology courses especially absorbed her. Stern directed his students' attention to the nature of individual differences and the unitary structure of the personality whole. His emphasis on essential individual uniqueness influenced Stein's subsequent thought pervasively. As in most of her classes, discussion in Stern's seminars flowed openly and freely; Stern welcomed his students' zest for credible knowledge. Stein recalled the U-shaped seminar table surrounded by students who in frequent unison responded to their professor's thought with "a very decided and resounding 'No!' "[30]

Classmates contributed to Stein's intellectual growth in unexpected ways. Stein became the youngest member of a tight-knit group affectionately called the Cloverleaf. It included one man, Hans Biberstein, Erna's husband-to-be, whom Stein described as a rare bird for his feminist ardor. With these friends Stein read Kant's *Critique of Pure Reason*. Despite being often bored with seemingly "highly ridiculous" experiments, they also, "[w]ith death-defying fervor, during one semester, . . . plowed through all of Meumann's *Experimental Psychology*."[31]

While at Breslau, Stein joined and benefited intellectually and personally from diverse political groups and circles. An offshoot of Stern's seminar, the "Pedagogical Group," met to discuss questions of educational reform, practical pedagogical issues ignored in the university's curriculum. Spurred by its active societal conscience, the group also arranged visits to schools and homes for children with special needs. With regard to nonacademic matters, Stein singled out the Pedagogical Group's founder, Hugo Hermsen, for alerting her to her judgmental, sarcastic, and what some called " 'enchantingly malicious' " tendencies.[32] Cherishing her probing intellect and zeal for truth seeking, Stein did not generally direct her critical mind at herself. She grappled for years with her quick wit and ease in mimicry that cut in both constructive and harmful ways. She considered most students "a negligible quantity."[33] Her intellectual self-assurance, indeed arrogance and stubbornness, likely essential for a woman of her time to hew a bold and unconventional path, warred with her maturing sense of the limits of her knowledge and the complicated lives of many she had previously dismissed. Similarly, untainted by gender-acculturated modesty, Stein retrospectively lamented that her remarkable gifts of comprehension and her "extraordinary facility in inserting myself into the other's thought process" enabled her to skip introductory courses and seminars she should have covered.[34]

While at the University of Breslau Stein found ample opportunity to advance her pedagogical skills. A member of the Women's Student Union, which Stein also joined, introduced her to the Academic Branch of the Humboldt Society for Adult Education. Students in this branch volunteered to teach workers' classes. Stein taught spelling and English one evening a week. Independent of her branch work, she also undertook private tutoring. Since Auguste Stein subsidized her daughter's board, tuition, and more, Stein did not need paid work; she simply was unable to resist repeated requests to help prepare a pupil for a higher class at the gymnasium.[35]

In addition to her formal studies and teaching, myriad cultural events—theater, concerts, animated discussions with relatives and friends—stimulated Stein's university life. The intensity of her curricular and extracurricular learning experience, the "constant exertion of all my powers," gave Stein "an exhilarating feeling of living a very full life, and I saw myself as a richly endowed and highly privileged creature."[36] Her sense of special privilege arose from multiple sources. Aware of both her unusual mind and women's recent right to higher education in Prussia, Stein also belonged to an upwardly mobile family background. Although sensitive to the plight of those less fortunate, she did not ally with her feminist peers whose politics were socialist. Although liberal, feminist, and critical of conservative Prussian state policies as well as of nationalists and jingoists in her midst, she expressed gratitude to the Prussian state for her educational and cultural bounty, and her study of history inspired optimism about the prospects of more sweeping egalitarian reform.

Although Stein hailed her two years at the University of Breslau as a time of "general euphoria,"[37] she suffered occasional bouts of deep depression and by the end of her second year felt the need for new academic challenges. Since she had far from exhausted the university's offerings, Stein had become frustrated with prevalent psychological methods of the time, which, she felt, lacked clear conceptual foundation. She was restive with psychologism—that is, a reduction of individual experience to empirically quantifiable generalizations. What clinched her decision to leave Breslau was her discovery via a guest speaker at the Pedagogical Group, Dr. Georg Moskievicz, of Edmund Husserl's trailblazing second volume of *Logical Investigations (Logische Untersuchungen)*. Published in 1901, this volume and its predecessor, out in 1900, established the philosophy of phenomenology, which decisively transformed twentieth-century philosophical approaches. As Stein waded through Husserl's influential tome, she concluded that "Husserl was *the* philosopher of our age."[38] As late as 1939, Stein revered Husserl as "one of those real giants who transcend their own time and who determine history."[39] She resonated to his demand that scholars undertake precise clarification and discrimination of ideas and forge the "mental tools for the task at hand."[40] Moskievicz's remark that at the University of Göttingen, where Husserl taught, students "philosophize, day and night, at meals, in the street, everywhere"[41] sparked her interest still more ardently.

Additional incentives fueled her decision to go to Göttingen for the single semester she expected she could afford. She learned that Husserl's circle welcomed women, one of whom, Hedwig Conrad-Martius, became Stein's closest Göttingen friend, a bond to last the rest of Stein's life. She also received a letter from the wife of her cousin Richard Courant, a distinguished mathematician at the University of Göttingen, urging her to study there and add female intellect to their family circle. With invariable support for her daughter's intellectual pursuits, a very sad Auguste Stein, reluctant to part with her youngest daughter, assured her, "If you need to go there to study, I certainly won't bar your way."[42] Auguste Stein was even willing to subsidize her daughter's friend Rose Guttmann to join her, though Guttmann found she could finance the semester herself. Helpfully, Moskievicz, who later returned to Göttingen as well, sent ahead a letter of introduction concerning Stein to Husserl's chief assistant, Adolf Reinach, a privatdocent in philosophy.[43]

Twenty-one-year-old Stein arrived in Göttingen on April 17, 1913, and quickly fell in love with the town and its university. She waxed rhapsodic about the glory of the town: its countryside, architecture, historical artifacts, and unmistakable academic and intellectual identity. With Rose Guttmann, she found living quarters along a quaint street. The day she arrived and following Moskiewicz's advice, Stein set out to Adolf Reinach's home. Reinach and several other Munich philosophers had moved to Göttingen in 1905 to study with Husserl, whose students referred to him as "the Master." With Husserl they launched the Göttingen School and its more intimate circle, the Phenomenological Society. Reinach warmly greeted and oriented new students and prepared them for Husserl's classes. As Reinach facilitated Stein's entry into the Phenomenological Society, Stein and Guttmann, "unaware of our audacity," joined this elite group with alacrity. Unlike most newcomers, who kept their mouths shut, Stein "was impudent enough to join the discussion at once."[44]

In Göttingen, Stein found the "home" for which she longed.[45] She was neither socially nor culturally ostracized for being Jewish or female. Many of her professors at Göttingen, as at Breslau, were Jews, though some, like Husserl, had converted to Christianity. Her intense and lifelong comradeship with those in the Philosophical Society was based on joint intellectual commitment and not on accidents of gender and ethnicity. She did not doubt that she would one day secure a position as professor of philosophy. Discriminatory job hurdles would topple, just as they had in education. Stein believed that women's equality would soon reign, even in marital and sexual attitudes. A lofty rationalism, humanism, and moral idealism pervaded her views on personal relationships. Stein planned to marry and raise children, but she warded off sexual overtures as debasing her dignity as an intellectual. Since adolescence she had found the sexual double standard abhorrent. Needless loss of rational objectivity upset her, as with people under the influence of alcohol or subject to angry outbursts, unexamined prejudices, and narcissistic self-interest. She expected men of whatever religion, ethnic background, and sexual appetite to treat her as their equal, in the same way they treated other men whose mental life they respected. Most men treated her accordingly.

Stein's political hope and ethical idealism were utterly compatible with Husserl's phenomenological vision. Since phenomenology became the cornerstone of Stein's subsequent thought, indeed the faith that oriented her life, some brief comments are in order. The foundational texts to critique prevalent sciences of the mind and introduce phenomenological theory and methods were Husserl's two volumes of previously mentioned *Logical Investigations* (1900–1901) and his "Ideen zur einer reinen Phänomenologische Forschung I" (Ideas Pertaining to a Pure Phenomenology), published in 1913 as the lead article in his *Jahrbuch für Philosophie und phänomenologische Forschung (Yearbook for Philosophy and Phenomenological Research)*. Given major tensions in Husserl's thought and in his approach over time, different schools of phenomenology emerged.[46] What I outline here is phenomenology as Stein first encountered it.

Husserl defined phenomenology as "the science of every kind of object."[47] Its goal is knowledge of the true essence of things or objects, whether a chair, a color, a mental act (such as willing), or an emotion—whatever is given to or encountered in consciousness. Its realist and rationalist assumption is that things do exist inside and outside our mind and that their nature is objectively knowable. Husserl optimistically believed that we can know truly how a thing enters our head, how it appears to us, and how our mind mediates and constitutes it— in short, the full structure and activity of our consciousness. This realism marked a radical rejection of the dominant nineteenth-century neo-Kantian idealism and contemporary academic discussions of philosophical problems. It excited adherents to return to concrete, lived human experience in all its vitality and plenitude.

Husserl was particularly intrigued with specific acts of intention. Whether or not the object of our love exists, for example, that particular turn toward the object, that act of intention, has meaning in our understanding of the mind and needs to be understood in relation to other mental acts. A truly knowing mind, however, is not easily acquired. Phenomenology challenged those who would "know" to abandon all inherited notions, traditions, and prejudices and to bracket—that is, to suspend all prior assumptions and ideas about—each thing under study. Its method required the knower to investigate a thing from as many angles as possible, delineating all ways in which a specific thing was distinct from kindred things, thereby ultimately determining its unique essence. A rigorous observational and self-critical scrutiny was to underpin every mental act. Presumably, neither our contingent historical circumstances nor our unconscious needs and predispositions prevent our truth-grasping ability. Central also to Husserl's philosophy is the assertion that all comprehensive description requires communication with other truth seekers in order to discern and check one's subjective bias and to amplify the range of angles possible in knowing a thing. Husserl's confidence in the results of radical skepticism, open inquiry, and intersubjective processes profoundly attracted and stirred Stein's intellectual fervor.

A salient feature of phenomenology was its inheritance from Descartes of the primacy of reason and the indeterminate lower status of body. Although Stein would come to insist on the unity of mind and body in perception, the rationalist tradition of body subordination served her and other female and Jewish intellectuals interests insofar as the Jewish body and the female body were commonly invoked as evidence for Jewish and female inferiority. Phenomenology, in its glorification of reason, contributed to the humanistic universalism that many Jewish and female thinkers favored.[48]

Beyond class sessions, Husserl held a weekly afternoon "at home," where students could discuss their questions and concerns with him. But Stein's study of phenomenology crucially benefited from occasions that featured the work of other phenomenologists with views that clashed with Husserl's. Since in 1913 Husserl was moving in a direction at odds with aspects of his earlier thought and unconvincing to his students, his followers struggled with a growing tension between Husserl's realism, with its focus on things as objective phenomena, and his heightened idealism that placed objects of consciousness and our modes of their perception as pivotal to the determination of things outside the mind. This tension was manifest in the rivalry between Husserl and Max Scheler. Not long after Stein's arrival at Göttingen, the Philosophical Society chose for close study Max Scheler's *Formalism in Ethics and Nonformal Ethics of Values*—a work, Stein claimed, of immense intellectual influence. The society invited Scheler to

Göttingen to guest-lecture. Denied campus lecture space, Scheler lectured in cafes and hotel social rooms, where "for hours" he continued to discuss philosophy well after his formal lecture had ended.[49] Scheler insisted that his phenomenology owed no debt to Husserl and, a dogged realist, opposed Husserl's new direction. Further, unlike Husserl's diligent training of his students' "radical intellectual honesty" as applied to abstract matters, Scheler's radiant genius lured and dazzled students with his expressive, though often, Stein felt, superficial, eloquence. Stein was intrigued with Scheler's ideas on the phenomenon of sympathy. Since Stein's interest in an allied phenomenon, empathy, was then emerging, Scheler's ideas had instant impact. Scheler, who also espoused Catholic ideas, introduced Stein to the phenomenon of faith, which both extended and challenged the rationalist boundaries of her prior assumptions.

It may sound otherwise, but phenomenologists did not exclusively monopolize Stein's time. She studied with a number of philosophers who were not phenomenologists and who further honed her critical skills. As she dedicated the lion's share of her time to the study of philosophy, Stein sustained research in psychology and her study with Göttingen Germanists and historians.

As her first semester at Göttingen advanced, Stein became clearer and more purposeful about her future. Her initial provisional plans gave way to her decision to remain in Göttingen and study for a doctorate in philosophy, completing her state boards for a teaching position along the way. Again, she could count on family support. Her earlier mentioned interest in the phenomenon of empathy evolved into her dissertation topic and owed much to her study of Husserl's philosophy of intersubjectivity. Stein observed that we establish the existence of others as persons and understand their experience through our capacity for empathy. Since philosophers lacked an adequate explanation of the phenomenon of empathy, Stein resolved to tackle this lacuna.

Stein's second semester differed strikingly from her first. It was academically more rewarding. She delighted in Husserl's course on Kant and Reinach's "Exercises for the Advanced," held in his home study, a space that entranced Stein. From Reinach, Stein learned the phenomenological method thoroughly. But she began to suffer acute bouts of depression. In part the cause was an explicable overexertion. Concurrent with her courses in philosophy, Stein prepared the various subjects required for her state board's teaching exams. Relieved that her preliminary work on empathy met the board's philosophy requirement, Stein found herself pushed to the edge by Husserl's demand that she examine all previous theories of empathy and, most importantly, differentiate in depth between his views on empathy and that of the primary other theorist of the subject, Theodor Lipps. Finding that both Husserl's and Lipps's views eluded her mastery, she underwent an "excruciating struggle to attain clarity" that agitated her daytime hours and disturbed her sleep.[50] She sank into suicidal despair. After some months, Stein brought her concerns to Reinach. He buoyed her spirits, assuring her that she had made good progress, and encouraged her to persevere. She brought to him a draft of her work on Husserl and Lipps, which he also complimented. Responsive to his urging, she remained in Göttingen during interterm and wrote uninterruptedly, completing her manuscript within a week. He predicted that her work would fully satisfy the state boards examination in philosophy.

In the spring and early summer of 1914 Stein busily prepared for the state board examinations. Although rumors of war were in the air, Stein and her comrades "found it inconceivable" that war would come and rend their taken-for-granted security.[51] They were tragically mistaken. Within weeks, Stein's educational path dramatically swerved. On July 30, while reading Schopenhauer's *The World as Will and Idea,* Stein heard a knock on her door and learned from friends that a state of war had been declared. Fearful that Breslau, not far from the Russian border and a key eastern fortification, would soon be besieged by Russian troops, Stein immediately rushed home.

In response to Reinach's question about her plans, Stein replied that she would join the Red Cross. Quickly upon her return to Breslau, Stein put her academic studies on hold and registered for nurse training at the huge urban All Saints Hospital. There she attended lectures on surgery and communicable diseases in wartime and learned practical nursing skills. At home, Stein studied anatomical and medical textbooks. Soon she apprenticed at tuberculosis and surgical wards as well as a surgical polyclinic until a severe bout of bronchitis ended her volunteer activity. Patriotic, eager to serve, anxious to share as equally as possible the risks of warfare with her male colleagues and kin, Stein hoped to be stationed at a field hospital at the front, but no military hospital summoned her.

When Breslau escaped Russian invasion, Stein resumed her studies in Göttingen. Though consumed with anxiety about her male friends at the front and busily preparing care packages for them, Stein dubbed winter 1914–15 as possibly "the happiest time of all my Göttingen student years."[52] Besides her course work, she took over the office of vocational counselor for women students, a position established by the feminist Society for Women's Education and Women's Studies. In mid-January 1915, after submitting much earlier the requisite forms and theses, Stein took the state board exams, passing both written and oral requirements with highest honors.

Returning to Breslau, Stein finally received her call to duty. Since the need for nurses was greatest in Austria, she agreed to a Red Cross assignment at the

Military Hospital for Contagious Diseases in Mährisch-Weisskirchen in eastern Czechoslovakia, where she traveled on April 7, 1915. Although Auguste Stein opposed her daughter's decision, Stein persisted, and her mother wisely relented. Stein maintained her intellectual life, taking with her to the front Husserl's *Ideen (Ideas)* and Homer's *Iliad,* but she learned even more from her experience with soldiers, physicians, and nursing sisters. Mährisch-Weisskirchen, though staffed by German nurses and aides, operated under a Czech director, Czech and Polish doctors, and Czech military command. The war victims Stein treated not only came from diverse realms of the Austro-Hungarian empire but also on occasion included Russians and Turks as well as gypsies. To communicate with patients and doctors, Stein relied on a manual in nine languages. Her compassion and admiration for non-German staff and war victims led Stein to cast off her presumptions about nationality traits and German superiority. Her wartime practice of empathy later provided illustrative support for her dissertation, evidence of the need to suspend all presuppositions and of the nature of empathy itself.

Crucially, Stein's wartime nursing experiences, combined with the fate of close friends and relatives who were soldiers, forced her to confront the reality of acute suffering and death. No doubt her father's death hovered as an inexplicable fate, its impact compounded during her youth by the death and suicide of various relatives; but not until the war did she, as a dauntless, efficient, and caring nurse (later awarded the Medal of Bravery), come face to face with the agonies of severe injury and dying. After a hasty account of "the first time I ever saw anyone die,"[53] she described the second instance of death in vivid detail. Through hourly injections of camphor she had kept a man alive for several days. Her capping experience occurred when she came upon a scrap of paper in her patient's belongings. His wife had written down her prayer for the preservation of his life. "Only when I saw that did I fully realize what this death meant, humanly speaking."[54]

In the course of the war, Stein suffered the loss of cousins, beloved friends, and teachers—Eduard Metis, Hugo Hermsen, Fritz Frankfurter, Rudolf Clemens, Husserl's son Wolfgang, and, perhaps above all, her adored mentor Adolf Reinach. Neither phenomenology nor Homer nor her limited knowledge of Judaism sufficed for Stein to make sense of this. Like countless Europeans, she underwent a spiritual crisis, desperate to find a shred of cosmic meaning in relentless physical pain and the wholesale slaughter of millions. Her existential despair prepared the way for her to newly examine the phenomenon of faith. Wartime misery also exerted an impact on her subsequent philosophical work, either as argumentative illustration or, more centrally, in her analyses of death.[55]

After six months of strenuous nursing, Stein took a furlough in Breslau, expecting to return to Mährisch-Weisskirchen. Since, however, her lazaretto was closed when Germany wrested Galicia back from the Russians, Stein had to look for wartime work elsewhere, even in a munitions factory.[56] In the meantime, she prepared for and passed Greek examinations requisite for her doctorate and proceeded with her dissertation. While in Breslau, with so many men fighting at the front, she found indirect wartime service as a teacher in the Victoria School, a position ordinarily restricted to Protestants. Auguste Stein delighted in her daughter's return home, but for Stein the double day of teaching and doctoral study was as intellectually overtaxing as her nursing had been physically and psychologically. Lacking all appetite, a condition that "recurred nearly every year thereafter," she lost weight rapidly.[57] Her health at risk, Stein temporarily resigned from her teaching post to channel her energies toward the dissertation alone.

In early 1916, Stein's academic path veered again. She learned that Husserl had accepted the position of professor of philosophy at the University of Freiburg im Breisgau, thus filling one of the most renowned chairs in philosophy in Germany. Husserl encouraged Stein to join him at Freiburg, culminating her doctoral studies there. Although her doctoral examiners would be strangers and preparations for the ordeal all the more arduous, she consented. In July, having a few months earlier completed and mailed to Husserl her enormous dissertation, a formidable typing task undertaken by two of her cousins, she set out for Freiburg.

Anxious about Husserl's verdict on her dissertation, Stein discovered he had yet to read it. After much prodding from his wife, he agreed to do so soon and encouraged Stein to set a date for her doctoral exams. Since her teaching duties required her return to Breslau by August 6, she arranged for August 3. During the summer, Stein attended her examiners' lectures and fit into her schedule of almost constant study some excursions and social events. On one occasion at the Husserls, Stein met Martin Heidegger, who had become Husserl's assistant in academic duties. Although Stein came to differ with Heidegger on various major phenomenological matters, their relationship then and for many years to come was cordial.

Husserl read Stein's dissertation closely but never gave her notes. He applauded her work, looked forward to its publication, and even admitted her effect on his writing sections of *Ideas II*. Her dissertation, *Zum Problem der Einfühlung (On the Problem of Empathy)*, was published at Halle in 1917. Stein's volume on empathy remains pioneering to this day, a necessary launch point for any philosophical or psychological account of the phenomenon. Painstakingly methodical, lucid, and compelling, it takes the reader through a series of questions that pinpoint distinctions among a spectrum of allied feelings, sympathy foremost, to climax in her determination of empathy's essence. Starting with the incontrovertible existence of her perception of self, Stein guides the reader to understand how empathy is the fundamental act that confirms our sense of the existence of other persons. She proceeds to attribute to empathy our means of grasping further another's consciousness, including emotions. It is a complex and singular act, for when we enter into another's state of emotion and mind—joy, for instance—we experience both a derivative joy (the feeling of joy is different for the one who first experienced it) and our own joy in the person's joy. The two feelings are interconnected but distinct. Stein's presentation of empathy, though to some degree consonant with and synthesizing ideas of other philosophers, was utterly new. Unlike philosophers and psychologists who assumed a direct correspondence between a person's empathic experience and the experience of the other, Stein carefully identified multiple forms of false empathy and how these arose. She examined the way others' empathy with us challenged and corrected our perceptions of ourselves. She discussed the *will* to attend and the *act* of attending to another person and how each related to our values. In what amounted to heresy with respect to Husserl's ideas at the time, Stein insisted that the human body and the natural world were integral to the structure of a person (she referred to each person as a psycho-physical individual) and to his or her empathic process.[58] In his later writing, to some extent Husserl moved notably toward Stein's perspective.[59]

Husserl's praise of her dissertation emboldened Stein to propose working as his philosophical assistant and collaborator. The wartime death of Husserl's younger son the previous year, compounded by the injury of his older son and the loss of so many of his students, had sapped Husserl's energy for work.[60] As a result of weakened eyesight, he had also to contend with deciphering his scribbled and scattered notes. Given the lack of eligible males to assist him, Husserl gladly accepted Stein's offer. Husserl's salary would fall short of Stein's needs, but her mother financed the gap.

On August 3 Stein, now nearly twenty-five, sailed through her doctoral exams with highest honors. The chance to work with Husserl and her summa on her exams and dissertation marked the pinnacle of Stein's student career. An elated Stein returned to Breslau to complete her teaching commitment before settling into her position with Husserl in Freiburg.

Stein's excitement about working with Husserl soon ebbed when she found Husserl reluctant to review his notes that she had organized and revised. Nonetheless, Stein assembled and prepared a coherent version of Husserl's scraps of paper on time-consciousness, facilitating his *Zur Phänomenologie des inneren*

Zeitbewusstseins (On the Phenomenology of the Consciousness of Internal Time), but Husserl did not acknowledge Stein's success in making his ideas more coherent. Nor did he acknowledge her contributions to his thought in *Ideas II* and *III*. Similarly, Husserl further failed to acknowledge Stein's contribution to his 1920s social philosophy. Venerating Husserl's work, Stein still believed that she should feel gratitude for her time with him, but her self-respect and autonomy were at stake. If Husserl had once served as her surrogate father and an irresistible genius, that idolatry was at its end. Her lone compensatory activity was what she called a "philosophical kindergarten" that she initiated to introduce students to phenomenology. This activity also contributed to her *Einführung in die Philosophie (Introduction to Philosophy)*, a work in progress until 1932.

By early 1918, Stein could no longer tolerate being less than as Husserl's collaborator.[61] She resigned, managing to maintain their close friendship. Her goal now was early acceptance for *Habilitation,* a professorial post, requiring a second doctoral thesis, done at the university where one was to teach. As Stein sought *Habilitation* at the University of Göttingen, she agreed to contribute to a *Festschrift* for Husserl on his sixtieth birthday (1919), for which she completed a thesis on the philosophical foundations of psychology and the humanities, intended to double as her *Habilitation* thesis. Published in Husserl's *Jahrbuch für Philosophie und phänomenologische Forschung (Yearbook for Philosophy and Phenomenological Research)* in 1922 (economic hardships of the postwar period forced a delay), *Beiträge zur philosophischen Begründung der Psychologie und der Geisteswissenschaften (Contributions to the Philosophical Grounding of Psychology and the Humanities),* conveyed Stein's approach to the nature of the psyche. Two treatises composed this hefty thesis: one on sentient causality, which plumbed the dynamics of human motivation and behavior, and the other on the interconnections between the individual and community.

The historical significance of Stein's two treatises lies in its original and penetrating analysis of personhood through the perspectives of empirical natural science and the humanities. Stein articulated the respective, complementary, and overlapping contributions of these ordinarily segregated and competing fields of study as she probed the nature of the individual and her relationship to other individuals and to communities. Based upon a preliminary distinction between natural causation (knowable through empirical science) and human motivation (knowable through empathy), her investigation fused both dynamics of influence to define and depict a person's identity, consciousness, and behavior.[62] At a time of fresh, radical, and challenging ways to comprehend human consciousness and behavior (e.g., forms of psychoanalysis), Stein chose the phenomenological method of microscopic clarification. Stein presented nuanced definitions of specific mental acts, such as attitudinal will, purposeful will, and efficacious will.[63] She finely dissected the continuum of action—impulse, drive, striving, desire— taking into account and sharply particularizing multiple and permeable layers of the individual experience—physical, sensate, mental, spiritual. Meticulously she demarcated the realm of human freedom, a matter of keen importance to her. But she explained that her inability to ground free will in individual strength and natural tendencies "opened the door to the philosophy of religion in whose domain further investigations must take place."[64]

A key element in her analysis of human psychology, anchored in her commitment to the humanities, was her insistence upon the uniqueness and mystery of each person's life force. Acknowledging certain universal elements present in each individual, she held that the inner core of each individual was unclassifiable, affecting motivation and behavior in unpredictable ways. Stein's thesis showed her inching toward a concept of the soul, grappling with questions about the singular unity of an individual's mind, body, and spirit.

In her second treatise on the individual and community, Stein extended the existing boundaries of phenomenological analysis of the person and intersubjectivity to wider orbits than the single individual. Stein expanded the nineteenth-century German sociologist Ferdinand Tönnies's distinction between an association of individuals (a group of individuals sharing a place or a job who enter into instrumental relationships in which they treat each other as means to some end) and a community (in which the individuals treat others as ends in themselves, sharing common values and goals). Proceeding beyond Tönnies's discussion of the origins of associations and communities, Stein detailed how communities function, especially with respect to the irreducible uniqueness of each individual. No one is "typically German," she argued; such a being would lack a genuine personality.[65] Although physical environment and the values of a given community shape its members identity and values, Stein argued that a community originated in each individual's unique being, not the reverse. Between the individual's and community's energy a mutuality flowed. Noting the pivotal role of imaginative individuals in imparting their ideas and experiences, she emphasized that a community must be receptive to such individuals' perceptions. Some of Stein's most interesting and original discussion was of positive and negative group contagion.

More optimistic about Germany's future when the war ended than many of her friends and relatives, Stein anticipated a new constructive spirit emerging in Germany.[66] She hailed new art forms, such as expressionism, that like phenomenology pierced beneath the surface of things to essential emotional and psychological reality. Predicting that rampant prewar materialism would fade and a greater moral astuteness and complexity would arise, she looked forward to a more tolerant, liberal, and democratic homeland. Stein had long combined both German and western European concepts of liberalism, upholding fundamental individual rights and freedom against an interventionist state while hailing the values of a powerful state that provided for its citizen's education and social welfare. Stein had an abiding interest in political history, particularly that of nineteenth-century Germany, which had been her significant course work focus at the Universities of Breslau and Göttingen. Her feminist political activism and wartime service grounded her assertion "My love of history was no mere romantic absorption in the past. Closely associated with it was a passionate participation in current political events as history in the making."[67] Concurrent with her work on her *Habilitation* thesis, she began *Eine Untersuchung über den Staat (On the State)*, completed in 1921 though not published in Husserl's *Yearbook* until 1925.

Intrigued by the phenomena of nations and states, Stein in her thesis etched the distinctions between communities, states, peoples, and nationalities. In light of later Nazi hegemony, her political thought is of particular importance in its opposition to dominant nineteenth- and early-twentieth-century German theory that posited the state as an inevitable expression of the nation and an instrument of each individual's moral development and freedom. By contrast, Stein interrelated state and community, their origins both natural and elective, involving individual consciousness and choice. Correspondingly, she drew emphatic distinctions between people *(Volk)*, their ethnic consciousness, their sense of national identity, and the state. Her vantage point as a woman and a Jew probably inspired Stein's abhorrence of simplistic equations of the majority ethnicity with the nation and the state. Upholding a pluralist universalism, arising, she boasted, from her "extraordinarily strong social conscience, a feeling for the solidarity not only of all mankind but also of smaller social entities,"[68] she objected to authoritarian governments that presumed to speak for all their constituents. The state, she asserted, sprang from the intentions of its multiple populations to share nationhood. Elucidating the nature of sovereignty, Stein underscored that the state was an instrument of individuals and communities, deriving its authority from popular consent. Placing primacy on individual conscience, Stein repudiated absolute obedience to the state. Relatedly, she insisted that secular and religious public life be kept separate. The state's role was to safeguard religious freedom.

Stein's optimism about the new Germany experienced its first major setbacks in her career aspirations. Her application for *Habilitation* at the University of Göttingen was not even taken up by the faculty, a decision she attributed to her

gender and her challenge to dominant psychological theories. Her second attempt at the University of Kiel was equally futile. She did not suggest that her
ethnicity factored in, yet she chose not apply to the University of Hamburg,
"since philosophy in Hamburg is already represented by two Jewish professors."[69]
She tried to take these rejections in stride, finding them "rather amusing," as she
added, "So much for the world in general."[70] Acting on feminist beliefs Stein appealed to the Prussian Ministry for Science, Art and Education to end sexual
discrimination in *Habilitation*. On February 21, 1920, the Prussian Ministry issued a landmark ruling that removed sex barriers to *Habilitation*, but sexist discrimination persisted in the field of philosophy, no enforcement policies having
followed upon the ruling.[71]

While Stein took some satisfaction in lecturing privately on phenomenology
to college students and in spending time with her Breslau family, she had lost
her professional moorings. Nor had she any longer a professional "home." Husserl's abode was no longer a place of comfort, and the Göttingen Phenomenological Society and its inner circle had scattered, with Husserl in Freiburg and
others elsewhere or dead. Hans Lipps had radically challenged Stein's treatises,
and Anna Reinach, admitting her inability to judge Stein's philosophical work,
encouraged Stein to consider whether the intellectual shortcomings that Lipps
pointed out in Stein's work might reflect "far deeper personal shortcomings."
Revered members of the society were mired in scandal. Memories of Husserl's
behavior along with observations now of other phenomenologists convinced
Stein that intellectual virtue did not guarantee moral virtue.

Stein's private world, too, was in disarray. Her personal life was in a crisis that
lasted until summer 1921. She tumbled into a deep depression, accompanied
by much physical illness. Control over a life that she had hitherto enjoyed now
eluded her. Her braided self had unraveled. Disagreeing over names, Stein biographers claim Stein suffered from possibly several unrequited love relationships. In 1920, Stein's planning for and being in the late December wedding of
her beloved sister Erna to Hans Biberstein had an edge to its joy. At thirty, Stein
was getting on in years for a woman who aspired to marry and bear offspring.
The specter of continued dependency on her mother no doubt stung her independent spirit. The passion driving Stein's treatises on personal identity, community, and the state arose from this concurrent personal and professional crisis.
Life questions bombarded her from all sides. At this juncture Stein's philosophical
life took a more decidedly religious turn.

Stein's shift toward Christianity, rather than Judaism, owed much to her
relationship with Reinach's widow, for whom she was arranging her deceased
husband's papers and notes. Study of Adolph Reinach's writings deepened her

understanding of religious faith and expanded her grasp of Christian concepts of love and death. The confidence of Reinach's widow in the soul's immortality, symbolized for her through Jesus on the cross, greatly inspired Stein when she first reconnected with Anna Reinach following her husband's death. With increasing fervor, Stein pored over the Bible, metaphysical books, and religious writings and discussed religion with her Jewish and Christian friends and with the provocative Gerda Walther, whose interests spanned mysticism and parapsychology.

The catalyst for Stein's decision to convert to Roman Catholicism occurred during her summer 1921 visit to her Evangelical (Lutheran) friend Hedwig Conrad-Martius in Bergzabern. Drawn to the autobiography of Teresa of Avila, she stayed up an entire night thoroughly engrossed. Turning its final page at dawn, she declared, "This is the truth."[72] Stein never explained the nature of her epiphany, just what the word *truth* meant to her that day. Scholars have speculated on many possible reasons for Stein's affinity with Teresa of Avila. That Teresa's father and grandfather were Jews who converted to Catholicism was then unknown. Surely, Stein identified with Teresa's deep depression and psychological exhaustion, her wrestling with death that led to her religious transformation. Stein likely found appealing Teresa's gender nonconformity, her entrepreneurial and risk-taking radical reform and expansion of the Carmelite order in the face of the terror of the Inquisition. Easily, Stein would also be drawn to Teresa's dedication to a contemplative life, her intellectual and psychological acuity combined with her deep emotionality and mystic relation with God, her experience of God as love, and her mix of demanding control over her circumstances with her absolute surrender to divine support.[73]

Stein's decision to become a Roman Catholic rather than convert to the predominant Christian religion in Germany, the Evangelical Church, the denomination of her Bergzabern hosts, despite her closeness with Conrad-Martius, stemmed, too, from her unease with the bellicose and nationalist features of German Lutheranism. Stein's universalist outlook was more compatible with Catholic internationalism, and her experience as a minority stirred her sympathy for a religion the German state had marginalized and persecuted in the preceding century. It didn't hurt that Stein prized Catholic churches being open to worshippers beyond set services. A student of Stein's at the time of her conversion observed, too, her relish in Latin texts: "It was because the Lutheran Church had none of this that she could never be a Lutheran."[74]

In swift order, while still in Bergzabern, Stein purchased a catechism and missal, attended her first mass, and prepared for her baptism and Holy Communion, which took place on New Year's Day, 1922, at the parish church in Bergzabern, with Conrad-Martius present as godmother. As part of her re-creation of self, Stein added to Edith the names of Theresia and Hedwig, respectively in honor of Teresa of Avila and of her closest friend and philosophical comrade. Hedwig was also the name of an older sister who had not survived infancy. For the momentous occasion, she wore her godmother's wedding dress. Her mother and siblings were not apprised of Stein's conversion until she returned to Breslau. Predictably, they were shocked and pained. Their dismay, however, did not cause Stein to break relations with her family, nor they with her. Although she desired to enter a Carmelite convent, she could not bear hurting her family still further. She remained a devoted daughter, returning home regularly, accompanying her mother to synagogue, and expressing her unaltered love for her and her siblings.

For the next eight years, to earn a living, Stein taught German language, history, and literature in the Dominican sisters' St. Magdalena's, a girls' secondary school and teacher-preparation institute for the sisters and novitiates in Speyer. Initially at Speyer, Stein devoted herself to teaching and religious contemplation. Seeking as well to blend her life of prayer and teaching with inquiry into the intellectual foundations of Catholicism, Stein sought spiritual guidance from an array of Catholic leaders and scholars both in Speyer and beyond. Notably, in 1925, Stein met Erich Przywara, SJ, a progressive Catholic with an intense interest in Judaism who later became an outspoken anti-Nazi. Recognizing Stein's philosophical gifts, he urged her to translate from English into German a volume of the letters and journals of John Henry Newman written prior to his conversion to the Catholic Church. Stein's translation appeared in 1928, followed by her translation of Newman's *The Idea of a University* and a few years later by her published translation of Thomas Aquinas's *De veritate (Disputed Questions on Truth)*. Przywara also arranged for Stein's retreats for prayer and contemplation at the Benedictine monasteries of Beuron and Maria Laach, centers for the decade's liturgical movement, where, with the movement's stress on inward emotional expression, Stein found a spiritual home anew.[75]

Though a religious apostate, Stein was not an apostate philosopher. Staying loyal to phenomenology and convinced of its compatibility with her Catholic convictions, she dedicated herself to synthesizing Husserlian logic and Aquinas's thought.[76] (Despite the demands of teaching and translation, she continued her writings in philosophy as well. For the celebration of Husserl's seventieth birthday she composed an imaginary dialogue between Husserl and Thomas Aquinas.[77] At Heidegger's prompting, she recast the dialogue into an article for a commemorative issue of Husserl's *Yearbook*, published in 1929.)

Stein's philosophical endeavors rekindled her earlier interest in learning theory and practice. Her teaching experience at Speyer deepened her thought on gender

and its implications for pedagogy and curriculum. She became a leading advocate for school reform. Before long, as her reputation as distinguished teacher
and scholar grew within Catholic circles, she received invitations from large national Catholic women's organizations to lecture in different parts of Germany
and Switzerland. Her favorite topic was the nature and role of women and their
education. These lectures were subsequently collected in a posthumous volume
Die Frau (Essays on Woman).[78]

Stein's lectures on woman provided the most thoughtful presentation of
Catholic feminism of the time. Though Stein discussed being a woman as a phenomenon, parsing it phenomenologically, seeking its gender essence, her remarks
were accessible to her nonphilosophical audience. She sought to arouse her female listeners to a sense of public calling, stressing the urgency of enlightened
female participation in all occupational realms and political endeavors. Stein
followed the course of many European interwar feminists. She integrated arguments for women's equality based wholly on women's similarity with men with
arguments emphasizing sex difference. Balancing her recognition of women's
proclivity toward nurturant professions with her insistence on the primacy of
individual talent and full equality of female opportunity (including the priesthood), she discerned positive/negative masculine/feminine components in each
individual to varying degrees. Calling for full self-realization of a woman's "masculine" as well as "feminine" qualities, her lectures marked the forefront of interwar Catholic feminism.

Juggling the demands of her intellectual and spiritual life was not easy. By 1930
Stein was at another life turning point, one scantly studied by her biographers. In
1931 she left teaching to devote her time to a philosophical writing. Still longing
for a professorship, she hoped her new treatise *Potenz und Akt (Potency and Act)*
could serve as another *Habilitation* thesis. When she consulted with Professors
Eugen Fink and Heidegger about the possibility of her habilitating at the University of Freiburg, they refused assistance. She also tried in vain to apply to the
University of Breslau. Although Stein had vastly upset her mother and family,
Auguste Stein welcomed her daughter's efforts to teach publicly as a Catholic in
Breslau. Having Stein home took top priority. Casting about in other directions,
Stein also appealed for permission to enter the Carmelite order but was turned
down; her superiors invoked not only her effective work as a lecturer but also the
needs of her mother.

Thwarted in attaining *Habilitation* and convent entrance alike, Stein accepted
the position of chair of scientific pedagogy at the German Institute for Educational Theory at Münster. There, in spring 1932, she began teaching. Her first
series of lectures was on her lifelong focus, the structure of the human person.

Stein steeped herself in the institute's library of writings on pedagogy, discovering Montessori literature on childhood education that she found "very significant."[79] In September, she attended a conference entitled "Phenomenology and Thomism," held by the Société Thomiste at Juvisy. At this gathering of eminent French and German philosophers, Stein, impressively fluent in French, was treated as a leading authority. Despite this professional recognition and the satisfactions of her new position, she felt frustrated, unable to create firm intellectual foundations for pedagogy and unable to bring others to her views on pedagogical reform. Stein was aware, too, of changing political tides. She warned friends of ominous signs of the rise of anti-Semitism and the growth of the Nazi party. Although she was not in her psychological shipwreck of the immediate aftermath of the war, her life flow was soon again to hit the rapids.

Stein's control over her future abruptly ended in January 1933 when the Nazis seized power and Hitler became chancellor of Germany. Nazi anti-Jewish laws were swiftly enacted. All non-"Aryan" professionals faced immediately job dismissal. On February 25, 1933, Stein gave her final lecture. Shortly thereafter she planned to travel to Rome to seek a private audience with Pope Pius XI (his pontificate lasted from 1922 to 1939) to convince him to issue an encyclical condemning anti-Semitism. When she learned that she could not see the pope privately, she placed her encyclical request in writing, which the pope received but refused to act on.[80] An alternative route to professional activity emerged when Stein received an invitation to teach in South America. Preferring to remain near her friends and family, she declined.

During this tumultuous spring, Stein began her autobiography, initially intended as a memoir of her mother and a defense of German Jews. In the preface of this unfinished work, *Aus dem Leben einer Jüdischen Familie: Das Leben Edith Steins: Kindheit und Jugend (Edith Stein: Life in a Jewish Family, 1891–1916: An Autobiography)*, Stein, who readily affirmed her Jewishness before and after her Catholic conversion, attacked anti-Semitism with passionate eloquence. The work's initial chapters detail the main lines of her ancestry, describe family members, especially her mother, and recount her early years. Subsequent chapters present her own life story, though always within the rich texture of her immediate- and extended-family tapestry. The Stein who emerged within these pages oscillated between displays of pride and humility; as she matured, she became increasingly serious and critical of her witty, gregarious youth. Stein did not hesitate to expose highly private family matters, but she assiduously protected her own privacy. With stunning recall, and deploying remarkable skills in phenomenological description and portraiture, Stein composed one of the most compelling autobiographies of early-twentieth-century Germany. Together with her letters, this work, despite its incomplete state, remains the most important source for understanding Stein and her education.

Still, even as she began her autobiography, without a job and no longer capable of serving the church in the public arena, Stein applied again to enter the Cologne Carmel. Taking various new initiatives, including a visit there in June, she at last received the longed-for telegram "Joyful assent. Regards, Carmel."[81] She could not fully rejoice. An agonizing phase lay ahead, which in 1938 Stein graphically set forth in "How I Came to the Cologne Carmel." In mid-August, she traveled to Breslau to break the news that she would never see her family again outside a cloister. Stein agonized over the pain she would bring especially to her mother, and she contracted a viral intestinal flu; but she took comfort in the knowledge that the order planned to establish a Carmel in Breslau to which she would be transferred by the following year (these plans never materialized).[82] Such a prospect provided no comfort to Auguste Stein, who viewed her daughter as an apostate and as turning her back on her mother and family during the most perilous times.

On October 14, 1933, Stein entered the Carmelite convent in Cologne-Lindenthal, became a postulant the next day, and received her newly selected name, Sister Teresa Benedicta of the Cross. She took her temporary vows the following year, and then, on April 21, 1938, her perpetual vows. Her intense closeness to her sisters and mother, her friendship with the nuns doing nursing in wartime, her bond with Hedwig Conrad-Martius, and her years among women at Speyer prepared her to enter into another world of sisters. As she fulfilled the various domestic tasks as a nun and sustained the Carmelite tradition of two hours each day for prayer and contemplation, Stein was able to resume her scholarly pursuits. Adrienne Rich's perceptive remarks about Emily Dickinson's nunlike retreat from the world apply no less to Stein: "[G]enius knows itself; . . . Dickinson chose her seclusion, knowing she was exceptional and knowing what she needed . . . a life deliberately organized on her terms."[83] While cloistered, Stein completed the index for her translation of Aquinas's *De veritate*. Building on her treatise *Potency and Act,* she undertook her premier metaphysical opus, *Endliches und ewiges Sein (Finite and Eternal Being),* which she completed early in 1937. Since Nazi censorship prevented its publication, Stein, having looked in vain for a publisher in Holland or Belgium, sought a publisher overseas. Former Göttingen comrades who had emigrated to the United States, attaining professorial positions there, attempted to help her, but the work, lacking an English translator, did not appear in either German or English until after her death.[84]

Finite and Eternal Being, an inquiry into the nature and meaning of being, is the glorious fruit of Stein's study of classical, medieval, and modern philosophy. Her illuminating footnotes variously underscored agreements and differences with past and contemporary philosophers—particularly, among contemporaries, Husserl, Heidegger, Hering, and Conrad-Martius. Through a step-by-step rational ascent from one's finite human self, the I, Stein inferred the First Being as infinite cause and meaning for all being. In singular fashion, she linked Husserl's and Conrad-Martius's concepts of actuality and time, the inner subjective flow of time within consciousness, and the experience of time's finite duration to Aristotelian-Thomistic doctrines of potency and act. Stein tackled the question of the sources of conscious being and our sense of stable self, given the ephemerality of time, memory, and experience. Unlike medieval philosophers who began with faith and moved to understanding, Stein began with reason, pursued natural knowledge to its farthest reach, and only then introduced faith but with the intent to extend philosophy, not turn it into theology. Her footnote 35 reads, "Grace does not exempt Christian scholars from the need for a solid scientific and philosophic erudition . . . just as it does not in other respects absolve them from their natural vocational duties.[85] Baseheart observed that Stein's metaphysics, specifically her linkage of faith and reason, "is not original in twentieth-century philosophy, as the works of Jacques Maritain and others show; but she has her own way of proceeding which is singularly concrete and existential."[86] Crucially, Stein acknowledged that both philosophy and faith are limited by the inexplicable.

While at work on *Finite and Eternal Being,* Stein added an appendix, "Martin Heidegger's Existential Philosophy," comparing and contrasting her views with Heidegger's pivotal works: *Being and Time, Kant and the Problem of Metaphysics,* and *On the Essence of Ground: What Is Metaphysics?* She simultaneously proceeded with her autobiography and composed smaller biographical sketches, biblical exegeses, poems, and a history of the Carmel. As ever, she read voraciously. *Finite and Eternal Being,* for example, required her to consult various sources. For this reason, on July 9, 1935, she wrote Hedwig Conrad-Martius that she "badly" needed to read her article on substance and soul, which had appeared in *Recherches philosophiques* (Paris, 1932–33).[87] Somewhat later she asked to borrow from Conrad-Martius *Die Seele des Menschen (The Human Soul)* (1933), by the phenomenologist Alexander Pfänder.[88] Not confining what she read to philosophical and theological treatises, she also read dramatic literature. As befit her lifelong interest in theater, she even helped mount religious plays.

While Stein was cloistered, her thoughts often dwelt on the world outside the convent.[89] She maintained a steady correspondence with religious leaders, scholars, friends, and family. After Auguste Stein's death in September 1936, Stein's sister Rosa converted to Catholicism and joined her in the convent at Cologne.

Both sisters were deeply concerned about the fate of their family, some of whom chose to leave Germany while others were to be gassed in concentration camps. Stein eagerly voted anti-Nazi herself and urged the other nuns to follow suit. After *Kristallnacht*, Stein sought refuge outside Germany for her own sake and to protect the sisters from Nazi reprisal for her presence among them. Unsuccessful in arranging a transfer to a Carmel in Palestine, Stein found sanctuary at the Carmel in Echt, Holland, which the Cologne Carmel had founded during Bismarck's persecution of Catholic institutions. The house physician of the Cologne Carmelites drove Stein across the border on New Year's Eve 1938.

With the spread of Nazi control into Holland, Stein had again to seek refuge for herself and her sister Rosa, an extern at the Echt convent in 1940. Her application to transfer to the safer Swiss Carmel at Le Paquier, with the United States as her ultimate destination, got ensnared in Nazi and Vatican red tape and foot dragging.[90] Despite her feared homelessness, Stein stayed anchored in her philosophical and contemplative life. While at Echt, she completed an article, "Ways to Know God," for the American Dominican journal *The Thomist* and undertook a study of St. John of the Cross, *Kreuzeswissenschaft (Science of the Cross)*.

Intended for a forthcoming celebration of the feast of St. John, this biographical account of St. John's life, with its thorough, deeply meditative, albeit uncritical exegesis of St. John's earliest work, *The Ascent of Mount Carmel*, offers an indispensable introduction to St. Teresa's trusted advisor and co-reformer. Much influenced by P. Bruno's classic treatment of St. John, Stein also relied on the indispensable studies of the French agnostic Jean Baruzi. By the mid-1930s Stein had come to regard St. John's psychological analysis of the way to purify one's heart for total love of God as a guide for her own spiritual path. The aspects of St. John's instructions that resonated with her personal historical situation were those that counseled detachment from earthly bonds and consolations, leading to complete submission to God's will. Both Stein and St. John believed that only when one felt the cross empathically while comprehending its meaning intellectually could one imitate Christ and declare with authenticity the ecclesiastical motto *Ave, Crux, spes unica* (Hail, Cross, our only hope).[91]

Ultimately, Stein's life of intellectual and spiritual contemplation met an insuperable obstacle. On August 2, 1942, the Gestapo reacted to a Catholic bishops' pastoral letter attacking Nazi policies by rounding up previously spared Catholic Jews for deportation. Edith and Rosa Stein were hauled to a prison camp at Amersfoort. Two days later they were transported to a concentration camp in Drente-Westerbork and from there to Auschwitz. There, along with countless other German Jews, they were murdered in the Birkenau gas chambers on August 9, 1942.

For many, Stein, beatified in 1987, canonized in 1998, and subsequently declared Patroness of Europe, continues active in the world. These papal decisions have stirred heated controversy. But whether or not one believes in a personal afterlife or in Teresia Benedicta of the Cross's saintly powers, Edith Stein won an earthly immortality. Her body of philosophical work survived the "Final Solution" owing to the love of Stein's sisters at the Echt Carmel. They hid Stein's extensive writings at a neighboring monastery in Herkenbosch, and though this monastery was destroyed, most of Stein's papers were rescued. Stein's intellectual passion and tenacity live on through her bold and brilliant writings to inspire later generations of thinkers to contemplate and address the fundamental and perennial questions of human existence that Stein knew all too well.

NOTES

1. Edith Stein, "The Spirit of St. Elizabeth As It Informed Her Life," in *The Hidden Life: Hagiographic Essays, Meditations, Spiritual Texts,* ed. Lucy Gelber and Michael Linssen, OCD, trans. Waltraut Stein, vol. 4 of *The Collected Works of Edith Stein* (Washington, DC: ICS Publications, 1992), 21. Originally published as "Lebensgestaltung im Geist der heiligen Elizabeth," in *Verborgenes Leben: Hagiographische Essays, Meditationen, Geistliche Texte,* vol. 11 of *Edith Steins Werke* (Freiburg: Herder, 1987). The original manuscript represents a lecture that Edith Stein gave on January 24, 1932, in Zürich.

2. Edith Stein, *Life in a Jewish Family, 1891–1916: Her Unfinished Autobiographical Account,* ed. Lucy Gelber and Romaeus Leuven, OCD, trans. Josephine Koeppel, OCD, vol. 1 of *The Collected Works of Edith Stein* (Washington, DC: ICS Publications, 1986), 73–74. Originally published as *Aus dem leben einer jüdischen Familie, Das Leben Edith Stein: Kindheit und Jugend,* vol. 7 of *Edith Steins Werke* (Louvain: Archivum Carmelitanum Edith Stein, E. Nauwelaerts, 1965). Published in a new edition as *Aus dem Leben einer jüdischen Familie und weitere autobiographische Beiträge,* ed. Maria Amata Neyer and Hanna-Barbara Gerl-Falkovitz, vol. 1 of *Edith Stein Gesamtausgabe* (Freiburg: Herder, 2002).

3. Maria Amata Neyer, OCD, *Edith Stein: Her Life in Photos and Documents,* trans. Waltraut Stein (Washington, DC: ICS Publications, 1999), 75, originally published as *Edith Stein: Ihre Leben in Dokumenten und Bildern* (Würzburg: Echter, 1987).

4. Stein, *Life,* 177.

5. Neyer, *Edith Stein,* 75.

6. Joyce Antler, *The Journey Home: Jewish Women and the American Century* (New York: Free Press, 1997), xi, cites novelist Marge Piercy's widely applicable term *braided lives.* See, too, the poet Adrienne Rich's discussion of Jewish female identity fragmentation in "Split at the Root," in *Nice Jewish Girls: A Lesbian Anthology,* ed. Evelyn Torton Beck (Boston: Beacon Press, 1982, 1989), 89.

7. The first half of this essay relies heavily on Stein's *Life.* Only quotations from the *Life* appear here. In addition to quotations, key biographical information from other sources than the *Life* will be fully cited.

8. Stein, *Life,* 55.

9. Ibid., 112.

10. Ibid., 277.

11. Ibid., 319.

12. Marion A. Kaplan, *The Making of the Jewish Middle Class: Women, Family, and Identity in Imperial Germany* (New York: Oxford University Press, 1991), 144.

13. Stein, *Life,* 173.

14. Ibid.

15. Ibid., 187.

16. Ibid., 64.

17. Ibid., 116.

18. Ibid., 77.

19. Ibid., 65.

20. Ibid., 148.

21. Nancy Fuchs-Kreimer, "Sister Edith Stein: A Rabbi Reacts," in *Never Forget: Christian and Jewish Perspectives on Edith Stein,* ed. Waltraud Herbstrith, trans. Susanne Batzdorff (Washington, DC: ICS Publications, 1998), 162, originally published as *Erinnere dich—vergiss es nicht: Edith Stein—christlich-jüdische Perspektiven* (Essen: Plöger, 1990). This essay was a reprint of an article in the Winter 1991 issue of *Lilith: The Independent Jewish Women's Magazine.* See, too, Harriet Pass Friedenreich, "Gender Identity and Community: Jewish University Women in Germany and Austria," in *In Search of Jewish Community: Jewish Identities in Germany and Austria, 1918–1933,* ed. Michael Brenner and Derek J. Penslar (Bloomington: Indiana University Press, 1998).

22. Till van Rahden, "Words and Actions: Rethinking Social History of German Antisemitism, Breslau, 1870–1914," *German History* 18, no. 4 (2001): 413–38.

23. Stein, *Life,* 157.

24. Ibid., 155.

25. Kaplan, *Making,* 8–12, 53; Ruth Gay, *The Jews of Germany: A Historical Portrait* (New Haven, CT: Yale University Press, 1991), 182, 202–3.

26. Susanne M. Batzdorff, *Aunt Edith: The Jewish Heritage of a Catholic Saint* (Springfield, IL: Templegate Publishers, 1998), 180.

27. Stein, *Life,* 162.

28. Ibid., 178.

29. Ibid., 132

30. Ibid., 197.

31. Ibid., 122.

32. Ibid., 196.

33. Ibid., 202.

34. Ibid., 199.

35. Ibid., 208. Stein delighted in handing over some of her earnings to her mother; they were put into the lumber business and "credited" to her in her individual account in the business. Stein's deposits grew in value as the lumber business flourished and land was acquired. Stein writes, "During the years I studied elsewhere, and later, when doing research without compensation, I met my expenses out of this fund." World War I loans and inflation, however, depleted it.

36. Ibid., 215.

37. Ibid.

38. Ibid., 219.

39. Ibid., 410.

40. Ibid., 222.

41. Ibid., 218.

42. Ibid.

43. A privatdocent has passed a special examination and presented a scientific thesis beyond the doctoral dissertation. Though university-authorized to lecture, the privatdocent does not receive a salary from the university; instead, students pay fees directly to the teacher.

44. Stein, *Life*, 252.

45. Mary Catharine Baseheart, SCN, *Person in the World: Introduction to the Philosophy of Edith Stein* (Dordrecht: Kluwer Academic Publishers, 1997), 22.

46. My chief source for understanding the various schools of phenomenology is Dermot Moran, *Introduction to Phenomenology* (New York: Routledge, 2000). Unfortunately, Moran pays scant attention to Edith Stein.

47. Ibid., 82.

48. A disproportionate number of philosophers of Jewish descent constituted the first generation of phenomenologists and formed the Göttingen Circle; they included, in addition to Husserl, Adoph Reinach, Max Scheler, Hans Lipps, Fritz Kaufmann, Dietrich von Hildebrand, and Alexander Koyré, and Stein's closest female friend, Hedwig Conrad-Martius.

49. Stein, *Life*, 258.

50. Ibid., 277.

51. Ibid., 293.

52. Ibid., 303.

53. Ibid., 338.

54. Ibid.

55. Antonio Calcagno examines Stein's views on death in "*Die Fülle oder das Nichts? Edith Stein and Martin Heidegger on the Question of Being*," in *American Catholic Philosophical Quarterly* 74, no. 2 (2000): 277–78. Calcagno draws heavily on Stein's appendices to her *Endliches und Ewiges Sein* [Finite and Eternal Being] (Freiburg: Herder, 1950), specifically *Die Seelenburg* [The Castle of the Soul] and *Martin Heidegger's Existential Philosophy*, which appeared in another volume, *Welt und Person* [World and Person] (Louvain: Nauwelaerts; Freiburg: Herder, 1962). For the English translation, see *Finite and Eternal Being*, vol. 9 of *The Collected Works of Edith Stein*, ed. Lucy Gelber and Romaeus Leuven, trans. Kurt F. Reinhardt (Washington, DC: ICS Publications, 2002). Allusions to her war experience and remarks on death also appear in Stein's writings on empathy and on community. See also chap. 7 of this volume.

56. Stein, *Life*, 499. Edith Stein to Fritz Kaufmann, December 13, 1916, in *Self-Portrait in Letters, 1916–1942*, ed. Lucy Gelber and Romaeus Leuven, OCD, trans. Josephine Koeppel (Washington, DC: ICS Publications, 1993), 2–3. Originally published as *Selbstbildnis in Briefen*, pt. 1, *1916–1934*, and pt. 2, *1934–1942*, vols. 8 and 9 of *Edith Steins Werke* (Druten: De Maas und Waler, 1976, 1977).

57. Stein, *Life*, 396.

58. Stein to Roman Ingarden, March 20, 1917, in *Self-Portrait in Letters*, 13.

59. See chap. 14 of this volume.

60. Moran, *Introduction to Phenomenology*, 32.

61. Stein to Roman Ingarden, February 19, 1918, in *Self-Portrait in Letters*, 210–11.

62. Marianne Sawicki, in her introduction to Edith Stein's *Philosophy of Psychology and the Humanities*, ed. Marianne Sawicki, trans. Mary Catharine Baseheart and Marianne Sawicki, vol. 7 of *The Collected Works of Edith Stein* (Washington, DC: ICS Publications, 2000), originally published as "Beiträge zur philosophischen Begründung der Psychologie und der Geisteswissenschaften," *Jahrbuch für Philosophie und phänomenologische Forschung* 5 (1922): 1–283, underscores that Stein differentiated between person and human individual (xv).

63. Ibid., 56, as defined in Sawicki, introduction, n. 82.

64. Stein to Fritz Kaufmann, September 16, 1919, in *Self-Portrait in Letters*, 31–32.

65. Stein, *Philosophy of Psychology*, 263.

66. Stein to her sister Erna Stein, July 16, 1918, in *Self-Portrait in Letters*, 27–28.

67. Stein, *Life*, 190.

68. Ibid.

69. Stein to Fritz Kaufmann, November 8, 1919, in *Self-Portrait in Letters*, 35–36.

70. Stein to Fritz Kaufmann, November 22, 1919, in *Self-Portrait in Letters*, 37–38.

71. Stein to Fritz Kaufmann, March 31, 1920, in *Self-Portrait in Letters*, 43–44.

72. Waltraud Herbstrith, *Edith Stein: A Biography*, trans. Bernard Bonowitz, OCSO (San Francisco: Ignatius Press, 1992), 65. Originally published as *Das Wahre Gesicht Edith Steins* (Munich: Gerhard Kaffke, 1971).

73. According to Thomas F. O'Meara, OP, in his *Erich Przywara, S.J.: His Theology and His World* (Notre Dame, IN: University of Notre Dame Press, 2002), 121, Przywara, a prominent German Catholic intellectual who was one of Stein's religious mentors, reported a different catalyst for Stein's conversion. Przywara recalled that Stein told him that "while still an atheist she found in the bookstore she frequented a copy of the *Spiritual Exercises*. It interested her first only as a study of psychology but she quickly realized that it was not something to read but to do. So as an atheist, she made, along with the little book, the long retreat and finished the thirty days with the decision to convert'" (121). O'Meara cites Przywara's "Die Frage Edith Stein," in *In und Gegen* (Nuremberg: Glock und Lutz, 1955), 72, and his review of a Festschrift for Hedwig Conrad-Martius, "Zwischen Metaphysik und Christentum," *Philosophisches Jahrbuch* 66 (1958): 181–93.

74. Recollection of Professor Gertrud Koebner, quoted in Herbstrith, *Edith Stein*, 71.

75. O'Meara, *Erich Przywara*, 121–22. See chap. 8 of this volume for Gerl-Falkovitz's account of Stein's translation of John Henry Newman.

76. Stein to Sr. Adelgundis Jaegerschmid, March 23, 1938, in *Self-Portrait in Letters*, 272. This letter includes Stein's much-quoted statement "God is truth. All who seek truth seek God, whether this is clear to them or not."

77. O'Meara, *Erich Przywara*. Przywara encouraged Catholics "to employ but not idolize Aquinas" (123). Przywara lauded Stein's "astonishing confrontation between Husserl and Aquinas." For this quotation O'Meara cites Przywara, "Husserl et Heidegger," *Études philosophiques* 16 (1961): 55, nn. 109, 223.

78. These lectures now appear in two volumes in the new Herder edition of Stein's work, *Edith Stein Gesamtausgabe*, as *Die Frau* [Essays on Woman] (vol. 13, 2000) and *Bildung und Entfaltung der Individualität* [Education and Development of the Individual] (vol. 16, 2001).

79. Stein to Elizabeth Nicola and Helene Lieb, Düsseldorf, December 20, 1935, in *Self-Portrait in Letters*, 221–22.

80. Edith Stein, "How I Came to Cologne Carmel," in *Edith Stein: Selected Writings*, ed. Susanne M. Batzdorff (Springfield, IL: Templegate Publishers, 1990), 17. On February 22, 2003, the Vatican released archived documents, including Edith Stein's letter seeking papal intervention against the Nazis. Her letter called upon Pope Pius XI to speak against the extermination of the Jews and argued that papal silence did not promote positive change in Germany and damaged the church's image worldwide.

81. Ibid., 22.

82. Stein to Mother Petra Brüning, September 17, 1933, in *Self-Portrait in Letters*, 156–57. Also see discussion in Batzdorff, *Aunt Edith*, 85.

83. Adrienne Rich, *On Lies, Secrets, and Silence: Selected Prose, 1966–1978* (New York: W. W. Norton, 1979), 160.

84. Steven Payne, OCD, "Foreword to the ICS Publications Edition," in *Edith Stein, Finite and Eternal Being: An Attempt at an Ascent to the Meaning of Being*, ed. Lucy Gelber and Romaeus Leuven, trans. Kurt F. Reinhardt (Washington, DC: ICS Publications, 2002), originally published as *Endliches und Ewiges Sein: Versuch eines Aufstiegs zum Sinn des Seins*, vol. 2 of *Edith Steins Werke* (Freiburg: Herder, 1950).

85. Ibid., 551.

86. Baseheart, *Person in the World*, 127.

87. Stein to Hedwig Conrad-Martius, July 9, 1935, in *Self-Portrait in Letters*, 212.

88. Stein to Hedwig Conrad-Martius, October 10, 1936, in *Self-Portrait in Letters*, 239–40.

89. See my extensive discussion in chap. 9 of this volume.

90. Herbstrith, *Edith Stein*, 176–77; Batzdorff, *Aunt Edith*, 163; Baseheart, *Person in the World*, 18.

91. Stein to Mother Ambrosia Antonia Engelmann, OCD, Echt, December, 1941, in *Self-Portrait in Letters*, 341.

Chapter 2

In Search of Edith Stein
Beyond Hagiography

DANA K. GREENE

The storm over the canonization of Edith Stein was probably inevitable, given the timing and politics of the event and the seeming contradictions in Stein's life itself. The elevation of another Carmelite, Therese of Lisieux, earlier in this century raised no such furor. Unlike the "Little Flower," whose holiness was rooted in ordinary life lived out in the cloister, Stein's life is intimately connected to the dramatic historical events of the twentieth century. Gaining perspective on her personal history will take time. The rush to judgment on her life after only fifty-six years brings its own burdens, one of which may be to obscure its meaning. It is understandable that the aging John Paul II, eager to offer contemporary models of sanctity to a world he perceives to be off course, would have pushed through her case. As a young intellectual he read her work, and the political events that shaped her life helped determine his own. John Paul's Carmelite sympathies must have been a factor too, as well as his acute realization that he had little time left to aid her cause.

Declaring Edith Stein a martyr of the church made her canonization possible in the short term. No matter how technically legitimate that designation, it obviated the fact that it was her Jewishness that was the basis of her death in the first place.[1] To address Jewish consternation over declaring her a Christian martyr, the pope claimed that Edith Stein died both as a faithful daughter of Israel and as a martyr of the church.[2] Because the history of Jewish-Christian relations is so strained, these claims and counterclaims will persist. However, what is lost in this skirmishing are the more fundamental questions of how the meaning of Stein's remarkable life should be constructed and who is to determine that meaning—Edith Stein herself? Those who have canonized her? Or some combination of past, present, and future interpreters?

To construct a full account of Edith Stein, a number of tasks need to be undertaken. Questions about her life and work must be resolved.[3] What is her contribution to philosophy,[4] spirituality,[5] education,[6] and feminism?[7] Is her work on empathy and her attempted integration of phenomenology and Thomism of enduring significance? Does she have original insight into women's condition as distinct from men's? Is there merit in her understanding of the function of the state? What is the literary and historical value of her autobiographical memoir of her Jewish family, and how is it connected to her philosophical work on empathy? While there is a growing body of biographical material on Stein, it does not address these questions, which are critical to an understanding of Stein's life story.

But simply adding new material to the existing work on Stein's life will not be sufficient. What is needed is a fundamental reframing of her life, which up until recently has been largely captive to the hagiographical tradition.[8] This essay will address a number of issues connected with the writing of Stein's life story. It will propose that her life can be more appropriately examined through a thoroughly secular biography that emphasizes development and contextualization and honors complexity and ambiguity. At the same time, it will address the limits of the biographical tradition, which often is preoccupied with examining external achievement. Can biography grasp a subject like Edith Stein, whose significance may principally be in the dynamic of her inner life? Can it take on the question of sanctity, which has historically been the purview of hagiography? Can it add to the discussion of the meaning of a subject's life?

The hope of those supporting Stein's canonization was that her sanctified status would draw interest to her. But this hope cannot be realized if her life story continues to be explored within a hagiographic tradition. The limits of hagiography were eloquently critiqued by John Henry Newman more than a century ago:

> I ask something more than to stumble upon the *disjecta membra* of what ought to be a living whole. I take but a secondary interest in books which

chop up a Saint into chapters on faith, hope and charity, and the cardinal virtues. They are too scientific to be devotional . . . They do not manifest a Saint, they mince him into spiritual lessons. . . . Such reading is not history, it is moral science; nay, hardly that: for chronological considerations will be neglected; youth, manhood and age, will be intermingled. I shall not be able to trace out, for my own edification, the solemn conflict which is waging in the soul between what is divine and what is human, or the eras of successive victories won by the powers and principles which are divine. I shall not be able to determine whether there was heroism in the young, whether there was not infirmity and temptation in the old. I shall not be able to explain actions which need explanation, for the age of the actors is the true key for entering into them. I shall be wearied and disappointed, and I shall go back with pleasure to the Fathers.[9]

The hagiographic tradition Newman criticized is fixed on teaching spiritual lessons; the life itself is of secondary importance, and as such it is presented in a fragmented and ahistorical form. By subordinating the development of a life to spiritual instruction, the hagiographer collapses its tensions that serve as the locus for incremental growth. While Newman's critique reflects his own nineteenth-century preoccupation with development and personal and historic conflict, he understands the limits of hagiography for the modern mind. Because the purpose of hagiography is to teach virtue, the saint's life is important only as a container for such virtue. One-dimensional and monochromatic, the life lacks vitality. What emerges is a plaster saint, one seemingly fated for holiness. Tensions in the life are flattened out; personal flaws and limitations are minimized. Unrelated to the human condition, this life neither inspires, challenges, nor educates.

The hagiographer begins with the assumption of holiness, and the life is understood as an illustration of that assumption. In the case of Stein, her hagiographers see her life through a lens of redemptive suffering. Confirmed in that view by her death at Auschwitz, they read suffering back into the whole of her life itself to give it meaning; suffering becomes its preeminent virtue. Her story then is a search for clues that prepare her to sacrifice herself for the Jewish people. According to this telling, her freedom, fated from the outset, is diminished, and the meaning of her life is narrowed to conform to a preordained destiny. The canonization of Edith Stein as martyr confirms this and makes alternative interpretations of her life even more difficult.[10]

If the hagiographic tradition, with its didactic purpose and ahistorical interpretation, has failed to capture Stein's life, it is clear that the humanistic genre of biography has much to contribute to illuminating it. The biographer's task is to explore a subject's life developmentally, rather than teleologically as a hagiographer might, and to select from among myriad facts those that have not been fully considered. In an effort to compensate for what has not yet been included in the extant studies of Stein's life, the biographer must both show the link between her personal history and contemporary events and explore the considerable complexity in her individual life. To contextualize Stein's life, consideration must be given to German history: the emergence of the modern German state, its participation in the Great War and its subsequent alienation, the evolution of its educational system, the rise of anti-Semitism and its aftermath, the development of modern German philosophy, the rise of feminism, the history of the German Christian churches and their relationship to Jews, the social and economic buildup to the Second World War, and the implications of that war for daily life in Europe. The biographer must set Stein's life within this larger context, evaluating the impact of these events on her[11] and her contribution to them.

A biography of Stein must also examine the complex interaction of social, intellectual, and psychological factors that shaped her responses to a variety of situations and questions, including her early formation as the youngest child in a large fatherless family, her dropping out of school, and her transformation from the daughter of a devout Jew, to a nonobservant Jew, to one who gave up praying altogether.[12] Greatly influenced by German patriotism, and longing to give herself to some great cause and to share the suffering of her male peers, she joined in the war effort. "My love for history," she wrote, "was no mere romantic absorption in the past. Closely associated with it was a passionate participation in current political events as history in the making."[13] She wrote: "[I]t was suddenly crystal clear and evident to me: today my individual life has ceased, and all that I am belongs to the state."[14] Are these claims the result of youthful hyperbole, psychological orientation, or cultural influence? What were the sources of her sense of social responsibility? What explains why, as a university student drawn to psychology and history, she chose instead to study philosophy? What was the impact on her of the heady university life of Göttingen and participation in Husserl's phenomenological circle of disciples? What explains the selection of the problem of empathy as her dissertation topic, and how does this influence her subsequent thinking? How did her problematic relationship with Husserl affect her? And what of the impact of others in Husserl's phenomenological circle, namely Max Scheler and Adolf Reinach? She had many friends but few male intimates. What was her relationship with fellow student Hans Lipps, and would she have married him if he had been interested in her?[15] How did she deal with her failure to achieve a university position? What were other consequences of her double marginality as a woman and as a Jew?

These ordinary themes of family and student life, love of country, and loss of opportunity are played out against the backdrop of Edith Stein's lifelong search for meaning. The documentation of this search must be a central consideration of any biography. Because Stein was above all an intellectual, it was the pursuit of truth that first attracted her. But even this was no mere rationalistic quest. The biographer must explore how she was moved from a quest for intellectual to religious truth. Certainly, her study of phenomenology played a major role in redirecting her. Mary Catharine Baseheart argues that phenomenology, with its emphasis on openness and objectivity, prepared her for religious experience.[16] The biographer's task is to show how this happened. What role did her experience of peers and colleagues have in this? Stein alludes to three separate incidents in which she perceived transfigured persons: in 1916 she glimpsed a woman in prayer in a Catholic church; in 1918 she was impressed by the peacefulness of Anna Reinach after the death of her husband; and in 1921 she read Teresa of Avila's autobiography in one night and proclaimed that it was "the truth." The biographer needs to examine these incidents closely, note their consequences, and show the relationship between them and her ongoing philosophical probing of what it means to be human person.

Stein's search for religious meaning created significant tension in her life. First, there was the continuous, unresolved hostility of her mother, who was incapable of accepting her daughter's decision to become a Christian. This mother-daughter relationship needs to be more fully explored. At least initially Stein believed that her conversion meant she must retreat from the world and from scholarship.[17] Why did she change her mind and continue her intellectual work, through translations first of the letters and journals of John Henry Newman and then of Aquinas's *Questiones disputatae de veritate*? How did this work deepen her understanding of her new faith? And what was the impact of her years teaching in Speyer and living with the Dominican nuns there? How and why did she take on a very public role as a lecturer on women? What was the consequence of this for her? What finally brought her to enter religious life, and why did she choose the Carmelites rather than the Dominicans or another religious order? At each step—as a university student, as a translator, as a teacher who failed to gain a university post, as an aspiring Carmelite—there were events, circumstances, relationships that redirected her. She made choices that moved her away from her past and opened up the possibility of a new future. These subtle decisions, these seemingly chance experiences, are the stuff of biography, the story of how a life is shaped. What is important is the interplay between the pressures of circumstance, talent, character, and personal freedom. The work of the biographer is to surround that interplay with detail, to hem it in, to point to it, and, in so doing, to illuminate it.

One of the most potent themes in Stein's life is her continuous attempt to reconcile seemingly contradictory realities involving intellectual commitments with her new faith. The biographer must focus on these attempts and the conflicts they created. In the ten years prior to her entrance into the Carmelite order, Stein tried to integrate phenomenology and Thomism, the two systems of thought that shaped her life. She also attempted to integrate feminism with Catholic teaching and Thomistic philosophy in a series of lectures given to Catholic women's groups throughout Germany between 1928 and 1933. In these she explored her belief in the political and social equality of women and her desire to protect their needs in a male-dominated world. These lectures, published subsequently as *Die Frau (Essays on Woman)*,[18] sprang from her deepened faith and her sense of social responsibility to change the degraded attitude toward women. In them she showed herself to be a precursor of contemporary feminists like Carol Gilligan who support women's political and social equality but underscore both similarities with and differences from men. How successful was Stein in reconciling her early commitments to phenomenology and feminism with Thomism? Whatever her contribution in these two areas, this corpus provides the biographer extensive evidence of her thinking at a particular point in her development.

Stein's work of philosophical and pragmatic reconciliation is superseded in importance by her attempt to reconcile her commitments to Judaism and Christianity. Did she, as some have argued, cease to be a Jew when she became a Christian?[19] If not, to what degree was she able to reconcile these two commitments, and how did she carry out the reconciliation? How did the anti-Semitic context of her life complicate this? Did she, as the pope has claimed, die as a faithful daughter of Israel as well a daughter of the church? Or is this reconciliation always fragile, illustrated most fully by the enigmatic image of Stein swathed in the black habit of Carmel with a yellow star of David affixed to the sleeve?

Reconciliation between Judaism and Christianity was not merely personal and internal for Stein. It had consequences for her relationships with friends and family, particularly her mother, as well as for her attitude toward the German state, which she loved but which became increasingly anti-Semitic after 1933. The tensions surrounding these relationships must have been extraordinarily difficult. She tried to be supportive and understanding of her mother and to do what she could to counter anti-Semitism. She wrote to the pope requesting an audience during which she hoped to persuade him to write a special encyclical defending the Jewish people. There was no response. When she entered Carmel she continued her work on a manuscript that was published posthumously as *Life in a Jewish Family*. In this extraordinary document, a work of empathy and compassion, she honors her past and presents Jewish family life in all of its humanity.

The themes of integration and reconciliation must be central to any biography of Edith Stein. They cannot be considered independent of the history of the early twentieth century, nor can they be addressed simplistically. The given is that they produced tension, and the biographer must capture this. Unlike hagiography, biography has no need to eliminate tensions or resolve conflicts. Neither is it responsible for solidifying the meaning of a life. That meaning must remain open-ended and incomplete. In the case of Stein, the biographer's task is complicated by the fact that the subject offered her own interpretation of redemptive suffering as the meaning of her life. In Stein's own words, she was both a *holocaustum*[20] and a modern Queen Esther who offered herself to save her people.[21] But her self-understanding is neither definitive nor complete; the biographer must recognize it for what it is—another artifact to be interpreted. The meaning of Stein's life is unfinished; it is not controlled by her, by official saint makers, or by interpreters past, present, or future. Biography itself points to the irreducible freedom in a life that can never be fully grasped, contained, or expressed.

Finally, and perhaps most difficult, a biography of Edith Stein must at least be willing to take up the claim of her holiness. How is this to be done? What is holiness, and how might it be documented? The etymology of the word *holy* may provide some clues to a new criterion for sanctity. The word *holy* is related to the notion of wholeness, a state of being in which inner and outer selves are congruent. As such, wholeness represents a coherence of being, an integrity lived out authentically, which gives evidence of the transformation called holiness.[22] Can this measure of holiness be applied to the life of Edith Stein?

Recently, there have been some incipient attempts to rethink the organizing themes and hence the meaning of Stein's life. For example, Patricia Hampl has argued that Stein is a riddle containing seeming contradictions and that "she is a life waiting to be read."[23] The theme that Hampl sees in Stein's life is a passion for greatness. Certainly, Stein herself gives abundant evidence of this passion. Reflecting on her early life, she wrote: "In my dreams I always foresaw a brilliant future for myself. I dreamed about happiness and fame, for I was convinced that I was destined for something great and that I did not belong at all in the narrow bourgeois circumstances into which I had been born."[24] If this is a defining theme in Stein's life, the biographer will need to inquire about its origin. Did it arise from her marginality, her sense of intellectual superiority, romantic sentiment, or an acute sense of destiny? And what are the implications throughout her life of this desire for greatness? The contribution of Hampl's brief reflection on Stein's life is to recast the question of its meaning, to open it up to a broader interpretation. Likewise Steven Payne, a fellow Carmelite, suggests that the way to understand Stein's life is as a series of failures.[25] How and why did Stein fail, and what ramifications did that have for her life? Finally, Rachel Feldhay Brenner, in a comparative study of four women confronting the Holocaust, depicts Stein's life as one of resistance.[26] She argues that Stein's great concern for the world shaped her scholarly interests and her actions. She spent her life trying to make her beliefs and actions cohere. Brenner contends that Stein's reconciliation of her Jewish and Christian selves, her empathetic defense of Jews in her family memoir, and her efforts to examine the nature of women in positive terms were all acts of resistance in a world of increasing inhumanity. Following the theological interpretation of Paul Tillich, Brenner links Stein with her three Jewish contemporaries— Simone Weil, Anne Frank, and Etty Hillesum—all of whom lived in a world that denied the existence of God. Each resisted that world and acted as if God did exist. In so doing they contributed to maintaining values of justice without the support of the divine. In Stein's case, by empathetically taking up the cross for her people she reached beyond them to a suffering God. While these brief interpretations of Brenner, Hampl, and Payne are limited and partial, they signal that the hagiographic interpretation of Stein's life may have an alternative.

One goal of the canonization of Edith Stein is to increase attention to this remarkable woman. Whether that goal will be realized is still an open question. What is clear is that unless an alternative to the hagiographic interpretation of her life is developed, interest in her case will remain limited to sectarian believers. Not only will Edith Stein's life not be subject to broad scrutiny, but the opportunity to create interest in it will be lost.

The identification and recognition of holy persons or saints in the Christian tradition have evolved over time. In the earliest centuries of the Christian Church the local community proclaimed saints. In the medieval period, this became the prerogative of bishops, and in the last few centuries canonization of official saints has increasingly been controlled by the Papal Curia.[27] As a result, in contemporary society these official saints have become remote and inaccessible. Likewise, the criteria for selection have become suspect. While the miracle may have had currency in the past, it presents a problem for the modern mind. In fact, miraculous power may not be the most convincing illustration of the transformed life of holiness. Some other means to verify sanctity may need to be defined. A nonhagiographic approach to Stein's life might be useful to believers as an example of what Kenneth Woodward calls "primary theology."[28]

If evidence for holiness is to be found in the life of Edith Stein, the biographer must look for it in her subtle and slow development—not in the act of death but in the process of living that makes a certain kind of death possible. Because the biographer is limited to external evidence, all that can be hoped for is to clarify when moments of transformation occur. By pointing to those moments, the biographer honors the freedom of the subject, recognizes the constraints on her, and shows the mysterious inner dynamic that can only be described but not proven—what Christians call grace. The purpose of biography is humble, not grand; it cannot prove or proclaim holiness or sanctity, neither does it assume it. Biography aims merely to open up a life to ongoing interpretation and to provoke the reader to self-reflection. If Edith Stein's life invites readers, as John Coleman argues the lives of saints do, to conceptualize their lives "in terms other than mastery, usefulness, autonomy or control,"[29] then she will have made a contribution to human possibility. It will be of value both to remember her life and to record it.

NOTES

1. Stein was declared a martyr of the church, one who was killed expressly in retaliation for the July 1942 Dutch bishops' public condemnation of Nazi activities. For accounts of her beatification and sanctification, see John Sullivan, "The Path to Beatification," in *Never Forget: Christian and Jewish Perspectives on Edith Stein,* ed. Waltraud Herbstrith, OCD, trans. Susanne Batzdorff (Washington, DC: ICS Publications, 1998), 7–14, and Kenneth Woodward, *Making Saints* (New York: Simon and Schuster, 1990), 127–44.

2. John Paul II, "Homily at the Beatification of Edith Stein," in *Edith Stein Symposium: Teresian Culture,* ed. John Sullivan, OCD, Carmelite Studies 4 (Washington, DC: ICS Publications, 1987), 298–306.

3. The recent publication of Marianne Sawicki's *Body, Text, and Science: The Literacy of Investigative Practices and the Phenomenology of Edith Stein* (Boston: Kluwer Academic Publishers, 1997), is a major contribution to Stein studies. In addition to treating a number of important philosophical and historical issues, Sawicki considers many of the interpretations of Stein. Her bibliography is extraordinarily inclusive of articles written in English and all European languages.

4. Two of Stein's philosophical works available independently in English are *On the Problem of Empathy,* trans. Waltraut Stein (Washington, DC: ICS Publications, 1989), and *Essays on Woman,* trans. F. M. Oben (Washington, DC: ICS Publications, 1987). For secondary works, see Mary Catharine Baseheart and Linda Lopez McAlister, "Edith Stein," in *A History of Women Philosophers,* ed. Mary Ellen Waithe (Boston: Kluwer Academic Publishers, 1995), 4:157–87; Mary Catharine Baseheart, *Person in the World: Introduction to the Philosophy of Edith Stein* (Boston: Kluwer Academic Publishers, 1997); James Collins, "Edith Stein and the Advance of Phenomenology," *Thought* 17 (1942): 685–708; Roman Ingarden, "Edith Stein on Her Activity as an Assistant of Edmund Husserl," trans. Janina Makota, in *Philosophy and Phenomenological Research* 23 (1962): 155–75; Ralph

McInerny, "Edith Stein and Thomism," in Sullivan, *Edith Stein Symposium*, 74–87; Jan N. Nota, "Edith Stein and Martin Heidegger," in Sullivan, *Edith Stein Symposium*, 50–73.

5. Her only work in spirituality published in English is *The Hidden Life: Hagiographic Essays, Meditations, and Spiritual Texts* (Washington, DC: ICS Publications), 1992.

6. Mary Catharine Baseheart, "Edith Stein's Philosophy of Woman and of Women's Education," *Hypatia* 4, no. 1 (1989): 118–31, and "On Educating Women: The Relevance of Stein," *Continuum* 4 (1966): 197–207.

7. Joann Wolski Conn, "Edith Stein and Authentic Feminism" (review of Stein's *Essays on Woman*), *Cross Currents* (1988): 223–26, and Linda Lopez McAlister, "Edith Stein: Essential Differences," *Philosophy Today* 37, no. 1 (1993): 70–77.

8. Hagiography is idealized biography written for purposes of veneration of the subject. In this case the writer begins with certain uncritical assumptions of the subject's saintliness and proceeds to find evidence in the life to confirm them. While the following works in English have made a contribution to scholarship on Stein, that contribution has its limitations: Hilda Graef, *The Scholar and the Cross* (Westminster, MD: Newman Press, 1956); Waltraud Herbstrith, *Edith Stein: A Biography* (San Francisco: Harper and Row, 1971); Josephine Koeppel, *Edith Stein: Philosopher and Mystic* (Collegeville, MN: Liturgical Press, 1990); Teresia Renata Posselt, *Edith Stein*, trans. C. Hastings and Donald Nicholl (New York: Sheed and Ward, 1952). The work of Baseheart, Berkman, Brenner, Hampl, Payne, and Sawicki, cited elsewhere in this chapter, is more critical.

9. Woodward, *Making Saints*, 369, quoting from John Henry Newman, "Ancient Saints."

10. Stein was beatified and canonized both for heroic virtue and for martyrdom. It is her designation as martyr that has caused concern and may have the lasting injurious effect.

11. In a recently published portrait of Stein, her niece, Susanne Batzdorff, describes Stein's early Jewish heritage, including Jewish life in Breslau and university life in Göttingen. See Susanne Batzdorff, *Aunt Edith: The Jewish Heritage of a Catholic Saint* (Springfield, IL: Templegate Publishers, 1998). A more promising treatment can be found in Joyce Avrech Berkman's "'I Am Myself It': Comparative National Identity Formation in the Lives of Vera Brittain and Edith Stein," *Women's History Review* 6, no. 1 (1997): 47–73.

12. Edith Stein, *Life in a Jewish Family: Her Unfinished Autobiographical Account*, ed. Lucy Gelber and Romaeus Leuven, OCD, trans. Josephine Koeppel, OCD (Washington, DC: ICS Publications, 1986), 148.

13. Ibid., 190.

14. Edith Stein to Roman Ingarden, February 9, 1917, in *Self-Portrait in Letters, 1916–1942* (Washington, DC: ICS Publications, 1993), 10.

15. Hedwig Conrad-Martius, "Edith Stein Remembered," in Herbstrith, *Never Forget*, 265–66.

16. Baseheart, *Person in the World*, 13.

17. Stein to Sr. Callista Kopf, OP, Feb. 12, 1928, in *Self-Portrait in Letters, 1916–1942*, 54.

18. The helpful introduction by Lucy Gelber to Stein's *Essays on Woman* includes consideration of Stein's general philosophy, pedagogy, and spirituality as it relates to women.

19. Daniel Polish, "The Canonization of Edith Stein," in Herbstrith, *Never Forget*, 171–75.

20. Stein to Sr. Adelgundis Jägerschmid, O. S. B., in *Self-Portrait in Letters*, 60.

21. Stein to Mother Petra Brüning, O.S.U., Dorstenf, October 31, 1938, in *Self-Portrait in Letters*, 291.

22. Here I draw from two provocative chapters, John Stratton Hawley's "Introduction" and John A. Coleman's "After Sainthood?" in *Saints and Virtues*, ed. John Stratton Hawley (Berkeley: University of California Press, 1987), xi–xxiv and 205–25 respectively.

23. Patricia Hampl, "Edith Stein," in *Martyrs*, ed. Susan Bergman (San Francisco: Harper, 1996), 201.

24. Stein, *Life*, 77.

25. Steven Payne, "Edith Stein: A Fragmented Life," *America* 179, no. 10 (1998): 11–14.

26. Rachel Feldhay Brenner, *Writing as Resistance: Four Women Confronting the Holocaust* (University Park: Pennsylvania State University Press, 1994).

27. In her introduction to a biography of Philippine Duchesne, Catherine M. Mooney provides an interesting history of saint making. See Catherine M. Mooney, *Philippine Duchesne: A Woman with the Poor* (New York: Paulist Press, 1990), 1–31.

28. Woodward, *Making Saints*, 396.

29. Coleman, "After Sainthood?" 209.

Chapter 3

Edith Stein (Poland, 1942)
A Book Sealed with Seven Seals

PATRICIA HAMPL

I have no private life anymore, I told myself. All my energy must be devoted to this great happening. Only when the war is over, if I'm still alive then, will I be permitted to think of my private affairs once more.

    The year is 1914, summer. Edith Stein is twenty-two, a graduate student in Göttingen studying philosophy with the phenomenologist Edmund Husserl. In this passage from her autobiography, *Life in a Jewish Family,* she is instructing herself on her place in the First World War, not the Second, though that is the war that finally claimed her and has fixed her in history as one of "the six million."

    Yet it is all there already—the stern high-mindedness barely concealing a raw passion, the longing to plunge into an existence more compelling than a "private life," the urge to be used, even used up, by a consuming reality. There is nothing morbid: the innocent grandiosity—"I have no private life anymore . . . if I'm still alive"—ripples with excitement. This girl, reading Schopenhauer in her rented room on a July afternoon, when a friend runs in with the news that war has been declared, might just as well have been saying, "At last—I can *live.*"

    She says that she slapped shut *The World as Will and Idea* ("Oddly enough, I never took up that particular book again") and headed home to Breslau—not so much because it was home but because "Göttingen was in the heart of Germany and there was little likelihood it would get to see any of the enemy except possibly prisoners of war. Breslau, on the contrary, was but a few hours' distance from the Russian border and was the most important fortification in the east. That it might soon be besieged by Russian troops was distinctly possible. My decision was made."

The destination she chose was not home, but history. A flight from the personal into—what? Thrilling danger? But also into a truth more encompassing than "private life." She wished her own life to be absorbed by a vast plot. The first such grandeur she encountered was the Great War. She ran to it. This was only partly a matter of patriotism (though she and her family were fiercely pro-German, then and much later, so assimilated that the anti-Semitism of the prewar National Socialist period struck her mother as implausible, demented, ridiculous). It was clearly Edith Stein's desire to disappear into devotion to a greater good. When a fellow student asked their friend Adolf Reinach, a young philosophy professor at the university, if he too must go to war, Reinach replied, "It's not that I *must*; rather, I'm permitted to go."

"His statement pleased me very much," Edith Stein noted. "It expressed so well my own feelings." What appealed to her was the surrender of individual life to a massive reality encompassing everyone. The self was no good if it was merely personal, merely "personality." Rather, as she wrote in her first book, "The self is the individual's way of structuring experience." The self was necessary—but not for itself. It was necessary as the experiencer of "phenomena," of reality as it is absorbed by a life. Self was meant, in a real sense, to be lost. A kind of blessed anonymity attended the most genuine life, the most realized self.

The desire for anonymity is a desire for greatness. True anonymity, of course, is unconscious, unsought. But the instinct, made conscious, to bury the self's small story in the overwhelming text of history—this is a passion for greatness. In her autobiography, Edith Stein emphasized her "conviction that I was destined for something great." Such greatness should not be confused with ambition, for ambition revolves endlessly, and finally hopelessly, around the individual's sense of stardom. Its engine is self-reflexive—whether the ambition looks like arrogance or self-loathing, or sheer willfulness.

The urge toward greatness, on the other hand, is oddly aligned with humility. The purpose is not the "fulfillment" of a self, nor its aggrandizement, but the deft insertion of the self into an overwhelming design. Hence, the sensation of "the loss of self." This quest for greatness always carries as well a charge of relation, of service: at the earliest opportunity, Edith Stein rushed, against her mother's strenuous objection, to work as a Red Cross nurse's aide in a camp hospital for soldiers suffering from infectious diseases. Ultimately, a life seeking greatness is about the loss of the self in the service of a more complete reality. It is a disappearing act. It is, sometimes, a martyrdom. That, finally, is how it came to be in the unlikely life of Edith Stein.

This is the plot: A woman, born into a warm German Jewish family, converts to Catholicism several years after she earns her doctorate in philosophy with a brilliant dissertation published under the title *On the Problem of Empathy*. She teaches and lectures at Catholic colleges in German-speaking Europe for a decade. Soon after her teaching career is ended by the Nazi decree against Jewish teachers in 1933, she enters a Carmelite monastery in Cologne and becomes a contemplative nun. After Kristallnacht, as conditions worsen in Germany, she is moved to a Carmel in Holland on New Year's Eve, 1938. Three years later, two SS officers raid the Dutch monastery and arrest her. A week after that she is sent in a transport to Auschwitz. She perishes in a gas chamber soon after her arrival there.

That is the life. There is a posthumous existence as well, with its own drama. In 1987 Pope John Paul II beatified Edith Stein as a martyr of the church in a ceremony in a Cologne stadium filled with 70,000 people. There was, not surprisingly, a backlash of protest, mostly from Jewish groups, but also from some chagrined Catholics: what was the church doing appropriating as a martyr a woman who, while she died a committed Christian, was murdered precisely because she was Jewish?

Some of Edith Stein's descendants declined to go to the ceremony. But her niece, Susanne Batzdorff, who lives now in California, did attend. Over the years, she has offered sympathetic help to the Carmelite editors and translators of her aunt's work. But as she sat in the stadium that day, she has since written, "Suddenly it hit me: All these people are gathered here to witness my Aunt Edith Stein declared a blessed martyr of the Catholic church. Yet in August 1942, when a freight train carried her to her death in a gas chamber, no one would help or cry out to stop the horror."

Hers is the inevitable accusation. And interestingly, the question of the propriety of the church's claiming Edith Stein as a martyr of the church rests fundamentally on "the problem of empathy," Edith Stein's defining subject. For if the church cannot see itself as it is reflected by another suffering population, and if it refuses to acknowledge the judgment of that gaze, then it fails in this essential spiritual relation of empathy. For the purpose of empathy is the fullness of reality, of truth. "Empathy," Edith Stein wrote, "offers itself to us as a corrective for self-deception." The point of empathy: I allow myself to be seen through the judgment and clarity of your gaze, acknowledging, as Edith Stein says, that "it is possible for another to judge me more accurately than I judge myself and give me clarity about myself." Empathy seeks truth, and along its difficult way it makes the stunning discovery of compassion as well.

In pursuing Edith Stein's canonization, the church not only displays a troubling insensitivity to Jewish experience but, even more strangely, denies itself and its people the real benefit of contemplating her death. For if the church relinquished its claim on her martyrdom, Edith Stein could become for Christians the focal point of an act of contrition still desperately needed by the Western world in response to the midcentury horrors committed against Jews and Jewish life in Christian Europe.

As a Catholic saint, she is folded into the canon of church history. But where she is needed is exactly where she placed herself: in between. The Catholic church needs Edith Stein—that's true. Not as a saint of the church, but as a presence who, against all the odds, stands at the midpoint of the evils of midcentury. She should remain a ghost, a figure forever calling Christians toward contrition—the proper Christian response to the Holocaust. What would her niece's response have been at a gathering of Catholics in the Cologne stadium if the occasion had been not a beatification ceremony but a giant open-air act of contrition on the part of the church, extended to Jews living and dead? Catholics must accept the fact that sainthood is not simply a way of honoring a great life; it is inevitably a way of claiming it. The act of contrition must begin with the willingness to relinquish that claim.

Yet this contentious question of Edith Stein's formalization as a martyr of the church, proper to any discussion of the church's habits of cultural appropriation, does not belong to Edith Stein. If there is a problem (and the essays and letters published on the subject make it clear that there is a problem), it is not hers. This ethical question belongs to the church's life, not to Edith Stein's. She remains the riddle containing her seeming contradictions. She, not her "cause" (on either side of the debate), is the fascination. For she is an enigma. That is, she is a life waiting to be read.

Edith Stein bore a crushing burden of paradox with simplicity, certainty, and humility. She went where she had to go—into the Catholic communion when commanded by faith; then, even deeper, into the cloister of Carmel; and finally, crammed into a fetid boxcar, to Auschwitz. For her, the paradox of her life was not a contradiction to be debated but a truth to be lived. She understood quite early that she would be doubly implicated in the crimes of the age as a Christian Jew: "I will always be close to you, to my family, to the Jewish people," she said to her niece Susanne Batzdorff when, as a girl, she asked her aunt why she was entering a Christian monastery *now*, just as attacks on Jews were growing. "And don't think my being in a convent is going to keep me immune from what is happening in the world."

If her life is one of the great conundrums of twentieth-century faith, the mystery does not begin when she converted to Roman Catholicism at the age of thirty. She was one born for mystery, it seems, as genius always is. Jan Nota, a Jesuit priest who knew Edith Stein in her final years in the Carmel in Echt, Holland, has written that the "fascinating thing to me about Edith Stein was that truth did not exist as an abstraction for her, but as something incarnated in persons, and therefore as inconceivable apart from love."

From childhood, when she perceived something to be "true," she had to pursue it, do it, be it—whatever it was. She had been a notoriously riotous, unruly child. "I was mercurially lively, always in motion," she writes, "spilling over with pranks, impertinent and precocious, and at the same time, intractably stubborn and angry if anything went against my will. My eldest sister, whom I loved very much, tested her newly-acquired child-training methods on me in vain."

Then, at about the age of seven, she says the "first great transformation took place in me." It was not the result of an external force, she was sure. She could not explain it, she writes in her autobiography, except to say that "reason assumed command within me." She distinctly remembered that "from that time on, I was convinced that my mother and my sister Frieda had a better knowledge of what was good for me than I had; and because of this confidence, I readily obeyed them." Her "old stubbornness" left her. No one could explain the transformation, but for her it was a natural response to an internal recognition: her behavior changed the instant her perception of "the truth" changed.

Later, the same precise register between perception and action would compel her to behavior far more flagrant than the childhood furies that once caused her mother such pain. But these changes, so inexplicable and even dismaying to those who loved her, were incontrovertible. Once she seized upon the truth, it claimed her and required action. As a result, she wrote, "I was able to sever the seemingly strongest ties with minimal effort and fly away like a bird escaped from a snare."

But if she could so easily "fly away," she flew alone and into skies darker than her protective family could have imagined. In the midst of an unusually close family, she remained inscrutable. "In spite of the great closeness between us," she wrote, "I couldn't confide in my mother more than in anyone else. From early childhood I led a strange double life that produced alternations of behavior which must have seemed incomprehensible and erratic to any outside observer."

The truth was, she wrote, that "within her, another hidden world was emerging, where I would assimilate on my own the things that I saw and heard during the day." As a child she had a naturally heightened sensitivity to suffering, and any observed inequity was writ large in her heart. "Whatever I saw or heard throughout my days was pondered over there"—in her "hidden world." She could not understand how people could laugh at a stumbling, incoherent alcoholic. If anyone spoke of a murder in her presence, she would "lie awake for hours that night, and, in the dark, horror would press in upon me from every corner. . . . I never mentioned a word to anyone of these things which caused me so much hidden suffering. It never occurred to me that one could speak about such matters."

No one else had access to this hidden world whence all the "incomprehensible and erratic" behavior came. Her adoring older sisters, already in awe of her grave intelligence and her fierce integrity, despaired of understanding her. So great was her native reserve that they called her, teasingly, "the book sealed with seven seals."

Edith Stein was born in Breslau, Germany (now Wroclaw, Poland), October 12, 1891, on Yom Kippur—a fact, she always thought, that played into her being her mother's favorite. She was the youngest of seven children, some of them nearly adult when she was born. She and her sister Erna, only eighteen months her senior, were the babies, brought up almost as twins.

When Edith was two, her father died suddenly of a heat stroke while he was away on business. Thus began the career of his widow, Auguste Courant Stein, who, against the counsel of her own family, took over the management of her husband's lumber business. The older children helped raise the younger ones, while Auguste kept them all going with her tireless devotion to them and to the business. Against significant odds, she prospered.

A photograph of Auguste, circa 1925 (she was seventy-six and would live another eleven years): The stout body, always dressed in black after her husband's death, suggests solidity rather than anything as frivolous as fat. The face is a stone of certainty, not hard but absolute. The jaw is set, the mouth the most telling feature: lips closed in a firm, almost fierce line, giving away nothing. It is not the tense face of a petty domestic dictator, but all the more resolute: a woman used to command, of necessity.

In a facing photograph in *Life in a Jewish Family,* taken at the same time (when she was thirty-four), Edith sits, hand to deep-clefted chin, gazing at the camera neutrally, not feeling compelled, apparently, to offer any expression. She is an attractive woman, her mouth surprisingly voluptuous in repose. She is waiting to return to her reading: her index finger is inserted in the closed book on her lap, marking her place during this brief intrusion.

By the time these two photographs of mother and daughter were made, much had already been decided. Edith, who was a convinced atheist at fifteen in the liberal idealist way her older brothers and sisters had brought to bear in their mother's orthodox home, had eventually come to belief during her university years, probably influenced by the largely Christian—though not Catholic— circle around Husserl. The Master (as Stein and his other devoted students always called him) was Jewish, though he had become a nominal Lutheran, apparently as a professional protection long before Nazi times.

The decisive moment for Stein occurred, however, when she was visiting philosopher friends in Bergzabern during the summer of 1921. One morning, by chance, she picked up a copy of the autobiography of Saint Teresa of Avila on a bookshelf. Reading it occasioned one of her galvanizing moments of truth. She was unable to put it down, and sat up all night reading. When she put it down the next morning, she said, "This is the truth." She was baptized in the Catholic church on New Year's Day, 1922.

Auguste was appalled, deeply repelled. "She particularly rejects conversions," Stein wrote to a Catholic friend later. "Everyone ought to live and die in the faith in which they were born. She imagines atrocious things about Catholicism and life in a convent." Going off, against her mother's wishes, to serve in a lazaretto during the war had been one thing, but this was a bizarre infatuation, a monstrous disloyalty.

Worse was to come. On October 15, 1933, three days after her forty-second birthday (on the feast day of Teresa of Avila), Edith Stein entered the Carmelite monastery of Cologne as a postulant. Her conversion to Catholicism and her conviction of her vocation to Carmel had come virtually together. Before her baptism, she "still cherished," she says, "the dream of a great love and of a happy marriage." Earlier, there had been a fondness (apparently chaste) between Stein and a fellow philosophy student, Hans Lipps. But she was never willing to sacrifice her profession to marriage. Later, after Lipps married and had two small children and his wife suddenly died, he approached Edith Stein again. "Too late," she is reported to have said. This was not the romantic "too late" of disappointed dreams, however, but quite simply the acknowledgment that she was already committed: by then she was baptized, and with her conversion came her vocation to Carmel.

The eleven-year wait between baptism and entrance into the monastery was largely a form of obedience to her spiritual advisers. They cautioned against hasty action on the part of enthusiastic converts. No doubt they also felt Stein's talents as lecturer and teacher had a place in the world. She was willing to be guided in this and was a diligent intellectual worker, turning her philosophical gift now toward Thomas Aquinas, writing and lecturing to Catholic audiences about medieval mysticism and the place of women in the world and in the church. Her writing of the period is lucid, sensible, progressive (she makes a cogent case for sex education in the schools, for example, and argues with uncanny prophecy about the importance of a wider role for women in religion).

There was another reason to wait. She admitted that at first she had thought of her baptism as "preparation for entrance into the [Carmelite] Order." But several months later, seeing her mother for the first time since her baptism, she realized that Auguste "couldn't handle another blow for the present. Not that it would have killed her—but I couldn't have held myself responsible for the embitterment it would have caused."

Before her conversion, she had tried to follow her brilliant *summa* doctorate with a regular university appointment, but the rigidly hierarchical German academic system was not ready for a woman. No one was willing to sponsor her *Habilitation,* the necessary second thesis required for university appointment. The fervent feminism of her youth met the hard wall of habit and entrenched power. She spent her professional career at Catholic colleges and became a much-sought-after lecturer in Germany, Austria, and Switzerland, in particular.

But clearly, already by 1922, she knew she was a contemplative nun. She lived in a room adjacent to the nuns' quarters at the college where she taught, and she attended daily mass, following as well the daily prayers of the Divine Office. In effect, she managed to mimic a monastic life years before her entrance to Carmel.

When Edith Stein was asked to reveal the nature of her religious conversion, she refused. There is no essay or memoir, not even a letter to a trusted friend—nothing—that sheds light on what exactly caused her decisive action. What we know: she read Teresa of Avila—and recognized there "the truth." And so she followed it. This had been her pattern since her "first transformation" when she was a willful seven-year-old and suddenly, inexplicably, felt that "reason assumed command" within her. Now it was not her mother and her older sister who "had a better knowledge of what was good" for her. Now it was the Spirit itself.

What she found in Teresa she also kept to herself, though certainly she is not the first person to have been profoundly affected by that ardent personality. Even today, almost four and a half centuries after she wrote it, Teresa's autobiography remains the most vivid personal document in the history of Christian testimony, more spirited and immediate even than Saint Augustine's *Confessions.* These three—Augustine, Teresa, Stein—form a fascinating linked-chain of conversions, each in turn liberated from what Teresa calls in her autobiography "the shadow of death," which had left them utterly worn out with interior struggle.

As Waltraud Herbstrith, one of Edith Stein's biographers, notes, the three "shadows" were different for each of them, but the sense of liberation was the same: for Augustine the snare was unbridled sensuality; for Teresa, the surface pleasures of "society" and its tendency to skim over life lightly. For Edith Stein, it was the twentieth-century existential burden: a rationalist, materialist worldview that did not permit the freedom to offer oneself to God. From carnality, to society's distractions, to heady intellectualism: these three figures are cameos of Western civilization's history of spiritual dilemmas.

Edith Stein's reticence about her conversion is striking even in this context of Catholic memoir. It sets her apart from Augustine and from Teresa, for her autobiography does not touch on Christian themes, whereas Augustine and Teresa tremble with the news. Edith Stein's silence bears the particular stamp of her faith—and of her solidarity with her Jewishness. There is nothing "apostolic" about Edith Stein; not a whiff of evangelism pervades her writing. She has no desire to convince anyone of anything—nor to persuade, and absolutely not to convert. What had happened to her, what continued to happen to her thanks to the daily grace of liturgical and contemplative prayer, was a mystery. It was simply to be lived.

That was not only enough, it was hard enough. It is often difficult for Catholics to understand what "contemplative life" is about—or for. But Edith Stein was entering this hidden world (literally, an "enclosure") against a backdrop of incomprehension and even antagonism from her family and professional friends. What on earth was she doing this for? As her mother cried in frustration at her Christianity, "Why did you have to get to know him? He was a good man—I'm not saying anything against him. But why did he have to go and make himself God?"

In fact, it was the full-time nature of the compelling occupation of prayer that sent Edith Stein to Carmel. What is often overlooked, especially in recent times, about the Catholic tradition: in spite of its glaring refusals and inequities regarding women, it remains the only Western tradition that has an unbroken history of providing a respected way of life for women outside the domestic role of wife-and-mother. The work of a nun and of a monk is identical: the *Opus Dei*, the work of God—to pray. Specifically, to pray without ceasing. If this was the call, then Edith Stein must go where that was the business of each day. Such faith had nothing to do either with dogma or with convincing other people of anything. In addition, the choice of Carmel is telling: Edith Stein chose the one

Catholic contemplative order whose roots extend past Christianity back into the hermetic tradition of the Old Testament. Carmelites, though they take their rule from Teresa and much of their tradition of contemplative practice from John of the Cross, look back to Elijah as the first "Carmelite."

Perhaps the most striking example of Edith Stein's unwillingness to meddle in the spiritual lives of others (which of course contains the converse: her absolute commitment to following her own conviction, against all inducements otherwise) concerns Edmund Husserl, her revered Master. Though he did not die until 1938, five years after Stein entered the Cologne Carmel, he was already pondering his death and considering religious as well as philosophical questions in 1930 when, in February, Stein wrote an important letter to a mutual friend about him.

Stein was living at the time with the Benedictine nuns at Saint Magdalena college at Speyer, where she taught literature and history; Husserl was in Freiburg, retired but still writing. They rarely saw each other, and the intimate teacher-student relationship was a thing of the fond Göttingen past. The friend to whom she wrote, a Benedictine nun named Sister Adelgundis Jaegerschmid, was living in Freiburg and so had access to Husserl there. Stein's letter is a response to Sister Adelgundis's mention of a conversation with the Master in which she had managed (she felt) to nudge him along the path of considering "the last things" (in Catholic doctrine: death, judgment, heaven, and hell).

Stein is clearly alarmed by this intrusion into the old man's spiritual process. "I believe one must be on one's guard against illusions," she writes back (immediately) to Sister Adelgundis. "It is good to be able to speak to him so freely about the last things. But doing so heightens his responsibility as well as *our* responsibility for him. Prayer and sacrifice are surely more important than anything we can say to him."

She goes on to make a broader association, distinct from her concern about Husserl: "There is a real difference between being a chosen instrument and being in a state of grace. It is not up to us to pass judgment, and we may confidently leave all to God's unfathomable mercy. But we may not becloud the importance of these last things. After every encounter in which I am made aware how powerless we are to exercise direct influence, I have a deeper sense of the urgency of my own *holocaustum*."

It is eerie, of course, to see that word—*holocaust*—employed here, almost as if it were a prophetically macabre job description Edith Stein had written for herself. It would be a mistake to make too much of it. But neither should it be passed over as simply a coincidence, haunting but without significance. For Edith Stein clearly understood—as mystics of all faiths and "ways" do—that the end point of contemplative life is the oneness that unites the individual with the fullest reality. With God, yes. But with the suffering world as well. This is why Buddhist monks incinerated themselves on the streets of Saigon and before the United Nations in New York during the Vietnam War. They too understood—so literally—that their own sacrifice would unite evil and its helpless victims in a liberating instant. The collision of radical evil with radical atonement—"my own *holocaustum*"—is redemption. Edith Stein was irresistibly drawn to it, as she had been drawn to the earlier conflagration of the First World War when she declared as a passionate university student, "I have no private life anymore." She was still trying to "lose her life," now in a frankly religious sense.

This is not to say that she longed for death or imagined foolishly that she could change anything. The opposite: she saw that even to *speak* to another, to evangelize harmlessly as her Benedictine friend so naively reported doing, was a misguided action, dangerous even, spiritually and personally for both sides of the equation. She felt that such discussion jeopardized the root enterprise of active faith: the personal atonement that every day she saw grow more necessary as the evil took hold of Germany.

As the political situation in Germany worsened for Jews, her focus on sacrifice grew. "Though she never complained outwardly," one of her students reported later to Waltraud Herbstrith, "nevertheless it was heartrending to have to see her gentle face contorted in pain. . . . I can still hear her saying, 'One day this will all have to be atoned for.'"

The silence she felt was incumbent on her has made her, strangely enough, a peculiarly contemporary believer: one whose respect for the range of beliefs (and disbeliefs) is so strong that "proofs" seem childish. Only the living, incontrovertible experience itself, mystical and unbidden and therefore unspeakable, will do. The contemporary believer, even one wrapped in the mantle of the established church, living within a cloister, must give witness in a culture of disbelief, in a secular and, in her case, lawless culture.

This silence did not extend to the repression of her own protest against what was happening, however. Before entering the Cologne Carmel, she wrote— twice, apparently—to Pius XI, requesting an audience to discuss the plight of the Jews, urging him to make a strong statement against this lawlessness. He denied her request for an audience and sent her in reply a papal blessing. Pius XI was very sick at the time, which perhaps mitigates somewhat how history regards this incident. He died soon afterward and was followed by Pius XII, the pope who reigned during the Second World War.

One more thing about Edith Stein's sense of her own sacrifice: it is significant that she used the Latin word—*holocaustum*—and not the vernacular. She was a brilliant Latin scholar and had been drawn to the language from her first study of it. Her use of Latin here and elsewhere is not the flourish of an intellectual fop. In *Life in a Jewish Family,* she says she felt, when she began studying Latin, "it was as though I were learning my mother tongue." This was long before she prayed in Latin or thought of it as the language of the church. Just as the precision of Bach and his elegant resolution of great complexities made him her favorite composer, so it was that of all her languages (and she was a gifted linguist, easily adding Greek and English, French and Dutch, as she went through life), Latin was the tongue that best suited her.

In her autobiography and in the letters, it is clear that when her passion quickens at the edge of the inexpressible, she resorts instinctively to Latin and its crisp, minimalist beauty. It was not for her a brittle, lost language, but the supreme mode of taut expression. Her most intimate revelations revert to Latin, as if there she could be relieved, finally, of the burden of her meaning. And so it is no surprise that when her closest philosopher friend, Hattie Conrad-Martius, asked her the question that every reader now asks—*What caused your conversion?*—Edith Stein replied, *Secretum meum mihi,* my secret is mine (literally, "my secret to me").

Josephine Koeppel, the splendid and meticulous translator of the autobiography and letters, calls this an "amazingly abrupt" response, and yet it is the right one for the new, converted Stein. The great Teresa herself, Koeppel notes, encouraged her nuns "to talk together about spiritual subjects in general, but she frowned on making a display out of one's prayer, or of 'the secrets of the King.'"

Edith Stein, the book her family said was "sealed with seven seals" even when she was a child, remained loyal to mystery and spoke of herself only to the limit of usefulness. The rest, she knew, belonged to her future, her *holocaustum.* It was, in any case, as she said to her closest friend, *secretum meum mihi.*

And what, finally, of that *holocaustum?* Especially the Jewish anguish she saw firing all around her, the anguish that she knew would claim her too. What did this do to her Christian conviction? Where was her solidarity? And did she understand her life as a martyrdom?

Everything suggests that Edith Stein was an unusually integrated person, capable of a high state of contemplative prayer. It seems clear that she adapted naturally to the core of prayer: she understood her vocation as an act of solidarity (or, her old word, empathy) with the suffering of the world. She chose, for her name in Carmel, Sister Teresa Benedicta of the Cross. The cross was where she stood. Of all the Christian mysteries—the incarnation, the resurrection—none magnetized her as the cross did. It was *her* mystery, and she made it her name. It was not for her an empty or merely edifying metaphor, but the image of shared, and ultimately redemptive, pain.

Yet in her most telling book, *Life in a Jewish Family,* she does not touch on Christian imagery, on her conversion, or on the story of her struggle. The book covers the years from her birth in 1891 (with backward looks at earlier family history) until 1916. That is, it covers the period before her conversion. But that does not in itself explain the absence of Christian reference, for she was obviously writing it from the standpoint of a Christian life (indeed, she wrote most of it in Carmel and began it at the insistence of a Jesuit friend).

The history of the book's composition is instructive. In January 1933 the Nazis seized power in Germany. Within a few weeks, Edith Stein, like all Jewish teachers, lost her job. She left Münster, where she had recently taken a position, and returned home to Breslau. There, during the next six months, she wrote the first part of the book. She felt "the new dictators" of Germany had so caricatured Jewish life that many Germans, especially younger people, "being reared in racial hatred from earliest childhood," had no idea of the truth. To all who had been thus deprived of the truth, "we who grew up in Judaism have an obligation to give our testimony."

Nowhere in Edith Stein's writing is there the troubling distaste for Judaism and Jewish life that sometimes betrays itself in Simone Weil's work. For Edith Stein, Judaism and, more to the point, Jews are not subject to judgment. They *are*—and are human. Therefore, to be honored in their persons and in their beliefs. And of course, treasured in her own personal life and memory.

In October of 1933, when she entered Carmel, she took up the work of the autobiography again almost immediately and wrote the majority of the text in the next eighteen months in the Cologne novitiate.

A strange project for a postulant to undertake, at her superiors' urging, as her first work in a Carmelite monastery: a detailed memoir of a Jewish upbringing. But her faithfulness to her specifically Jewish identity precluded any diversion from the task she saw as another strict part of her calling: the representation of a real Jewish family to an ignorant (she wished) and hostile (she knew) audience.

She never completed the book, though she tried to return to it. But circumstances intervened. In an effort to find safety for herself and also for her community, she requested to be transferred to a Carmel in Palestine. Too late: the British had already closed that escape route. In the end, she moved to the Carmel in Echt in 1939, aware that she was also transferring to the Dutch monastery the very risk she had brought into the Cologne enclosure. It was impossible for her, carrying Jewish identity papers, to take the manuscript of *Life in a Jewish Family* across the border. But once in Echt, she asked if someone could be found to bring the manuscript from Germany into Holland. A young Marianhill missionary, Father Rhabanus, volunteered. At the border, the police searched his car after all and picked up the bulky manuscript, flipping through the pages idly. "Your doctoral thesis, evidently," the policeman said, and tossed it back in the car, letting him pass through.

Time was running out. Edith Stein wrote only a few pages before the Nazis invaded and occupied Holland. The manuscript had again become a fearful liability. If it was found in a Nazi search (and monasteries were suspicious places), the book would put the entire community at risk. At one point, she buried it on the monastery grounds. Then, fearful of the effects of moisture on her carefully wrapped package, she dug it up again and had a sister hide it elsewhere. It caused her much worry; she was troubled, as well, that her presence jeopardized her community. She also had another pressing project under way: she desperately wished to complete *The Science of the Cross,* her study of John of the Cross, in time for the 400-year anniversary of the father of Carmel in 1942.

She and her superiors began a search for a new sanctuary for her. They were working feverishly on efforts to remove her (and her older sister Rosa, who had also converted to Catholicism and was sheltering at the Echt monastery as a refugee) to a Carmel in Switzerland. Then, on Sunday, July 26, 1942, almost three years after her arrival in Echt, a pastoral letter from the Dutch bishops was read in all Catholic churches, denouncing the Nazi policies toward the Jews.

The next day, "because the Bishops interfered," *Reichskommissar* Seyss-Inquart ordered all Catholic Jews to be deported before the week's end. The official Nazi memorandum listed 722 Jews registered as Catholics throughout the country. A further memorandum, dated July 31, claimed that 4,000 Jews registered as Christians had been gathered in one camp. This information was seen as a threat to induce the bishops to stop their protest of the general deportations.

On August 2, 1942, at 5:00 P.M., after Edith Stein (Sister Benedicta) had, as was the custom, read the point of meditation, the evening hour of mental prayer began. The silence was interrupted several minutes later by a loud pounding on the door that echoed into the nuns' choir. The SS had arrived. Before the nuns realized what was happening, Edith Stein and her sister Rosa were being taken away.

Rosa, terrified, at first became hysterical. Her younger sister turned to go and gently told her to follow. "Come," Edith said to Rosa, "let us go for our people."

Not "to our people," but "for" them. Her *holocaustum* had begun.

They were taken to the transfer camp at Westerbork, from which all Dutch Jews were sent east. They were with other Catholics, some of them also professed religious. On August 6, from Barracks 36 at Westerbork, Stein sent a card to the

Echt Carmel, requesting a few necessary items: "woolen stockings, two blankets. For Rosa all the warm underwear and whatever was in the laundry; for us both towels and washcloths. Rosa also has no toothbrush, no Cross and no rosary." Then, strangely radiant, "So far I have been able to pray, gloriously."

It was her last written communication. There was a brief, false, hope of release or "deferments" for these Catholic Jews. Then came news that all such releases were revoked. An Ursuline nun (also a Jewish convert) wrote later of observing Edith Stein when she received this news: "I saw the German Carmelite. Her release had also been cancelled. Pale but composed, she kept on comforting her fellow-sufferers."

A few days later when a group of men sent from the Echt Carmel managed to visit the prisoners in Westerbork, they reported that Stein related everything "in a calm and quiet manner." They had been smoking as she spoke, "and after she finished, in the hope of relieving the tension a little, we jokingly offered her a cigarette. That made her laugh. She told us that back in her days as a university student she had done her share of smoking, and dancing too." They were surprised by her "lighthearted happiness." Later, when the SS patrol signaled the prisoners back into their barracks with a harsh whistle, Stein said, "I am prepared for whatever happens." Apparently, she expected to be sent to a forced labor camp in her native Silesia, to work in the mines.

On August 7, 1942, she and Rosa, along with many of their fellow prisoners, were conveyed by cattle car from Westerbork toward the east.

Final sightings: In 1948 the prioress of the Cologne Carmel wrote that in August 1942 Valentin Fouquet, the stationmaster in the town of Schifferstadt, reported that he heard himself called from the transport that had stopped briefly in the station. A "lady in dark clothes," who said her name was Stein, asked him to tell her friends that she sent greetings and was on her way to Poland.

Then, in 1982, a man named Johannes Wieners published a piece claiming that on August 7, 1942, he had spoken with Edith Stein. There is no proof, only his testimony. He had been working as a postal driver and was assigned to an army post office in Breslau. A freight train came in on the track alongside his and halted. The guard opened the sliding door, and he could see people penned up, "listlessly squatting on the floor. There was a horrible stench coming from the car."

A woman who was dressed in a nun's habit came to the door. "I guess because I looked sympathetic to her, she said to me, 'It's terrible. We don't even have containers to relieve ourselves.' After that, she looked into the distance at Breslau and said, 'This is my home; I'll never see it again.'"

Wieners says he stared at her, and then she said, "We are going to our death."

"That really shook me," Wieners wrote. "I remember that I asked her, 'Do the other prisoners know about this?' She answered very slowly, 'It's better for them not to know.'"

An engine was hooked up to his mail train then, and it pulled out, headed also toward Poland. "But when I got back from internment in 1948," he says, "I read about Edith Stein in a magazine. The minute I saw the picture, I knew it was the sister from August 7, 1942."

That is all there is. Maybe—because the account by Johannes Wieners has no corroboration—it is more than there is. On June 2, 1958, the Bureau of Information of the Netherlands Red Cross sent the nuns in Echt and Cologne a final certification concerning Edith Stein, with information dated February 15, 1950:

FOR REASONS OF RACE, AND SPECIFICALLY BECAUSE OF JEWISH DESCENT
ON 2 AUGUST, 1942, ARRESTED IN ECHT.
ON 5 AUGUST, 1942, HANDED OVER IN K.L. WESTERBORK AND
ON 7 AUGUST, 1942, DEPORTED FROM K.L. WESTERBORK TO K.L. AUSCHWITZ.
THE ABOVE NAMED PERSON IS TO BE CONSIDERED AS HAVING DIED ON
9 AUGUST, 1942 IN AUSCHWITZ.

Nothing more. The mind goes back instinctively to the brief flashes that spark from her memoir as if to live again in her life rather than her death, jots of personal life indelibly inscribed in her account of her "life in a Jewish family." They are the small moments she chose to rescue and reveal as evidence of simple humanity—family parties, mountain hikes with her student friends, as idyllic as scenes out of a German operetta ("No one growing up during or since the [First World] war can possibly imagine the security in which we assumed ourselves to be living before 1914"), dances and jokes, the heated arguments and reconciliations of young intellectuals, the months at the lazaretto, seeing physical suffering and desperation as she never had before, the intensity of her philosophical inquiry, the thrilling proximity to Husserl.

Taking the whole of Edith Stein's life into mind, it is impossible not to see this memoir as part of her sacrifice as well: she is offering up the enormous fact of her family's reality, its appeal, its humanity, to the hostile gaze of a world lit by racial hatred. The Greek root of the word *martyr* is often invoked: it means to witness. But in a deeper recess of the word's etymology there is also a related Sanskrit derivation—from *smar,* to remember. A fierce act of memory then—the will to remember—is the hidden kernel of the martyr's calling. And naturally, the martyr's literary form would be the autobiography.

The strangely instinctive solitude of this woman even as a girl is threaded through this family history. Even when she was quite young, she radiated the dignity of her "hidden world" when she encountered the edge of death by accident one morning when the flame went out in the gas jet of the bedroom she and her sister Erna shared. They lay in their beds, "deathly white, . . . in a heavy stupor." When her sister Frieda discovered them and opened the windows, letting fresh air rush into the room, Stein "returned to consciousness out of a state of sweet, dreamless rest." To her surprise, she says, "what flashed through my mind upon coming to and grasping the situation was the thought: 'What a shame! Why couldn't they leave me in this deep peace forever?' I myself was shocked to discover that I 'clung to life' so little."

She clung, finally, to something firmer than life. But what is the name of that thing? The truth of revelation? Was it the redemptive value of suffering that sustained her? Did she really smile and move through Westerbork "like an angel," as the reports say, playing with the children, helping to knit up the shreds of courage torn from the adults? Did she appear at the cattle-car door, did she know she was heading to her death?

It is gone now with her into the gray mid-century smoke she became. How it all happened, what it meant to her, how she understood it—these are hidden away with the mystery of her conversion, which, as she told Hattie Conrad-Matius, she kept as the *secretum meum mihi*, refusing to divulge, even to her best friend, what she knew each person must find alone.

NOTE

This chapter appeared originally as "Edith Stein (Poland 1941): A Book with Seven Seals," in *Martyrs: Contemporary Writers on Modern Lives of Faith*, ed. Susan Bergman (San Francisco: HarperSanFrancisco, 1996), 197–215, copyright © by Susan Bergman. It is reprinted here by permission.

Chapter 4

Some Instances of Edith Stein's Humor and Compassion

JOHN SULLIVAN, OCD

Most experts on Edith Stein would agree that all her professional activities, philosophizing, and religious questing had a deeper understanding of the human spirit as their preeminent goal. Her own best summary of this preoccupation is the statement she put into her autobiography *Life in a Jewish Family*: "The constitution of the human person was something personally close to my heart."[1] According to neoscholastic philosopher Daniel Feuling she "had a yearning to attain to the deeper sense of our human being and existence that kept her constantly on the watch, both personally and as a scholar, for the great interconnections which permeate existence—in men and women, in the world and in being itself."[2] The prospects and the projects of the human scene were what sustained her interest as she worked to increase human freedom around her.

Those familiar with her life and writings also recognize that she seldom spared herself in her "incessant search for the truth," as Pope John Paul II said in his homily for her beatification.[3] They would agree that she demonstrated a great deal of earnest zeal, intellectual rigor as well as vigor, and unflagging seriousness in the task. Such traits are certainly admirable. Yet they could easily convey an image of Edith Stein as an acutely earnest person, "all work and no play." At least one informed European Stein commentator seems to suggest that the photos from a particular phase of her life betray a "melancholic" Edith.[4]

Does there lie in Edith Stein, nevertheless, not only a sense of dogged pursuit of the truth but a sense of humor as well? Or did she, the distinguished philosopher and recognized saint of the Catholic Church, allow deep and serious thoughts to crowd out expressions of humor? The response to this need not be tentative; and a number of works in translation provide clear indications of a positive answer to the first question, and of a negative one to the second. Edith Stein's life and writings *do* reveal a woman of humor. To show this, however, we need to begin with a working definition of humor.

Preliminary Remarks about Humor

Clearly, humor is more than mere joke-telling. Indeed, theories of humor are as varied as those who have proposed them, from the ancient Greeks down to Henri Bergson and contemporary authors.[5] Many definitions of the past, and much of what passes for comedy today, might seem to suggest that "the emotions discharged in laughter always contain an element of aggressiveness" and sometimes even of cruelty.[6] In these pages, however, we follow a more benign tradition, well expressed by Stephen Leacock in his article in *Encyclopaedia Britannica:* "Humor may be defined as the sense within us which sets up a kindly contemplation of the incongruities of life, and the expression of that sense in art. . . . The element of kindliness is essential to humor: there must not only be perception of the peculiarities, the contrasts and the shortcomings which lend to any character or circumstance an incongruous aspect, but there must be a tolerance or acceptance of them. Where indignation is aroused the humorous conception is lost and amusement ends."[7]

In other words, authentic humor implies the ability to resonate with the pathos in Shakespeare's famous observation on the lips of Puck in *A Midsummer Night's Dream:* "Lord, what fools these mortals be!" (act 3, scene 2). The Bard's advice to us is to take ourselves for what we are, not as something greater than life but rather as a small piece of that baffling puzzle which will oftentimes lead us to smile at our inadequacies. What we're expected to produce in others or induce in ourselves are not gales of laughter but good, "kindly" admissions of the foolishness and incongruity we frequently cause and witness around us. That is what having a sense of humor involves.

A few scattered and unscientific examples tend to confirm this view. My copy of *The Complete Works of Shakespeare* includes the word *fool* in its glossary and defines it as "a term of endearment or compassion"; true humor moves us to feel with (*com* + *pati*), and not just laugh at or about, others. TWA's April 1989 *Ambassador* magazine conjured up this same connection between humor and compassion when it characterized the works of Samuel Beckett as "tragicomic, absurd, haunting, bitterly misanthropic yet filled with compassion for the human condition." A saint, well before she was declared a saint, was overheard sighing to be spared the burden of non-humorous people: "God, deliver me from sour-faced saints." As many know, the source of that memorable oneliner was Teresa of Avila. And mention of a "churchperson" like St. Teresa reminds one of what Umberto Eco tried to illustrate in *The Name of the Rose*—regardless of whether Aristotle's manuscript on comedy ever did exist[8]—that true holiness actually springs to the defense of humor, and that only a basically uncharitable attitude would consider it both unseemly and subversive.

Humor pervades the thoughts and emotions of any healthy human being; humor, in fact, characterizes us as humans and even distinguishes us from all the other species on earth. One should therefore expect numerous instances of humor in the writings of a philosopher of the human person like Edith Stein, and our examination of some of the places where she uses it will reassure us of how well she grasped its nature. In addition, since compassion is included in the understanding of humor used here, the second part of this article will attempt to show its presence both in the freedom-generating actions of her life and in passages from her writings.

Humor in Edith Stein

Edith Stein's autobiographical *Life in a Jewish Family* offers ample material, and several stories in it will do justice both to Stein and to our topic. We begin with some vignettes from the days of her university studies. Two further passages from her doctoral dissertation in philosophy will complement events described in that part of her autobiography.

Texts from Life in a Jewish Family

The opening chapter of the autobiographical account (where members of her family are introduced some time previous to her birth) shows her aunt by marriage, Mika, helping to write little plays for family "feasts." The narrative indicates that "the persons in these plays were portrayed with loving humor and keen insight."[9] The expression "loving humor" breathes through the texts to come, and the qualifier *loving* deserves a place alongside the word *humor* wherever true humor is found.

Edith Stein and Her Cousin

Just as the very title of her autobiography bespeaks family life, so family members figure in the first two selections. A cousin is the protagonist of the first, and her description of his reaction to her talents gives us the chance to see what a well-rounded person she herself was at the age of twenty.

> This time my cousin Erich was also at home. He was a year younger than I and had just begun the *Oberprima*. Now my successful *Abitur* was held up to him as a pattern: this was not at all to his liking. Once, thoroughly vexed because he had verified that I had read Part II of "Faust," he declared: "People like you only have so much time to read because you're too lazy to take part in any sports!" [Erich either didn't know or had just conveniently forgotten she was an avid tennis player, as she noted earlier on in that same chapter.]
>
> Otherwise, we got along fine together. One afternoon when I returned from somewhere with my aunt, he and another young man were practicing some dance steps to the music of a record-player. As soon as Erich saw me, he asked me whether I could dance. My aunt scolded him for his audacity; but I was both happy and ready to show how accomplished I was.
>
> Thanks to Hans Biberstein [her tennis partner from earlier on], I knew all the latest steps. Erich had to admit he was outclassed and remarked in sincere admiration: "A girl who's made her *Abitur* and been excused from the orals, who has read 'Faust,' and who can waltz around to the left, should be featured at the Hansa Theater (the theater with the largest variety show in Chemnitz)!"[10]

How familiar the story sounds: school achievement rivalry between young family members; their competitiveness abetted by the admiring approval of success from their elders; an attempt to take revenge by embarrassing the rival; and some prudish shock over youthful informality.[11] The narrator adds just the right dose of irony: her interest and skill in both sports and dancing, and her deft closing of the trap Erich thought he was setting. Just the same, the outcome provides a warm resolution as the cousin overdoes his admiration, even urging a vaudeville appearance on her.

Edith Stein and Her Mother

The second story centers on Edith Stein's beloved mother, Auguste Courant Stein. One ought to preface the following narrative with a few background remarks on the importance of Frau Stein to the autobiography's elaboration.

By showing that Jews find the same pleasures in life as others, the same problems and pains, Edith Stein made her narrative function also as a refutation of the Nazi anti-Semitic propaganda current in Germany in the 1930s. She began drafting it, in fact, in 1933, when she found herself removed from her teaching job in Münster because of the discriminatory laws against Jews.[12] To demonstrate the "ordinariness" of her own family life, she places her mother at the center of the book, borrowing some of her mother's recollections and even calling the first chapter "My Mother Remembers, 1815–1891."[13]

She goes on to mention Frau Stein up to and including the last page of the last full chapter (the *Life* remained unfinished due to the arrest and subsequent murder of its author by the Nazis), where she provides her daughter with nighttime refreshments during her difficult university studies, leaving her only "after a good-night kiss." Father John Donohue, an editor of *America* magazine, recognized the importance of this close relationship in an article that appeared only a month before the Vatican authorized Stein's beatification in 1987: "If Edith is beatified, her picture of Auguste Courant, by a divine and tender irony, is likely to rank first in the gallery of portraits drawn by saints of their mothers. It is more complete and memorable than the image of Monica in Augustine's *Confessions* or of Zélie Guérin in Thérèse of Lisieux's *Story of a Soul.*"[14]

The story of mother and daughter comes from the year 1915, when World War I was raging. Soldiers were dying, and the philosopher, surrounded by the books of her graduate studies, wanted to do her share and help her homeland. She had plans to volunteer as a Red Cross nurse and go to a contagious disease hospital. Frau Stein's youngest daughter wanted to convince her widowed mother that her desire was a good idea:

> I had heavy opposition from my mother. I did not even tell her it was a lazaretto [i.e., for those with contagious diseases]. She was well aware that no suggestion of hers that my life would be endangered could ever induce me to change my plans. So as an ultimate deterrent, she told me all the soldiers arrived from the front with clothes overrun with lice and that I could not possibly escape infestation. Naturally that was a scourge I dreaded—but if the people in the trenches all had to suffer from it why should I be better off than they? (A note: the delousing in Weisskirchen was organized so well that

I was spared this ordeal. Occasionally I did find some of the little creatures on people's linens, indeed on washed pieces just taken out of closets.)

When this tactic failed, my mother declared with all the energy she could muster: "You will not go with my permission." My reply was every bit as determined: "Then I must go without your permission."

My sisters were downright shocked at my harsh retort. My mother was totally unaccustomed to such opposition. True, Arno or Rosa may often have used harsher language with her. But that happened only in the heat of anger while they were beside themselves and was soon forgotten again. Now, however, granite was striking granite. My mother said no more and was very silent and depressed for several days, a mood which always affected the entire household. But when subsequently I began making my preparations, she, as a matter of course, undertook to provide the complete nurse's outfit called for. Frieda, who was the most knowledgeable about such things, had to make all the purchases and do all the sewing required.[15]

Despite the apparently confrontational, almost distressing, character of this account, when read in context it conveys "the kindly contemplation of the incongruities of life" mentioned above. The humor is there, and intentionally so: a little bit to show the daughter's emancipation as she continued growing up (then at the hardly tender age of twenty-four), and a little to justify hope's triumph over the unrealized fears of her loving mother.

Since this scene was being memorialized almost two decades after the fact, the seemingly sharp edge to the struggle of wills between mother and daughter had already disappeared, nor was it being glamorized. Rather, as she tells the story, Edith Stein is already a Catholic, preparing to move out once again, this time to the cloistered existence of a Carmelite nun, a decision making the argument over volunteer service seem relatively minor by comparison. We can imagine her explaining: "True, nineteen years ago my mother was 'unaccustomed to such opposition.' But now, however, she has grown used to other acts of independence from me, and . . . she has always survived. Hadn't she already at that time, heard even 'harsher' language from my brother and sister? If we were both so vehement then, our exchange was ultimately to *their* benefit; so they could see the youngest of the seven surviving siblings assuming adulthood with a sense of initiative *exactly like that of mother,* who was forced to assume leadership of the family when poor father died unexpectedly. I use the image of 'granite striking granite' to show how equally resolute we were then, but how resilient we subsequently turned out to be, with no real damage or hurt inflicted. True, mother reverted to silence and acted 'depressed' for a few days, but then 'as a matter of course' she resurfaced and arranged for my nurse's outfit."

As the final touch, neither Mother Stein nor the nurse volunteer actually had to fret over the practicalities involved with assembling the nurse's outfit. Stein's sister Frieda was assigned the task of purchasing and sewing those items, at her mother's behest, in the wake of the meeting of minds.

Admittedly, this story may evoke a gentle smile rather than gales of laughter, but it shows Edith Stein in possession of that essential element of humor: a loving acceptance of the shortcomings and incongruities of events and individuals. The subsequent stint at the contagious disease hospital ultimately gave Frau Stein reason to be proud of her daughter; and the next selection comes from the chapter of the *Life* that describes her service there.

Edith Stein as a Nurse

The *Life* records Stein's departure date for the Red Cross work as April 7, 1915. She stayed at Mährisch-Weisskirchen in Moravia for about six months until a furlough and eventual release from service came through. Chapter 8 of the *Life* is a valuable historical document since there are so few surviving eyewitness accounts of what went on in those "lazarettos," as they were called.[16] In spite of all the sufferings listed perhaps the funniest description of the entire book is found in this chapter, thus proving the previous point about the nature of humor:

> On one occasion the arrival of a fresh transport kept us busy until late in the evening getting the new arrivals properly adjusted in traction. The officer's room which so far had housed only two occupants was now filled to capacity. Going down the corridor very late, I encountered a most remarkable transport: a gigantic figure lay stark naked on the gurney; a rimless pince-nez perched on the sharply aquiline nose; the head was resting on a red silk pillow. A Polish cavalry-captain was being transferred from the operating room to the officers' room. He had refused to allow them to put a hospital gown on him but had positively insisted that he retain those two items.
>
> . . . I was informed that the cavalry-captain required private nursing throughout the night. . . . He was wide awake and gave orders in ringing tones which prevented the other officers from sleeping. They were half amused, half despairing. . . .
>
> Repeatedly, my patient asked me to cool his hands and arms with water. Since I had no one else to care for during the night, I was able to perform for him any service he fancied. To be sure, when the other nurses arrived in the

morning, I was free to leave to freshen up a bit. When I returned, I found every-one in an uproar. The badly wounded officer was a nobleman, the nephew of one of the government's ministers who had already inquired about his con-dition. One could not satisfy the patient. He made one impossible demand after another and filled everyone who approached him with mortal dread. It was time for one of the girls to bring him his breakfast. Not daring to do so, she asked me to take it for her. While she provided for the other officers, I went over to the fearsome one.

"Good morning, little sister," he called out to me. Evidently what he recalled of my services during the night was pleasant. After we had left the room, the maid said to me in respectful awe: "He likes you, Sister. He called you 'Little Sister.'"

When I went back into the officers' room, a captain summoned me to his bedside. He had also come in only the night before. "Little Sister," he begged, "see to it that this fellow gets moved into another room. One hasn't got a moment's rest."[17]

Although her mother worried about lice, Edith Stein had much different chal-lenges to face. And quite evidently she relished the chance to stress how humor-ous was the poor wounded man's insistence on "wearing" just the pince-nez set of glasses and keeping the red silk pillow. Her choice of the words "uproar," "mortal dread," "not daring," "the fearsome one" and "not a moment's rest" is a fine exercise in hyperbole to strengthen the tragicomic strain of her reporting. A little later in the chapter she adds that the Polish officer died of his wounds, so it would be wrong to think she was painting the scene totally at his expense. Rather, she deftly played up the incongruities and shortcomings shared among the staff as well—nurses ("sisters" in continental usage, just as in England), aides, and doctors alike.

The entire passage not only reveals the self-sacrificing patriotism of its author but also reassures readers of the basic realism which undergirds many of the philosophical and spiritual writings she drafted later on in life. Some of them came after she entered a Carmelite cloister, so her reflections on life and death could be dismissed as so many pious abstractions. In *Life,* the sobering effects of Edith Stein's wartime service on others were recorded in the follow-ing dialogue of a Christmastide dinner party: "So I was back in Göttingen after being away for nearly a year. As in former times, Liane Weigelt sat opposite me at the dinner table. 'You haven't changed a bit, Fräulein Stein,' she remarked. Frau Gronerweg declared, 'I don't agree. One can tell just by looking at her that Fräulein Stein has experienced the serious side of life.'"[18]

However brief this stint in the wartime hospital had been, Edith Stein looked long and compassionately into the depths of human suffering. The First World War gave her an understanding of death within life; the Second brought her own life to an untimely end, when she was only fifty-one years old, at Auschwitz, with hundreds of other Catholic Jews, among them her sister Rosa.

Texts from *On the Problem of Empathy*

Two brief passages from her thesis, defended less than a year after ending the World War I Red Cross service, fill out the picture by showing that a sense of humor was not foreign even to Doctor Stein's most serious philosophical endeavors.[19] The first comes from a section called "The Deceptions of Empathy," and alludes to an art form very dear to her, viz., classical music: "But as we said, this deception can only be removed again by empathy. If I empathize that the unmusical person has my enjoyment of a Beethoven symphony, this deception will disappear as soon as I look him in the face and see his expression of deadly boredom."[20]

The second is found in a section entitled "The Phenomenon of Expression," with a final line that suits the American scene fairly well: "As is well known, we civilized people must 'control' ourselves and hold back the bodily expression of our feelings. We are similarly restricted in our activities and thus in our volitions. There is, of course, still the loophole of 'airing' one's wishes. The employee who is allowed neither to tell his superior by contemptuous looks he thinks him a scoundrel or a fool, nor decide to remove him, can still wish secretly that he would go to the devil."[21] The contrast between controlled bodily expression of "civilized" people and what they're *really* thinking couldn't be more perfect, nor more timely today as we seek the greater psychic freedom that "being in touch with" our emotions provides. Once again, Edith Stein's ability to combine profound philosophical reflections on the human person with a light touch of humor is evident.

Compassion in Edith Stein

Another facet of the same sympathetic view of reality that humor represents for Edith Stein is contained in her compassion for others. "Compassion" is pursued by many spiritual traditions, especially by Buddhism. It has become a predominant spiritual catchword of our time, as any glance at current religious literature confirms.[22] This increasing emphasis on compassion is a positive development, provided the term does not become emptied of all meaning through over-use. No need, however, to argue over definitions. For our purposes, it is enough to say that compassion itself and the ability to be compassionate are crucial to an understanding of the human person, which so fascinated and preoccupied Edith Stein. The human spirit, involved in so many instances of tragicomic happenings, reveals its truly human side in compassion or solidarity with/in suffering. The compassionate person is always ready to identify with the pain of others as they go struggling along.

To grasp Edith Stein's appreciation of compassion we ought to return to the *Life*, then pass on to the letters since they fill out the autobiographical narrative that breaks off abruptly at the year 1916. By including the selections from her correspondence, we view Stein before World War I, during the war, between world wars, and during World War II.

"All Were Deeply Moved"

The first illustration of compassion brings us back to her cousin Erich and to his brother Walter. Just after the accolade she received for her ability to "waltz around to the left" from the former, she tells about the latter—an apparent ne'er-do-well and failure in the family. His story is laid out succinctly:

His [i.e., Erich's] older brother Walter had always given his parents cause to worry. . . . [He] was apprenticed to a respectable business firm as far away from home and from his old influences as possible. But neither there nor in a subsequent job did he last long, for soon he was deep in debt and mixed up in all kinds of shady deals. His father sent him to America, but before long he turned up again. When the war [World War I] started, he was dispatched to the front at once. A daredevil soldier, he was almost immediately home again with an Iron Cross and a serious injury to his jaw. The old way of life began again. My uncle had no alternative but to cut off all contact with him and to forbid him entry into his paternal home. . . . He finally married a Christian girl with a lower middle-class background. He lived in the crowded workers' apartment which belonged to his father-in-law, a respectable cabinet-maker. Walter's parents were not happy with his misalliance and continued to ignore him and his family. But it was a good marriage, and the young wife was inconsolable when he died after a very short illness. She was left with two small children. His parents went to the funeral. On the way to the grave, his daughter-in-law clung to Uncle's arm. When the rabbi had said the final prayers and the whole group of mourners turned to leave, the young woman knelt down at the grave and, in her grief, prayed the Lord's Prayer aloud. Naturally, that was something totally unheard of in a Jewish cemetery but, instead of being offended by it, all were deeply moved.[23]

This passage is a masterful piece of writing, also concise in setting out the personality traits of the persons involved. It deftly establishes a tension involving real opposition, resolved in a beautiful dénouement the reader would hardly have expected. There is drama in the ebb-and-flow of the cousin's activities: from the small victories to defeat, to serenity in married life (however humble the surroundings), on to the ultimate tragedy of dying soon into his marriage. Paralleling this are the ups and downs of his parents' reactions to his exploits, especially the alienating force of marriage to a non-Jew; then, the turn-around of interment in a Jewish cemetery after a Jewish burial service, crowned by yet another turn-around—the Lord's Prayer recited aloud by the grief-stricken wife which led, not to consternation, but to inclusion and acceptance by the blood relatives of her deceased husband. The simplicity of her spontaneous gesture and the equally simple humanity of the Jewish mourners—"deeply moved" as they all were— have no need of further analysis; the compassion is evident. Still, before we turn to the next selection, it is worth mentioning how poignantly ecumenical Edith Stein was in passing on this scene. She wasn't writing her autobiography to prove the strength of her own faith. She always maintained modest reserve regarding belief and unbelief in setting out her story. Intensely aware from her own personal experience of what it meant to live without any faith at all, she remained circumspect in examining the usages of either Judaism or Christianity and avoided criticism of either tepidity or overzealousness in others. Consequently, the moment of prayer at the cemetery acquires a special cogency that favors, all the more, inter-religious openness, mutual assistance, and respect.

Stein Comforts a Friend

The next text describes an act of compassion for a close friend. Near the time of Stein's doctoral exams Erika Gothe came to Freiburg for a little visit, thus offering the doctoral candidate an excuse to take a break from all her studies. She never needed much of an excuse to leave on excursions into the mountains, so she gladly complied with her friend's stratagem.[24] This was during wartime, and her narrative provides an insight into the psychological ravages of hostilities on non-combatants. The story is situated in town before they leave for their trip:

But we came away with more than memories of happy outings, for impressions of a more serious nature were made, also [in Freiburg]. The first or second night after Erika's arrival there, we were awakened by an air raid. I was accustomed to that by this time and made little of it. Erika slept in another room; her bed was against the wall adjoining the room occupied by the landlady's elderly in-laws. During the night, suddenly, the man knocked at my door and told me in his Baden dialect that my companion was weeping. I dressed immediately and went over to her. She was, indeed, shedding tears but not for herself. She had been told that from Freiburg one could hear the artillery fire from the Vosges Mountains and her brother Hans, a lieutenant, was stationed there.

> Now she heard shells exploding and said, "If it sounds so terrible here, what a hell it must be there!"
> I knelt beside her bed and comforted her. What we were hearing were the anti-aircraft guns from the *Schlossberg* which protected the entire city. All one could hear from the Vosges mountains was a very dull rumbling. Thereupon the tears stopped at once. Erika was completely comforted. She even noticed the dress I had thrown on so rapidly.
> "You have found the style that suits you," she said.[25]

Distress over the danger, aggravated by anxiety for a loved one placed in a similar or even greater peril, was what was discovered when Erika was found crying "but not for herself." Edith Stein quickly realized that she in turn must sympathize with her friend. A nice twist to the story comes from the way she relied on her knowledge of her surroundings to apply a factual explanation to her comforting gesture: she didn't offer hollow platitudes, but provided a solid reason for hope instead. Interesting, too, the way her realism brought Erika back to focus on their immediate surroundings and to notice her friend's dress. As a result, the intervention earned Edith Stein a compliment for her sartorial taste—a story with a happy ending (and an implicit touch of humor) after all.

"To Be of Some Help to Them"

The next story focuses on another setting in which the "Fräulein Doktor" had to watch what she wore because of a most discerning audience, i.e., a class of young women before whom she stood as teacher. Teaching young laywomen as a laywoman herself, she was well attuned to the life problems of her students.[26]

Many hours of counseling troubled individuals at the teacher's college of the Dominican Sisters of St. Magdalena in Speyer led her to write these golden lines that any teacher would be happy to own:

> Surely it is most important that the teachers truly have this spirit [of Christ] themselves and vividly exemplify it. At the same time they also need to know life as the children will find it. Otherwise there will be a great danger that the girls will tell themselves: "The Sisters have no notion about the world"; "They were unable to prepare us for the questions we now have to answer"; and the [danger] that then everything might be thrown overboard as useless. . . . You personally, though, have the advantage of not having entered too soon and of having belonged to the youth movement. That gives you access to much that others lack. However, it is necessary to keep up contacts. Today's young generation has passed through so many crises—it can no longer understand us, but we must make the effort to understand them; then perhaps we may yet be able to be of some help to them.[27]

Stein wrote this letter in what the Gregorian calendar designates the year 1932, but for the young German women of whom she speaks it was one of those "between-the-wars" years, when Germany lurched back and forth under the burden of the social and political upheaval that eventually paved the way toward the Nazis' seizure of power. W. H. Auden was staying in Germany at about this time. What he saw led him to coin the often repeated nickname for the century, an "Age of Anxiety." So, it was a time for great doubts and hesitations. The teacher was taking the proper measure of the young people entering her classroom when she claimed on their behalf the presence of "questions we *now* have to answer." Every generation has shifting matrices for its growth pains, but only the perceptive educators like Edith Stein have both the insight and the courage to declare candidly what they are. Yet, regardless of the shifts, the merit of those words is that they recognize what used to be called a "generation gap" and suggest that compassion requires extra efforts to ease communication, to take the initiative toward the alienated.

"So Many Persons Here Who Need Some Consolation"

The final quotation from her writings is from the next-to-last written communication she had with anyone on earth. Arrested on August 2, 1942, by the Gestapo, she died one week later in the Birkenau section of the Auschwitz extermination camp southeast of her home city of Breslau. In that last week of her life she was pushed through the infernal network of Hitler's "final solu-tion," thus visiting two intermediate transit camps in Holland, first Amersfoort, then Westerbork. In Westerbork her stay coincided with the tenure of Etty Hille-sum, the Dutch Jewish woman who has left behind a diary and some *Letters from Westerbork* that have made her a subject of recent discussion in some Chris-tian circles.[28] Hillesum devotes a lot of space in her writings (published post-humously because she too was killed by the Nazis) to the deep sense of despair which overcame women with children in the camp.[29] Understandably the chil-dren were neglected, and an eyewitness account informs us that Edith Stein, known by then as Sr. Teresa Benedicta, did much to look after them. Julius Mar-can, a survivor, testified that "[i]t was Edith Stein's complete calm and self-possession that marked her out from the rest of the prisoners. . . . Many of the mothers were on the brink of insanity and had sat moaning for days, without giving any thought to their children. Edith Stein immediately set about taking care of these little ones. She washed them, combed their hair and tried to make sure they were fed and cared for."[30]

From Westerbork Sr. Teresa Benedicta was able to send back a compelling message to the nuns in her monastery of refuge at Echt: "We count on your prayers. There are so many persons here who need some consolation and they expect it from the sisters."[31] This time the term *sisters* refers to the religious nuns and not nursing personnel, as during her volunteer service in World War I. She had no medications to dispense, nor could she deal with the other detainees from a nurse's position of authority. She had only herself to give: her attentiveness, the time she took away from her own worries. Supported by her sense of religious hope she gave all that she had. She was present *with,* present *to* the others, and she was willing to do as much as she could to share their burden of suffering so as to lighten the load. The freeing effects of her compassionate "consolation" did not go unnoticed. Mr. Wielek, a camp official who spoke with her in Westerbork, left a description which can serve as an eloquent epilogue to what she wrote, said, and did to add to this poor world's reserve of compassion:

I knew: here is someone truly great.

For a couple of days she lived in that hellhole, walking, talking and pray-ing . . . like a saint. And she really was one. That is the only fitting way to de-scribe this middle-aged woman who struck everyone as so young, who was so whole and honest and genuine.

At one point she said to me, "I never knew people could actually be like this . . . and I honestly had no idea of how my brothers and sisters were being made to suffer. . . . I pray for them continually."

... [T]hen I saw her go off to the train with her sister [Rosa], praying as she went, and smiling the smile of unbroken resolve that accompanied her to Auschwitz.[32]

These words of tribute hardly deserve comment. Still, it helps to realize they were published only ten years after the encounter they describe and were affirmed with conviction. A decade after her death someone was using the word *saint* to describe Edith Stein in the public forum of a Dutch newspaper. Mr. Wielek was a Jew and remained one. Most likely he had no inkling people would be gathering up proof of acts of virtue suitable to promote an official cause for canonization at the time he wrote his account—the diocesan process started officially a decade after that in 1962.[33] "And she really was one." In the final analysis, it was her compassionate concern for her "brothers and sisters" in the concentration camps that was the best indicator of the saintliness that emanated from her, bringing a visible measure of consolation to people in such a state of abandonment. She acted as a vessel of compassion even in the most trying days of her life. Her humane behavior won out over the inhumanity imposed on her and her companions by the Nazi persecutors of her church and of her people.

Notes

This text is an updated version of my article "Edith Stein's Humor and Compassion," *Spirituality Today* 43, no. 2 (1991): 142–60.

1. Edith Stein, *Life in a Jewish Family*, trans. Josephine Koeppel, vol. 1 of *The Collected Works of Edith Stein* (Washington, DC: ICS Publications, 1986), 397.

2. Daniel Feuling, *Edith Stein: Die Frau in Ehe und Beruf. Bildungsfrage Heute* (Freiburg: Herder, 1963), 162.

3. Pope John Paul II, "Homily at Beatification Eucharist," in *Holiness Befits Your House: Canonization of Edith Stein, A Documentation,* ed. John Sullivan (Washington, DC: ICS Publications, 2000), 23.

4. Romaeus Leuven, *Edith Stein: Mijn Weg naar de Waarheid* (Druten: De Maas & Waler, 1980), 121. But see, on the other hand, the testimonies gathered by Waltraud Herbstrith, "Die Freude im Leben Edith Steins," chap. 4 of *Edith Stein: Versöhnerin zwischen Juden und Christen* (Leutersdorf: Johannes-Verlag, 1987), 23–49; and Edith Stein's own long reflection on joy in *Science of the Cross*, trans. Josephine Koeppel, vol. 6 of *The Collected Works of Edith Stein* (Washington, DC: ICS Publications, 2002), 90–109.

5. Among philosophers, Aristotle in the *Poetics* lists the laughable as a subdivision of the ugly, while Thomas Hobbes defines "the passion of laughter" as "nothing else but sudden glory arising from a sudden conception of some eminency in ourselves by compari-

son with the infirmity of others, or with our own formerly" (*The Elements of Law,* 1.9.13 [1640]) and Immanuel Kant speaks of "the sudden transformation of tense [a strained] expectation into nothing" (*Critique of Judgment* [1790]). See also D. H. Munro, "Humor," in *The Encyclopedia of Philosophy,* ed. Paul Edwards (New York: Macmillan, 1967), 4:90–93, and *Argument of Laughter* (Cambridge: Cambridge University Press, 1951); Henri Bergson, *Laughter: An Essay on the Meaning of the Comic,* trans. Cloudesley Brereton and Fred Rothwell (New York: Macmillan, 1911); Arthur Koestler, "Humour and Wit," in *The New Encyclopaedia Britannica: Macropaedia,* 15th ed. (Chicago: Helen Hemingway Benton, 1974), 9:5–11.

6. Koestler, *"Humour and Wit,"* 9:6.

7. Stephen Leacock, "Humour: Its Theory and Techniques," in *Encyclopaedia Britannica,* 14th ed. (New York: Encyclopaedia Britannica, 1935), 11:883.

8. See Curt Hohoff, "Umberto Eco: Author of the Postmodern," *Communio* 15, no. 2 (Summer 1988): 255. Also Karl-Josef Kuschel, I, "Aristotle, Umberto Eco and *The Name of the Rose*" and "Laughter as the Signature of 'Postmodernity,'" in *Laughter: A Theological Reflection,* trans. John Bowden (New York: Continuum, 1994), 22–42.

9. Stein, *Life,* 35.

10. Ibid., 182.

11. In Edith Stein's time, the *Oberprima* was the educational phase just prior to university-level studies, and the *Abitur* was the final examination ("with written and oral portions") required before entering the university: see ibid., 470–73.

12. Ibid., 23–24.

13. Ibid., 27–61.

14. John W. Donohue, "Edith Stein's Early Years," *America* 151 (January 3 & 10, 1987): 9.

15. Stein, *Life,* 319.

16. Ibid., 318–67.

17. Ibid., 360–62.

18. Ibid., 378.

19. See Edith Stein, *On the Problem of Empathy,* 3rd rev. ed., trans. W. Stein, vol. 3 of *The Collected Works of Edith Stein* (Washington, DC: ICS Publications, 1989). It would require too much space here to discuss Stein's contribution to phenomenology in her doctoral dissertation. An introduction to her philosophical thought by Mary Catharine Baseheart has been published (posthumously) with the title *Person in the World: Introduction to the Philosophy of Edith Stein,* Contributions to Phenomenology 27 (Boston: Kluwer Academic Publishers, 1997).

20. Stein, *Empathy,* 87.

21. Ibid., 52.

22. Some essays on the notion of compassion come from Matthew Fox, *A Spirituality Named Compassion* (San Francisco: Harper & Row, 1979); Monika Hellwig, *Jesus, the Compassion of God* (Wilmington, DE: Michael Glazier, 1983), and Joan Puls, *A Spirituality of Compassion* (Mystic, CT: Twenty-Third Publications, 1988).

23. Stein, *Life,* 183.

24. See ibid., 130–32, 390.

25. Ibid., 407.

26. See Mary Catharine Baseheart, "Edith Stein's Philosophy of Woman and Women's Education," *Hypatia* 4, no. 1 (1989): 122.

27. Letter 123, Edith Stein to Sr. Callista Kopf, October 20, 1932, in *Self-Portrait in Letters, 1916–1942*, trans. J. Koeppel, vol. 5 of *The Collected Works of Edith Stein* (Washington, DC: ICS Publications, 1993), 122–23.

28. Judy Cannato, "Transformation in Etty Hillesum," *Spiritual Life* 40, no. 20 (1994): 88–96.

29. See Etty Hillesum, *Letters from Westerbork,* trans. A. J. Pomerans (New York: Pantheon Books, 1986), passim for the children and 28–30 for a haunting account of the arrival in the camp of Edith Stein's group of Catholic-Jewish detainees.

30. Waltraud Herbstrith, *Edith Stein: A Biography,* trans. B. Bonowitz (New York: Harper & Row, 1985), 105.

31. Letter 341, Sr. Teresa Benedicta (Edith Stein) to Mother Ambrosia A. Engelmann, August 5, 1942, in *Self-Portrait in Letters,* 352.

32. H. Wielek (orig. name W. Kweksilber, born in Cologne), "Doden die Leven," in *Als een brandende toorts* (Echt: Vrienden van Dr. Edith Stein, 1967), 158–59 and 276 n. 33 for personal background information. Appeared originally as an article in Amsterdam's *De Tijd* newspaper, August 5, 1952.

33. John Sullivan, "The Path to Beatification," in *Never Forget: Christian and Jewish Perspectives on Edith Stein,* trans. S. Batzdorff, Carmelite Studies 7 (Washington, DC: ICS Publications, 1998), 9.

Edith Stein's Passing Gestures
Intimate Histories, Empathic Portraits

SCOTT SPECTOR

Canons and Contexts

In a mass at St. Peter's Square on October 11, 1998, Pope John Paul II elevated the Jewish-born philosopher, nun, and Holocaust victim Edith Stein/Sr. Teresa Benedicta a Cruce to sainthood.[1] The announcement reawakened the controversy surrounding Stein's 1987 beatification, which depended upon a definition of her death at Auschwitz as a martyrdom of Christian faith, a declaration reiterated in the announcement of her elevation. On both occasions, the debate was described as a question of appropriate memorialization, or of "Stein's proper place in history."[2] Yet this was not the beginning of the dilemma of identifying the "proper" context for the Husserl student whose writings spanned phenomenology, feminism, theology, hagiography, and obscure mysticism. The recurring debate points rather to a persistent and difficult problem of the negotiation of subject positions and contexts that remained salient throughout Stein's own works and life, and that lingers on even now.

We begin at the end. At the Breslau railroad yard on August 7, 1942, as German soldiers on their way to the Russian front were waiting for their train to be refueled, they had a passing encounter with the prisoners on board a freight train bound for Auschwitz.[3] The report of one of the soldiers asserts that the train had originated in Holland, and that when the sliding doors were opened they revealed a squalid interior and a huddled mass of people penned within, including a woman in a nun's habit. In this report the nun exchanges words with the soldier; indeed, she is the only passenger represented as having a voice. She speaks first of the miserable conditions in the car, and then looks to Breslau in the distance and says, "This is my home. I'll never see it again. . . . We are going to our death." The shaken soldier asks whether the others know this terrible secret. The peaceful figure shakes her head — it is better that they remain in ignorance. They are in darkness, she is in light; they are squatting on the floor, she is standing; they are "listless," she is pensive and composed.

In this, as in other accounts of her last days, Edith Stein is portrayed in a manner that would pave the way toward her canonization: "resigned" and "composed," "the glow of a saintly Carmelite radiat[ing] from her eyes," a "heavenly atmosphere" emanating from her Christian faith and insight, prepared for whatever would come while those around her were ignorant and frightened, comforting and resolved among a mass of confused and despairing victims. "Every time I think of her sitting in the barracks [of the Dutch detention camp]," reads another testimony, "the same picture comes to mind: a *Pietà* without the Christ."[4]

These portraits of Edith Stein already point to the potential controversy of her canonization. A paradigmatic image of the historical Jewish tragedy — the crowded freight car on its way to the death camps — has become a *Pietà* without a Christ;[5] the story of the deportations and exterminations is diverted into a narrative of Catholic salvation and the making of a saint. The pope's beatification of Stein in Cologne in 1987 met resistance on a number of levels, but most pointedly because it rested, as beatifications in the absence of miracles must, on the definition of her extermination at Auschwitz as a Christian martyrdom.[6] The terms used by opponents are telling: the Catholic appropriation of the Shoah, the "Christianization" or even "universalization" of the Holocaust.[7]

The figure of Edith Stein is problematic in still other ways that might be particularly useful to broader inquiries of Jewish history and German-Jewish identity, and yet this problematic status has impeded such consideration. Indeed, her inclusion on the list of central German-Jewish cultural figures of the twentieth century has been disputed on the basis of her embrace of Catholic faith and entrance into the Carmelite order. Similarly, while her status as the first German woman to serve as a professorial assistant in philosophy and her continued engagement with the woman question might suggest her inclusion in another "canon," that of contemporary feminist history, the evident essentialism in her writing on the status of woman has apparently encumbered that move, while the same engagement has been troubling for those Catholic writers who read her feminist biblical interpretation as unorthodox.[8] Intellectual historians and literary critics who might be interested in the work of one of Husserl's most promising students have not known what to do with a phenomenology that moved seamlessly into Catholic theology and mysticism.

I would like to suggest that it is not accidental that Stein's status is problematic in each of these very different ways, and to argue that this uneasy status is itself useful for addressing questions of identity politics that are of interest to contemporary observers. This is not an argument for revising our canons to include more marginal elements, but instead for highlighting how an exceptional, idiosyncratic figure can call for a rethinking of categories of subjectivity, canonicity, and contextuality, which the focus on "representative" German-Jewish figures may well obscure. In Stein's case, for instance, an analytical framework placing her between the poles of assimilation and Jewish communal identity is utterly useless. How subjects are situated in—and situate themselves within—historical contexts is obviously a central issue for the cultural historian, yet that issue's complexity is stunningly underexamined. It is worthwhile to bring the current critical interest in "identity" (in this case, Stein's self-identification as a Jew or as a martyr for her "unbelieving" people)[9] back to the culture-historical study of contextualities: how does a subject's consciousness of her placement within her own historical contexts work to inflect or control those contexts? How do historical actors work to inform or to trouble the future memory of themselves? While the term *passing* is a loaded one, evoking the suspicion of oppressed individuals' inauthentic appropriation of privileged or majority identities, it also contains associations that disturb assumptions of authentic, irrevocable, and unexchangeable identity. Stein's phenomenological account of empathy, in her 1916 dissertation on the topic, offers a model of "passing" between self and other that is prerequisite to the experience of the self. In manifold ways, the figure of Edith Stein seems to pass between categories assumed to be hostile to one another, so that her appropriation within scholarly feminist, German-Jewish, philosophical, and theological canons is necessarily fraught. I am interested in the degree to which this troubled status prefigured the agendas of late twentieth-century "canonizers"—secular and clerical—and belonged to an unruly self-representation of Stein's own making.

To identify the structure of this self-fashioning and its implications for the positioning of subjects within contexts, it will become necessary to focus on the very tensions which most contemporary writing on Stein has felt obliged to resolve. Stein's self-portraits brush against the grain of familiar models of identity and representation, just as she seems to offer "intimate histories" which, in contrast to the rhetorical strategy of most memoir-writing, resist being understood as personal narratives representing grand narratives in microcosm. Thus I will explore how the "intimate history," in its rejection of consonance with forceful master narratives, is not a sub-genus of history as much as it is a challenge to it. In this sense it is similar to the "literary self-portrait," which, according to Michel Beaujour, operates on a different level from the autobiography or memoir: "It is no longer a question of standardizing the individual's memory to fit a cultural model but, on the contrary, of working with fragments that do not conform to the stereotype and out of which the subject can fashion an idiosyncratic ensemble of metaphors where he will find himself (again) or get lost."[10] In Stein's case, it is valuable to trace the ways in which this self-fashioning takes form, and to keep in mind the contexts or "big pictures" it reconfigures in the process. These include the narratives supporting a German academic context that systematically marginalized a promising philosopher on the basis of gender, a religious Christian theological context that identified Judaism either as completely alien or else as a necessary precursor to be overcome, and, most saliently, the rise of the racial state. Both instances and instruments of these subversions can be identified in Stein's rather idiosyncratic formulations of phenomenological empathy at one end (her 1916 dissertation under Husserl) and in the equally original theological and mystical writings from the end of her life at the other. Centrally, though, I will be referring to the rich and under-read text from late in Stein's life, her draft memoir entitled *Aus dem Leben einer jüdischen Familie (Life in a Jewish Family).*[11] This text, more than any other, has informed my notion of "intimate history."

Family Portraits

In turning to Stein's memoir *Life in a Jewish Family,* we encounter the twin concepts "empathic portraiture" and "intimate history." Central to these is the sublation of several sets of oppositions: self and other (through empathy, the subject of Stein's dissertation), private experience and official narratives or histories (through "intimate" accounts such as *Life in a Jewish Family*), and synchronic image and diachronic narrative ("portraits" and "histories"). Indeed, the stated intention of Stein's memoir manuscript, written chiefly in the first year after the Nazi seizure of power, is to provide an alternative history of German-Judaism, a counter-narrative to the National Socialist vision of Jews in German history.[12] But Stein's narrative is also generically informed by an early modern central European tradition of writing on Jewish life and Judaism by apostates; use of the rhetorical force of knowing the Jewish world from within, and then coming out of it into the light, was an important strategy of Judaism's Christian opponents.[13] In her foreword, Stein subtly articulates this dual source of her book: a priest's suggestion that Stein commit to writing her "insider's" knowledge of Judaism is first taken up years later, when an unbearable Nazi image of Jews dominates the scene and calls for repudiation.[14] Indeed, the book's title *Aus dem Leben einer jüdischen Familie* syntactically contains this double movement, claiming authenticity—*aus* points in this sense to an originary source—while also suggesting that the author has emerged from that world, come "out" of it. Of course one can take the expression *aus dem Leben* (from the life of) in a more pedestrian sense; yet the memoir constantly returns to this structure of passing between intimate, immediate experience and the perceptual experience of the oppositional outsider. Attention is called to the binary of internality/externality, in/out, a structure of identity and alienation which is dissipated within this intimate history, so that it seems as if the goal of "intimate history" itself were to do away with these dichotomies, or to render meaningless the segregation of the most private experience from public narratives of peoples and politics.

From the Life is a kind of autobiography, but its impetus and its first chapter is the story of another life, that of Edith's mother, Auguste Courant Stein. The powerful identification between mother and daughter is unmistakable in the text. On the other hand, this most important relationship in Edith Stein's life is also seen to be conflicted and adversarial: it is the single obstacle to her surrender to Christian faith. Fearing her mother's reaction, she keeps her Catholic enlightenment a secret at first; then she conceals her desire to become a nun, and her sister's subsequent conversion. The narrative construction of this mother as an external obstacle to Christian faith while at the same time a model very clearly prefiguring it is a symptomatic gesture of Stein's memoir text, in ways I will trace more closely.

This brings us to the shift alluded to above between histories or narratives and images, or "portraits." Stein claimed her first idea for the memoir was to tell her mother's story, to reproduce her inexhaustible story-telling. But the "stream of memories" could not be domesticated in a narrative which would offer "order and clarity" to the reader standing outside of Jewish life; tangible and reliable facts proved impossible to verify.[15] This apologia serves to prepare the reader for a narrative which not only treats foreign and unfamiliar experience but calls for an innovation of form. In place of the expected narrative, Stein offers "short sketches" of her mother's reminiscences, out of which should emerge a "life-image" of her mother. This transition from narrative to image conforms to what a French critical tradition has identified as a subversive move (sometimes unconscious) in certain literary self-portrayal, where fragmented analogic correspondences, cross-references, superimpositions, and collage disrupt the logical sequence of autobiography or historical narrative.[16] This move is not incidentally related to the structure of epiphany, where mechanically sequenced logic is displaced by more synchronic revelation.[17]

Thus Stein foregrounds the element of intimacy in her own text and, with the pretext of apologizing for it, breaks down the boundary between rational narrative and impressionistic image-making. In fact the Nazi story this narrative is intended to rebut is also principally a series of images. The speeches and programmatic writings of those in power had constructed an unbearable portrait of the Jew: "From these sources, as though from a concave mirror [*Hohlspiegel*], a horrendous caricature [*Zerrbild*] looked out at us."[18] The distorted image, or horrendous caricature (*Zerrbild*), the image from a distorting mirror (*Zerrspiegel*), is intended to be shattered by the detailed picture of life in a Jewish family which follows the preface. The text is clearly written with a Christian German public in mind, although these references may also imply the text's utility as a mirror for Jews, like the texts called "mirrors" for Renaissance princes—a model, a strategy, and a warning on how to behave. Already in this first page, Stein admits a certain anti-Semitism or Jewish self-hatred into her text which continues throughout: the caricatures were "possibly copied from living models," the manifest examples of "powerful [Jewish] capitalists, insolent [Jewish] literati, or restless [Jewish] revolutionaries." She objects principally to the thesis that the exaggerated image applies to all Jews, as an inevitable consequence of Jewish blood. But there is more at stake in both Stein's conjuring of anti-Semitic images and her self-distancing from them than an answer to National Socialist propaganda. Built into the claim of painting a portrait from the inside out is the possibility of constructing an alternative Jewish image and self-image, reconcilable with German Christianity, indeed a Jewishness which passes into figures German and Christian, and which allows these to pass in turn into itself.

Empathy, in Passing

Stein's portrait of a Jewish family is carefully engineered to be an intensely "empathic" text, and for this reason we will need to return to the complex dynamics of empathy outlined in Stein's dissertation, *On the Problem of Empathy*. For now it is worth noting that the phenomenological term empathy (*Einfühlen*) is conceptually and philologically linked and simultaneously contrasted to the related term sympathy (*Mitfühlen*). The terms share the root "feeling" and differ in the prepositional prefixes of *ein* ("in" or "into") and *mit* (with). Sympathy—

"feeling-with," or "fellow feeling"—may have noble origins and charitable out-comes, but it also guarantees the discreteness of self and other: one does not feel or move or act "with" oneself, of course, but with another.[19] Empathy—"feeling-into"—on the other hand is an experience of being led by the foreign experi-ence, of identifying *as* another.[20] In empathy Stein finds a moment of fusion of perception and sensation, a "double mode of experiencing" which overcomes dichotomies of inside and outside, native and foreign. Thus these Jewish por-traits are not designed as sympathetic depictions of a fellow community on German soil; rather, they seduce the reader into seeing herself in portraits that nonetheless retain the mark of an exoticized other. The figure of the Jew in this text thus passes into figures of Christian faith, German patriotism, or German bourgeois values at respective moments; similar moves in Stein's feminist texts, as we will see, perform provocative passing gestures in the field of gender. Thus empathy informs a narrative pattern in Stein's texts in relation to the triptych of spiritual, national, and gender identities, each troubled within by empathic al-ternations with their others and stressed from without by hostile Weimar and Nazi contexts.

The first section of the memoir, the one focusing on the memories of Auguste Courant, stresses images of piety, respectability, and German loyalty. In the ear-liest description of Stein's great-grandfather's home she focuses on his strictness as father and teacher, the patriarchal order of the home, and the prayer-room in the family house where sons-in-law and patriarch congregated for intimate wor-ship. The great-grandmother, too, is described as a "truly pious woman" whose religiosity is closely associated with her intense suffering; she ends each prayer with the plea "Lord, send us only as much as we can bear." If these romantic con-structions of Jewish piety contain more than a touch of orientalism, which Stein continues in her descriptions of Jewish religion throughout the memoir, they resist anti-Semitic and older anti-Jewish stereotypes of Judaic religion as me-chanical, legalistic, and empty ritual. The reader senses a touching authenticity of faith, even if it seems a naive and somehow unresolved faith. It is a primor-dial Christianity, a Judaism to remind the reader of Christian faith's Jewish roots. Hence in her lengthy description of the Passover observance she points out to "unaware" Christians that the feast "continues to be celebrated today in the identical manner in which it was celebrated by our Lord with his disciples when he instituted the Blessed Sacrament and took leave of his followers."[21] This fact colors the exoticizing description of the Passover rituals, which suddenly seem more immediate to the life of Christ than they are alien to modern Christians. The theme of secularization is at work in the three-page description of holiday practices, as Stein confesses relief at having others perform religious duties after her "enlightenment" (put in skeptical quotation marks), and the passing of her father leaves the duty of prayer recitation in the unreliable and disrespectful hands of assimilated brothers. So in this sense, the modern Christian's remoteness from the mystical moment of the Sacrament/Passover ritual is mimetically reproduced in the assimilated Jewish environment. In spite of the visceral response of many Jewish observers to the figure of the Jewish nun, Stein's turn to Christianity was never described by herself in terms of disavowal; to the contrary, she insisted upon the close kinship of her Catholic spirituality and her Jewishness[22]—but as in other close kinships, the relationship was complicated.

In the same passage of the text, for instance, two references to Jewish ritual serve as vessels for figures that are not supposed to share a single space: the Jew and the Christ. The first of these is the Pascal lamb, the sacrificial creature so symbolically significant for both ancient Judaism and early Christianity. To some degree, it could be argued, even this strange overlaying of symbols proceeds from a convention in the anti-Jewish theological literature, granting a primordial authenticity to the ancient Jewish tradition whose manifest legitimate heir is the Christian one. Even stranger is the reference in Stein's description of Yom Kippur to the "'scapegoat' [*Sündenbock*] upon whose head, symbolically, the sins of all the people had been laid [and which was] driven out into the desert." Stein resists sanitizing Jewish ritual as kindred religious celebration, and locates it instead as a site of authentic and originary Christian experience, even as Christ's own experience. Just as the Carmelite nun knew that the task of the Christian life was to enter the life of Jesus himself, her Christian readers were positioned to see Jewish religion as a key to revelation rather than as alien to Christian faith. The word *scapegoat* conjures the figure of a vessel for the sins of others which is ritually expunged or sacrificed, and it is a vessel which in this textual setting contains several objects corresponding to parallel historical moments: the original creature sacrificed by the ancient Jewish community, the Christ (whether as scapegoat of the Jews, or as the lamb who dies for the sins of humanity), and now the Jews, victims of a contemporary cleansing ritual uncannily identical to the one they created. Stein's own birth on the Day of Atonement is given some gravity in this passage, and allows not only her own prophetic identification with the *Sündenbock* but also the key to her special intimacy with her mother. The complexity of this mother-daughter relation rests on this tension between identification and opposition. Stein's piety is her mother's, but the latter's more instinctive and unprocessed faith is transformed (or "converted") in the daughter into a Catholicism run through with phenomenological philosophy, with thinking.

As striking as the ellipsis from Jewish to Christian identity is in this portrait, the Jewish family's intimate bond with Germanness is no less impressive, similarly containing the radical ambivalences of double gestures which subvert no more than they collude. In particular, we continually encounter a representation of a fervent and threatened German patriotism. The most familiar moments of this representation include listing relatives who sacrificed their lives in the First World War, or the tale of the Jewish hero uncle who slipped through enemy lines in disguise to save important papers and enlist in the army.[23] Descriptions such as these were common in the efforts of Jews to contradict the *völkisch* challenge to their Germanness in the Weimar Republic and the Third Reich. But this "sympathetic" model of Jewish Germanness (or the "me-too" structure of such descriptions) is different in kind from the patriotism of Edith's mother and of herself: a veteran defending his country is somehow standing apart from it. "I can be in love with Germany," Stein wrote to Roman Ingarden in 1917, "so little as I can be in love with myself, for I am indeed [Germany] itself."[24] Thus from the sympathetic assertion of fellow-German patriotism, Stein passes, or claims to pass, into "Germanness," to elide herself and her country; in doing so, she escapes the possibility of "loving" her country in the way that she might love someone else's. As with Jewish religion, a powerful identification is constructed in the text as inherited from her mother, yet refracted in a complicated way through the empathic dynamic. Her mother is the most zealous of German nationalists, setting her wedding song to the tune of "The Watch on the Rhine," and "she finds it incomprehensible that anyone should dare to dispute her German identity."[25]

Stein recounts the story of the loss of the homeland after World War I, when a plebiscite turned the Courant hometown of Lublinitz over to Poland.[26] The family's patriotic struggle to keep the German homeland, and the impossibility of their staying once it was no longer German, operate in this text in the same way the figure of the *Auslandsdeutsche* and *Volksdeutsche* (ethnic German communities outside the Reich) operated within Nazi propaganda leading up to 1939. That is to say, the issue of ethnic Germans facing the loss of their German homeland or the integrity of their German identities to Poles, Czechs, and Russians played an important role in the inscription of German national identity in the heartland and thus played a role quite out of proportion to their numbers. A certain priority was given those Germans whose nationality was under fire, and who could not take their national identities for granted, or who had to fight for it. In Stein's text, the Polish threat to the German Courants is set against a second and present challenge to the Courants' German legacy represented by "those [racialists] who would dare to dispute" it. It is not that Auguste Courant was more German than the Germans; but by empathizing with the figure of Auguste Courant, a German identity under siege, the German reader is invited to come to a more active realization of his/her Germanness—empathically to experience the terrible possibility of its slipping away even as one, as German Christian outsider, sees why it is slipping away from these Jews. This empathic portrait is structured to allow an experience of identification with the plight of the othered figure at the same moment that its otherness is brought into relief.

Empathy, as a section title of Stein's dissertation asserts, is the condition of possibility of constituting the individual self (*das Ich*).[27] In making this point, Stein defines the dual nature of the body with twin terms: the *Leib*, or living body, which is the subject of immediate or "primordial" experience, and the *Körper*, or physical body, such as those bodies one perceives around oneself. But the experience of the living body is not purely primordial; it is itself subject to the empathic relation. The experience of touching involves both the sensation of the living body—internal sensation—and the perception of my hand touching an object that I know from seeing other bodies touching other objects—an act that I therefore can identify as "touching." This dual nature of corporeal experience is called "reiterated empathy," and "is at the same time the condition making possible that mirror-image-like givenness of myself" which belongs to a host of primordial experiences, such as memory, fantasy, expectation, and so forth. All are "primordial as present experience though non-primordial in content."[28] The double mode of experiencing is crucial to the possibility of emergence of "the pure self" or "the pure 'I,'" which, without the empathic relation to other selves, cannot be given to itself—its "selfness" first appears through the empathic encounter with "the otherness of the other."[29]

It is obviously not my concern to locate the innovation of Stein's analysis of empathy within the field of phenomenology, but rather to bring her discussion of empathy to bear on our readings of her life and work. Yet, because of the issue of "history" at stake in Stein's intimate and empathic turn, it is worthwhile to take a moment to look at one of her precursors and her reaction to him: the philosopher of the human sciences Wilhelm Dilthey. Dilthey is addressed in force, and for the first time in her dissertation, in its final chapter, "Empathy as the Understanding of Spiritual Persons." Stein identifies Dilthey's life work as a search for the ontological foundation of the human sciences (*Geisteswissenschaften*, the German term, foregrounds its relation to Stein's subject, the spirituality of persons). Stein's interest in Dilthey makes sense, given his connection of historical knowledge to the notion of subjective experience and empathy.[30] In Dilthey she finds a philosopher who is working through an empirical system which will yield natural laws of culture, or of spirit.[31] This approach to history, which she defines as "empathic comprehension," is already taken further in the 1916 dissertation and used as the way to steer her text away from its systematic review of the relationship of subjectivity and the apperception of others, toward an unresolved conclusion on religious consciousness and revelation. ("*Non li-quet*," she interpolates in the argument, "It is not clear.") The "intimate histories" she would spin out after her conversion would go even a step further, moving from Dilthey's empirical empathic comprehension toward mystical experience which defies observation, for it is hidden from view.

Redressing Subjectivity: Jewishness as a Masquerade

If the pedestrian association of empathy with the feminine was already close to the surface of the text even as it was being written, its connection to Jewish identity, and further, to Jewish history, is exposed in the Jewish memoir. Yet neither of these identifications is constructed in ways that simply appropriate a discrete space of canonical philosophy for these marginalized elements—each contains the complex and sometimes unsettling double movement I have been describing, where innovative cross-identifications and appropriations reiterate and reinforce the rules of the game. For instance, to refer briefly to Stein's writings on "the nature of woman," while empathy is delineated within the feminine province, the philosophical career would seem, according to her apparently strictly essentialist essay "'The Calling of Man and Woman According to the Orders of Nature and Grace," to be practically reserved for men: "overwhelmingly abstract reasoning ability" being, along with physical strength, the most exclusively masculine quality.[32] In a manner that rather remarkably parallels her moves between Jewishness and Christianity (and that evokes similarly visceral reactions in contemporary readers), Stein's inscriptions of a space for women in spheres from which they have been excluded are continually accompanied by the reinscription of the boundaries which have excluded them. These newly inscribed boundaries, however, are passable: in her reading of masculine and feminine essences, she incorporates the notion of the influential misogynist philosopher-psychologist Otto Weininger that all beings are located on a spectrum between male and female ideal poles. Via this fairly orthodox adoption of his system, Stein opens a passage between incontrovertibly male and female spheres, and passes. That is, in the same essay on the vocation of the genders, she stresses that the professions should *not* be reserved for men or for women in light of (and here she practically quotes Weininger) the "strong individual differences" which make some women "closely approach the masculine type [*Typus*]", and some men the feminine. Weininger's ideal types are placed in service of the delegitimation of assumptions of gendered ability, as they take on quotation marks in Stein's text: "Hence every 'masculine' profession may also be very satisfactorily filled by certain women, and every 'feminine' one by certain men."[33] The close proximity of this passage to the characterization of the philosophical profession as "masculine," coming as it does in a woman philosopher's essay, marks the whole as another self-portrait which constitutes a gesture of passing, or identifying across gender lines.[34]

This gesture is usefully set against the figure of "masquerade" that has informed recent gender studies. A text that is contemporary with Stein's and has been discussed in that literature is a psychoanalytic essay of 1929 by Joan Riviere, "Womanliness as a Masquerade."[35] Riviere also works off of a spectral model of gender and sexuality partially founded by Weininger, according to which "we all" figure as to some degree "bisexual," or "intermediate" figures along the line between oppositional poles of the ideal masculine and ideal feminine.[36] The case study Riviere presents in her essay is meant to represent one particular type of homosexual woman, the intellectual who fulfills classical feminine roles but who excels in "masculine" arenas. In Riviere's essay, the "masquerade" is constituted by an enacted, exaggerated femininity to mask the possession of the masculine object (in psychoanalytic discourse this is obviously the phallus, the possession of which implies the castration of the father).[37] There are several directions in which this thinking could take the phenomenon of Stein's textual passing. It turns out that the least convincing model is that represented by the most immediate association of the figure of passing: the anxiety about passing expressed by hegemonic subjects, the response to a woman (Jew, black) inauthentically clothing herself as a privileged subject. The Riviere text, written just as Stein was working on issues of gender and vocation, posits an antithetical relation between exterior identity and interior (psychic) life; the feminine mask is a symptom of the possession of the phallus. Is Stein positing her role of philosopher, then, as a masculine essence in feminine guise (the objectionable implication of the essay on the vocation of the genders)? Or do we have to look further to get at the prickly question of selves and identities, of truth and disguise?

The special status of the photograph, Roland Barthes famously asserted, is that it appears to be a message without a code, the perfect *analogon*.[38] The well-known power of photographic images to deceive rests on this assumption of the special status of the medium. In three photograph portraits taken of Stein (figures 5.1–5.3), we see the subject looking at the camera/spectator/public, her head tilted at the same angle downward and to the left, her dark eyes aimed in a

FIGURE 5.1. *Edith as a student. Photograph courtesy of Edith-Stein-Archiv, Karmel "Maria vom Frieden," Cologne.*

FIGURE 5.2. *Edith on her Clothing Day (1934). Photograph courtesy of Edith-Stein-Archiv, Karmel "Maria vom Frieden," Cologne.*

FIGURE 5.3. *Passport photo (1938) before her transfer to Echt. Photograph courtesy of Edith-Stein-Archiv, Karmel "Maria vom Frieden," Cologne.*

pensive glance up and to the right, at the viewer, with an arguably inscrutable expression. The first is Edith the seated student, with short hair and some work in her lap, her head resting thoughtfully on her hand. One is reminded of a style of female intellectual we think of in relation to her contemporary, Hannah Arendt—a self-presentation which leans toward the androgynous. A second portrait hails from two years after writing the essay on woman, at her clothing day of entry into the Carmelite order in the spring of 1934. The same face in angle and expression glances out from a traditional bridal gown, and she holds in her hand a white scepter, signifiers of her weddedness to Christ until her death. The last is the best known image of Stein, clothed in her Carmelite habit; it is the passport photograph taken in 1938 before her transfer to the Echt convent. On the one hand, these three images together could be read as gestures of passing, in their surrender to clearly cited conventions. Or, as Linda Haverty Rugg has suggested in her recent book on photography and autobiography, such a series could be said to "supply a visual metaphor for the divided and multiple ("decentered") self."[39] Yet, if Stein could have had control over these images and the way they work against one another, they might have looked like this: as though a powerful, if somewhat inscrutable, self survived throughout these transformations, a hidden life independent of exterior identity.[40] The clothing ceremony itself is interesting because of its self-conscious surrender of a certain kind of subjectivity (while simultaneously claiming the priority of an essential, inner and hidden subjectivity). The novice surrenders her name—and to the last, Stein would prefer her works to appear under the name she chose for her life in Carmel, Sr. Teresa Benedicta of the Cross.[41]

The surrender of the name and the "redressing" of the subject are consistent with Stein's increasing devaluation of external identities and given narratives, just as they resonate with contemporary discussions of gendered subjectivity. These have circulated in large part around Judith Butler's work on gender performance and the so-called sex/gender distinction, which again emphasizes the contingency of a central category of identity. Butler herself points out that the performativity of these identities is less controversial than what lies, or does not lie, behind them, or what the masquerade masks.[42] In a contribution to these discussions, Slavoj Žižek has referred to Hegel's notion that subjectivity itself is something *angezogen*, dressed-up or worn, and hence the association of femininity with masquerade privileges rather than denies female subjectivity.[43] What we have been tracing in Stein's writing can be seen as a redressing of identities through an empathic identification and simultaneous surrender, or a "giving-itself-away."[44] The redressing (and a degree of surrender) of the subject takes place chiefly through Stein's textual device of "empathic portraiture." In fact, as Stein promised in her introductory reference to "sketches," *Life in a Jewish Family* is full of portraits, chiefly of women in her family. Some such sketches are taken from portraits and photographs from the family home: Stein describes the portrait of her grandmother that hung there, her "small, delicate features" reflecting a profound "nobility of spirit." Another portrait, a photograph of her Aunt Mika, demonstrates a "wonderful graciousness, maidenly purity and her deep seriousness." Thus these portraits serve as counter-images to anti-Semitic stereotypes, just as these two women are strongly associated in the text with preservation of Jewish identity and reinforcement of a Jewish foundation to family life. This piety, too, takes forms familiar to Christian German readers: reading psalms in German, a family life based on principles of simplicity and thrift. The dominance of empathic portraits of women in the family is particularly notable in light of the relative dearth of such portraits of men. The father, who died suddenly in 1893 when Edith was still a small child, is described hardly at all, or appears as a sort of phantom. Her brother Arno's paternalistic posing is mocked as form without content, as the family (and Stein, throughout the memoir) refers to him as der "*Chef*" ("the 'boss'"), framed by ironic scare quotes. The matriarchal order of the household is naturalized in the memoir, even as it remains disguised, for this is a household that seems to match every model of stereotypical German bourgeois (i.e., patriarchal) life.

Stein's intense identification with her mother in the portrait (the whole first part of the memoir) renders it a strange sort of self-portrait—strange because young Edith herself appears in the text as the other, yet occasionally also the eyes through which the life of the mother is seen. Central here is the image of Auguste as matriarch and patriarch of the family after the early death of the *paterfamilias*—her powerful role driving the successful family lumber business, culminating in the chapter's final note on an overheard comment in a Breslau streetcar: "Do you know who is the most capable merchant [in German the term is more clearly gendered as masculine: *der tüchtigste Kaufmann*] in the whole trade in the city? Frau Stein! [*Das ist die Frau Stein!*]"[45]

This passing between gender roles, mentioned above in the context of Stein in the "masculine" role of philosopher, is interestingly set against a family photograph portrait of 1895 (see figure 5.4). On the surface, this seems to be a typical, traditional family portrait, with the seven children around the *paterfamilias*, the tall sons framing the back row, the young girls in front, and the dutiful mother seated deferentially by her husband's side. But Herr Stein had died, we know, two years earlier. Upon the sudden death of Auguste's husband, or rather upon reflection at least a year after his death, the absence of an image of the family with the father at the center was felt (presumably by Auguste).[46] The mother and children

FIGURE 5.4. *Stein family, 1895 (father superimposed). Photograph courtesy of Edith-Stein-Archiv, Karmel "Maria vom Frieden," Cologne.*

positioned themselves around an unoccupied space in the center of the composition, into which a passport photograph of him was superimposed. The photograph effected a powerful illusion of the patriarchal order of the family which was eerily at odds with the fact that no one could doubt: that the center of this family circle was occupied by the figure Edith Stein identifies in her own text, Auguste Courant Stein.

Empathic portraiture brings us around again to the figure of "passing" in a provocative way. If this text is, as the preface confesses, meant to be in dialogue with an "unsympathetic" image of the Jew promulgated by the Nazis, the question of passing takes on sinister implications. A central didactic goal of Nazi anti-Semitic propaganda was of course to redraw the boundaries of difference between Jew and German that had become invisible in the post-emancipation period: one thinks for instance of the famous scene from Hippler's *The Eternal*

FIGURE 5.5. *Edith Stein (right) with sister Erna. Photograph courtesy of Edith-Stein-Archiv, Karmel "Maria vom Frieden," Cologne.*

Jew where East European Hasidic Jews, presented as radically and unappealingly foreign, are groomed as if to "pass" in German society, and the successive dissolve to a bourgeois cocktail party of Berlin Jews. Even this specifically racialist valence of "passing" is touched upon in the memoir. Stein recalls her large family as a series of pairs, negative doubles. Her own negative double is the sister Erna (see figure 5.5), darkly complected, overanimated in her gestures, and garrulous in contrast with the young Edith, described as blonde, deep thinking, and reserved. The apparently unironic description of Edith as an Aryan double of a Jewish Erna is startling in the same way as other moments in Stein's texts, appearing to shore up the contemporary anti-Semitic contexts the memoir was intended to attack. But this apparent discursive complicity is not easy to sort out. What could it mean to figure her relationship with her closest sister in terms of "racial" opposition, to paint "Aryan" portraits of herself and other women in her family? Does it subvert the foundation of the notion of "race" (blood is character) through an acceptance of the normative values of contemporary racism? Does it represent a crossing, or a passing gesture, that fortifies or that attacks notions of authentic identity and difference? Is it an example of the famous copy which authorizes the original?[47] Or perhaps the question we should be asking is whether we can be satisfied with the uneasy way these meanings are overlaid and confounded *as an integral component of their construction,* so that a radically malleable vision of identity is—unmistakably, irredeemably—fused with a conviction in an irreducible, certainly "essential," if hidden, truth.

Hidden Histories

Between the portrait of life in a Jewish family written chiefly in the Cologne Carmel and the image of the nun in the freight train bound for Auschwitz, Stein left a series of additional portraits: the hagiographic pieces written in the Echt Carmel.[48] Collected in a slim volume under the title *The Hidden Life* (*Verborgenes Leben,* the word for "hidden" being connected with the notion of a diversion into the invisible, or to a safe haven) in the year of her beatification, these sketches of the holy lives focus mainly on women: St. Elizabeth of Thuringia, St. Teresa Margaret of the Sacred Heart, Sr. Marie-Aimée de Jésus, and Stein's inspiration to convert to Catholicism, St. Teresa of Jesus (Teresa of Avila).[49] Neither the predominance of sketches of women nor their status as "empathic portraits," or even thinly veiled self-portraits, was lost on the German and Dutch editors of the original volume. In their preface and introduction, they note that in these portraits "she frequently finds a mirror image of herself": her encounter in the image of Marie-Aimée of "her own self," the focus in the sketch of St. Teresa Margaret on "the saint's spontaneous empathic ability" which was Stein's own strength, and the possibility of reading "between the lines" how the lives of Edith Stein and her Catholic namesake St. Teresa of Avila "have all along been parallel."[50] Thus these sketches, they contend, are more autobiographical than her memoir and the correspondence they published under the title *Self-Portrait in Letters.*[51]

The value of these insights lies in their recognition of the rhetorical construct we have been recognizing in Stein's writings all along: a dialectic between interiority, the "hidden" true spiritual life of the subject, and the often deceptive apprehension of exterior life, social and political contexts, or "history." Conceiving what seem to be problematic narrative strategies in this way permits a reassessment of the troubling double movement in Stein's texts, where exclusionary narratives on race, gender, and religion are buttressed at the same moment as they are undermined. If the rethinking of contextuality that Stein's work engenders indeed entails a dialectic of selves and contexts, we can begin to make sense of simultaneously linked and antithetical poles, such as spiritual subjectivity and the world of politico-historical objects, interior selves and exterior identities, the hidden and the represented.

It is not surprising that a sketch of Teresa of Avila should be found among these empathic (self-)portraits. As I have mentioned, Stein's construction of her own epiphany turns around the image of a furtive reading of the saint's famous autobiography, and this experience led her not only to Christian faith but of course to Carmel, where she would take the name Teresa. Yet the editors' description of these sketches as "mirror images" of the author reminds us, as Stein did herself in her reflection on images of Jews, that the mirror reflects at the same time that it reverses; some mirrors distort, and others invert. What is the nature of the "parallel lives" of the two Teresas? The sketch reflects upon the way the moment in which it is being written (February 1934) mirrors the moment of Carmelite reform:

> While outside in carnival's frantic tumult people get drunk and delirious, while political battles separate them, and great need depresses them so much that many forget to look to heaven, at such still places of prayer hearts are opened to the Lord. . . . The desire for new foundations is surfacing in the most varied places. One almost feels transported into the time when our Holy Mother Teresa, the foundress of the reformed Carmel, traveled all over Spain from north to south and from west to east to plant new vineyards of the Lord. One would like to bring into our times also something of the spirit of this great woman who built amazingly during a century of battles and disturbances.[52]

While this opening explicitly suggests a parallel between these periods and between these women's lives, this model of allegory proves somewhat deceptive. Both Teresas live in embattled times and battle for the spirit, both ceaselessly seek the truth and know that the journey is a spiritual one. Just as Stein is put on the path to truth in her reading of Teresa's autobiography, in that same autobiography we learn of the young future saint's identification with the subjects of the classical hagiographies she reads (the *Lives*). With the knowledge that the easiest path to God is martyrdom, the young Teresa runs away from home with the wish to perish for her faith among the Moors.

The portrait of Teresa is set against the backdrop of sixteenth-century Spain. The walled city of Avila is a fortress of Christianity, the heart of the "castle" or fortress of Christendom which is Castile. The Castilian knights were a crusading army of faith—from "such a race of heroes" came Teresa, the "bold warrior for God."[53] It is difficult to disregard Stein's uncolloquial description of Teresa's

wandering "from west to east" to crusade for her faith, or to read this mirrored—
or reversed—image of Stein's voyage as a "parallel"—unless the author's clear
identification with the "centered" figure of Teresa is a signal that, in a world
turned on its head, we need to look for centers in the most unlikely of places:
from the heart of Castile to Breslau the borderland, from a fervent Catholic to
a pious Jewish upbringing.

The central inversion in the piece has to do with history. The identification of Teresa's turbulent century with the 1930s seems sensible in the opening
quoted above, but this correspondence is, again, vexed. Teresa's embattled time
is identified with the proximity of her birth to the expulsion. The "disturbance"
of her century is not named as the battle of Reformists and Catholics, for instance, but is associated with the struggle against the Moors (and with them, of
course, the Jews), as though the Catholic Reformation were a continuation of
the ongoing battle with the infidel. To comprehend the strangeness of this move
in Stein's text we need to recall that, in 1934, a comparison to the same historical
period—the Inquisition—would be the commonest rhetorical move by a critic
of the new German regime. But here Stein presents an unequivocally affirma-
tive image of that battle against Europe's and Christianity's others, and she openly
identifies with the Castilian crusader. The hidden, spiritual truth (all Stein's words,
frequently repeated in the Carmel writings) of this figure is a life independent
of, even in opposition to, the apparent "history" surrounding it. Intimacy again
appears as a counter-figure of history in a time demanding such a move. To illuminate this operation of the "hidden life" we turn finally to the brief mystical
work with that title, a 1940 meditation on darkness and light, concealment and
revelation, entitled "The Hidden Life and the Epiphany."

In this piece written for the Feast of Kings in the dark months of winter, Stein
begins with the image of the advent candles providing a feeble but unceasing
consolation and illumination of an increasingly dark and fallen world. The origin of this light, like the dark history it challenges, is not paradise but the expulsion from it. In the following account Stein carefully maintains the opposition of this inner light to external history, even as she charts the equally hidden
relation between the two:

> A ray of this light fell into the hearts of our original parents even during the
> judgment . . . an illuminating ray that awakened in them the knowledge of
> their guilt. . . . Hidden from the whole world, it illuminated and irradiated
> them. . . . Seen by no human eye, this is how living building blocks were and
> are formed and brought together into a church first of all invisible. . . . [I]t fi-
> nally comes down to inner life; formation moves from inner to the outer.

The deeper a soul is bound to God, the more completely surrendered to grace, the stronger will be its influence on the form of the church. Conversely, the more an era is engulfed in the night of sin and estrangement from God the more it needs souls united to God. And God does not permit a deficiency. The greatest figures of prophecy and sanctity step forth out of the darkest night. But for the most part the formative stream of the mystical life remains invisible. Certainly the decisive turning points in world history are substantially co-determined by souls whom no history book ever mentions. And we will only find out about those souls to whom we owe the decisive turning points in our personal lives on the day when all that is hidden is revealed.[54]

Oddly, this oblique and unsystematic piece posits explicitly what earlier texts at best implied. For the unseen and unseeable subject here is not merely prior to the visible one, authentic in contrast to the latter, if not verifiable; these two (inner and outer life, as well as the most covert spirituality of the individual and the broadest outlines of human history) are powerfully united. Since external form never reflects this inner reality, but more often opposes it, the relationship between the two is almost always illegible. The darkest historical moment, Stein writes in 1940, masks the most brilliant spiritual light; the decisive souls of such periods, saints of the present, remain unrecognized in the exterior world. These are the paradoxes represented by the figures of (inner, spiritual) light and (external, historical) darkness above. The true life is spiritual, hidden, virtually inaccessible, and as often obscured as it is exposed by exterior living. It reveals itself even to the subject only through the empathic relation, through the encounter with a simultaneously discrete and identical other. As was already recognized before her conversion, in the dissertation on empathy written by an agnostic Stein, this single path to the self is simultaneously the unique way of encountering God.

Stein's mystical turn, her faith in a hidden and immutable truth, and the encounter with God may seem irreconcilable with contemporary critical approaches to modern philosophy, German-Jewish identity construction, and feminist writing. But this is only so if we forget the way the "true subject" actually emerges in Stein's work: it is utterly invisible, an inversion or else an utter reconfiguration of the way subjects appear within their historical and social surroundings. It emerges out of a network of contradictory relations, patterned by negative doubles and unidentical selves, compelling an inescapable intimacy with the other and a link between dissimulation and authenticity which brushed perhaps no more against the grain of Stein's historical moment than it does our own. This is a subjectivity that confects itself in ways that protect it from and allow it to defend itself against hostile contexts. The controversies associated with Edith Stein's afterlife in public historical consciousness—her contextualization within competing histories of the Holocaust, canonical appropriations of her work and herself as a figure—seem overdetermined in light of these self-constructions. That is why focusing on issues such as "identity" and "essentialism," both of which appear particularly relevant to the Edith Stein case at first glance, may lead readers astray. Stein's work may be better served by the notion of "contextuality," or by a rethinking of contextuality that takes seriously not only historico-political influences, but also contexts of reception, including those anticipated by subjects: by attending to the ongoing project in which many figures engage—if not all as relentlessly and creatively as Stein—to create contexts for themselves.

NOTES

For our good discussions and/or their direct contributions to this chapter I thank Lauren Berlant, Crisca Bierwert, Todd Endelman, Sander Gilman, Barbara Hahn, Michael Steinberg, and Julie Skurski. Above all I acknowledge the staff and anonymous reviewers for *New German Critique*, where this essay originally appeared under the same title (*New German Critique* 75 [Fall 1998]: 28–56), and which has graciously permitted this reprint.

1. Reports of the canonization stressed the controversy surrounding it and the "contradictions and ambiguities" associated with the new saint. See, e.g., "A Saintly Controversy," *Chicago Sun-Times*, 11 October 1998, 38; "Vatican Rushes to Canonise a Catholic Jew," *Independent* (London), 11 October 1998, 23; "A Jew's Odyssey from Catholic Nun to Saint," *New York Times*, 11 October 1998, 1; "Contention Trails Nun's Elevation to Sainthood," Associated Press report, 11 October 1998; "Jewish Groups Object to Nun's Canonization," *Chicago Tribune*, 11 October 1998, C9; "Fury as Jewish Nun Who Died in Auschwitz Is Made Saint," *Times* (London), 12 October 1998. The official approval for the canonization process came from Pope John Paul II on 22 May 1997, on the basis of the miraculous recovery of a Massachusetts two-year-old after swallowing a near-lethal dose of Tylenol a decade earlier. The child, Benedicta McCarthy, had been named for the Auschwitz martyr, and her family had prayed to Edith Stein for her recovery. News reports of the May 1997 announcement focused on the miracle rather than on the controversy over the status of Stein's martyrdom (see below).

2. S. Heilbronner, "Canonizing of Jew Still Debated," *Religion News Service*, 24 May 1997. The *Jerusalem Post* strikes a similar chord: "The heart of the dispute over Stein is whether she should be properly remembered as a Christian martyr or as one of the countless Jewish victims of the Nazi death machine." C. Ben-David, "The Saint of Auschwitz," *Jerusalem Post*, 2 May 1997, 4.

3. Report from Johannes Wieners, "Meine Begegnung mit Edith Stein," *Kölnische Rundschau*, 9 August 1982, quoted and trans. in Waltraud Herbstrith, *Edith Stein: A Biography*, trans. Bernard Bonowitz (New York: Harper and Row, 1985), 111.

4. Many such testimonies are recorded in Teresia Renata Posselt, *Edith Stein: Eine große Frau unseres Jahrhunderts* (Freiburg: Herder, 1963), 188–215, and Herbstrith, *Edith Stein*, 104–8.

5. The absence of the Christ figure in the peculiar representation of "a Pietà without the Christ" is worth some consideration. In the first place it seems to signal something of the paradox of the ultra-Christian figure of the saint embodied by a Jewish woman (foreshadowing the press's recent hyperbole that Stein is "the first Jewish-born saint . . . since the Virgin Mary"; see *Detroit News*, 10 October 1998, C3). Another provocative parallel is offered by Sigrid Weigel in her analysis of the controversial selection of an enormously enlarged reproduction of the Käthe Kollwitz sculpture *Mutter mit Sohn* for the Berlin "Neue Wache" national memorial to "Öpfer des Krieges und der Gewaltherrschaft." In the context of a broader discussion of the symbolic place of women within Holocaust memory in Germany, Weigel argues that the Pietà figure shifts the focus of national memory from the victims (the "silent ashes," in the quotation from Auschwitz survivor Cornelia Edvardson's memoir opening Weigel's article) to the perpetrators-as-victims. This particular use of gendered symbols pertains to a "universeller Opferkonzept" or "überhistorischer 'Existenzmetapher'" eclipsing a perpetrator-identification unavoidable in thematizations of father figures. See Sigrid Weigel, "Der Ort von Frauen im Gedächnis des Holocaust: Symbolisierungen, Zeugenschaft und kollektive Identität," *Sprache im technischen Zeitalter* 135 (September 1995): 260–68.

6. Either two miracles or such a martyrdom is required for beatification. Once a person is beatified, a miracle is prerequisite to canonization.

7. See, e.g., "An Unnecessary Saint," *Jerusalem Post*, 20 October 1998, 10; "Pilgrimage to Auschwitz," *Los Angeles Times*, 19 August 1989, 8; "Again, the Pope Has Disappointed Jews," *New York Times*, 26 September 1987, sec. 1, 27; "Church Putting Christian Stamp on the Holocaust," *Jerusalem Post*, 13 June 1989; "A Papal Act Ruffles Jewish Community," UPI commentary, 15 May 1987.

8. The issue of Stein's essentialism is discussed below. The tensions between her feminist interpretation and conventional Catholic doctrine become apparent in several editorial correctives to texts collected in a 1956 edition of selected writings in English translation, culminating in this symptomatic note: "Here the author's feminist tendencies have evidently carried her too far in her criticism of the Apostle and allowed her to forget that his words are inspired." See *Writings of Edith Stein*, ed. and trans. Hilda Graef (London: Peter Owen, 1956), 111. There has indeed been a recent *Toronto Sun* article titled "Let's Claim Edith Stein for Women Everywhere," accompanied by her photograph with the caption "EDITH STEIN . . . A feminist saint," but the suggestion is made chiefly tongue-in-cheek, and the article in fact focuses on the difficulty of appropriations of Stein; see Liz Braun, *Toronto Sun*, 18 October 1998, C13.

9. One of the flagrant tensions informing the current controversy takes form in the contrast between Stein's last recorded words, to her sister as they were being deported to the camp, "Come, Rosa, we are going on behalf of our people," and the reference in her Carmelite spiritual last will and testament to her penance "for the sins of the unbelieving people." See, e.g., *Chicago Tribune*, 11 October 1998, C6.

10. See Michel Beaujour, *Poetics of the Literary Self-Portrait*, trans. Yara Milos (New York: New York University Press, 1991), 197.

11. Edith Stein, *Aus dem Leben einer jüdischen Familie. Das Leben Edith Steins: Kindheit und Jugend,* ed. Lucy Gelber, vol. 7 of *Edith Steins Werke* (Louvain: E. Nauwelaerts, 1965).

12. Any relation of this anti-Semitic account to the theologically based anti-Jewish accounts of early modern Christian thought is eclipsed in Stein's narrative by another discourse on the relation of Jewish to Christian religion: that Judaism is the necessary forerunner of Christian faith, an authentic, primordial form of faith that needed and needs to be overcome, but that cannot have been done without. We will see how Stein's assertion of this more complex relation disables the simple adversarial relation of Jew against Christian (or German).

13. See Sander L. Gilman, *Jewish Self-Hatred: Anti-Semitism and the Hidden Language of the Jews* (Baltimore: Johns Hopkins University Press, 1986), 22–67. In fact, one of the concerns surrounding the canonization expressed by Baltimore Cardinal William Keeler was that the Church might be seen to be glorifying "a public apostate" from Judaism; see *Los Angeles Times,* 10 October 1998, B4.

14. Stein, *Aus dem Leben,* 3.

15. Ibid., 4: "Ich mußte bestimmte Fragen stellen, um in den Strom der Erinnerungen so viel Ordnung und Klarheit zu bringen, wie für einen fremden Leser zum Verständnis unerläßlich war, und oft war es nicht möglich, greifbare und zuverlässige Tatsachen festzustellen. Ich stelle im Folgenden die kurzen Aufzeichnungen im Anschluß an die Gespräche mit meiner Mutter voran. Darauf soll ein Lebensbild meiner Mutter folgen, wie ich es selbst zu geben vermag."

16. See the excellent discussion in Beaujour, *Poetics,* 1–21. In *L'autobiographie en France,* Philippe Lejeune writes that in Montaigne "there is no continuous narrative nor any systematic history of the personality. Self-portrait rather than autobiography" (quoted in Beaujour, *Poetics,* 2). Michel Riffaterre writes of Malraux's *Anti-Memoirs* that memoirs follow a "chronology" or "logic of events" ("then they are narrative"), whereas the *Anti-Memoirs* "rest on analogy" and Malraux's "superimposition method," "therefore they are poetry" (quoted in Beaujour, *Poetics,* 3).

17. An incidence of this is offered in the recent obituary of the historian Donald Nicholl, which stresses the deceased's shift to a concern with spiritual rather than material truth, as he increasingly came to identify thinking with the Fall and to replace it with "gazing" at a portrait of Edith Stein, among other exemplars. See "Obituary," *Daily Telegraph,* 20 May 1997, 23.

18. Stein, *Aus dem Leben,* 3. Translations are adapted from Edith Stein, *Life in a Jewish Family: Her Unfinished Autobiographical Account,* ed. Lucy Gelber and Romaeus Leuven, OCD, trans. Josephine Koeppel, vol. 1 of *The Collected Works of Edith Stein* (Washington, DC: ICS Publications, 1986).

19. The description of sympathy to work with in this case is that explicated at length by Max Scheler. Scheler, another Jewish convert to Catholicism who had also (for quite different reasons) been marginalized in the academy, was the most prestigious figure in the circle around Husserl in Freiburg in the period of Stein's dissertation. See his *Sympathiegefühle,* in translation as *The Nature of Sympathy,* trans. Peter Heath (London: Routledge and Kegan Paul, 1954); cf. Edith Stein, *On the Problem of Empathy,* trans. Waltraut Stein, vol. 3 of *The Collected Works of Edith Stein,* 3rd ed. (Washington, DC: ICS Publications, 1989), 27–34.

20. Stein, *On the Problem of Empathy*, 16–18, cf. translator's introduction, xviii.

21. Stein, *Aus dem Leben*, 38, and *Life*, 69. In a later text, Stein writes at greater length on the space shared by the Seder and the Last Supper, or the Old and New Covenants. See Edith Stein, "The Prayer of the Church," in *The Hidden Life: Hagiographic Essays, Meditations, Spiritual Texts*, ed. Lucy Gelber and Michael Linssen, trans. Waltraut Stein, vol. 4 of *The Collected Works of Edith Stein* (Washington, DC: ICS Publications, 1992), 7–8.

22. Part of the problem of appropriating Stein into a contemporary Jewish studies canon must be attributed to this somewhat unreflected and visceral response, demonstrated in an exemplary way by a highly charged exchange in the spring of 1996 on a Jewish studies Internet discussion group over the appropriateness of discussing her in that setting. Stein's most striking contrast to the provocatively comparable figure of Simone Weil, for instance, must be the former's continued identification with Judaism. See Erich Przywara, S.J., "Edith Stein et Simone Weil: Essentialisme et existentialisme," trans. Henri Leroux, *Cahiers Simone Weil* 6 (September 1983): 249–58.

23. Stein, *Aus dem Leben*, 6.

24. Edith Stein to Roman Ingarden, Freiburg, February 20, 1917, in *Selbstbildnis in Briefen*, pt. 1, *1916–1934*, ed. Lucy Gelber and P. Fr. Romaeus Leuven, vol. 8 of *Edith Steins Werke* (Druten: De Maas und Waler, 1976), 18.

25. Stein, *Life*, 47.

26. Stein, *Aus dem Leben*, 11.

27. Stein, *On the Problem of Empathy*, 63.

28. Ibid., 63.

29. Ibid., 38.

30. Dilthey's concept of the historian's relationship to the past as a "re-experiencing" or "Nacherleben," for instance, contains both empathic and experiential qualities which seem to inform Stein's encounter with history. See, e.g., W. Dilthey, "Das Verstehen anderer Personen und ihrer Lebensäußerungen" (1910), in *Gesammelte Schriften* (Stuttgart: Teubner, 1961), 7:205–20.

31. See W. Dilthey, *Einleitung in die Geisteswissenschaften*, in *Gesammelte Schriften*, 1:3–120.

32. See Edith Stein, "Beruf des Mannes und der Frau nach Natur- und Gnadenordnung," in *Die Frau: Ihre Aufgabe nach Natur und Gnade*, ed. Lucy Gelber and Romaeus Leuven,, vol. 5 of *Edith Steins Werke* (Louvain: Editions Nauwelaerts; Freiburg: Herder, 1959), 40–41.

33. Ibid., 40. Translation adapted from *Writings of Edith Stein*, 122. It might be pointed out here that while this argumentation and rhetoric is, as I have stressed, a rather orthodox embodiment of the principles outlined in Otto Weininger's *Geschlecht und Charakter: Eine prinzipielle Untersuchung* (Vienna: W. Braumüller, 1903), the Weininger text itself oscillates between an insistence on mutability and the fluidity of the scale from the ideal points "M" and "W" and the reification of these ideal types with the actual genders: thus his conviction that, despite the potential masculinity of individual women, no woman can be far enough from the "W" pole to produce true art, for instance. Stein is, from a certain perspective, more strictly Weiningerian than Weininger himself.

34. In considering what today's readers readily identify as Stein's essentialism, the constantly reinscribed figures of passability and passing would seem to be a crucial issue, yet one that has not been considered in the literature on Stein's feminism. For the ques-

tion of essentialism and Stein's feminist writing, see Linda Lopez McAlister, "Edith Stein: Essential Differences," *Philosophy Today* 37 (Spring 1993): 70–77 (reprinted and edited for this volume); Przywara, "Edith Stein et Simone Weil," 249–58.

35. Joan Riviere, "Womanliness as a Masquerade," *International Journal of Psychoanalysis* 10 (1929): 303–13, reprinted in *Formations of Fantasy*, ed. V. Burgin, J. Donald, and C. Kaplan (London: Methuen, 1986), 35–44; see also Stephen Heath, "Joan Riviere and the Masquerade," in Burgin et al., *Formations of Fantasy*, 45–61; Mary Ann Doane, "Masquerade Reconsidered: Further Thoughts on the Female Spectator," *Discourse: Journal for Theoretical Studies in Media and Culture* 11, no. 1 (1988–89): 42–54; and Judith Butler, *Gender Trouble: Feminism and the Subversion of Identity* (New York: Routledge, 1990), 43–57. The Stein text has been dated 1931; see Stein, *Die Frau*, xxv.

36. Riviere's spectral model cites not Weininger but Ernest Jones, whose typology of female sexuality has the same structure as Weininger's, even appropriating the term *intermediate types*, but gives much more attention to the specificity of the female subject.

37. While Butler provides a nuanced reading of this essay in *Gender Trouble*, 53, it is most useful to the general work of her book (with its subtitle *Feminism and the Subversion of Identity*) and to Stephen Heath's "Joan Riviere" in its refusal to posit "a femininity that is prior to mimicry," since Riviere, at the end of her text, confesses that the homosexual woman's compulsive masquerade is "the same thing" as "genuine womanliness" (3).

38. Roland Barthes, "The Photographic Message," in *Image-Music-Text*, ed. and trans. Stephen Heath (New York: Hill and Wang, 1977), 17–18.

39. Linda Haverty Rugg, *Picturing Ourselves: Photography and Autobiography* (Chicago: University of Chicago Press, 1997), 1.

40. Rugg bases her study on precisely this tension within both photography and autobiographical portraiture: the "double consciousness" of the self as "decentered, multiple, fragmented, and divided against itself in the act of observing and being," on the one hand, and "the simultaneous insistence on the presence of an integrated, authorial self, located in a body, a place, and a time," on the other. Rugg, *Picturing Ourselves*, 2, cf. 19. Self-imaging plays on the border between these competing claims of artifice and authenticity, as between public ("identities") and private ("selves"): "Images can represent the most *intimate* expressions of ourselves . . . and images allow the escape of our private or guarded sphere into the unguarded public" (4, italics mine).

41. This choice of name could be discussed at length. In short, one notes figures which are central in Stein's subject construction: Teresa of Avila, the reformer of Carmel, whom I discuss below; her follower John of the Cross, another saint and the first male Discalced Carmelite, and finally the figure of "the cross" itself. Stein's most sustained mystical work was *Kreuzeswissenschaft: Studie über Joannes a Cruce (Science of the Cross: Studies on St. John of the Cross)*, vol. 18 of *Edith Stein Gesamtausgabe* (Freiburg: Herder, 2003), a very interesting text which has been discussed by Hanna-Barbara Gerl-Falkovitz. The combination of male and female figures in this chosen name is worth noting, particularly since the masculine figure is himself associated with a certain gender-crossing. The image of the cross is pervasive in the late writings; a fascinating valence it has (for our purposes) is its coupling with Jewish suffering under the Nazis, implying the very gesture (conflation of the Jewish Kiddush Hashem with a martyrdom of Christian faith) which informs the current debate: "I said to the Lord that it was His Cross that was now laid on the Jewish people. Most of my people did not understand that, but those who did

had to bear it willingly in the name of all the others. I wanted to do that. . . . But I did not know in what way my bearing of the Cross would happen." Edith Stein, cited in Philip J. Scharper, "Edith Stein," in *Saints Are Now: Eight Portraits of Modern Sanctity,* ed. John J. Delaney (Garden City, NY: Doubleday, 1981), 128.

42. Butler, *Gender Trouble,* 47–48. The Lacanian answer seems to be that the mask disguises a lack, there is nothing behind the mask, or, "the secret is there is no secret."

43. See Slavoj Žižek, *The Metastases of Enjoyment: Six Essays on Woman and Causality* (New York: Verso, 1994). I am both more convinced and more comfortable with Butler's account, but this particular description of the nature of subjectivity is most relevant here. Cf. Judith Butler, "Critically Queer," *glq: A Journal of Lesbian and Gay Studies* 1, no. 1 (1993): 17–32, and "Lana's 'Imitation': Melodramatic Repetition and the Gender Performative," *Genders* 9 (Fall 1990): 1–18.

44. I take the phrase from Stein: "God is love, and love is goodness giving itself away." Stein, *Hidden Life,* 38.

45. Stein, *Aus dem Leben,* 32.

46. The photograph appears in an English edition of Stein's works with the date 1893, indicating it was taken just before the death of the father (July 1893). The later date is confirmed by close examination of the photograph, where the montage is apparent, and because Edith (seated in foreground) cannot be one year and eight months old in the photograph. In a letter to me, archivist Sr. Maria Amata Neyer, OCD, reports on the account of Edith's sister Erna, confirming that the photo-montage was constructed using a passport photograph of the father when, after his death, members of the family regretted the lack of a family portrait.

47. On these cross-currents of masquerade and gender performativity one needs to read *Gender Trouble,* and especially the spate of articles citing it, against Butler, "Critically Queer," esp. 21–24; cf. Judith Butler, "Imitation and Gender Insubordination," in Diana Fuss, *Inside/Out: Lesbian Theories, Gay Theories* (London: Routledge, 1991), 13–31. This literature suggests the danger of celebrating Stein's passing gestures, or performativity, as unqualified subversion of identities, at the cost of glossing over the complicity of these moves with their ultra-nationalist, sexist, and racist discursive contexts.

48. Until now, of all the contexts and canons into which Stein might be subsumed, the theological is the only one in which a very serious attempt has been made to resolve contradictions and inconsistencies (and indeed literally to canonize Stein). If a single justification is to be found for this, it must be found in chronology: for Christian canonizers, the move from secular literary and philosophical to theological and hagiographic writing follows the pattern of revelation, whereas modern literary canons are founded on the assumption of a reverse chronology of a corpus of secular texts emerging from the Renaissance onward. A productive antidote to this literary-canonical version of the fraught "secularization thesis" is to be found in Julia Lupton's analysis of a dialectic of secularization and Christianization, or hagiography and modern literature, in *Afterlives of the Saints: Hagiography, Typology, and Renaissance Literature* (Stanford, CA: Stanford University Press, 1996).

49. It may be salutary not to succumb too quickly to the temptation to read Stein's turn to Catholic religion—and eventually the cloth—in terms of her academic and intellectual marginalization. Yet the forms taken in her thought from this point on cannot be seen apart from this experience of exclusion, particularly those relating to the "exter-

nal world" of society and of history and their complex relation to spiritual life. In any event, an interest in Christian thought and mysticism inspired by religious friends was set aflame one night in 1921, according to her own much-repeated account, as she read straight through the autobiography of Teresa of Avila, and her decision to convert to Catholicism was sealed. Edith Stein, *Verborgenes Leben: Hagiographische Essays, Meditationen, Geistliche Texte,* ed. Lucy Gelber and Michael Linssen, vol. 11 of *Edith Steins Werke* (Freiburg: Herder, 1987). Translations are taken from Stein, *Hidden Life.*

50. Lucy Gelber and Michael Linssen, introduction to Stein, *Hidden Life,* xi–xv.

51. Michael Linssen, preface to Stein, *Hidden Life,* ix.

52. Stein, "Love for Love: The Life and Works of St. Teresa of Jesus," in *Hidden Life,* 29.

53. Ibid., 30. Another provocative "parallel" is suggested by the probable Jewish origins of Teresa of Avila's family, but it cannot be established that Stein had any inkling of these origins.

54. Stein, "The Hidden Life and the Epiphany," in *Hidden Life,* 109–10.

Chapter 6

The Complex Modernity of Edith Stein
New Gender Relations and Options for Women in Early-Twentieth-Century Germany

THERESA WOBBE

Edith Stein grew up during a period of profound transformation in gender relations within Germany. An understanding of her life calls for an analysis of both newly widened opportunities and continued restrictions on women's career paths during her formative and adult years. Stein's choices in relation to these realities are the focus of this chapter. By viewing Stein not singly but as part of a generation of female pioneers and warriors, we understand her better, and the story of her life takes on enhanced historical significance.

Prelude

Whereas at the beginning of the twentieth century in Germany equal opportunity for women in politics, the professions, and in economic life was highly contested, by the end of the century German gender equality had become an accepted and legal cultural pattern.[1] More broadly, a worldwide transition took place, "the transition from social models in which women were defined as 'property,' as 'minors,' or only in relation to their reproductive capacities, to those models in which they are defined as persons and, as such, entitled to participate in public institutions."[2] If, for centuries, women were subjected in their personal lives to numerous, including violent, forms of subordination, by the late twentieth century the norm of gender equality within the personal domain had gained solid acceptance in most nations. Although women still suffer from economic discrimination and sexual violence, these injustices are now widely recognized and deplored.[3]

As early as 1926 the cultural studies scholar Margarete Susman described fundamental shifts taking place in gender relations in Germany: "The former world disappears with the former imagery of woman."[4] Susman proceeded to describe a new gender struggle. Previously, women, she claimed, had carried the burden of the world men had constructed, including its symbolic order of gender representation. "Only now the struggle over speech and representation breaks out."[5] Women's challenge to historic interpretations of culture and its gendered symbolic system inevitably not only led to reconstellated gender relations in social and political institutions but transformed the overall understanding of culture.

Edith Stein belonged to the first generation of young, self-confident German women who entered the terrain of higher education and science, politics, and the professions. That generation was shaped by and shaped the gender transformations of the twentieth century.[6] Though benefiting from new modern societal opportunities, Stein set these aside in 1933 when she decided to enter a Carmelite convent. Why did a young, ambitious intellectual make this choice, a choice to spend her life in a "total institution"?[7] Was her decision a reaction to the unchanged obstacles to her professional goals? Or was it primarily a response to anti-Jewish Nazi laws? How may this choice and her many previous choices have reflected both the transformation in gender relations of her time and the increasing individualization of modern lives as that affected both religion and gender relations?

In many ways Stein's life partook of a modern societal movement enabling both new forms of female-female and cross-sex association and greater individualization in women's lives. The foremost theorist of this double-pronged movement is Georg Simmel. Charting the relationship between shifting boundaries in gender relations and changes in social structures, Simmel shows how men's lives within the traditional gendered division of labor altered under the impact of increasing specialization and differentiation of work functions. Possibilities arose for males to enjoy greater social mobility, adopt new roles, and form new kinds of male-male associations as well as exercise wider individual agency and choices. Indeed, a correlation existed between the burgeoning of new kinds of associational membership and the expansion of individual agency such that the intersection and multiplication of "social circles" became an indicator of individuality and modern culture.[8]

These societal changes remained male-specific, women being family focused, until the mid–nineteenth century, when the groundwork for similar changes began for women. As evident in the unequal inclusion of women in citizenship and higher education, female role differentiation and individualization had greater obstacles to surmount and developed asymmetrically in relation to progress for men. Yet the dynamics of change were similar: when social differentiation opened new possibilities of association for women as a group—for example, through the women's movement—it simultaneously expanded female individualization.[9]

Decisive for these modern advantages for women was higher education. Since the mid–nineteenth century the women's movement had astutely set women's higher education at the top of its agenda, aiming toward female economic independence and entrance into the professions.[10] Stein was quick to pursue both goals.

The First Generation of Women Scholars in Germany

Karl Mannheim's concept of generation (1928) is useful in understanding Stein's cohort of female scholars who were able to pursue a university career. According to Mannheim, these women formed a generation through their specific joint relationship with political events and social opportunities of their time. Their entry into academia took place within shared parameters: only in 1908 did women gain entry into the universities of Prussia, Germany's largest state. Together they experienced the First World War's accelerated gender modernization, most notably its speeding of women's integration into the workforce.[11] Likewise, they enjoyed the widening opportunities of Germany's political revolution from empire to republic. Among the Weimar Republic's many reforms, women in 1920 gained the right to the procedure of *Habilitation* needed to become university professors. The *Habilitation* thesis, the main requirement in obtaining the Venia Legendi and with it a professorial appointment, served as the academic community's most powerful instrument of self-recruitment and social closure.[12] Edith Stein played a key role (soon to be discussed) in the decision of Carl-

Heinrich Becker, the highest official in the Prussian Department of Education, to issue a decree that stated that women would no longer be excluded from *Habilitation*. Along with the right of *Habilitation,* Weimar Republic reforms opened gates to women's tenured positions in the civil service *(Berufsbeamtentum)*, although with certain restrictions. The requirement of female celibacy in the professions was only partly abolished.[13]

Of course, the first generation of women scholars lacked professional precursors and mentors. Marianne Weber calls the heroic German female students who had to fight without administrative and professorial models for their entry into the university "female warriors."[14] The national and international women's movements inspired their resolve and persistence and created a cultural and political context for female solidarity.[15] Weber deems this solidarity a collective and "powerful virginity."[16] The friendships and feminist networks that emerged among these women promoted individual moral strength and innovative choices, fostering these women's ability to resist conventional concepts of womanhood and female roles, especially the primacy of family duties.

This heroic generation of women shared an optimism about the many changes taking place in Germany's succession from empire to republic, but the advent of National Socialism abruptly ended their professional careers and shattered their dreams. Like Stein, many of the first generation of women scholars were dismissed from their university positions. Out of the seventy-two female teaching scholars at German universities, thirty were forced to leave their posts by decree of the Nazis' Law for Re-Creating the Tenured Civil Service *(Gesetz zur Wiederherstellung des Berufsbeamtentums).*[17]

Widening Women's Opportunities in Religion

As women made strides to enter institutions of higher education and the professional positions within them, they also sought access to professional positions within the churches. Traditionally, women had been invisible not only as citizens and political actors but as members of religious communities, where their fathers, husbands, and ministers spoke "for" them. The liberal and socialist feminist movements that formed in mid-nineteenth-century Germany prepared the way for religious women's movements to emerge as the century turned. The German-Protestant Women's Council formed in 1899, the Catholic German Women's Council in 1902, and the German Jewish Women's Council one year later.[18] These councils pressed for women to have a greater voice in their religious mixed-sex organizations and in religion-sponsored community groups.

The appearance of these councils coincided with new approaches in Christian theology. In 1900, the Protestant historian of religion Adolf von Harnack published his essay on the importance of women within early Christendom. Harnack's student Leopold Zscharnack undertook further research on women's positions in this nascent Christian era. Demonstrating that in the early church the teaching profession *(lehrampt)* did exist for women, Zscharnack's research became an important reference point for feminist theology in the second part of the twentieth century.[19]

Concurrently, women scholars began to gain access to the academic field of theology. At Jena University in 1908, Carola Barth became the first woman to do her dissertation in the field of biblical scholarship. She spearheaded the movement for women's claim to the ministry. At the onset of the Weimar Republic, the Protestant theological faculties opened their doors to women for examination in theology. Within Catholicism Franziska Werfer in 1929 became the first woman to take examinations in theology at the University of Tübingen. Only after 1945, however, did Catholic theological faculties admit both lay people and women.[20]

Similar feminist currents rippled through Judaism. In 1930, at the Hochschule für die Wissenschaft vom Judentum, Regina Jonas completed her thesis "Can a Woman Hold the Function of the Rabbi?"[21] For Jonas this was more than a theological question. She received her rabbi's diploma in 1935, becoming the first female rabbi, even transcending the bounds of the Jewish Women's Council, which advocated female emancipation within the institutions of their religious community but not in the realm of religious ritual. Jonas's quest to become a rabbi was heatedly opposed by Orthodox Jews. The controversy could have served as a fruitful point of departure for Jewish thought and practice, but Nazi persecution ended that potential. Rabbi Regina Jonas continued her duties even in Theresienstadt until 1944, when she was deported with her mother to Auschwitz. Not until three generations later could Jewish women reconnect with the striking precedent set by Regina Jonas.

Stein's religious development and choices need to be understood in the context of this broader effort by women to gain inclusion and equality within religious (as within other) institutions. The religious women's and religious youth movements as well as liturgical and ecumenical movements transformed hierarchical structures and boundaries between experts and lay people: women were gaining recognition as experts, just as they were in science, politics, and other professions, surmounting barriers between experts and lay people across the board.[22]

Edith Stein's Secular Choices

When in 1911 Edith Stein began her studies of literature, history, psychology, and philosophy with William Stern and Richard Hönigswald at Breslau University, she had decided for the "temple of scholarship." Ernst-Wolfgang Orth calls the university the "new church" that young people in the early twentieth century entered to endow their lives with meaningful and modern perspective.[23]

While at Breslau University Stein joined various associations. Within the female student association Stein discussed with her friends once a week aspects of life from education and professional concerns to marriage and love. She belonged, too, to the radical Prussian Association for Women's Suffrage, a group committed to women's equal citizenship.

After reading Edmund Husserl's *Logische Untersuchungen* during Christmas vacation in 1912, Stein opted to leave Breslau to study with Husserl, "the master" of phenomenology, at the University of Göttingen. When she arrived at Göttingen, the phenomenological movement was at its zenith. Hedwig Conrad-Martius (1888–1966), who became Edith's closest friend, carefully depicted Husserl's disciples: "A distinctive and shared way of thinking and communication created . . . a relationship among Husserl's students that I can describe only as an organic birth of a shared spirit *(Geist)*, which was the exact opposite of an ideology. We shared neither a specialized language nor a scholarly system. What connected us was only our openness to apprehending being in all its possible modes."[24]

Göttingen introduced Stein to philosophical communication within a scientific community. Her lifelong friendships emerged there. From the philosopher of religion Adolf Reinach she received her basic socialization as a philosophy scholar. Göttingen also opened her eyes to the world of religion. Inspired by her meetings with Max Scheler (1874–1928), who at that time ranked among the most well-known and esteemed Catholic intellectuals, Stein recalls, "This was my first encounter with this hitherto totally unknown world. It did not lead me as yet to the Faith. But it did open for me a region of 'phenomena' which I could then no longer pass blindly. With good reason we were repeatedly enjoined to observe all things without prejudice, to discard all possible 'blinders.'" Directly linking her interest in the phenomenology of all things *(Sachen an sich)* with her interest in the phenomenon of faith, Stein adds, "The barriers of rationalist prejudices with which I had unwittingly grown up fell, and the world of faith unfolded before me."[25] Her move from Breslau to Göttingen ushered in a shift in the coordinates of her scholarly and personal existence.

After earning her doctorate, Stein worked as Husserl's assistant in Freiburg, a position that would seem to mark the beginning of a dynamic academic career. Indeed, while her male comrades were fighting in the war, Edith Stein occupied a position with Husserl ordinarily held by male scholars, such as Adolf Reinach earlier and Martin Heidegger later. But her relations with Husserl were neither easy nor direct, and in time Stein broke off her collaboration with him.

At roughly the same time, Stein despaired of her efficacy within the political arena and turned solely to philosophy. As the German empire ended in 1918, Stein, as one of the founders of the German Democratic Party in Breslau, championed the republic and committed herself to win women voters for the democratic parties. She went frequently to Berlin to help the Women's Council prepare for impending elections.[26] But after the election of the National Assembly she retreated from politics. "I haven't any tools for politics," she said, and highlighted two: "a robust conscience and a thick skin."[27]

Returning to philosophy, Stein took the risk of submitting her second thesis (i.e., her *Habilitation* thesis) to the University of Göttingen. Consider that Stein attempted *Habilitation* before any woman had been accepted for it in Germany. Ordinarily, a professor backed a scholar for *Habilitation*. Given his conventional ideas concerning women in science, Husserl did not support Edith Stein's *Habilitation*, nor did any of Göttingen's philosophy faculty. They refused her thesis, arguing that women had no access to *Habilitation*.

Stein did not capitulate to this rejection. She wrote a protest letter to the above-mentioned Carl-Heinrich Becker of Prussia's Department of Education, a leading reformer of Germany's system of higher education. With Becker's response to Stein came the landmark decree to eliminate sex as a basis of *Habilitation*. Though Stein's letter was the catalyst of the ending of this academic obstacle to women's academic careers, she, alas, did not benefit from that reform.

Now Stein took another remarkable step, no less risky than her submitting of a *Habilitation* thesis. She started a "private academy" of philosophy, writing Roman Ingarden, "As you may notice, failures will under no circumstances get me more undemanding."[28] Without university authorization, Stein determined to be a lecturer in philosophy. As of the summer of 1920 she taught fifty students, one of these the young Norbert Elias, later a renowned sociologist. Stein enjoyed her academy, even though it lacked institutional status and could neither advance her professional career nor serve as a basis for an independent professional position elsewhere. She remained economically dependent on her mother just as when she had worked with Husserl. Her professional frustrations with Husserl, her inability to gain *Habilitation*, and a series of personal crises coincided with her growing religious orientation, which as we know led soon to her Catholic conversion.

Neither her conversion nor her self-styled teaching position ended her ties to the phenomenological movement. She contributed essays to the *Jahrbuch in Phänomenologie* and remained in contact with many of her phenomenological friends. Importantly, she translated into German writings by Thomas Aquinas and the English convert John Henry Cardinal Newman. In addition, she became deeply engrossed in issues in Catholic women's education and lectured widely on the subject. In her 1930 essay "The Ethos of Women's Professions," prefiguring later twentieth-century perspectives, Stein regarded Mary as a symbol of women's diverse roles in public and private realms: "Whether she is mother in the home, or occupies a place in the limelight of public life, or lives behind quiet cloister walls, she must be a *handmaid of the Lord* everywhere."[29] Taking changed historical circumstances into account, Stein focused on new challenges for nuns, housewives, and professional women alike.

In her *Essays on Woman,* Stein also examined the status of women within the church. She found the status of women in early-twentieth-century Germany worse than in early Christendom. Stein attributed the removal of women deacons and the lower status of women to legal strictures of the Old Testament and of Roman law. She considered these strictures mutable, and she took note of many positive legal changes within her lifetime.[30] Regarding women's ordination and priesthood, Stein, influenced by the liturgical renaissance and reform-minded groups within the Catholic Church, held that religious dogma posed no obstacles to women's ordination, though she realized that practical implementation was understandably controversial.[31]

Edith Stein's Religious Choices

Prior to her conversion Stein had already undergone shifts in her religious outlook, but none as momentous, of course, as what occurred when she encountered the autobiography of the Carmelite Teresa of Avila (1562–1582). Stein was much drawn to Teresa's idea of contemplation and prayer. Teresa's central reform of convent life was her integration of contemplation into the Carmel convent daily discipline. According to Teresa, the path to internal prayer promised freedom for every sister, "as it must be a consolation for you to enjoy yourself in the internal castle which you can enter and within which you can walk around without the approval of authorities."[32] With kindred sensibility, Stein wrote her friend Sister Callista Kopf, "The only essential is that one finds, first of all, a quiet corner in which one can communicate with God as though there was nothing else, and that must be done daily."[33]

The Carmelite day is highly structured, with many set times for contemplation. The rule of the Carmelite order dictates that "[e]verybody should stay in one's own cell . . . contemplating day and night following the law of the Master and lively-mind in one's prayer, as long as one is not prevented by further legitimate work."[34] The matter of legitimate work is unclear. The rule's very regulated day does not offer much time for action, a strain that Stein experienced as tugs between contemplation and scholarly work. Fortunately, her Catholic mentors encouraged her to continue her scholarly work, and she received exemptions from tasks to make that possible. Besides dispensation from collective recreation after lunch, she was freed from collective housework: "Peeling potatoes, cleaning windows, and writing books carry equal value in the Carmel. In general, people are assigned to those tasks in which they have talent. Thus I am assigned to peel potatoes rarely so that I can write books instead."[35] Provincial Theodor Rauch urged her to prepare her manuscript *Potenz und Akt* for publication. Since Stein was not allowed to visit libraries, Rauch procured the literature she needed. Until her flight from Cologne to the Carmel at Echt, Stein was engaged in scholarly labor as her religious choice of activity, specifically her study *Kreuzeswissenschaft*. She never abandoned the goal of her scholarly work: her open-minded approach to truth. After 1935, the Hamburg political science scholar Dr. Ruth Kantorowicz, also a convert, transcribed Stein's manuscripts and edited them for publication.

Conclusion

Is Stein's choice to become a Carmelite at odds with female modernity? Consider her circumstances. Edith Stein grew to adulthood at a time of many new options for women. She took advantage of many of these and campaigned to open doors women found still closed. After her Catholic conversion, she sought ways to reconcile her spiritual life with her persistent philosophical scholarly pursuits. Unwilling to resign herself to societal limitations, she persevered in her struggle for a professorial post in the face of sexist opposition. Having failed after several efforts to gain *Habilitation* and then permanently foreclosed from realizing her secular ambitions by Nazi Aryan Laws, she shifted gears and entered a Carmelite convent. Despite ardent family opposition to her decision and family willingness to support her financially were she to remain in Breslau, despite her age of entry into the convent at forty-two, despite her Jewish descent and her professional and scholarly commitments, she remained firm.

Since by entering Carmel Stein knew that her participation in other institutions was no longer possible, her decision appears to contradict modern concepts of women's lives as preserving maximum choice and autonomy. Her entrance, however, enabled her to exercise options for scholarship and religious practice not possible elsewhere for German Jewish women at that time. Crucially, Stein's entry into Carmel underscores that belief and unbelief belong among a woman's individual choices. Whereas in the nineteenth century a woman's religious orientation emerged in the context of separate gender spheres in which piety was a primary expectation for women,[36] Stein made her decision within a context for women of greatly expanding expectations, when many women chose unbelief and when religious vocation vied with many other possible female careers. Stein's modern agency in making her choice to enter a Carmelite convent carries a distinctive historical relevance.[37]

NOTES

An earlier, more extended version of this chapter has been published as "Edith Stein: Der Wandel von Geschlechterordnung und Religion im frühen 20. Jahrhundert," in *Religion and Geschlechterverhältnis* (Opladen: Westdeutscher, 2000), 49–68. I am most grateful to Joyce Avrech Berkman for her helpful comments and encouragement.

1. Ute Frevert, *Women in German History: From Bourgeois Emancipation to Sexual Liberation* (Oxford: Berg, 1989).

2. Nitza Berkovitch, *From Motherhood to Citizenship: Women's Rights in International Organizations* (Baltimore: John Hopkins University Press, 1999), 14.

3. Shahara Razavi and Carol Miller, *Gender Mainstreaming: A Study of Efforts by the UNDP, The World Bank and the ILO to Institutionalize Gender Issues* (Geneva: United Nations Research Institute for Social Development, 1995).

4. Margarete Susman, "Das Frauenproblem in der gegenwärtigen Welt," in *Das Nah- und Fernsein des Fremden* (Frankfurt: Jüdischer Verlag, 1992), 146.

5. Ibid., 144.

6. Theresa Wobbe, "On the Horizons of a New Discipline: Early Women Sociologists in Germany," *Journal of the Anthropological Society of Oxford* 26 (1995): 283–97.

7. Erving Goffman, *Asylums: Essays on the Social Situation of Mental Patients and Other Inmates* (New York: Doubleday, 1961).

8. Georg Simmel, *Soziologie: Untersuchungen über die Formen der Vergesellschaftung*, 6th ed. (Berlin: Dunker und Humblot, 1983).

9. Theresa Wobbe, *Wahlverwandtschaften: Die Soziologie und die Frauen auf dem Weg zur Wissenschaft* (Frankfurt a. M.: Campus-Verlag, 1997), chap. 1; Theresa Wobbe,

"Elective Affinities: Georg Simmel and Marianne Weber on Differentiation and Individuation," paper presented at the International Sociological Association World Congress, Montreal, Canada, 1998.

10. Frevert, *Women in German History.*

11. Ibid.

12. Martin Schmeiser, *Akademischer Hasard: Das Berufsschicksal des Professors und das Schicksal der deutschen Universität, 1870–1920* (Stuttgart: Klett-Cotta, 1994).

13. James Albisetti, "Women and the Professions in Imperial Germany," in *German Women in the Eighteenth and Nineteenth Centuries: A Social and Literary History,* ed. Ruth-Ellen B. Joeres and Mary Jo Maynes (Bloomington: Indiana University Press, 1986), 94–109; Claudia Huerkamp, *Bildungsbürgerinnen: Frauen im Studium und in akademischen Berufen, 1900–1945* (Göttingen: Vanderhoeck and Ruprecht, 1996).

14. Marianne Weber, "Vom Typenwandel der studierenden Frau," in *Frauenfragen und Frauengedanken* (Tübingen: Mohr, 1919), 179.

15. Mineka Bosch and Annemarie Klostermann, eds., *Politics and Friendship: Letters from the International Suffrage Alliance, 1902–1942* (Columbus: Ohio State University Press, 1990); Nancy Cott, *The Grounding of Modern Feminism* (New Haven, CT: Yale University Press, 1987).

16. Weber, "Vom Typenwandel," 179.

17. Wobbe, *Wahlverwandtschaften,* chap. 1.

18. Ursula Baumann, *Protestantismus und Frauenemanzipation in Deutschland, 1850 bis 1920* (Frankfurt: Campus-Verlag, 1992); Gisela Breuer, *Frauenbewegung im Katholizismus: Der Katholische Frauenbund, 1903–1918* (Frankfurt: Campus-Verlag, 1998); Marion Kaplan, *Die jüdische Frauenbewegung in Deutschland: Organisation und Ziele des juedischen Frauenbundes, 1904–1938* (Hamburg: Dölling und Galitz, 1981).

19. Luise Schottroff et al., *Feministische Exegese: Forschungseriträge zur Bibel aus der Perspektive von Frauen* (Darmstadt: Primus, 1995), 8.

20. Ibid., 9.

21. Regina Jonas, *Kann die Frau das rabinsche Amt bekleiden?* (Belins: Klapheck, 2000) (PhD diss., Hochsule für die Wissenschaft vom Judentem, 1930).

22. Karel Dobbeläre, "Secularization: A Multi-Dimensional Concept," *Current Sociology* 29 (1981): 3–213. Dobbeläre argues that the shifting boundaries between clerical experts and lay people indicate the process of secularization in the long run. She applies Niklas Luhmann's framework in *Die Religion der Gesellschaft* (Frankfurt: Suhrkamp, 2000). This framework is useful to conceptualize modern changing gender relations within various social institutions, taking into account different institutional rationales and codes. With respect to religion, the distinct formulations of transcendence and immanence should be linked to changing gendered boundaries between experts and lay people. Additionally, this framework relates to Susan Starr Sered's distinction between "Woman" and "women" as well as her study on religious change in Israel. See her "Women and Religious Change in Israel: Rebellion or Revolution," *Sociology of Religion* 58 (1997): 1–24, as well as "'Woman' as Symbol and Women as Agents: Gendered Religious Discourses and Practices," in *Revisioning Gender,* ed. Myra Marx Ferree, Judith Lorber, and Beth B. Hess (Thousand Oaks, CA: Sage Publications, 1998).

23. Wolfgang Orth, "Richard Hoenigwalds Neukantianismus und Edmund Husserls Phaenomenologie als Hintergrund des Denkens von Edith Stein," in *Studien zur Philoso-*

phie von Edith Stein: Internationales Edith Stein-Symposion Eichstätt 1991 (Freiburg: Alber, 1993), 107–39.

24. Hedwig Conrad-Martius, "Meine Freundin Edith Stein," in *Denken im Dialog: Zur Philosophie Edith Steins*, ed. Waltraud Herbstrith (Tübingen: Attempto-Verlag, 1991), 176.

25. Edith Stein, *Life in a Jewish Family: Her Unfinished Autobiographical Account*, ed. Lucy Gelber and Romaeus Leuven, OCD, trans. Josephine Koeppel, OCD (Washington, DC: ICS Publications, 1986), 260.

26. Andreas Mueller and Maria Amata Neyer, *Edith Stein: Das Leben einer ungewöhnlichen Frau* (Zurich: Benziger, 1998).

27. Edith Stein to Roman Ingarden, December 27, 1918, in *Briefe an Roman Ingarden, 1917–1938*, ed. Lucy Gelber and Michael Linssen, vol. 14 of *Edith Steins Werke* (Freiburg: Herder, 1991).

28. Edith Stein to Roman Ingarden, March 15, 1920, in *Briefe an Roman Ingarden.*

29. Edith Stein, *Essays on Woman*, ed. Lucy Gelber and Romaeus Leuven, OCD (Washington, DC: ICS Publications, 1987), 52.

30. Edith Stein, "Problems of Women's Education," in *Essays on Woman*, 106–7.

31. Edith Stein, "The Separate Vocations of Man and Woman According to Nature and Grace," in *Essays on Woman*, 83–84. Also see Birgit Sack, *Zwischen religiöser Bindung und moderner Gesellschaft: Katholische Frauenbewegung und politische Kultur in der Weimarer Republik, 1918/19–1933* (Münster: Waxmann, 1998), for a discussion of the Catholic feminist movement during the 1920s with respect to women's political orientations and concepts, as well as her discussion of the Catholic feminist and youth movements, "Katholische Frauenbewegung: Katholische Jugendbewegung und Politik in der Weimarer Republik: Standorte, Handlungsräume, und Grenzen im Kontext des Generationenkonflikts," in *Frauen unter dem Patriarchat der Kirchen: Katholikinnen und Protestantinnen im 19. und 20. Jahrhundert*, ed. Irmtraud Goetz von Olenhusen (Stuttgart: Kohlhammer, 1995), 120–38.

32. Teresa von Avila, *Das Leben der heiligen Theresia von Jesu*, trans. P. Aloysius Alkoser, OCD (Darmstadt: Kösel, 1979), 216.

33. Edith Stein to Sr. Callista Kopf, OP, February 2, 1928, in *Self-Portrait in Letters, 1916–1942* (Washington, DC: ICS Publications, 1993), 54–55.

34. Mueller and Neyer, *Edith Stein*, 223.

35. Edith Stein to Roman Ingarden, summer, 1937, in *Briefe an Roman Ingarden*, 237.

36. See von Olenhusen, *Frauen unter dem Patriarchat.*

37. Sered, "Women and Religious Change" and "'Woman' as Symbol."

Chapter 7

Moments in Edith Stein's Years of Crisis, 1918–1922

ANGELIKA von RENTELN

translated by Antonio Calcagno

At a time of widespread national upheaval, Edith Stein once wrote to her sister Erna, "I am in no way a saint, and I even have my hours of weakness. Incidentally, I believe that it is not necessary for a saint to renounce all wishes, hopes, and joys of the world."[1] This was written in July 1918, when World War I had come to an end and when it was apparent that not only the German Reich but also the old social, business, and cultural orders were breaking down. It was at this time of national crisis that Edith Stein found herself in a long personal crisis, which led to her discovery of faith and to her conversion to Roman Catholicism in 1922.

Since Edith Stein's canonization on October 11, 1998, it has been particularly important to present a comprehensive picture of her decisive years of crisis extending from 1918 to 1922. We must, therefore, equally record and take into account, in light of the above-cited passage from Edith Stein's letter, her personal disappointments, misfortunes, wishes, and hopes, as well as the resulting reflections contained in her early work and the development of her philosophical thought.[2]

External life circumstances were important markers that contributed decisively to Stein's discovery of faith. The difficulties that Stein encountered made her stronger on her spiritual path. For anyone who searches for a deeper understanding of Edith Stein's conversion and is not satisfied with the explanation of her conversion as a sudden supernatural experience, it is important to know the nature of these difficulties. Consequently, pivotal moments, such as her hope for an academic career and for a fulfilling marriage, must be examined. Edith Stein herself did not deny these circumstances and regarded the painful experiences that she had in this respect as an important asset, which led her to new insights. It is also surely in the spirit of her life that "Saint Edith Stein" should receive human characteristics and be freed from the idealized interpretations and moral representations of others. Only once her humanity and her very human struggles and doubts receive an adequate place in her biography, can today's reader be brought nearer to Stein's life; and only then can her life also be pioneering for others.

It would exceed the framework of this essay to present a comprehensive picture of Stein's years of crisis together with the development of her philosophical and spiritual thought. Instead I will focus on certain significant aspects, keeping in mind that the external life circumstances that will be delineated here cannot be seen as the only valid motives for Stein's conversion. Rather, they should be considered more as a contribution to the story, just as the small tile of a mosaic is understood as contributing to the whole.

Adolf Reinach: Preparing the Way

The death of Stein's teacher Adolf Reinach on November 16, 1917, was the trigger and beginning of a long crisis in her life. We know that she was in Freiburg when news of his death became public. She traveled to Göttingen en route to Breslau to attend his funeral on December 31.

In Freiburg, she left for her friend the Pole Roman Ingarden an exceptional and, since then, oft-cited love letter. This is the only source from the period of any clue of the deep shock felt by Stein following the death of Reinach. This letter also let Roman Ingarden know of Stein's deep affection for him, though he did not reciprocate these feelings. For the first and only time she addressed her friend by the more familiar "you" *(Du)* form of address, Stein wrote:

First [I would like] to beg forgiveness, since for a while, under the pressure of the difficult days that have passed and those that lie ahead, I have been incapable of happiness. . . .

What I seek now is peace and the restoration of my totally shattered self-confidence. As soon as I have the feeling of again being something and of being able to give something to others, I wish to see you [*Dich*] again.

She ended the letter with "And so my final farewell! [*Damit endgültig Lebewohl!*] Yours [*Deine*], Edith."[3] It has often been asked, why Stein closed with the words "final farewell," when in fact the correspondence continued. Certainly, she saw, at that turbulent moment, the possibility that the friendship could no longer proceed as it had hitherto. It was Roman Ingarden who made the correspondence continue. He did not want to lose his good friend, who also possessed a wealth of information concerning phenomenological activity in Germany and who was the energetic corrector of his German-language works. So Ingarden continued his contact with Stein, but without addressing her love letter or her state of mind. Since nothing of Ingarden's correspondence on this matter has been preserved, we can turn only to the few comments found in Stein's subsequent letters to understand his reaction to and her disappointment with his rejection. Ingarden proceeded to ask Stein a "few matter-of-fact things," and at first she had no desire to respond to such a cold and "horrid letter."[4] She was also disappointed and upset fourteen days later that Ingarden gave only a glimpse of his own "bleak mood" in his letters, without reference to what had occurred and to her likely state of mind. Ingarden sought support and understanding from her, of all people, which must have reinforced her "feeling of incapacity" in relation to him, since he allowed her neither to be close to him nor to help him. The feeling of "absolute powerlessness" that she addresses in the letter was in the following years a recurrent theme that she tackled with new intensity.[5]

Edith Stein resumed her usual correspondence with Roman Ingarden after a few clarifying words and accepted his implicit demand that the correspondence continue on a purely friendly basis and deal with more matter-of-fact topics. We cannot measure how Ingarden's rejection continued to affect Stein's state of mind and her ongoing crisis precisely because the most important source of information about her disposition at the time are to be found in her letters to Ingarden. Stein did now try to be reserved, so as to preserve the distance for which Ingarden had called. She writes: "[F]or my part, I had always forcibly to hold myself back, never writing to you with the full force of my personality."[6]

At the same time, that February Edith Stein made a further decision, which had already been looming for some time. The work of being Edmund Husserl's assistant, which she commenced in October 1916, had quickly proven to be unsatisfactory. She had hoped that this position would enable her collaboration with Husserl. Instead she was entrusted with the mindless reworking and sort-

ing of a tremendous number of the "Master's" old notes. After lengthy consideration, Edith Stein came to the conclusion that she had to resign from her position as Edmund Husserl's assistant. This was a difficult decision to make because she feared a breach with her beloved Master, who represented the center
of phenomenology and therefore of the world in which she felt most at home.
In case she were to "fall out of grace" with Husserl, she considerd going for a
period of time to Göttingen, where, "if anywhere at all," she felt "somewhat at
home."[7] Without a quarrel, Husserl accepted Stein's resignation in good grace.
Stein wrote to Ingarden: "I am therefore now free, and I think it is good to be so,
even if, for the moment, I am not exactly happy."[8]

Free from all external pressures, Stein now proceeded to find clarity regarding her personal path in life, its professional as well as private aspects. Closely
related to this was her interior search and exploration of her own person. This
theme of "person" was one of Stein's ongoing scholarly interests, although in
this situation the theme attained existential relevance. Her old home of Breslau,
however, did not provide the support and fertile ground necessary for her to arrive at such a clarification. She felt strange and cramped in her own family circle.
She missed the philosophical exchange, the discussions and arguments with like-
minded people that she had become accustomed to in Göttingen.

At this delicate moment of her life, she received on February 12, 1918, the
religio-philosophical notes of Adolf Reinach. The notes were written between
April and the end of June 1916 under the influence of his experience of the war
while serving at the front.[9] The effect of these notes on Edith Stein is indis-
putable. Not only was she presented with a dear memory of the deceased, but
she also gained rich insights into the change that Reinach had undergone as a
result of his experiences at the front, experiences that led him to his conversion
to Protestantism.

To understand fully the meaning of Reinach's writings for Edith Stein, one
must consider the profound respect and admiration she felt for him. This is most
clear in Stein's memoirs, where the figure of Reinach receives a very idealized
characterization. She recounts various episodes that convey a deep bond and reciprocal understanding with her mentor.[10] Although not the focus of this essay,
other Reinachs besides Adolf Reinach influenced Stein's path in life. As other
scholars have amply demonstrated, Stein's association with Reinach's wife Anna
and his sister Pauline, who gave Stein her first personal contact with Reinach's
family, were also influential.

A comparison of the religious lives of Adolf Reinach and Edith Stein reveals
certain similarities as well as differences caused by their completely different life
circumstances. For Reinach, both his experience of the war and his proximity to

death awoke in him religious feeling; for Stein, religious feeling emerged from the slow breakdown of her life ambitions and hopes, a process that began with the above-mentioned events of 1918. Both Reinach and Stein had in common a "feeling of powerlessness" that forced them to capitulate before the events, but given their different circumstances, the intensity of this feeling and the ensuing change were quite different. For Reinach, it was a sudden and brutal rupture in his life, whereas for Edith Stein the development was slower and more gradual. This contrast is manifested in both philosophers' work. Under the influence of his experiences of war, Reinach came to the conviction of the utter importance of leading human beings to God, and he wanted from that point on to orient his work in a religio-philosophical direction. His earlier work provided no starting point for this new direction of his thought. In contrast, a definite continuation of method and thought characterizes Edith Stein's writing. Her texts from 1918 to 1921 build upon one another, but the theme of religious belief is far from in the foreground of her work, unlike was the case quite suddenly in Reinach's work.

Prompted by her perception of the beautiful and deeply moving writings of her deceased teacher, Edith Stein took her first few steps in the direction of an active faith. She wanted to empathize with Reinach's experience, which had given him the strength and calmness that she herself so greatly desired. The most important passage to make clear Stein's religious experience and her new understanding of faith comes from her 1918 text "Sentient Causality."

There is a state of resting in God, of complete relaxation of all mental activity, in which you make no plans at all, reach no decision, much less take action, but rather leave everything that's future to the divine will, "consigning yourself entirely to fate." This state may have befallen me after an experience that exceeded my power, and that has completely consumed my mental life power and deprived me of all activeness. Compared to the cessation of activeness from the lack of life-power, resting in God is something completely new and unique. The former was dead silence. Now its place is taken by the feeling of being safe, of being exempted from all anxiety and responsibility and duty to act. And as I surrender myself to this feeling, new life begins to fill me up, little by little, and impels me—without any voluntary exertion— toward new activation. This reviving infusion appears as an emanation of a functionality and a power which is not my emanation and which becomes operative within me without my asking for it. The sole prerequisite for such a mental rebirth seems to be a certain receptivity, like the receptivity supporting the structure of the person.[11]

Even though Edith Stein here speaks expressly of a personal experience, her words contain overtones of Reinach's notes on "being safe in God." Edith Stein begins in the first sentence with a description of what she means by the state of "resting in God." Employing an example taken from her own personal experience, Stein wishes to explain both the circumstances that can lead one to such a state and the experience in itself. Stein remarks, "This state has been more or less [*etwa*] apportioned to me." *Etwa* ("more or less" but also "perhaps" or "in a way") can be taken to mean that she is invoking her own experience but also has another description in mind.[12] It could well apply to the experience described by Reinach. Stein doubtless had his notes in mind when she was writing this text, since she cites passages from them in a footnote of the preceding page of her own text.[13] Her wish to empathize with and to draw closer to the experience of her beloved teacher, to identify with the origin of the immense power that emanates from his writings, certainly contributed to her increasing sensitivity and openness to religious experiences. An increased receptivity, however, did not lead her inevitably to the experience she desired. It is important to remark that though Stein's reflections and descriptions rely greatly on the writings of Reinach,[14] she also separated herself more and more from Reinach's example and began to find her own way.

The year 1918 was a very intense year of work for Edith Stein, in which she traveled frequently between Breslau, Göttingen, and Freiburg. In just a few months, she put together Reinach's writing "on the essence of movement," participated in the organization of the planned memorial volume in honor of Reinach, and worked on her own essay "Sentient Causality." She also spoke often of interesting talks and discussions given within the phenomenological circle. As to her own state of mind, Stein gives us only a few hints in her letters to Ingarden, which make up the major part of the extant correspondence. In May, she found herself back in Freiburg. From there she wrote to Ingarden that after being surrounded for a time by loved ones, she feared being alone in Freiburg. Things however went better than she had expected. Perhaps her being alone precisely at this time was fruitful and important for the transformation that was slowly taking place. She wrote: "And I have found a support that gives me a certain degree of independence from external conditions."[15]

Is Edith Stein perhaps referring here to the state described in "Sentient Causality" as an invigorating stream that, without one doing anything oneself, serves to regenerate one's vitality? It is not easy to determine which of the two texts cited, the letter or "Sentient Causality," was written earlier. Further clues, however, can be found in Stein's correspondence to indicate a steady change. In a letter to her sister Erna from July 6, 1918, Stein speaks again of her experience of a source of invigorating strength: "I would like so much to instil in both of you some of what, after every new blow, gives me fresh strength. I can only say that after everything I went through in the past year, I affirm life more than ever."[16] The most significant clue for understanding the change that Stein had undergone can be found in a letter to Ingarden from October 10, 1918. As in "Sentient Causality," Stein speaks here of "rebirth," which at the very least can be seen in relation to her upcoming birthday—the letter is a reply to an early birthday letter from Ingarden:

> I do not know whether you have already ascertained this from earlier things I have written, but I have forced my way to a thoroughly positive Christianity. This has liberated me from the life that had overcome me and has also given me the strength to resume my life in a new and thankful way. I can therefore speak of a "rebirth" in a very deep sense. But this new life is for me so intimately tied to my life experiences last year that I will never be able in any way to disassociate myself from them.[17]

These few texts enable us to suspect that Stein already had in 1918 an important and fundamental experience that brought her closer to Christianity. But, although the letters clearly express the hope for a new beginning, this experience can be considered only a first step. Edith Stein could not have known that her crisis was not soon to be overcome.

The Value of Community

The most important source for understanding the events of 1919—Stein's correspondence with Roman Ingarden—is unfortunately less than fruitful. Despite her urgent plea for signs of life from him at the beginning of 1919, nine months passed before he made contact again. In that letter he communicated to her the news of his marriage. He wrote no doubt with some discomfort and apprehensiveness concomitant with a bad conscience, given how long he had waited to tell her this news. For Stein, this meant a further distancing from him, which explains why Ingarden received only four letters, compared to the forty-one letters he had received in the preceding year. At exactly the same time, Stein experienced two further failures. At the end of 1918 and the beginning of 1919, she expressed the wish and hope for *Habilitation*,[18] which she thought would not present "serious difficulties" in the "new Germany."[19] With this goal in mind, Stein added to her essay "Sentient Causality" a second part entitled "Individual and Community." She submitted this to various universities as her *Habilitations-schrift* in October 1919.[20] She learned soon however that her wish to habilitate had failed, despite an intensive effort on her part, since the habilitation of women brought with it as many difficulties as it had prior to 1918. Her hope of an academic career was dashed irrefutably, and she was forced privately to swallow yet another disappointment. We experience this disappointment in a later letter to Ingarden from 1925:

> First, I must tell you that just around the time I got news of your marriage, the memories from Freiburg were nullified by fresh impressions, by a story that demonstrated in many respects an uncanny analogy to the story you know. You'll certainly allow me to skip the details. The experiences were at least as painful, but my inner powers of resistance had grown so that I got through them more easily and, so I believe, have thereby attained inner freedom. I am now convinced that I am where I belong and am simply grateful that I have been led on this path; I travel it with the most joyful dedication and without any trace of "resignation."[21]

The "story" that Edith Stein mentions no doubt concerns her friendship with Hans Lipps, a fellow student whom she had met in the winter semester of 1913–14. In the summer of 1919 they met each other again at Anna Reinach's, where they became closer. Edith Stein was living at the home of Anna Reinach, who was at the same time a good friend of Hans Lipps. At the end of August, Stein traveled back to Breslau in order to dedicate herself to the second part of her proposed *Habilitationsschrift*. Arriving there on September 16, she received Ingarden's letter containing news of his marriage. Hans Lipps had worked as a physician before he came to Freiburg to habilitate under Husserl. When his plans for habilitation failed due to a disagreement with Husserl, it was only through Stein's mediation that Lipps received a second opportunity for habilitation at Göttingen. Edith Stein took complete care of his plans and dreamed of a shared future with Lipps, yet she had a presentiment that this might not come to pass. By the summer of 1921 at the latest, she must have realized that yet again a valuable colleague and discussion partner, who had become a friend, did not however reciprocate the affection she as a woman felt for him.

After Lipps received his *venia legendi*[22] on July 30, 1921, he found himself in such a hopeless mood that he decided to "emigrate" from Göttingen[23] and to work again as a ship's doctor for a year. This repeated disappointment marked the end of Stein's deeply rooted hope for a happy marriage. In the already cited letter to Ingarden from 1925, she writes: "Do you remember when you said that

I was 'too Catholic?' At that time I did not understand what you meant. Today, I understand, and I know how right you were. I actually felt Catholic. But since Catholic dogma with its practical consequences was alien to me, I could not justify what I felt, so my mind and my senses joined forces to do violence to my heart."[24] Edith Stein clarifies the meaning of these words with a quotation from her own memoir: "Though totally dedicated to my work, I still cherished in my own heart the dream of a great love and of a happy marriage. Though I had no inkling of Catholic doctrines on faith and morals, I fully espoused the Catholic ideal of matrimony."[25]

This ideal of marriage along with the no less important hope for an academic career came to seem more and more unrealizable and distant. Edith Stein was once again compelled to reconsider her powerlessness and to think concretely about future opportunities and the shape her life was to take. But what kind of opportunities awaited her? Perhaps a life within the circle of her family, such as other unmarried sisters had had? She definitely could not imagine this. Even though she loved her family dearly and supported family unity, her family could not provide the environment necessary and important for her personal development.

Though few letters from 1919 give us information about Edith Stein's state of mind and the questions of faith that she was contemplating, an essay written during this time, "Individual and Community," does provide an insight into these matters. Many parts of the text have an autobiographical value. In this text, she attempts, for example, to obtain clarity about the soul and its darkest depths, and she gives powerful expression to the spiritual torments that occur when no "awakening" of the soul, or "dawning of consciousness" in the soul *(Bewußtwerdung der Seele)* takes place.[26] Her considerations of the limits of the intellect are also illuminating, where up until this point she had regarded the phenomenological method as such an important accomplishment that she had ruled out any other kind of knowledge for herself. Specifically, Stein raises the interesting theme of the immanent value of the community for the individual. Since issues of community are involved in her years of crisis, I will briefly sketch her philosophy of community.

The investigation of the individual as a microcosm, which Edith Stein had undertaken in "Sentient Causality," is extended to the community. The community is to be understood as the organic combining of unique individuals. In the case of the individual, as in the case of the community, Stein recognizes an analagous structure of lived experiences concomitant with a flow of lived experiences and a life force. These fundamental elements are, however, always linked to individual persons, who together nurture the communal lived experiences and life force of the community. Stein seeks to bring to light both this interaction and the value of a life in a community for the individual. She also seeks to clarify how the individual handles him- or herself within the context of various communities, including the family, religious, or other communities. It is in this context, according to Stein, that such terms as *social stances (soziale Stellungnahmen)*, acquire meaning. These are found only in a community and not in an individual, isolated life, can have both a positive and a negative nature, and include, for example, love, hate, and trust. Each type of stance can have consequences both on the person toward whom it is directed and the person from whom it originates. For example, Stein writes: "The love which I meet with strengthens and invigorates me and grants me the power for unexpected achievements. The distrust that I run into disables my creative power." On the other hand, such a stance works in a different way in one who loves: "Love operates within the one who loves as an invigorating force that might even develop more powers within him than experiencing it costs him. And hate depletes his powers far more severely as a content than as experiencing of hate."[27]

A given stance is produced or "sparked" by latching onto a value. This can be influenced both by taking on a certain value *(Wertnehmen)* and assuming a certain stance of value *(Wertstellungnehmen)*. Stein remarks, "Love is based on the apprehended value of the beloved person, but on the other hand the worth of a person is fully and completely accessible only to the love."[28] Just as there are social stances, we can also find "social" virtues and vices that can likewise develop only among a union of persons: for example, "humility and pride, servility and defiance, power lust and affability, team spirit and helpfulness."[29] This means that only in a communal life with others can the immanent dispositions of a person come to the fore; and only in a communal life can they unfold. If and to what extent these dispositions are cultivated depend on the one hand on the personal environment, which can exert both a positive and negative influence, and on the other on the will of the affected person, who has the freedom, within certain boundaries, to choose and shape his or her own environment as well as to avoid certain influences. The value of community is such that, through interaction with others, interaction corresponding to the form and depth of the unity, the unfolding of original dispositions, and personal development can happen, even to the extent of a transformation *(Umbildung)* of the individual person. Further, the community "releases individuals from their natural loneliness and in the new super-individual personality that unites in itself the powers and abilities of the discrete [members], turns them into its own functions, and through this synthesis can produce achievements."[30] These reflections on the value of community, in reference to Stein's momentary situation, bring to light the relevance of her question: What is the right form of life to aid personal development? The wish to be supported in a community of like-minded people also resonates in her essay, but without a distinction being made as to whether this is a principally intellectual or spiritual elective attraction *(Wahlverwandtschaft)*.

Stein spent most of 1920 in Breslau for family reasons. She wanted to be close to her "favorite" sister Erna, whose engagement to Hans Biberstein was threatened because of differences between the families involved. For Erna, this time was excruciatingly painful, and Edith, acting as a mediator, tried to bring some resolution to the difficulties. But she concealed her own crisis and spiritual struggles from her family. Only after the wedding in December did she begin to feel free again to look after her own needs and prepared herself for a trip to Göttingen and Bergzabern, where she wanted to visit with the phenomenologist Hedwig Conrad-Martius. The two women had become acquainted personally a few months earlier and from the start got on well. Stein traveled to Bergzabern on May 21 and remained there until the beginning of August. The Conrad family home served as a "general home base for phenomenologists," a meeting point and center for followers of phenomenology, a desired community.

During this time, the two women became very close. Edith Stein departed only because her sister requested her presence. The relationship, according to Hedwig Conrad-Martius, was more than a usual friendship. Uniting the two women were both their phenomenological training and the fact that both women found themselves at the time in religious crises, which were ultimately resolved in different ways. The communal work around the orchard in Bergzabern was punctuated and accompanied by stimulating discussions and conversations about Christian life and confessions, which had a clarifying impact on both women.[31]

When Edith Stein traveled back to Breslau, she had already decided to convert to Catholicism. During her summer visit at Bergzabern she had read *The Life of St. Teresa of Avila,* which was the final spur leading to her conversion. Yet she wished wholeheartedly to return quickly to Bergzabern and there to pursue further her academic work. From Breslau, she wrote on August 30, 1921:

> As soon as everything is done here I am returning to the Conrads—for an indefinite period of time. I helped work in their orchards all summer long. And it is absolutely essential that Frau Conrad get some relief; she's worked beyond her strength for years now, and it just can't go on this way. If each of us does half, both of us still have enough time left over for academic work. The main thing is that we get on with each other so well that we'd both

hardly thought it possible before that one could relate to another person in such a way. Naturally, we wish to live together, as long as it's at all possible. I get along superbly with Conrad as well, which is of course a necessary part of it.[32]

It is clear how happy Stein felt at Bergzabern. We have seen that for Stein life in a community presented her with the opportunity to overcome her natural solitariness and to develop further personally. Perhaps, for a time, Stein believed herself to have found the community she searched for among this circle of phenomenologists. These were the people to whom she felt particularly united and whom she sought to be near. She remarks, "It is so beautiful how the connection between phenomenologists, which at an earlier time I worked for in vain, is now gradually being established entirely on it own."[33] In Hedwig Conrad-Martius, Stein found a companion who likewise wanted to lead her work in a religio-philosophical direction. Even after her baptism into the Catholic faith on January 1, 1922, Stein stayed principally at Bergzabern, where she met many phenomenologists. While there, as she wrote in a letter to Ingarden from September 30, 1922, she worked with Hedwig Conrad-Martius on a translation of a book by Koyré about the idea of God in the philosophy of Descartes.[34]

At this point, a gap appears in Stein's correspondence, and one can only speculate as to what motivated her to turn her back on these surroundings and on the people whom she found at Bergzabern. For it should be noted that the true beginning of Stein's new life does not stem from the date of her baptism but from the beginning of her new job as a teacher with the Dominican sisters in Speyer in Easter 1923.[35] Decisive for Edith Stein in accepting the position at Speyer was "the religious basis of the entire life" she would find there.[36] Although Bergzabern was not so far away, Stein traveled there only from time to time for a "few days."[37] But it was now in the community of the Dominican convent where she felt most at home and to which she was always glad to return. At this same time, Edith Stein distanced herself from phenomenology and phenomenologists, both of which only a year earlier had been so significant for her. Perhaps she had recognized that she could not find in phenomenology that thing for which she really searched? Perhaps her collaboration with Hedwig Conrad-Martius led to more differences rather than to more common ground? Even though we are unable to understand Stein's individual motives, it is clear that only once detached from her phenomenological surroundings—a detachment that represented less a definitive renunciation than a liberating distance—did she embark on an entirely new chapter in her life.

NOTES

I cite directly from Edith Stein's German texts. The translator has taken Stein's quotations, where possible, from the extant English translations.

The original version of this essay appeared as "Momente der Krisenjahre Edith Steins," *Edith Stein Jahrbuch 7* (2001): 343–54.

1. Edith Stein to Erna Stein dated July 29, 1918, in Edith Stein, *Aus der Tiefe leben,* ed. Waltraud Herbstrith (Munich: Kösel, 1988), 64.

2. This was the theme of my Italian dissertation, Angelika von Renteln, "La conversione di Edith Stein," submitted to the Faculty of Humanities at the University of Florence in 1998. This dissertation investigates important preparatory moments in Stein's conversion process, including, for example, Stein's Jewish upbringing and her relationship to her mother. The main part of the dissertation then investigates the events of Stein's crisis years between 1918 and 1921 as well as her inner development, as ascertained from letters and excerpts from her texts.

3. Edith Stein, letter no. 25, December 24, 1917, in *Briefe an Roman Ingarden, 1917–1938,* vol. 14 of *Edith Steins Werke* (Freiburg: Herder, 1991).

4. Stein to Roman Ingarden, letter no. 26, January 29, 1918, in *Briefe an Roman Ingarden.*

5. All quotations from Stein to Roman Ingarden, letter no. 27, February 12, 1918, in *Briefe an Roman Ingarden.*

6. Stein to Roman Ingarden, letter no. 32, May 12, 1918, in *Briefe an Roman Ingarden.*

7. Stein to Roman Ingarden, letter no. 28, February 19, 1918, in *Briefe an Roman Ingarden.*

8. Stein to Roman Ingarden, letter no. 29, February 28, 1918, in *Briefe an Roman Ingarden.*

9. The notes with commentary and critique of texts were first published in *Adolf Reinach: Sämtliche Werke,* 2 vols., ed. Karl Schuhmann and Barry Smith (Munich: Philosophia Verlag, 1989).

10. See, e.g., Edith Stein, *Aus dem Leben einer jüdischen Familie, Das Leben Edith Stein: Kindheit und Jugend,* vol. 7 of *Edith Steins Werke* (Freiburg: Herder, 1965), 225 ff., 262, 264, 343, 345.

11. Edith Stein, *Philosophy of Psychology and the Humanities,* trans. M. C. Baseheart and M. Sawicki (Washington, DC: ICS Publications, 2000), 84–85.

12. This distinction echoes the phenomenological practice of making a distinction between the content of an experience and the experience of living through a given experience in consciousness—that is, the phenomenological distinction between *noesis* and *noema.*—Trans.

13. See Stein, *Philosophy of Psychology,* 82 n. 111.

14. In her paper "Phänomenologie des religiösen Erlebens im Anschluß an Adolf Reinach und Edith Stein," delivered at the International Edith Stein Symposium in Rome in 1998 on the occasion of Edith Stein's canonization, Beate Beckmann recounts how Edith Stein relied on the model of Adolf Reinach for her own philosophical and existential concerns with religious experience.

15. Stein to Roman Ingarden, letter no. 32, May 12, 1918, in *Briefe an Roman Ingarden.*

16. Edith Stein to Erna Stein, letter no. 24, July 6, 1918, in *Self-Portrait in Letters, 1916–1942*, trans. J. Koeppel, OCD (Washington, DC: ICS Publications, 1993), 27.

17. Edith Stein to Roman Ingarden, letter no. 53, October 10, 1918, in *Briefe an Roman Ingarden*.

18. The process whereby one would become a university professor, acquiring a formal academic position at the university.—Trans.

19. Edith Stein to Roman Ingarden, letter no. 63, December 27, 1918, in *Briefe an Roman Ingarden*.

20. The *Habilitationsschrift* was a large academic work that served to demonstrate the academic competence of a candidate who wished to apply for a formal position at a German university.—Trans.

21. Edith Stein to Roman Ingarden, letter no. 93, November 29, 1925, in *Briefe an Roman Ingarden*.

22. Literally, the "right to read." This was the Latin name for the official right to teach at the German university, granted after one was officially habilitated.—Trans.

23. Hans Lipps describes his hopeless mood in a letter to his friend F. Kaufmann. See F. Rodi and K. Schuhmann, "Hans Lipps in Spiegel seiner Korrespondenz," *Dilthey-Jahrbuch* 6 (1989): 58. For further information about Hans Lipps's life and work, see Waltraud Herbstrith, "Hans Lipps im Blick Edith Steins," *Dilthey-Jahrbuch* 6 (1989): 31–51, which clarifies Stein's attitude toward him, using all her reference to him from her correspondence.

24. Edith Stein to Roman Ingarden, letter no. 93, November 29, 1925, in *Briefe an Roman Ingarden*.

25. Edith Stein, *Life in a Jewish Family*, trans. Josephine Koeppel, vol. 1 of *The Collected Works of Edith Stein* (Washington, DC: ICS Publications, 1986), 227.

26. Being awake is distinguished from consciousness in that the former refers more to sentience whereas the latter implies an inner awareness of one's sentience. Hence, with regard to the former, I can feel a certain sensation. In the case of the latter, I am aware of my feeling this sensation. I can describe what it means for me to be conscious of and live through such an experience. There is a higher sense of reflectivity in the case of the latter.—Trans.

27. Edith Stein, *Philosophy of Psychology and the Humanities*, trans. Mary Catharine Baseheart and Marianne Sawicki, vol. 7 of *The Collected Works of Edith Stein* (Washington, DC: ICS Publications, 2000), 212.

28. Ibid., 213.

29. Ibid., 266.

30. Ibid., 273.

31. See Angela Ales Bello, *Fenomenologia dell'essere umano: Lineamenti di una filosofia al femminile* (Rome: Città Nuova Editrice, 1992), and "Edith Stein und Hedwig Conrad-Martius: Eine menschliche und intellektuelle Begegnung," in *Phänomenologische Forschungen*, vol. 26/27 (Munich: Karl Alber, 1993), 256–84.

32. Edith Stein to Roman Ingarden, letter no. 76, August 30, 1921, in *Briefe an Roman Ingarden*.

33. Edith Stein to Roman Ingarden, letter no. 77, September 22, 1921, in *Briefe an Roman Ingarden*.

34. Edith Stein to Roman Ingarden, letter no. 82, September 30, 1922, in *Briefe an Roman Ingarden*.

35. The division of Stein's *Briefe an Roman Ingarden* into the sections "I. Paths and Detours (1917–1921)" and "II. Call and Profession (1922–1930)", based on the official date of her entry into the Catholic Church, suggests the date of her baptism as the decisive moment and beginning of her religious life.

36. Edith Stein to Roman Ingarden, letter no. 83, February 5, 1924, in *Briefe an Roman Ingarden*.

37. Ibid.

Chapter 8

"His Whole Life Consisted of a Search for Religious Truth"

Edith Stein in Conversation with John Henry Newman

HANNA-BARBARA GERL-FALKOVITZ

translated by Jonathan Knutzen

Edith Stein the Translator

Few are aware that Edith Stein devoted over three years of her early days in Speyer, from 1923 to 1925, to the writings John Henry Newman (1801–90). Despite hundreds of pages of translation work by Stein, however, the little that can be said about this "conversation" must be put together indirectly by coming to an appreciation of the tumultuous period around the 1920s.

After becoming a Christian on New Year's Day 1922, Stein was encouraged by the Jesuit Erich Przywara to translate some of Newman's works that had not yet appeared in German. She began by translating a collection of lectures, *The Idea of a University* (1858) (with the German title *Die Idee der Universität*), and then worked on what was entitled *Briefe und Tagebücher bis zum Übertritt zur Kirche, 1801–45*. The latter title is somewhat misleading, since besides letters the German volume contains not so much diary entries as explanatory texts that were intended for publication, for example, the preface to the French edition of *Apologia* and the "Brief Autobiography" that Newman wrote in 1874 specially for the edition of his letters dating from his Anglican period, which he had asked his sister-in-law Anne Mozley to edit *(Letters and Correspondence of John Henry Newman during His Life in the English Church, with a Brief Autobiography)*. The final letters in Stein's volume date from 1846, which means that, as it stood, the edition did not reflect accurately either the title or the number of years covered.

Przywara had been made aware of Stein's qualities through her fellow student Dietrich von Hildebrand (1889–1977).[1] Originally a Protestant, "Gogo" von Hildebrand had converted to Catholicism by 1914 (a fact that Stein mentions)[2] and by the early 1920s had founded a publishing company in Munich, Theatiner Verlag, with the ambitious goal of publishing a critical edition of Newman's collected works.[3] Admittedly, this project did not get very far, and the publishing house had been disbanded by 1930.[4] Stein held Hildebrand's phenomenological works in high esteem and reviewed his *Metaphysik der Gemeinschaft (Metaphysics of Community)* (1925) approvingly, though in secret she was also critical of it.[5]

Przywara became something of a mentor to Stein in the 1920s, and he undertook to introduce her to Catholic philosophy.[6] The relationship was all but one-sided, and he acknowledges with gratitude in the preface to his major work, *Analogia entis,* that "he had been drawn into Stein's work of placing Thomas and Husserl head to head. The fruitful connection to Husserl, which was opened up by Edith Stein, exerted an influence on the shaping of my methodology."[7] Nonetheless, as becomes apparent in Przywara's response, Stein was critical of *Analogia entis.*[8] The initial contact between Stein and Przywara regarding Newman was in the form of letters, until they met in the spring of 1925 in the house of Joseph Schwind, the vicar-general of Speyer.[9] Years later, upon the tenth anniversary of Stein's death in 1952, Przywara painted a curiously striking picture of his first impression of Stein: she seemed to him to be an "Uta von Naumburg," a comparison that makes sense given the historical context.[10] In the translations he made her stick to a very literal German, as will become apparent below. He chose Newman's *personal* texts from before his conversion, presumably for chronological reasons having to do with the projected critical edition, but doubtless also as an encouraging testimony for Stein, who had recently converted to Catholicism and was faced with a difficult separation from her family.

At the time the German Catholic Church unexpectedly entered a "Holy Spring," which was to yield much lasting fruit. The liturgical movement,[11] a simultaneous revaluing of monasticism,[12] the academic movement (which had its source in Maria Laach), neo-Thomism, numerous conversions following the

First World War, and the religious youth movement all contributed to a refreshing influx into what had long seemed to be a culturally inferior Catholic world.

Edith Stein not only managed to immerse herself in the work of Newman while she had teaching responsibilities in Speyer but on top of that (beginning in 1925) began working on Aquinas's *Questiones disputatae de veritate*,[13] with which she caused quite a sensation in neoscholastic circles. Her translation of Newman's *Idea of a University* has only recently been published, and her translation of Aquinas's *De ente et essentia* will be printed in 2007.[14] The amazing breadth of these postconversion translations tells us something about her desire to "think herself into" the world of Catholicism. In addition to these works, there is — strangely enough — Stein's first anonymous translation, which she completed together with Hedwig Conrad-Martius: *Descartes und die Scholastik (Descartes and Scholasticism)*, written by Alexandre Koyré, who was a student with Stein under Husserl. The book was published without additional publication details in Bonn with Cohen in 1923,[15] and the only way we know about this translation is from Stein's mention of it in her letters to Roman Ingarden.[16] In the text, Koyré attempted to expose the scholastic and Thomistic roots of Cartesian thought and to demonstrate thereby the proximity of modern epistemology *(Erkenntniskritik)* to medieval metaphysics, a goal Stein shared in her translations of Aquinas. Husserl's *Cartesianische Meditationen (Cartesian Meditations)* (1928), by contrast, reestablished an epistemological reading of Descartes.

Stein kept busy with translation work until the last years of her life. For her study *(Wege der Gotteserkenntnis) (Ways to Know God)* (1941) she translated works by Dionysius the Areopagite.[17] In addition she completed many shorter translations, some intended for in-house use in the Carmelite monastery.[18] What should be taken from this is that Edith Stein was working on other thinkers with a considerable degree of philological accuracy and with the intention of drawing them into the philosophical debates of her time.

The "Troublesome History" of Newman's Reception in the Germany of the 1920s

Apart from a few earlier isolated translations, John Henry Newman's voluminous work did not begin to appear in Germany until 1920. And even then it did not happen without conflict among the three main publishers—Herder in Freiburg, where Przywara published a selection from the collected works in eight short volumes;[19] Grünewald Verlag in Mainz, where Matthias Laros published *Ausgewählte Werke* (Selected Works) of Newman beginning in 1922; and the aforementioned and short-lived Theatiner Verlag in Munich, which was run in part by Przywara. Thus after 1920 Newman's work drew attention in an explosive and not uncontroversial way, particularly given the current controversy surrounding theological modernism *(der Modernismusstreit)*. Other translators and critics who helped to introduce Newman to Germany included such notables as Theodor Haecker (who made Kierkegaard available to German speakers),[20] Rudolf Kassner,[21] Maria Knoepfler (with the backing of Josef Weiger and Romano Guardini), and Ignatia Breme.[22] It is within the context of this in many ways uncoordinated reception of Newman that Guardini's puzzling sentence from his postscript of Newman's *Briefe aus der katholischen Zeit II (Ausgewählte Werke* 10, 1931) makes sense: "And if someday the troublesome history of the German translation of Newman should be written—a history that includes much goodwill, much disunity, and many obstacles—then the name of this truly humble woman [M. Knoepfler] would have to be among the first to be mentioned."[23]

A little light can be shed on this passage, which hints at controversy, by Przywara's recollection: "Dietrich von Hildebrand told me immediately that he wanted to get Edith Stein to do the most important volumes [of the German edition of Newman's collected works]. So I wrote Edith Stein about how I imagined the form of the translation—not a so-called translation of sense, but one that was strictly faithful down to every last word and even capable of preserving the rhythmic sentence structure and word order of the original. While Maria Knoepfler, who is—so to speak—Newman's standard translator, would not countenance these demands, Edith Stein knew immediately what I wanted, because she too shared the same idea."[24]

Newman through Knoepfler, Weiger, and Guardini

Although for a long time little was known about Maria Knoepfler (1881–1927), she is currently coming into greater focus as a subject of research.[25] Knoepfler got to know the then-chaplain Josef Weiger (1883–1966), a friend of Guardini's and great admirer of Newman, during his residence in Wangen. Beginning in 1917 she ran Weiger's household, at which time he was the pastor of Mooshausen.[26] Weiger and Guardini, and as a result Knoepfler, had apparently been encouraged to study Newman by the theologian Wilhelm Koch during their studies at Tübingen in 1907–8. A copy of Newman's *Selected Sermons (Ausgewählte Predigten)*[27] still contains the original label of ownership: "Josef Weiger. 1908." At the time of his chaplaincy, Weiger had planned to translate Newman's *Fifteen Ser-*

mons Preached before the University of Oxford (*Universitätspredigten*), but the plan did not come to fruition.[28]

Knoepfler had begun working on Newman by 1912 at the latest.[29] She had been given a copy of Newman's posthumous *Meditations and Devotions* with a note of dedication by Guardini[30] and translated parts of it that year (probably at her father's mill in Wangen) under the title *Betrachtungen und Gebete* (published in 1924 by Theatiner Verlag). In 1915 she began a new translation of *Apologia pro vita sua* (Grünewald Verlag, 1922, *Ausgewählte Werke* 1) with the help of Guardini,[31] though it had already been translated by Matthias Laros.[32] Her next work was *St. Philipp Neri* (Theatiner Verlag, 1922) and the posthumous *Briefe aus der katholischen Zeit* (Grünewald Verlag, 1929 and 1931, *Ausgewählte Werke* 9 and 10), the first volume of which Weiger published with a long and insightfully balanced preface, while the second volume contained Guardini's moving obituary of Knoepfler.

Other translations remained among Knoepfler's unpublished works, including the translation of the letters from his Anglican period and also Newman's autobiographical sketches from the edition edited by Anne Mozley, which are the *same* pieces translated by Stein![33]

Guardini's own public interaction with Newman was limited to one short review.[34] In a letter to Weiger, however, the young Freiburg scholar emphasized the crucial importance of Newman to his own thinking.[35] Guardini's comment to the editor Richard Knies, who was instrumental in shaping Grünewald Verlag, reflects this: "And I am sad to think that Newman will probably be introduced programmatically here. Newman is not that sort of thinker, indeed he is not a theologian for a broad audience. He is someone who one must approach face to face, in a personal way, and with due respect as well as cautious critique; he is a name that fits into no discussion."[36]

How does the "team" of Stein and Przywara relate to that of Knoepfler, Weiger, and Guardini?

Newman through Edith Stein and Erich Przywara

Perhaps the fact that Stein translated Newman's *pre*-conversion letters without contacting Knoepfler, who had also worked on translating these letters as well as finishing the next thematically related volume, can perhaps be explained by the latter's unexpected death in August of 1927. However, as became clear above, Przywara did not get along well with Knoepfler. Equally perplexing is the fact that in all of her works, Stein refers to Guardini just once, namely to his "Gegensatzlehre," which she talks about in connection with the question of education.[37] Stein could have forged a link to Guardini through Przywara, either via the Academics' Conference held in Ulm in 1923, which I will make more detailed mention of below, or via Przywara's many positive reviews of Guardini.[38] Presumably, however, the lack of exchange is due to Guardini's reservation vis-à-vis Przywara.

Hundreds of Stein's handwritten pages, containing a fairly literal translation of Newman's *The Idea of a University (Idee einer Universität),* have, until recently, been collecting dust in the important archive of the Cologne Carmel. Newman had written this fundamental and extensive work in the context of plans to found a Catholic university in Dublin, a plan that was in the end taken out of his hands. Edith Stein was apparently deeply concerned with the concept of Catholic education, especially because of the shortcomings in this respect that existed in the Weimar Republic at the time. Stein was herself teaching in Speyer (1923–31) and she was also active on the public lecture circuit, though time and again she attempted to habilitate, despite in the end gaining only a professorship for two semesters (1932–33) in Münster. It remains a mystery why Stein's completed translation of Newman's *Idea of a University* was unpublished until 2004.[39]

Stein's translation of Newman's preconversion letters and diaries first appeared in 1928, published in Munich by Theatiner Verlag, which was shut down shortly thereafter.[40] This edition has long since been out of print, and the manuscript was not preserved. The title of the series, which was printed on the left inside page, reads: "John Henry Cardinal Newman, *Collected Works.* Commissioned by the Association of Catholic Academic Scholars for the Nurturing of the Catholic Worldview, edited by Frs. Daniel Feuling, O. S. B., and Erich Przywara, S.J., and Professor Paul Simon. Volume 1, 1928, Theatiner Verlag, Munich" (John Henry Kardinal Newman, *Gesammelte Werke.* Im Auftrage des Verbandes der Vereine Katholischer Akademiker zur Pflege der katholischen Weltanschauung herausgegeben von P. Daniel Feuling O. S. B.,[41] P. Erich Przywara S.J., Professor Paul Simon.[42] Erster Band 1928 Theatiner Verlag München). The translation is, as Przywara had demanded, truly word for word, which, in part, given the complexity of Newman's relative clauses, makes for somewhat awkward German reading. In contrast to Knoepfler, Stein offers almost no clarification on the context of the letters and limits notes to essential details, for example, translations of Latin and Greek phrases. She does not provide footnotes to explain the many names and allusions to the world of Oxford University life (the new 2001 edition tries to rectify this through extensive footnotes and an index of names and terms). Apparently she expected her readers to be familiar with these aspects and, as well, thoroughly knowledgeable about church history and the history of dogma *(Dogmengeschichte).* But because Stein had just recently converted and was extremely busy with teaching responsibilities and presumably also cut off from relevant literature, the job of providing notes and commentary would have fallen to Przywara. Moreover, Stein had to correct the galleys under time pressure and was therefore unable to proofread the final corrections, as the plentiful printing errors indicate; the last third of the book even contains a few errors of content.[43]

Regrettably, we have no systematic reflections (beyond these two translations) from Stein on Newman. In a letter to Ingarden from June 19, 1924, however, she makes some beautiful and important remarks: "I enjoy translating for its own sake. And besides, it is wonderful for me to get to come into such close contact, as happens when one is translating, with a mind like Newman's. His whole life consisted of a search for religious truth, and it led him with inescapable necessity to the Catholic Church."[44] She finds room for similar laudatory remarks in her (anonymous) obituary of Joseph Schwind, the truly pious and erudite vicar-general of the diocese in Speyer, with whom Stein had a little-known friendship, but one that was nevertheless vital for her spiritual growth: "Cardinal Newman often stressed that '[i]t is relatively easy to unfold just *one* part of the Christian life within oneself—strictness [*Strenge*] *or* tenderness, solemnity *or* joyfulness; but true Christian perfection comes only with the union of antithetical virtues.' Prelate Schwind has lived up to this challenge to the highest degree."[45]

In spite of her silence on the matter, Stein's selection of letters to translate is quite telling. For example, she translates a letter of lamentation written by Newman to his sister Jemima on March 15, 1845, around the time of his conversion: "I am distressing all I love, unsettling all I have instructed or aided. I am going to those whom I do not know, and of whom I expect very little. I am making myself an outcast, and that at my age. Oh, what can it be but a stern necessity which causes this?"[46] As Theo Gunkel movingly summarized the tenor of Newman's letters in the review of Stein's 1930 translations: "Get thee out of thy country, and from thy kindred, and from thy father's house, unto a land that I will shew thee" (Genesis 12:1).[47] This hints at a distant reflection of Stein's image in the shadow of her great predecessor.

The "Przywara Phenomenon" as a Reflection of the Religious Movements of the 1920s

In this section, I shall attempt indirectly to elucidate Stein's "internal" conversation with Newman with reference to the "Przywara phenomenon."[48] Erich Przywara (b. 1889 in Kattowitz, d. 1972 in Murnau) was from Upper Silesia (which, along with their birthday on October 12, was something that he had in common with Stein) and was of Polish and German descent. Because of Bismarck's *Kulturkampf*, he received his Jesuit formation in the Dutch town of Valkenburg. His training was primarily in scholastic thought, but he was also well read in patristic literature and German idealism. Along with Romano Guardini and Karl Adam he quickly ascended to the status of a notable figure in German Catholicism in the 1920s.[49] He published in *Kantstudien (Kant Studies)* and *Logos* (something previously unheard of for a Jesuit!) and from 1922 to 1941 was the editor of the famous Jesuit publication *Stimmen der Zeit (Voices of the Time),* which was disbanded by the Gestapo in 1941.[50] In his major work *Analogia entis* (1932), he attempted to establish a methodology that could do justice both to Aquinas's thought and contemporary trends in philosophy and theology.

Had Przywara limited his output to *Gottesgeheimnis der Welt (The World's Divine Mystery)* (1923) and *Ringen der Gegenwart (The Present Struggle)* (1929), both of which were collections of critical essays on the period of 1922–27 in Germany,[51] one could still have observed how he boldly dared to enter into the philosophical, theological, and literary debates of these tumultuous years. He not only referred to a multiplicity of significant names, schools, and movements like phenomenology, neo-Kantianism, the Protestant theology of Marburg, neo-Thomism, and the new departures in Catholicism, as well as the above-mentioned liturgical movement, the academic movement, and many more, but he also articulated his own judgment of them.

The latent religiosity of the 1920s emerged out of the tension between a thoroughly shaken postwar existence and a desperate search for meaning. Among the systems that promised this generation meaning, the religious, especially the Christian and Jewish, new departures, as well as new a-Christian mythologies such as that of Rilke, were primary. "The image of the present hour," writes Przywara, "is curiously fractured. On the one hand, the religious renewal movements are perhaps stronger than ever. On the other hand, the differences between them are becoming more glaringly obvious than ever, differences that are not infrequently tinged with dark fanaticism. It is like a stormy early spring during which heat and frost dance in an unpredictable rhythm."[52]

The largest renewal movement seems to have been within and toward the Catholic Church. "These are the years of the 'Catholic movement' . . . in the sense of a movement toward Catholicism, which at the very least can be witnessed in the form of a positive estimation of the Catholic spirit as a creative component of the contemporary intellectual life; a positive estimation of the Catholic movement but then above all of a stage of development within Catholicism itself, to the extent that a Catholicism of positive creativity, drawing on its own resources, began to take the place of the old dichotomy between Catholicism as *either* reactionary *or* conformist."[53] In 1945 Ida Friederike Görres (1901–71), reflecting on the past, remarked: "Today's generation cannot imagine what it was like when suddenly out of the arid intellectual desert, in which one had been able only to refer to bygone centuries — to Dante and the Gothic — appeared such names as Guardini, Adam, Lippert, Przywara, and Herwegen, who shone like stars and illuminated a new path for us. By 1920–30 it was again commonplace and taken for granted that there was such a thing as a Catholic intellectual culture, which outsiders revered and even envied. The spirit had returned and this caused great celebration."[54]

Conversions

The postwar years witnessed conversions *(Übertritte)* with outstanding frequency and great prominence. The majority belonged to this new "springtide of Catholicism," whereas the number of Protestant converts was considerably fewer; when Söderblom's disciple, the Catholic Friedrich Heiler, converted to Protestantism in 1920, this event drew considerable attention.[55] Among the great Catholic converts was the spectacular Hugo Ball, whose recommitment (in 1920) to the Catholic faith inspired him to write in 1923 the apologetic work *Byzantinisches Christentum (Byzantine Christendom),* in which he focused on the lives of three saints: John Climacus, Dionysius the Areopagite, and Simeon Stylites. It differed fundamentally from his earlier dadaistic work, although Przywara sensed a hidden connection.[56] Another occasion for public excitement was Gertrud von le Fort's 1924 book *Hymnen an die Kirche (Hymns to the Church).* Gertrud von le Fort had been a longtime student of the Protestant Ernst Troeltsch (1865–1923) but converted from Protestantism to Catholicism in 1926 in Rome. Other notable conversions during these years included Theodor Haecker, Werner Bergengruen, Ruth Schaumann, Edzard Schaper, and, in 1930, Erik Peterson.

At the same time, however, there were some who clearly distanced themselves from the Christian faith. Heidegger's turn away from the Catholic Church is a well-known example, although he did not completely denounce the church, as his continued relations with the arch-abbey of Beuron demonstrates. Rilke's "Brief eines jungen Arbeiters" (Letter of a Young Worker) (1922) passionately expresses theoretical objections and emotional opposition to Christianity. Later, calmer evaluations by Rilke showed no sign of reconciliation with the Christian faith but only reinforced his newly worked out post-Christian mythical consciousness.[57] Scheler's path, too, showed a minority trend away from the mainstream of newly awakened church-consciousness,[58] when, following his spectacular conversion, he drifted toward a theology without dogma, without a personal God, without liturgy, and without intellectual precision.[59]

Nevertheless, the conversions of intellectuals to Catholicism in Germany are remarkable, not least because a similar process was taking place in France, especially in the circle around Jacques and Raïssa Maritain (who had themselves been baptized in 1906). In 1925, Jean Cocteau was on the verge of converting.[60] The general sentiment can be summarized by the lament of a Protestant German in 1925: "Recently someone said at a gathering, '[I]n all of Germany, one cry is now heard: oh that we were all Catholic again!' This is indeed a widely shared feeling. . ."[61]

Astonishingly enough, the word *Catholic*—understood with its etymological meaning—seems to have been used beyond its ecclesiastical sense, or at the very least its connotations were construed in an approving way. By some, it was seen as "a password to a new epoch of German, even European, development. . . . From Stefan George's circle in Berlin, we hear talk of an 'intellectual Catholicism'; at a conference in Darmstadt in 1923, Keyserling spoke in his final address to his *Schule der Weisheit* [school of wisdom], and in various subsequent lectures at other times, of the 'Catholic man' as the new man, who is in the process of becoming. In the circles around Scheler there was talk of a new birth of a 'Catholic ethos.'"[62]

The Catholic Academic Movement

An important intellectual aspect of the broader Catholic movement was the academic movement, which Przywara regarded, though in a thoroughly approving sense, as symptomatic of the "spiritual crisis of the present." This academic movement, which published Newman's works with Theatiner Verlag, grew up around Ildefons Herwegen,[63] the abbot of Maria Laach, and brought with it the self-assurance of a new *ver sacrum catholicum*,[64] or, to use another metaphor, the self-assurance of a "return from exile."[65] "How can we rescue," asks Przywara, "the spirit of those years in the ascendant, that blossoming springtide, and carry it into the gray everydayness that wraps itself inescapably around us?"[66] The Academics' Conference in August of 1923 in Ulm gives us a glimpse of the emerging feeling about Catholicism. Przywara, who gave the conference's three main lectures, drew on Guardini as an exponent of a new sort of Christian thinking. It is characteristic of the overall intellectual atmosphere of these pivotal years that two thinkers who were otherwise so different could arrive at similar con-

clusions about the polarity of "living-concreteness" *(Lebendig-Konkretes)*. Przywara attempted to bring out this tension in his focus on Thomas Aquinas and
Newman.

It was Przywara's insight at Ulm to make a connection between three movements of the 1920s: phenomenology, the liturgical movement, and the youth
movement.[67] Of course, he did not think that phenomenology was distinctly or
even primarily a Christian movement, but he characterized it as an unexpected
turn from a German philosophy that had been dominated by Kant to the old
philosophia perennis. He saw the appearance of Thomas Aquinas in the sphere of
phenomenology as indicative of an attempt to overcome the narrow Cartesian-
Kantian focus on the knowing subject with a threefold will: the will toward the
object, the will toward being *(Wesenheit)*, and the will toward God.[68]

Przywara saw the liturgical movement as containing a very special ethos, or,
as he termed it, a "psychogram": "Will to form as opposed to free-flowing life,
will to community as opposed to one-sided individualism, will to an intrinsi-
cally valuable *vita contemplativa* that rests in God as opposed to the functualiza-
tion of an excessive *vita activa*."[69] This is a direct allusion to Guardini's "primacy
of Logos over ethos" with its explicit will to form. Przywara was no doubt also
thinking of Stefan George's "priestly aristocracy" and suggesting a bridge from
the loneliness of George's elite to a vision of the will to form and the already established shape of Catholic liturgy. In the latter he saw "the tension of opposites and the infinite expanses of streaming life"[70] harnessed by a vigorous will
to form.

As far as the youth movement was concerned, Przywara was of the opinion
that a mere rejection of the ordinary and the desire for revolutionary change,
as had been evident in the early activities of the Free German Youth, had been
overcome. In contrast, he believed that he recognized three components in the
Catholic version of the youth movements that provided an antidote to a prevailing sickness of the German spirit: "It is the will to discover the individual
value of the person, as opposed to enslavement to the material values of profession and office. It is, second, the will to the free, inner growth of love, as opposed to purely external enslavement to that which is duty alone. It is, third and
finally, the will to such forms and laws as are the outward expression of the inner
being of life, as opposed to forms and laws for which life is merely an enslaved
'area of use' [*Anwendungsgebiet*]. Will to person, will to love, will to form of life
[*Lebensform*]."[71]

What becomes noticeable is a continued emphasis on the complementarity of
polarities, through which one posture of the soul counterbalances another. Przywara pleads for an overcoming of all antitheses through a "both and" philosophy,

a philosophy of dynamic polarity. "Not object or subject, being or becoming, person or form, nor a once-and-for-all-time static equilibration of these antitheses. No. Rather, the philosophy of an active ebbing and flowing between both poles, the philosophy of a dynamic 'unity of opposites,' the philosophy of a 'harmonious tension.'"[72] Thus Przywara ends in 1923 with a reconciliation between object and subject, exemplified for him in the teachings of Aquinas and Newman, which he portrays as the complementary poles of a doctrine of being and a doctrine of concrete historical becoming. He thus saw Aquinas and Newman as guarantors of a reconciliation of perspectives that degenerated into the extremes of integralism and modernism, extremes that gravely endangered the life of the church.[73]

The Conditions of Newman's Discovery

I cannot here go into the manifold theological developments of the 1920s, but I will say a bit about the developments within Catholicism at this time, when the two aforementioned contrary *(gegenläufig)* streams—the one drawing on Aquinas, the other on Newman—began to have an impact. Przywara played a significant role in both currents, and in both he drew with him Edith Stein.

Catholic theology in the nineteenth and early twentieth centuries was deeply indebted to neoscholasticism, in which systematic analysis and rational investigation of the truths of faith set the tone and made theology a matter of "science" rather than "popular piety." At the same time, but opposed to this, the historical critical method, following the French exegete Alfred Loisy,[74] began scientifically to historicize Scripture and tradition. The intense repercussions of this method led to the crisis of modernism, the effects of which could be felt well into the 1920s.[75] It was precisely the latter movement that neoscholasticism was intended to bring under control. The Thomistic renaissance of those days was sealed by Pius XI's 1923 encyclical *Studiorum ducem,* but it was also rooted in a new awareness of the philosophical inheritance of the Middle Ages. This awareness had a theological as much as a philosophical background: since the end of the nineteenth century, Thomism had offered a superb resource of argumentation for Catholic schools of theology, especially as it contrasted with contemporary philosophy, which was dominated principally by the Kantian questions about the possibility of knowledge, as well as Schopenhauer's and Nietzsche's biting critique of religion. Neoscholastic and neo-Thomistic, Catholic theology had, as it were, a life of its own apart from the mainstream of philosophical thought. Psychologism, historicism, and neo-Kantianism had taken skeptical, subjectivist positions and had dismissed the question of being in favor of primarily knowledge-oriented questions. As serious and urgent as neoscholastic studies were, because of their ontological starting point and the metaphysic erected upon it, and because of their resistance to "modernist" currents, they became associated with confessional defense.

With phenomenology, however, a new, albeit revised, form of ontological questioning had reentered philosophy, which, especially at first, promised a mode of thinking that proceeded through and beyond Kant and that applied a skeptical approach to skeptical positions. In his essay *Philosophie als strenge Wissenschaft (Philosophy as Rigorous Science)* (1911), Husserl had demonstrated that psychologism and historicism, with their claims to be able to attain only relative knowledge, were self-refuting.

Thus in a unique and unexpected way the separate strands of Catholic philosophy and mainstream academic philosophy, i.e., phenomenology, were conjoined. Edith Stein's aforementioned translation of Thomas had as its goal that "this attempt to reproduce [his] system in the philosophical language of our time could be useful for interacting with modern philosophical thinking."[76] Instinctively at ease in Thomism, although certainly not completely at home in it, as she continually stressed, Stein thought that a genuine philosophical contact between the thirteenth and twentieth centuries was possible. Well-known critics like Koyré, Naber, and Dempf affirmed the success of the undertaking. Przywara did so most memorably: "Because of the nature of translation itself, everything today has become living philosophy. Thomas and Thomas alone is everywhere, but in such a way that he stands eye to eye with Husserl, Scheler, and Heidegger. The terminology of phenomenology, which Stein masters as a creative philosopher in her own right, has nowhere taken the place of Aquinas's, but with it, doors now open back and forth all the more effortlessly."[77]

The opposite "pole" of new theological developments, namely that rooted in Newman, was the *Jahrbuch der deutschen Katholiken (Yearbook of German Catholics)* (1920–21). In it, Guardini takes to task an essay by Friedrich Heiler, "Wesen des Katholizismus" (The Essence of Catholicism) from 1920. His answer to Heiler's historicism is clearly inspired by Newman: the mechanistic view of the church cannot be upheld in light of the idea of the church as a living whole in its identity of form from beginning to end. Not the parts but rather an organic development forms the living shape of the church. The modernistic opposition, which Heiler reiterates, between nature and supernature and between revelation and history is answered using arguments very much in line with Newman: "With all this, no harm is done to the supernatural and definitiveness of Christianity. The content, the seed, revelation, and grace are from God; so are the line of development, the logic of selection, and the law of construction;

history, however, offers plenty of material and the spur that causes certain already germinating potentialities to blossom."[78]

Przywara, too, defended Newman faithfully against the suspicion of modernism and ranked him alongside Thomas Aquinas, in the sense of Przywara's favorite concept of the "basic law" *(Grundgesetz)* of Catholicity:[79] "In the unity of Thomas and Newman there lies, as if symbolized in their two persons, Catholicism's mission for philosophy: I tell you, get up!"[80] Newman thus gave German Catholics of the 1920s a phraseology with which they could accept the challenges of a culturally Protestant modern age. What was so compelling about Newman was his unification of a naturally cultivated habitus with grace (rather than an unworldly holiness on the one hand or a relativizing skepticism on the other). In the noticeably rapid translation of Newman's work into German in the early twentieth century, one can tell something about the emerging intellectual climate: the "church father of the nineteenth century" stood as an exciting alternative to contemporary neo-Thomism. Among Newman's contributions were his biblical-anthropological personalism, his anchoring of revelation in the church, which he conceived with respect to historical development, the insight that the community of believers is a mystery and also a socially effective entity, and the forging of an intellectually responsible position that included the rational defense of Christian religious beliefs, showing Catholicism a path out of the narrow apologetic defensiveness, and the acceptance of the challenge of historicism, which excluded equally fideism and modernism.

Edith Stein represented a kindred type of mature faith. Newman's relentless dedication to truth constituted his life endeavor, even though it had the potential to lead into unintended territory, and found forceful expression in his pre-conversion texts. The fifteen-year-old Newman's life goals had been shaped decisively by the "old Calvinist" Thomas Scott in his book *The Force of Truth*. "My wish was to have truth as my closest friend and no other enemy than falsehood," said Newman in 1837. Or, as he said in 1845 in *An Essay on the Development of Christian Doctrine:* "[T]he human mind is subject to truth and not vice versa; that it is required to approach her in humility, rather than clothed in high and mighty talk; that truth and falsehood are offered as tests for our heart." Stein was characterized by a similar persistence; truth was the object that consumed her philosophical and religious life as well. A great and unforgettable statement testifies to this: "My longing for truth was my single prayer."[81] As one might have guessed, this is where the "conversation" between Stein and Newman takes place, and in this regard Newman's influence on the contours of Germany in the 1920s was indeed more profound than previously assumed. It reverberates in Stein's insightful declaration that "[t]he path leads from faith to seeing, not the other way around."[82] Here, once again, the wisdom of Newman is reflected: "*Ex umbris et imaginibus ad veritatem*" (Out of the shadows and images to the truth).

NOTES

This essay was first published in German with the title "'Sein ganzes Leben ist nur ein Suchen nach der religiösen Wahrheit gewesen.' Edith Stein im Gespräch mit John Henry Newman. Einführung," in Edith Stein, *Übersetzung von John Henry Newman, Briefe und Texte zur ersten Lebenshälfte*, vol. 22 of *Edith Stein Gesamtausgabe* (hereafter referred to as *ESGA*) (Freiburg: Herder, 2002), ix–xxvii.

    1. "Gogo" von Hildebrand, as he was called in Göttingen phenomenology circles, originally studied in Munich under Theodor Lipps and Alexander Pfänder before switching to Göttingen, where he studied under Husserl and graduated in 1912. It was in Göttingen that Stein got to know him. Hildebrand emigrated to the United States in 1933.

    2. Edith Stein, *Aus dem Leben einer jüdischen Familie und weitere autobiographische Beiträge*, *ESGA* 1 (Freiburg: Herder, 2002), 330.

    3. Erich Przywara, "Die Frage Edith Stein," in *In und Gegen* (Nuremberg: Glock und Lutz, 1955), 61.

    4. Edith Stein wrote to Ingarden on January 13, 1930: "Theatiner Verlag ceased to exist a long time ago." *Selbstbildnis in Briefen III: Briefe an Roman Ingarden*, *ESGA* 4 (Freiburg: Herder, 2001), 132.

    5. *Mädchenbildung auf christlicher Grundlage* 24 (1932): 690–95. Stein praised Hildebrand's introduction to the Reinach anthology in *Selbstbildnis in Briefen III*, letter 45, and praised his *Habilitationsschrift* "Sittlichkeit und ethische Werterkenntnis" (*Jahrbuch für Philosophie und phänomenologische Forschung* 5 [1922]), in *Selbstbildnis in Briefen III*, letters 52 and 80.

    6. Unfortunately, only a negligible portion of the correspondence is extant (Edith Stein, *Selbstbildnis in Briefen I (1916–1933)*, *ESGA* 2 [Freiburg: Herder, 2000], letters 160 and 218 from Przywara). See also n. 5 to Stein's letter 153, August 8, 1933, to Agnella Stadtmüller, in *Selbstbildnis in Briefen III:* "There [in Munich on April 3, 1932] Edith Stein also met Alois Mager, OSB, Erich Przywara, SJ, and probably Gertrud von le Fort as well." Thereafter, one finds only a few references to Przywara's sickness in Stein's letters, such as letter 735, April 10, 1942, to Hilde Borsinger (Edith Stein, *Selbstbildnis in Briefen II [1933–1942]*, *ESGA* 3 [Freiburg: Herder, 2000]).

    7. Erich Przywara, preface to *Analogia entis* (Munich: Kösel, 1932), vi.

    8. *Selbstbildnis in Briefen I*, letter 218, September 13, 1932.

    9. See Joachim Feldes's thorough researches on Edith Stein and her spiritual mentor Joseph Schwind in Feldes, *Edith Stein und Schifferstadt* (Schifferstadt: Geier-Druck, 1998), 9–27. Additional information can be found in Maria Adele Herrmann, "Wissenschaft als Gottesdienst," chap. 7 of *Die Speyerer Jahre von Edith Stein: Aufzeichnungen zu ihrem 100. Geburtstag* (Speyer: Pilger, 1990), 105 ff.

    10. Erich Przywara, "Edith Stein: Zur ihrem zehnten Todestag," in *In und Gegen*, 61 ff.

11. The deep impression that Beuron's liturgy made on Stein and her continued spiritual accompaniment, from 1928 onward, by Arch-Abbot Raphael Walzer can be traced back to suggestions made by Przywara.

12. See F. Imle, *Christusideal und katholisches Ordensleben* (Kempten: Kösel, 1922); Germain Morin, OSB, *Mönchtum und die Urkirche* (Munich: Kösel, 1922); Jean de Hemptinne, OSB, *Mehr Liebe* (Freiburg: Herder, 1922); Dietrich von Hildebrand, *Der Geist des heiligen Franziskus und der dritte Orden* (Munich: Kösel, 1921); Peter Lippert, SJ, *Zur Psychologie des Jesuitenordens* (Kempten: Kösel, 1923). These books are mentioned in Erich Przywara, "Religiöse Bewegungen," in *Ringen der Gegenwart*, 2 vols. (Augsburg: Benno Filser, 1929), 1:11 ff.

13. Stein writes to Ingarden on August 8, 1925: "I have just quickly finished the volume of Newman, which I had taken on, and have recently begun to study Thomas Aquinas's central philosophical work." Letter 89, in *Selbstbildnis in Briefen III.*

14. Stein's translation of *Quaestiones disputatae de veritate* was first published in 2 volumes (Breslau: Otto Borgmeyer, 1932–34); later it was published as *Des hl. Thomas von Aquino Untersuchungen über die Wahrheit (Quæstiones disputatae de veritate)*, vols. 3 and 4 of *Edith Steins Werke* (Louvain: Nauwelaerts, 1952, 1955), and soon it will be published as *Thomas von Aquin, De Veritate I* and *Thomas von Aquin, De Veritate II und weitere Übersetzungen*, ESGA 23 and 24 (Freiburg: Herder, probably 2007). Stein's translation of *De ente et essentia* will be published for the first time in ESGA 24. Her translation of Newman's *The Idea of a University* has recently been published as *Übersetzung von John Henry Newman, Die Idee der Universität*, ed. Hanna-Barbara Gerl-Falkovitz, ESGA 21 (Freiburg: Herder, 2004).

15. Printed by Bouvier in Bonn in 1923 and then by the WBG in Darmstadt in 1971.

16. Stein to Ingarden, September 30, 1922, no. 83, *Selbstbildnis in Briefen III.*

17. Edith Stein, *Wege der Gotteserkenntnis: Studie zu Dionysius Areopagita*, ESGA 17 (Freiburg: Herder, 2003).

18. Edith Stein, *Geistliche Texte I*, ESGA 19 (Freiburg: Herder, 2005).

19. John Henry Newman, *Christentum: Ein Aufbau*, 8 vols. (Freiburg: Herder, 1922).

20. John Henry Newman, "I. Belief in God. II. Belief in the Holy Trinity," trans. Theodor Haecker, in *Der Brenner* 6 (1920); *Essay in Aid of a Grammar of Assent*, trans. and postscript by Theodor Haecker (Munich: Kösel, 1921); *An Essay on the Development of Christian Doctrine*, trans. and postscript by Theodor Haecker (Munich: Kösel, 1922); "A New Form of Unbelief," trans. Theodor Haecker in *Der Brenner* 8 (1923).

21. See Rudolf Kassner, preface to John Henry Newman, *Apologie des Katholizismus* (Munich: Drei Masken, 1920).

22. John Henry Newman, *Verlust und Gewinn: Die Geschichte eines Konvertiten*, trans. Ignatia Breme (Bonn, 1928).

23. Romano Guardini, "Maria Knoepfler zum Gedächtnis," in John Henry Cardinal Newman, *Briefe aus der katholischen Zeit seines Lebens*, trans. Maria Knoepfler, *Ausgewählte Werke* 10 (Mainz: Grünewald, 1931), 374.

24. Przywara, "Die Frage Edith Stein," 61.

25. Alfons Knoll, "'In Officio Caritas': Leben und Werk der Newman-Übersetzerin Maria Knoepfler (1881–1927) 75 Jahre nach ihrem Tod,'" in Hanna-Barbara Gerl-Falkovitz, *"Herz spricht zum Herzen": John Henry Newman (1801–1890) in seiner Bedeutung für das deutsche Christentum* (Annweiler: Plöger, 2002), 71–128. The following quotations are

a result of my own researches in the Mooshausen Archive and draw from the unpublished letter exchange between Guardini and Weiger. Thanks to Alfons Knoll for helpful suggestions.

26. See Hanna-Barbara Gerl, Elisabeth Prégarier, and Annette Wolf, eds., *Begegnungen in Mooshausen, Romano Guardini, Maria Knoepfler, Maria Elisabeth Stapp, Josef Weiger* (Weißenhorn: A. H. Konrad, 1990).

27. John Henry Newman, *Ausgewählte Predigten auf alle Sonntage des Kirchenjahres und für die Feste des Herrn*, trans. Guido Maria Dreves (Kempten: Kösel, 1907).

28. Guardini writes to Weiger on August 27, 1916: "I like your plan to translate Newman's Oxford sermons very much. Think about it when the time is appropriate" (Mooshausen Archive, 1r).

29. Guardini, "Maria Knoepfler," 373.

30. Guardini writes to Weiger on May 10, 1914: "I wrote to D. Maria in the copy of Newman from his first Meditation: "May . . . that . . . is the month of *promise* and *hope*" (letter from the Mooshausen Archive, 2v; the copy of the Meditations that was originally dedicated to Knoepfler can also be found there).

31. Guardini writes to Weiger on March 28, 1915: "Today we received the finished portion of the *Apologia* that we had started. The translation is very beautiful. Newman would be delighted" (Mooshausen Archive, 1).

32. Guardini writes to Weiger on March 10, 1915: "D. M. seems to be losing courage on the *Apologia*, since Laros is wising up and translating more literally toward the middle and end. For Heaven's sake—her translations are as good as any! By the way, I am very sympathetic to the idea of publishing the translation with Reclam (in the event that Diederichs does not accept it). True, this will mean the edition will be very modest, but nevertheless it will be published with Reclam, and that means it will be for her translation that everyone will automatically reach, especially those who don't have that much money" (Mooshausen Archive, 2v).

33. There is a typescript in the Mooshausen Archive with corrections: "Autobiographische Aufzeichnungen," paginated 17–114, and a cover with the title *Anglikanische Briefe*, which are heavily corrected in Knoepfler's handwriting. The pagination is partially crossed through. Apparently, the pages remain unordered and regrettably also lack appropriate dating.

34. R. Guardini, "Sein Wesen prägte der 'Commonsense': Zu einer neuen Auswahl von Newmans Werken," [review of *John Henry Newman*, ed. Walter Lipgens (Frankfurt: Fischer, 1958)], *Allgemeine Sonntagszeitung* 31 (1958): 5.

35. Cf. Hanna-Barbara Gerl-Falkovitz, "Newman-Rezeption in den 20er Jahren in Deutschland: Edith Stein im Umkreis von Maria Knoepfler, Romano Guardini, und Erich Przywara," *IkZ Communio* 5 (2001): 434–49.

36. R. Guardini to Richard Knies, April 29, 1919 (Nachlaß Richard Knies, Diözesanarchiv Mainz).

37. Edith Stein, "Probleme der neueren Mädchenbildung" (1932), in *Die Frau: Fragestellungen und Reflexionen*, ed. Sophie Binggeli and Maria Amata Neyer, *ESGA* 13 (Freiburg: Herder, 2000), 158, with reference to R. Guardini, *Der Gegensatz: Versuche zu einer Philosophie des Lebendig-Konkreten* (Mainz: Grünewald, 1925).

38. The reviews can be found in Przywara, *Ringen der Gegenwart*. Guardini seems not to have responded to the reviews.

39. See Newman, *Die Idee der Universität.*

40. Stein read the proofs in 1927. See letter 59 to Callista Kopf, October 12, 1927, in *Selbstbildnis in Briefen I,* 84. Letter 63 to Fritz Kaufmann, in *Selbstbildnis in Briefen I,* 89, reports the publication of the work.

41. Stein became acquainted with Daniel Feuling, OSB (1882–1947), a monk at the arch-abbey in Beuron, through a phenomenology meeting in Juvisy, Paris, between September 10 and 12, 1932 (on the invitation of Jacques Maritain), in which they both participated. See *Selbstbildnis in Briefen I,* letter 217, n. 4.

42. Paul Simon (1882–1946), vicar of Paderborn cathedral, a close friend of Bernhard Rosenmöller (1883–1974), who was a philosophical colleague of Stein's at the Deutsche Akademie für wissenschaftliche Pädagogik (German Academy for Scientific Pedagogy) in Münster and who also participated in the conference at Juvisy. Simon was an important figure in the ecumenical movement. He was responsible with Stählin for the first official gathering of Catholic and Protestant theologians in Berlin. With Simon's cooperation, conversations with Karl Barth, who taught in Münster between 1925 and 1930, took place at Rosenmöller's house. Cf. Bernhard Rosenmöller Jr., "Bernhard Rosenmöller: Widerstand aus dem geistigen Erbe des Heiligen Augustin," in *Christlicher Widerstand im Dritten Reich,* ed. Hans Günter Hockerts and Hans Maier (Annweiler: Plöger, 2003).

43. A comparison of the German and English texts shows the following noteworthy passages (the page numbers refer to Edith Stein, *Übersetzung von John Henry Newman: Briefe und Texte zur ersten Lebenshälfte (1801–1846),* ESGA 22 [Freiburg: Herder, 2002]: p. 233, *persuaded*—"überrascht" (instead of "überredet"); p. 260, *moral*—"geistig" (instead of "moralisch"); p. 246, *items*—remains untranslated; p. 267, *Coleridge's . . . consideration*—"Coleridge's Bedeutung" (instead of "Überlegung", "Mitsorge"); p. 275, *It is the fear that there is some secret undetected fault, which is the cause of my belief which keeps me there, waiting*—"Gerade die Furcht vor einem geheimen, unentdeckten Fehler erzeugt ja den Glauben in mir, der mich wartend da festhält, wo ich bin" (instead of "Gerade die Furcht vor einem geheimen, unentdeckten Fehler ist ja der Grund für meine Vermutung, die mich warten läßt"); p. 282, *All is against me—may he not add himself as an adversary?*—"Alles ist wider mich—möge er nicht zu den Gegnern hinzukommen!" (instead of "—kann er sich nicht auch noch als Gegner hinzustellen?); p. 283, *persuasions*—"Erinnerungen" (instead of "Überredungen"); p. 292: *All this is quite consistent with believing, as I firmly do and consistent too, with thinking it highly unjudicious*—"all dies ist ganz vereinbar mit dem Glauben, von dem ich fest durchdrungen bin und auch damit vereinbar, daß man es für höchst unklug hält (instead of "und auch damit vereinbar, daß ich es für höchst unklug halte"); p. 292: *But it must be put on the ground of discretion*—"Doch muß es auf den Boden der Vernunft gestellt werden" (instead of "Doch es muß auf den Boden der Unterscheidung gestellt werden").

44. Stein, *Selbstbildnis in Briefen III,* 85.

45. [Edith Stein], "Praelat Joseph Schwind," *Korrespondenzblatt des Priestergebetsvereins im theologischen Konvikte zu Innsbruck* 62 (1927): 8, quoted in Feldes, *Edith Stein und Schifferstadt,* 9.

46. Quotation from *Letters and Correspondence of John Henry Newman during His Life in the English Church, with a Brief Autobiography,* ed. Anne Mozley (London: Longmans, Green, & Co., 1903), 2:411.

47. Theo Gunkel, a member of the famous and (in the German-speaking world) leading Oratory in Leipzig, wrote a review of Stein's and Knoepfler's translations of the Newman letters: "Bücher und Bilder zu John Henry Newman," *Die Schildgenossen* 10 (1930): 566–68. Regrettably, he concerned himself not with the style and quality of the translations but only with their content.

48. Bernhard Gertz, *Glaubenswelt als Analogie: Die theologische Analogie-Lehre Erich Przywaras und ihr Ort in der Auseinandersetzung um die analogia fidei* (Düsseldorf: Patmos, 1969), 573.

49. Karl-Heinz Wiesemann, *Zerspringender Akkord: Das Zusammenspiel von Theologie und Mystik bei Karl Adam, Romano Guardini und Erich Przywara als theologische Fuge* (Würzburg: Echter, 2000).

50. G. Wilhelmy, "Vita Erich Przywara," in *Erich Przywara, 1889–1969: Eine Festgabe* (Düsseldorf: Patmos, 1969).

51. In a review "Zum Kampf um den kath. Lehrer" [The Struggle around the Catholic Teacher] (1929), Stein writes: "Anyone wanting a comprehensive and vivid picture of all these movements should refer to the collected essays of Erich Przywara, SJ, which have been published this year with B. Filser in Augsburg under the title 'Ringen der Gegenwart.'" Edith Stein, *Bildung und Entfaltung der Individualität*, ESGA 16 (Freiburg: Herder, 2001), appendix.

52. Przywara, "Neue Religiosität," in *Ringen der Gegenwart* 1:48.

53. Przywara, preface to *Ringen der Gegenwart*, vii.

54. Friederike Görres, *Der Geopferte: Ein anderer Blick auf John Henry Newman* (Vallendar: Patris, 2004), 216.

55. Cf. F. Lelotte, ed., *Heimkehr zur Kirche: Konvertiten des 20. Jahrhunderts* (Munich: Kösel, 1956), and E. Reinhard's contemporaneous *Der Siegeszug der Katholischen Kirche: Die Konversionsbewegung in Deutschland in den letzten 100 Jahren* (Dortmund, 1920), as well as Przywara, "Konvertiten," in *Ringen der Gegenwart*, 1:146–54.

56. Cf. Przywara's discussion, *Ringen der Gegenwart*, 246 ff. It is noteworthy that in England Byzantium was praised as a transcendent, atemporal culture as well, as, for example, in Yeats's poems "Sailing to Byzantium" (1926) and "Byzantium" (1930). See Ulrich Schneider, "Yeats' Byzanz-Bild im Kontext seiner Zeit," *Anglia: Zeitschrift für englische Philologie* 95, nos. 3–4 (1977): 426–49.

57. See Walter Warnach, "Rilke und das Christentum," *Hochland* 6 (1950): 417–39.

58. See, among other works, Scheler's "Zur religiösen Erneuerung," *Hochland* 16 (1918–19): 5–21, later published as part of *Vom Ewigen im Menschen* (Leipzig: Neuer Geist-Verlag, 1921), and *Deutschlands Sendung und der katholische Gedanke* (Berlin: Aktien-Gesellschaft für Verlag und Druckerei, 1918).

59. In his 1925 article "Geist und Leben," Theodor Haecker characterized Scheler's inner turmoil and incomprehensible ambiguity harshly but appropriately: "Scheler is one of the more tragic figures of more recent intellectual history, widely known for his great gifts and works, some of which inherently merit and will retain the fame of, and give comfort to, a defeated and unjustly—beyond all measure—humiliated people. He is a tragic figure because at one moment he reached for the Highest and it appeared as if he had grasped it, only to let it fall from his hand in the next. But this is certainly not the case. Indeed, I never took him to be a Christian philosopher, not even when he was considered a Catholic and even to a certain extent considered an intellectual leader among

Catholics. For I never found in him what a good many Protestants nonetheless do have, what belongs to Christians, and therefore essentially belongs to Catholics: faith, the obedience of faith, the unconditional acceptance of revelation, [I] never sensed in him a hidden, invisible life of grace, never a trace of a prayer life. However, to an astounding degree, we find in him a 'natural' acceptance of a great, wide, and world-encompassing reason in the Catholic spirit, and *prima facie* a great similarity between Catholic thought and teaching and a hierarchically structured system of values, which he discovered with the gifts of natural intellect. Thus it appears as if again the nearly impossible case were the case: as if nature from its side did not completely comprehend the supernatural but came so close to it, and was so directed towards it, that nature could assume the supernatural as if there were no essential difference between them and without the intellectual and spiritual struggle that otherwise occurs. But this is certainly not the case any more. Unashamedly and almost brutally, Scheler approaches Creator and world, uncovers them and simply lays them bare: Ecce Deus!" In Theodor Haecker, *Christentum und Kultur* (Munich: J. Kösel & F. Pustet, 1927), 240 ff.

60. Victor Conzemius, "Eine komplexe Freundshaft: Charles Journet und Jacques Maritain im Briefwechsel," *Neue Zürcher Zeitung*, June 24–25, 2000, 53.

61. K. Heim, *Das Wesen des evangelischen Christentums* (Leipzig, 1925), 6, quoted in Alfons Knoll, *Glaube und Kultur bei Romano Guardini* (Paderborn: Schöningh, 1993), 48.

62. Przywara, "Custos, 'quid de nocte?'" in *Ringen der Gegenwart*, 1:37.

63. Ildefons Herwegen, *Lumen Christi: Gesammelte Aufsätze* (Munich, 1924).

64. On this expression, see Knoll, *Glaube und Kultur*, 57.

65. Peter Wust, "Die Rückkehr des deutschen Katholizismus aus dem Exil," in *Die Rückkehr aus dem Exil*, ed. Karl Hoeber (Düsseldorf: Schwann, 1926).

66. Erich Przywara, "Katholisches Schweig en," in *Ringen der Gegenwart*, 1:86.

67. Erich Przywara, *Gottgeheimnis der Welt: Drei Vorträge über die geistige Krisis der Gegenwart* (Munich: Oratorium, 1923), 9 (reprinted in Przywara, *Religionsphilosophische Schriften* (Einsiedeln: Johannes, 1962), 2:123–372.

68. Przywara, *Gottesgeheimnis der Welt*, 11.

69. Ibid., 32.

70. Ibid., 38.

71. Ibid., 48 ff.

72. Ibid., 137 ff.

73. Ibid.

74. Alfred Loisy, *L'Évangile et l'Église* (Paris: Picard, 1902).

75. Cf. Knoll, *Glaube und Kultur*, 48–51.

76. Stein, preface to *Endliches und ewiges Sein* (1935–36), in *Endliches und ewiges Sein I, ESGA* 11 (Freiburg: Herder, probably 2007).

77. Erich Przywara, "Rezension von E. Stein, Des hl. Thomas von Aquino Untersuchungen über die Wahrheit," *Stimmen der Zeit* 121, no. 11 (1931).

78. R. Guardini, "Universalität und Synkretismus," in *Jahrbuch der deutschen Katholiken 1920–21* (Augsburg, 1921), 154 ff.

79. See Przywara's extensive "Kant—Newman—Thomas," chap. 6 of *Ringen der Gegenwart*, 2:729–962.

80. Przywara, "Sendung," in *Ringen der Gegenwart*, 2:962.

81. Quoted in Theresia Renata Posselt, *Edith Stein. Eine große Frau unseres Jahrhunderts. Lebensbild einer Philosophin und Karmelitin* (Nuremberg: Glock und Lutz, 1954), 75.

82. Stein to Ingarden, November 20, 1927, in *Briefe an Roman Ingarden,* letter 117. Müller and Neyer make the careful observation that Stein's term for religious experience in this letter is similar to Newman's "proof of probability" for God in *Grammar of Assent.* See Andreas Uwe Müller and Maria Amata Neyer, *Edith Stein: Das Leben einer ungewöhnlichen Frau* (Zurich: Benziger, 1998), 171.

The German-Jewish Symbiosis in Flux
Edith Stein's Complex National/Ethnic Identity

JOYCE AVRECH BERKMAN

I would not want them to become totally alienated from their homeland.
Edith Stein to her brother-in-law,
Hans Biberstein, November 17, 1939

During the "turnip winter" of World War I, when the most efficiently organized continental war economies could not prevent wide-scale hunger, Edith Stein wrote to her close friend Roman Ingarden, the Polish philosopher, "I am very happy that your understanding of 'German-ness' is progressing. You are 'in love with the Polish soul'—that was the precise phrase that occurred to me also, as I sought recently to clarify what is essentially different in our approach to the State and to the People. You see, I can no more be in love with Germany than with myself for, after all, I am myself it, that is, a part of it." Stein proceeds to describe a *Volk* (a people) as a whole that is greater than its parts: "It is a life beyond our own, although it includes ours." Likening a *Volk* to an organism, she equates individuals with cells, but cells that can become conscious of their relationship with the whole, and that self-awareness she calls national consciousness.[1]

Stein's sense that "I am myself it" never diminished, even at the height of Nazi persecution of Jews. Although throughout her life she voiced sharp criticisms of the German state and in the 1930s lambasted Hitler and Nazism, she remained deeply, one may say inextricably, attached to Germany and the German people.

As late as November 17, 1939, with World War II tumultuously underway, Stein, by then a nun at the Carmelite convent in Echt, Holland, where she had fled in the face of escalating anti-Semitism in Germany, urged her brother-in-law, Hans Biberstein, who had emigrated to New York, not to let his children "become totally alienated from their homeland."[2]

Stein's identification with her homeland, her *Deutschtum* (Germanness), raises striking questions. In 1916 Stein declared in her curriculum vitae that accompanied her completed doctoral dissertation, "I am a Prussian citizen and a Jewess."[3] Despite her conversion in 1922 to Roman Catholicism, she remained throughout her life proud of her Germanness and Jewishness. Her presentation of her Germanness is characteristically complicated: many-sided, having both unusual and relatively common features, and occasionally inconsistent and confused. None of her criticisms of German and Jewish culture exhibited Jewish self-hatred. Whatever the object of her criticism, Stein aimed to be fair, frank, and objective.

Among key questions that spring to mind: What did her Germanness and Jewishness mean to Stein during successive phases of her life, and how did she express any shifts in perspective? Did Stein's femaleness and social class position inflect her national and ethnic identity in illuminating ways? Did the unusual features of her personality and life experience shape her German-Jewish identity? How did Stein reconcile her national and ethnic loyalties? How do her life and thought contribute to the immense body of disputatious scholarship on German Jews' national consciousness and the reality of a "German-Jewish symbiosis" before and after Nazi ascendancy? Do we find a harmonious melding or "a reciprocal instability of Jewish and German identity"?[4]

Stein's distinctive German and Jewish hybridity is best understood by separately analyzing each of her allegiances, placing her identity formation within an historical framework, and incorporating the ways in which her phenomenological outlook and her femaleness modulate and reconstellate each. Of course, the general issue of personal identity formation, and of national and ethnic identity formation in particular, has inspired much scholarship in recent decades. In accord with many contemporary scholars, I view a person's identity as protean and relational to other persons and groups and to diverse ways of understanding human differences and as constructed in available modes of discourse and within specific historical contexts. Individuals forge a viable sense of self from a chaotically shifting assembly of conflicting roles, experiences, and affiliations. Leaving open the question that absorbed Stein and many other intellectuals concerning an identity essence that marks a person's singularity from birth, I prefer to examine the ways historical realities, as experienced and conceptualized by individuals, form, direct, and determine motives, choices, and possibilities for self-realization.

Stein's Germanness

Although Stein's philosophical treatises on community and on the state present her ideas about national identity and consciousness in the abstract, the richest source for understanding how she viewed her German identity is her autobiography. Despite being a retrospective account subject to the vagaries of memory and dramatic changes in Stein's perceptions of herself, her society, and her world, *Aus dem Leben einer Jüdischen Familie (Life in a Jewish Family, 1891–1916: Her Unfinished Autobiographical Account)* remains a fertile source for gaining insight into Stein's experience and values. Begun in 1933 after Hitler's Aryan Laws had ejected Stein from her faculty position at the German Institute for Scientific Pedagogy, her autobiography testifies repeatedly to her own and her family's staunch devotion to their native land. Stein's expressions of family and personal patriotism were aimed at dramatizing to her readers the injustice of the Nazi refusal to view Jews as loyal and true Germans. She noted, for example, that during the post–World War I plebiscite that ceded part of Silesia to Poland, Stein's mother's entire family antagonized the Poles by their decisive pro-German partisanship. "More than fifty descendants of the Courant family who had been born in Lublinitz returned for the voting," Stein reported. ". . . The sad event after so much strain and effort was the more painful: Lublinitz became Polish." Stein added that her "relatives could not and would not think of remaining there [in Lublinitz]; they sold the family seat and left their homeland."[5] Various relatives moved to German sections of Silesia and to Berlin. Focusing on her mother's German pride, Stein's clincher is that her mother's wedding song was set to the popular patriotic melody of "Es braust ein Ruf wie Donnerhall" (Tumult and Cry Like the Thunder's Roll), written ca. 1840 to champion Germany against French challenges to the boundary of the Rhine.[6]

In the autobiography, Stein glides seamlessly back and forth between the beauty of Germany's landscape and the greatness of its cultural heritage. Like many German young people, Stein spent much of her leisure time hiking and mountain climbing. Later, when studying at the University of Breslau, she, her sister Erna, and their friends climbed the Sudetan mountains, most often the Riesenbirge, where Stein enjoyed both winter and summer sports. She also recounts climbing the Hartz Mountains near Göttingen, the Thuringian mountains near Weimar, and, during World War I, the Hegaür mountains, "rising like crests of foam" near Feldberg. She delights in evoking the cultural and historical associations of the landscapes and cityscapes that she describes: "It was wonderful to climb the mountain in the evening, to wander about in the ancient castle [*Hohentwiel*], to think of Ekkehart and of Schiller's youth, here where many a captive once languished in the fortress."[7] When she climbs the two hilltops (*Gleichen*) overlooking Göttingen, she exults in the "lovely landscape . . . carefully husbanded fields" and imagines "a wedding procession to emerge from the woods on the opposite hill, just as Ludwig Richter depicted in one of his paintings."[8] As she walks Göttingen's streets, she revels in the commemorative plaques on nearly every one of the older houses: "They told of famous persons who had formerly lived there . . . the Brothers Grimm, the physicists Gauss and Weber . . . . I thought that [Heine], too, had at one time been seated on these benches."[9]

In her mingling of landscape and culture, Stein placed greater emphasis upon culture, what in her 1920s treatise on community she called the "value world," as formative in a person's sense of identity.[10] Stein's reverence for German culture sprang from both her informal education at home and her formal schooling. In both settings, Stein read widely. Stein and her family were linguistically fluent Germans. Unlike Eastern European Jews whose natal language was Yiddish, German Jews identified from birth with the language of their nation. Stein's immediate and extended family encouraged her passion for German literature and art. She became familiar with Germany's vibrant literary and philosophical traditions—the diverse works of Lessing, Goethe, Schiller, Schlegel, Hebbel, Schopenhauer, Kant, Herder, Heine, and Nietzsche—as well as the brilliant historical writing of Leopold von Ranke. She admits that classical theater gripped her even more than reading, as evidenced most resoundingly by her passion for Grillparzer's *Jewess of Toledo,* Hebbel's *Agnes Bernauer, Judith,* and *Herod and Marianne,* and Lessing's *Nathan the Wise.*[11]

German composers no less exhilarated her. She rejoiced in her hours at the piano, often with her cousins in four-handed playing of Beethoven symphonies. Among German composers she was most moved by Bach's "world of purity and strict regularity."[12] Stein attended every single performance of the 1911 Bach Festival in Breslau. During her years at the gymnasium, theater and opera captivated her. When she heard *The Magic Flute* she bought the piano score and "soon knew it by heart"; so, too, with *Fidelio,* her favorite opera.[13] She also saw Wagnerian opera performed and "found it impossible wholly to evade its magic. Still I repudiated this music, with the sole exception of *Die Meistersinger.*"[14]

While her informal and formal education shaped Stein's pride in German culture, the sheer fact of her opportunity to pursue higher education fed her national devotion and identity. Grateful to the state "which had granted me

academic citizenship with its free access to the wisdom of mankind," she detailed
the impact of her academic privilege: "I regarded all the small benefits to which
our student pass entitled us, such as reduced prices for theatre and concert tick-
ets and the like, as the loving providence of the state for its favored children."[15]

Although in her autobiography and earlier 1920s philosophical treatises she
stressed that the state is not the nation—acknowledging, in fact, that a pernicious state government can betray the national spirit—Stein's sense of Germanness involved feelings of loyalty to Prussia and the German Reich. When she encountered an Anglophile history professor, she "became more conscious . . . of
the virtues of the Prussian character; and I was confirmed in my own Prussian
allegiance."[16] She did not specify the Prussian virtues she reified, but she insisted
that an individual's social responsibility to all members of the nation, an ethos of
citizen mutuality, was one of those virtues. In effect, Stein was exalting what historians have described as Germany's pride in their *Sonderweg,* their alternative
to Anglo-American understanding of the roots of freedom.[17] At a time when
British and American liberals opposed state intervention for the well-being of
its citizens, Germany was pioneering Europe's first social welfare legislation, ex-
emplifying the progressive potential of a positive, activist state. These were state
policies that Stein esteemed and that England and the United States would emulate decades later.

At the time of Edith Stein's birth, the German Reich was akin to the three
little pigs' straw-and-wood houses, a patchy, fragile, cobbled reality. Germany had
not become a nation state until 1871, and despite the 1871 consolidation of the
German Reich many Germans maintained a primary political loyalty to their
residential territory or city. The Reich was a hodgepodge of disparate and conflicting political forms and territorial languages. Still into the twentieth century
the question of German political identity and cohesion remained perplexed.
Stein's identification with the central government of Prussia and German Reich
was partial, always mediated through her emotional ties to Silesia and its capital city, Breslau, where she was born and raised.[18]

Stein was fortunate to grow up in Breslau, the most religiously heteroge-
neous and tolerant city in the German Reich, a city in which Jews exercised considerable economic, cultural, and political power. At the time of Stein's birth,
the chair of Breslau's City Council was Wilhelm Salomon Freund, a Left Liberal
Jew and board member of an array of Jewish associations. A key element of Breslau civic pride was its rejection of anti-Semitism and its emphasis upon harmonious relations among all its citizens. Stein and her family had many non-Jewish
close friends and trusted acquaintances from all walks of life. Stunned in the
early 1930s by the national wave of anti-Semitism, Stein, in her autobiography's

optimistic preface, declares that individuals from every stratum of the German nation who have "associated with Jewish families as employees, neighbors or fellow students, have found in them such goodness of heart, understanding, warm empathy, and so consistently helpful an attitude that, now, their sense of justice is outraged by the condemnation of this people to a pariah's existence."[19] Although, as will become evident, Stein was already aware of and appalled by anti-Semitism before and during World War I, she seldom had to confront this bigotry. Her years in Göttingen's intellectual circles (1913–15) reinforced her sense of interreligious and gender-equal cameraderie.

Except among conservative nationalists, German identity was not tethered to German laws and political institutions. Despite popular support for an activist German state, Germany's authoritarian, aristocratic, plutocratic, and patriarchal political and legal institutions alienated many liberal and radical Germans, but the rickety nature of the German Reich led Stein and her family, like many, to feel a duty to support it. Stein's sense of being part of, indeed a favored child of, the German Empire was quickly manifest with the outbreak of World War I. She fervently supported the German war effort: "with jubilant cries of victory, we followed our army into France."[20] She announced that her personal, private life had ended and, resolving to serve the state, volunteered as a Red Cross nurse on the Eastern Front. There she completed an arduous and courageous six-month term of duty for which she earned the Medal of Bravery. Later in the war she considered work in a munitions factory but opted against it. Stein's close friend Roman Ingarden perceived that Stein yearned for solidarity with her nation: "[T]he existence of such a community was . . . personally essential for her."[21] Like her Christian, Jewish, and atheist friends who also volunteered to serve their nation, and many of whom died at the front, Stein thrilled to the Kaiser's ringing declaration of civic truce, *Ich kenne keine Parteien mehr* (literally translated as "I no longer acknowledge parties"—i.e., factions and other social and political divisions—and widely understood to indicate the Kaiser's desire to unify the nation in a spirit of mutual respect). Sharing the optimism of many Germans who viewed the war as overcoming internal national conflicts and forging a more inclusive and invincible nation, Stein proclaims that "since Sparta and Rome there has never been as strong a consciousness of being a state as there is in Prussia and the new German Reich. That is why I consider it out of the question that we will be defeated."[22]

Stein's wartime ardor, however, was not intrinsic to her patriotism. Despite Stein's claim that "I am myself it," she emphatically distinguished between patriotism *(Patriotismus)* and nationalism *(Nationalismus)* or chauvinism *(Hurra-patriotismus)*.[23] Her distaste for nationalism arose quite early. Her pro-Prussian sentiments notwithstanding, Stein mocked her gymnasium principal's approach: "The entire history course was thoroughly conservative-Prussian. Brandenburg, Prussia, the new German Reich: that was the brilliant development offered to us. The Great Elector, Frederick the Great, and Wilhelm I were the three titans. But, he would add, it was still too soon to tell whether Wilhelm II might not put all the others in the shade! I was already very critical of this biased presentation . . . [and]the official patriotic chauvinism."[24] Deploring "blind idolization" of the Prussian royal family and Darwinist nationalism and nationalist celebrations, she found "most rankling" the annual Sedan Day Celebration in honor of Germany's triumph over France on September 1, 1870: "There in the open, a stirring patriotic speech would be delivered. . . . [W]e sang patriotic songs. . . . [T]hat type of emotional expression was foreign to me. . . . I had a deep antipathy to the mere idea of continuing to celebrate the victory over the French after so many years. I was not a pacifist, but such an attitude toward a vanquished foe seemed to me most unchivalrous . . . [and I] made a solemn resolution never again to take part in such an affair."[25] At Breslau University she praised her friends and professors, who, while as proud as she of the new Reich, were not "myopically Prussian."[26] Nor did she hesitate to criticize the emperor.[27]

As World War I's relentless death toll mounted, Stein's letters register her longing for peace. The Prussian state and German Reich lost her confidence. She cast a cold eye on her close friend and future brother-in-law Hans Biberstein's feelings; for him, "The war had retained its romantic glow to the very end." Following the armistice, Biberstein "intended to support the Kaiser enthusiastically; for him, it was unbelievable that no one dared to show allegiance to the monarchy."[28] In the wake of the war Stein and her family supported the Weimar Republic, and Stein joined the newly formed German Democratic Party.[29]

Further tempering and complicating Stein's national consciousness and loyalty was her keen European identity fostered by her informal and formal education. The *Abitur,* a rigorous state exam preliminary to university matriculation, required written and oral response to classical and modern literature and philosophy and to French, English, and German history and literature. Stein's comprehensive education kindled her esteem for Greek and Roman classics and such writers and thinkers as Spinoza, Shakespeare, Turgenev, Dostoyevsky, Ibsen, Descartes, Montesquieu, Rousseau, Locke, Hume, John Stuart Mill, William James, and Henri Bergson. As much as she esteemed German drama, she writes that "above all, Shakespeare became my daily bread."[30] Before Stein chose philosophy as her university major, she plunged into history, literature, and psychology. She relished, for example, Max Lehmann's course on the Enlightenment, an era in which cosmopolitan-minded intellectuals and artists traveled throughout Europe, affirming the exchange of ideas across borders and the transnational character of their thought—an outlook that prevailed among most intellectuals in prewar Germany.[31] The Göttingen philosophical circle epitomized an international spirit. Among Stein's close friends in that circle were Russian-born Alexandre Koyré, who spent most of his life in Paris, the Alsatian Jean Hering, the Pole Roman Ingarden, and the Canadian Winthrop Pickard Bell.

Stein's Europeanness is evident in the growth of her religious life. The catalyst for her conversion to Catholicism was the reading of the autobiography of the extraordinary Spaniard St. Teresa of Avila, who defied both church and state authority and risked death at the hands of the Spanish Inquisition. Stein's religious writings included her 1928 translation of the distinctively English John Henry Cardinal Newman's *Letters and Diaries until His Conversion to the Church*. Newman was championed by German Catholic modernists, a minority within the German Catholic Church. Max Scheler, Stein's comrade in phenomenological studies, and the Silesian Jesuit theologian Father Erich Przywara, her dear friend from the time of her conversion onward, led the Newman revival. Father Przywara not only was responsible for Stein's translation of Newman and St. Thomas Aquinas's *Questiones disputatae* but also arranged Stein's European lecture tours from 1928 to 1932.[32] Near the end of her life, Stein composed *The Science of the Cross*, a major study of the mystic theology of the Spaniard St. John of the Cross. Tellingly, too, she converted not to Lutheranism, the national religion of Germany, but to internationally minded Catholicism, with its history as a persecuted minority in Germany and, compared to Protestant Christianity, its more critical stance toward the German state. (Alas, that critical stance was lost during the 1930s when the notorious "prudent silence" of many in the Catholic Church hierarchy contributed to Nazi power.)

Like many Germans of her time, Stein was given to national stereotyping, though she readily admitted her mistaken generalizations. Her service as a Red Cross nurse at Mährisch-Weisskirchen, a huge military academy converted into a lazaretto in the Austro-Hungarian Empire, became a turning point in her life. The war victims Stein treated came from diverse regions of the Austro-Hungarian Empire and also on occasion included Russians, Turks, and gypsies. At Mährisch-Weisskirchen Stein discovered that her patients from the "'barbaric nations' were humble and grateful. . . . [T]he Czechs, hated for what was called their 'betrayal' of the German cause, [were] the most patient when sick and also the most ready to help others," while the German soldiers struck her as arrogant and demanding.[33] Whatever the range of her prewar European identity, Stein's wartime work stretched her capacity to develop respect for and empathy with soldiers from southern and eastern Europe.

If her European identity modulated her Germanness and her enthusiasm for the Prussian state, Stein's experience as a woman and her feminist outlook had comparable impact. An aching complication for Stein and many other German women—in fact, a problem for women throughout Europe—was their lack of genuine citizenship. For men, Germanness presumed citizenship, but where did that leave women, who lacked the vote, whose career and occupational choices were restricted, whose national identity depended upon their husband's nationality, and who until 1908 had no right to enter and receive degrees from universities? Scholars such as Sander Gilman and George Mosse have observed how anti-Semitic, racist German Christians and even some self-hating Jewish men (e.g., Otto Weininger) caricatured Jews, Slavs, and Africans as "womanish"—that is, irrational, morally deficient, and incapable of major forms of public leadership.[34]

These distortions were not peculiar to German men. The masculine construction of European and American identity confined women's strengths to their domestic capacities and religious piety. Women were expected to foster love, charity, and forgiveness, to act as peacemakers and healers, and to support men's decisions in the public realm. The primary female identity, then, was not national but familial, though volunteer community and church or synagogue service was also valid. This ideology, known as civic motherhood, always presumed essentially different male and female natures and destinies, including second-class citizenship for women. When Stein's gymnasium classmates teased her in verse, "Let woman equal be with man, / So loud this suffragette avers, / In days to come we surely can, / See that a Cab'net Post is hers,"[35] they envisioned an unconventional, indeed impossible, role for Stein, while expressing approbation of Stein's "masculine" talents and feminist outlook.

Stein's reform-minded Germanness typified liberal, ambitious German feminists. She argued for women's full citizenship and rights of nationality, which she linked to her "extraordinarily strong social conscience" that made her "decidedly favor women's suffrage." She joined the Prussian Society for Women's Right to Vote because "it advocated full political equality for women."[36] Since she thought both sexes were on earth to serve humanity, her work for the German Red Cross reflected a combined set of humanist, feminist, and patriotic values. She treasured Adolf Reinach's letter from the warfront that began, "Dear Sister Edith! Now we are comrades in arms."[37]

Frustrated after the war by sexist impediments to her *Habilitation,* the required step after completing a dissertation to become a faculty member at a university, Stein took political action. Her appeal to the Prussian Ministry for Science, Art, and Education led, on February 21, 1920, to a landmark ruling on *Habilitation* that removed sex as a disqualifier. Unfortunately, not until 1950 did a woman actually habilitate in Germany in philosophy. By the early 1920s the prospect of a gender-equal republic had dimmed. A woman's professorship in philosophy, let alone a cabinet post, was out of the question.

As crucial as Europeanist and feminist elements in the ensemble of her German identity was Stein's phenomenological self. Prior to her Catholic conversion, phenomenology took religion's place. Stein believed in the possibility of objective knowledge of both one's subjective life and the external world. This objectivity, as enunciated by Husserl and his students, was founded upon a dispassionate and comprehensive analysis of phenomena, a bracketing of any possible bias. Stein and her phenomenological peers were rationalists, scientific in their self-critical and open-minded application of reason to describing what their senses and thoughts perceived. Her identity as a phenomenologist was compatible with her conversion, since she saw no fundamental clash between it and her Catholicism. While Catholicism stirred her to pursue supernatural truths, she continued to examine natural phenomena through the rigorous rational and scientific method at the core of phenomenology. Even in the early 1940s as she composed her study of St. John of the Cross, she assured her convent mother, Johanna van Weersth, that it was important to include the insights of Jean Baruzi, a French agnostic whose various studies of St. John of the Cross Sanjuanist scholars still esteem.[38] Stein's lifelong commitment to careful logic and comprehensive, open-minded research roused her disgust with unscientifically examined patriotic or nationalist sentiment.

All of Stein's writings about the nature and meaning of community, society, national identity, and the nation-state were phenomenologically framed. Although eager for a unified state, Stein never accepted the prevalent German view that human identity is essentially defined by national identity. Unlike Herder, whose influential late-eighteenth-century ideas of the German *Volk* were later expanded in Troeltsch's renowned 1916 treatise, *The German Idea of Liberty,* Stein did not consider herself a human being or a woman through her membership in the *Volk,* even though she considered her identity inseparable from her nation. Ultimately, as we have seen, her idea of Germanness posited a larger selfhood that encompassed, as part of and as separate from Germanness, other fundamental identities.

Stein opposed the dominant German view that the nation was biological and historical necessity made manifest. Combining Anglo-American and French traditions that regarded national and state membership as elective with Germanic ideas of the state as an organic outgrowth of community and national development, she argued that individuals, though greatly influenced by their historical situation, choose their communities. A corollary was her unorthodox view of the *Volk* or ethnic community and its relation to the national community. While she agreed with many German theorists that a single *Volk* can constitute a nation, a nation, she insisted, can be composed of many *Volker,* and uniformity among them was not vital. Unlike conservative and liberal nationalists and anti-Semites of her time, Stein argued that separate, distinct ethnic communities and identities were not at odds with a cohesive nation and national well-being.[39]

Correspondingly, Stein rejected the dominant German view that the state was sacred, transcendental, with a destiny beyond that of its individual citizens. Nor did she accept the corollary totalitarian assumption that each individual's freedom, identity, and moral development depended upon obedience to the will of the state. For Stein, if a state failed to uphold justice, protect its people and communities, and act morally toward other states, its citizens were under no obligation to obey it and could exercise the right of resistance.[40] Stein's personal and philosophical aversion to servile, knee-jerk obedience to public and private authority allied her with German's radical tradition, a minority tradition even during the more open Weimar era.[41]

Stein's Jewishness

Stein's zest for objective and rational knowledge, her feminism and cultural pluralism, and her questioning of authority owed much to her unwavering Jewish ethnic identity and loyalty. One of many striking instances of her ethnic assertion took place on September 12, 1933, roughly a month before she entered the Carmelite Convent in Cologne, roughly five months after Hitler's Aryan Laws ended her lecturer position at the German Institute for Scientific Pedagogy in Münster. Stein was in Juvisy, France, as one of thirty distinguished philosophers and scholars invited by the Société Thomiste to take part in its Conference on Phenomenology and Thomism. A number of the participants were of Jewish descent. Father Daniel Feuling recalls a conversation at the conference in which Stein and Alexander Koyré, a professor of philosophy at the Sorbonne (a friend of hers since their Göttingen University days), kept invoking the names of philosophers of Jewish birth (Husserl, Bergson, Meyerson, et al.), each time gleefully remarking, "He is another of ours." Feuling adds: "It amused me a little to hear the way Koyré and Edith Stein speaking of Jews and Jewish matters would say simply 'we.' I had a vivid impression of that blood-brotherhood which was so strong in Edith, as formerly in Saint Paul, who, in his Second Letter to the Corinthians [11:22] spoke with such pride, 'Hebraei sunt—et ego' ['They are Hebrews, and so am I']."[42]

Our analysis of Stein's Jewishness brings us into the roiling controversies over who has authority to determine a person's ethnic identity. As befits their ideal of Talmudic debate, Jews disagree on the definition of Jewishness and who represents it. According to age-old Halachic decrees and current Israeli law, when Stein converted in 1922 to Catholicism, she lost, as any Jew would, all claim to being Jewish. Stein's apostasy was further heightened by her decision in 1933 to enter a convent and assume a new name, Sister Benedicta a Cruce. For traditional Jews, Stein died a Catholic. But other traditionalists differ on this matter, such as Professor David Novak, Shiff Chair of Jewish Studies at the University of Toronto, who holds that Stein's conversion does not eclipse her Jewish identity: "An apostate doesn't quit the Jewish community; rather, she is absent without leave. . . . Edith Stein is always a Jew."[43] His view is akin to that of non-traditional Jews, who argue that though Stein changed faith, she grew up a Jew, adhered proudly to many Jewish traditions throughout her life, affirmed herself a Jew, and thus died as fully a Jew as Catholic. Stein's surviving Jewish-identified family, wrestling with their lack of consensus, refrain from defining postconversion Stein as Jewish. They deem her, instead, a Catholic of Jewish heritage.[44] Expectably, Jewish Christians or Hebrew Catholics proclaim Stein one of their own, hailing her as a model for syncretic approaches to religious and ethnic identity.

If we assign authority to a state to define Jewishness, then the answer in Nazi Germany is tragically clear: Stein was a Jew. When Hitler came to power, the Nazi state branded races Aryan and non-Aryan (the broad usage of the term *ethnicity* in place of *race* is a post–World War II phenomenon). Stein's Carmelite garments did not protect her from extermination. Today the German state leaves to the Jewish community the authority to determine whom to include.

Most current scholars apply a loose ethnic criterion for Jewish identity, minimally descent from one or both Jewish parents. For example, Friedenreich, in her study on Jewish female college and university peers of Stein, sorts Jewish women into three categories: Former Jews, approximately 15 to 20 percent, women who officially left the *Gemeinde* (the German-specific legal entity that embraced all Jews within a particular geographical area); Just Jews, about two thirds, who were nominally Jews, lacked any Jewish religiosity, but remained within the Jewish community, socializing with both Jews and Gentiles (Stein was such during her university years); and Jewish Jews, approximately 10 to 15 percent, who avowed their religious and communal ties.[45]

I share the view of many feminist scholars who maintain that each human being has the ethical right and supreme responsibility, within the bounds of reason, to define her or his own identity. Admittedly this individualist placement of authority often ignores the politics of history and institutions, but it respects the integrity of personhood. Stein viewed herself her entire life as Jewish, and that prevailing fact determines my approach to her identity.

Stein's Jewishness, her sense of "we," involved two criteria of self-definition: one lineage (her Jewish descent); the other communal (her Jewish family/kin and her Jewish university friendships and intellectual circles). Although Stein often voices her pride in her Jewish ancestry, her view of lineage diverges from dominant nineteenth- and twentieth-century understanding of Jewish descent. European and American intellectuals of Stein's lifetime merged lineage with "race"; hence, people belonged to the Jewish race, the Irish race, the Slavic race, the Aryan race, and so on and were assumed to inherit racial characteristics. Scientists, political theorists, and nonprofessionals alike ranked races hierarchically. Stein repudiated these views, though many of her closest friends and associates held them. Jews were for her not a race *(Rasse)* but rather a lineage *(Stamme)*, or people *(Volk)* or Jewish humanity *(jüdisches Menschentum)*. Moreover, in her hylomorphic theory of form, type, and species, Stein never proposed *a priori* racial or ethnic characteristics as constituting the essence of "person." Her search for essences did not include ethnic and racial phenomena. Although she considered it valid to inquire into the ontology of "woman"—woman as human, woman as gender, woman as individual—she made no comparable effort for Jewishness or any racial or lineage category, including Germanness. Even when she wrote about typical characteristics of nations, she underscored that "[i]f somebody were 'a typical German' in his essence and nothing else, he wouldn't have a genuine personality; you'd even have to say whatever typically German character traits he'd be showing off couldn't be genuine. For the genuine being of the community has its origin in the personal distinctiveness of the individuals."[46]

Like many Jewish women of her time Stein sought to be a person, not "just" a woman or a Jewish, atheist, or Catholic woman. Rudolfine Menzel, Stein's contemporary, recalled of herself, "I want to become a person [*ein Mensch*], and not just a middle-class school girl."[47] Another contemporary, Rahel Straus, wrote of her days at the University of Heidelberg, "I look back fondly at our stimulating evenings in which interesting women sat together and participated in the construction of a new female identity."[48] Stein's autobiography is in many ways a study of Jewish heterogeneity. Originally intended as a biography of her beloved mother, it soon became a refutation of Nazi anti-Semitic propaganda. Outraged by Nazi efforts to demonize people of her descent, she defied the silence imposed on Jews by Nazi laws, titled her work *Life in a Jewish Family*, and boldly announced her Jewishness and solidarity with the Jewish people. In her effort to debunk anti-Semites' "horrendous caricature" of Jews, she presented her readers with a bountiful array of Jewish personalities, hoping thereby to stir appreciation for the fundamental individuality of Jews as well as their basic humanness.[49] These many portraits depict Jews in their multiple societal roles, their mix of achievements and shortcomings, their dignity and their complexity.

Stein's pride in her Jewishness extends beyond the fact of descent. She situates the formation of her self within the context of her family religious traditions, noting, on her maternal side, that her great-grandfather was a cantor and had a prayer-room in his own home. Her grandfather founded a Jewish private school, where his fifteen children received a basic Jewish education. Stein grew up in a home in which, as she recurrently informs her readers, her mother prac ticed a genuine Jewish piety.[50]

Within Stein's immediate and extended family, common middle-class liberal German-Jewish ethnic patterns shaped her upbringing. Paramount among these was the value placed on education and intellectual accomplishment, which by the time of Stein's birth applied to Jewish girls as well. Is it a mere coincidence that the first two women to earn doctorates in philosophy in Germany—Edith Stein and Hedwig Conrad-Martius—were of Jewish descent? Scholars note, in fact, the disproportionate percentage of Jewish women enrolled in higher education in early-twentieth-century Germany.[51] Stein's gymnasium and University of Breslau curriculum required study of eminent thinkers of Jewish descent whom Stein greatly admired, such as Spinoza, Lessing, and Heine. Earlier I noted the Jewish heroines and themes in the drama of Grillparzer and Hebbel.

Crucially, Stein children were raised to be open-minded about oppositional beliefs and lifestyles, liberality that encouraged development of comprehensive, critical thinking skills. Although obedience to parental authority was important, independence of thought and active assertion of will were no less supported, values characteristic of middle-class Jewish families of Stein's time and place.[52]

A traditional Jewish optimism about the power of personal will underpinned familial support for individual freedom. Stein's writing emphatically affirms individual agency—individual choice, the assenting "I can."[53] Jews are not alone, of course, among philosophers occupied with questions of agency and causation, but Stein's optimism about the role and range of free will strongly reflected her middle-class liberal Jewish upbringing.

At the same time, Stein's mother put aside personal material gain to enable her daughters to pursue higher education. Jewish mothers paradoxically exemplified self-denial and other-regarding traits as part of raising their daughters to become self-assertive, self-confident, and self-reliant. Family members were expected to sacrifice their interests to serve relatives in need. This common ethnic duality of self-realization and self-denial became integral to Stein's Jewish identity formation.

If Stein's Breslau family and friends helped form and strengthen her Jewish identity and pride, her mentors and friends at Göttingen furthered her sense of Jewish community. Though most, not all, of Göttingen Jewish phenomenologists converted to either the Lutheran or Catholic faith, it is striking that Husserl and many of his students were of Jewish descent: Adolf Reinach, Husserl's right arm; the brilliant mercurial Max Scheler; Hedwig Conrad-Martius, Stein's closest friend; and Stein's dear friends Fritz Kaufmann, Hans Lipps, Alexandre Koyré, all key early contributors to the phenomenological movement. Many of these philosophers were drawn to and became indebted to the thought of the French Jewish philosopher Henri Bergson. Fritz Kaufmann decades later remembered the "rare intimacy of symphilosophizing the like of which has never been reached again in the history of the movement."[54] Clearly, this ethnic commonality played a role in Roman Ingarden's remark about the communal intensity among Göttingen's philosophical circle: "We understood one another without saying a word. Even when we saw one another again after years, we know after only a few words what this or that one was concerned about."[55] Of course, Ingarden and others in the community not of Jewish descent most likely attributed this communal intimacy to their shared phenomenological outlook and views about Husserl; yet affinity among those with Jewish backgrounds must have further bonded the members of the circle. When, at Juvisy, Stein and her college friend Koyré delighted in the "we" and "us" of Jewish-born philosophers, they were re-enacting the nostalgic affinity of an innocent era as well as bolstering their Jewish pride during their current hard times.

Stein's affirmation of her Jewishness and solidarity with her Jewish family and with Jews also took political forms. During the early and mid-1930s she sought an audience with Pope Pius XI to urge him to issue an encyclical denouncing anti-Semitism. Her efforts proved fruitless. When, later, she received a British certificate that would enable her to flee from Germany to Palestine, she turned down its privilege because her sister Rosa was denied it. Further, she refused to publish her writings under an Aryan name when that was the only way to get her major philosophical and theological writing in print.[56] Trying, as she often did, to encourage Christians to unify with Jews, she warned a friend as early as 1930 that the German army will "persecute first the Jews, then afterwards the Catholic Church." Her friend was dubious, but Stein stood her ground: "Wait and you will remember my words."[57] After she entered the cloister in 1933, she urged her Gentile sisters to vote, and to vote against the Nazi party.[58]

Nor was her sensitivity to anti-Semitism a late development that influenced her attitudes only in the 1930s. Her autobiography recounts galling anti-Semitism of prior decades. Illustration one: two eminent scholars at the University of Breslau who numbered among her admired professors "were barred advancement in their academic careers because of their Jewish descent."[59] Illustration two: since Jewish women rarely obtained employment as teachers in the state school system, she and her sister Else knew that their teaching at the municipal *Victoriaschule* during World War I depended on the shortage of male and Christian teachers.[60] As the first postwar elections approached, Stein remarked that Jews "could expect no sympathy any further to the political right [than the German Democratic Party]."[61] To be sure, her 1930s personal and family experiences of anti-Semitism heightened her sense of Jewishness. After losing her university teaching position in 1933, she declared, "I was now caught up in the common fate."[62]

Stein's feelings of ethnic solidarity, however, also betrayed ambivalence. Her feelings were mixed toward both acculturated middle-class German Jews and, during her college years, the increasing numbers of poor Eastern European Jews arriving in flight from oppression. For the first part of the twentieth century, Germany was a haven for Jewish refugees, much as the country has become again since the fall of the Berlin Wall. Stein's World War I patriotism arose in part from the fact that Germany was less anti-Semitic than Russia. Nevertheless, for most German Jews, Eastern Jews *(Ostjüden)* were a horrid embarrassment, seen to jeopardize Jewish struggle for Gentile respect as well as occupational and social opportunities for German Jews in the Gentile world. In a telling comment, Stein revealed both her biases and her discomfort with these biases. Describing a fellow student, she observed, "Nor had he even the slightest trace of that unpleasant intonation common to uneducated Eastern Jews which irritated the German 'assimilated Jews' even more than it did the 'Aryans.'"[63] She refrained from saying that such intonation was unpleasant to her, only to "assimilated Jews" in general, references she carefully framed in quotation marks, as she did "Aryan." Yet she found hilarious her brother-in-law's ability to tell stories, verses, and Jewish jokes in "dialect."[64]

Despite Stein's self-consciousness in describing assimilated Jews, she celebrated many aspects of the acculturated bourgeois Jewish lifestyle, especially its cultural, intellectual, and artistic achievements. As Marion Kaplan and other scholars document, German Jews helped to shape *Bildung,* the German concept of the fully cultured person. After Jews—men, to be sure, more than women—gained legal and civic equality in 1871, Jewish cultural traditions of theoretical learning and Jewish middle-class aspirations enabled Jews further to define and more completely embody *Bildung. Bildung* became for Jews "a kind of intellectual and emotional home after the physical confines of the ghetto and the closed scholarly world of Jewish learning."[65] Not surprisingly, educated Jewish women and men brought expression and power to *Bildung* in multiple scientific and artistic forms. Since prevailing middle-class German cultural ideals contained mutual Jewish and Christian influences, *assimilation* is a porous term; Kaplan prefers the term *acculturation*. To be sure, the Gentile world was never disposed to integrate Jews fully on an equal basis in either public or private spheres. Crucially, most Jews valued and preserved major aspects of their religious and ethnic traditions and outlook even as they incorporated Gentile patterns of life and thought.[66]

As much as Stein admired Jewish contributions to and expressions of *Bildung,* she abhorred the bourgeois materialism, greed, sexual laxity, and egoism that she associated with many prosperous Jews. The same critical objectivity that she brought to other matters she applied to her description of individuals and communities, even if these were socially marginalized. She deplored wealthy Jews' ostracism of poor Jews. Despite her fondness for schoolmate Käthe Kleeman, who shared Stein's "serious search for truth," they parted after school because the Kleemans had moved to the south side of Breslau, "where, as in Berlin's West End, the newly wealthy Jews gathered; for my mother this was another example of typical behavior of the newly affluent. . . . [W]e were tied to the unfashionable north side."[67] Although her mother deplored this Jewish snobbery, she voiced elitist attitudes about the very poor. Her mother shared the family view, one common among many Jews and Protestants, that Catholicism appealed primary to the "lowest social class," whose ignorant servility was evident in their "grovelling on one's knees and kissing the priest's toe."[68] Whereas anti-Semites viewed Jews as racially inclined to self-centered status-seeking behavior, Stein faulted Christians and Jews alike for social snobbery and materialism but never viewed these traits as inherent.

Increasingly, and in an ironic take on the stereotype of the bourgeois Jew, Stein blamed loss of Jewish piety, rather than Jewish efforts at assimilation, for status-seeking egoistic behaviors. Never ceasing to revere her mother's Jewish piety, Catholic Stein grew increasingly impatient with the unbelief in God of many affluent Jews. She wished her siblings had more respect for Jewish rituals and beliefs. Stein lamented that religious education had become increasingly anemic with subsequent generations, observing that "the Jewish identity" of younger folk "had lost its religious foundation."[69] Her highly controversial last Will and Testament documents Stein's desire that God receive her death as a sacrifice for the unbelief of the Jews (meaning their unbelief in their Talmudic God, not their failing to be Christians). Her statements closer to the time of her death underscored that she wanted to sacrifice "for all who lost God from their hearts."[70]

The most powerful evidence of how Stein's Jewishness and communal roots shaped her identity is her positive attitude toward Judaism even after her conversion to Catholicism. Unlike those Jews who honored Jewish accomplishments but, whether unbelievers or converts, viewed Judaism as backward and primitive, Stein prized myriad Judaic features and preserved many after her conversion. She rejoiced in Jewish holidays and festivities, especially Purim and the High Holy Days. Until she entered her cloistered Carmelite life, Stein gladly accompanied her mother to Yom Kippur services. Although she had trouble with aspects of Judaism's approach to death, she exulted in the fact that she had been born on Yom Kippur, the High Holy Day of Atonement. She spent much of her life reflecting on the meaning of atonement. Affectionately describing Yom Kippur piety, she gloried in the "beautiful ancient melodies" that accompanied worship.[71] Stein delighted in the links between Jewish High Holy Days service and Catholic liturgy, and she frequently corresponded with her niece, Erika Tworoger, a Jewish theologian, regarding translation and commentary on Hebrew texts of the Torah.[72] Since Stein's attachment to her immediate and extended family remained intense her entire life and animated her ongoing sense of Jewishness, she hoped, in vain, upon entering the Carmel at Cologne-Lindenthal, that she could be transferred to the Silesian Carmel near her mother and sisters.[73]

Throughout her life, Stein enthusiastically identified with the Old Testament's Queen Esther, the intrepid advocate for Jews. Stein enjoyed performing Esther in family Purim celebrations. Her Esther identification appears throughout her writings, such as her letter of October 1938: "And [I trust] in the Lord's having accepted my life for all of them. I ... think of Queen Esther who was taken from her people precisely that she might represent them before the king. I am a very poor and powerless little Esther, but the king who chose me is infinitely great and merciful."[74] Two days before her deportation to Auschwitz, she composed a dialogue in which, as Esther incarnate, she returns to earth to her people anew. Stein alternately deployed her identification with Esther and Jesus as a Jewish martyr to frame her understanding of the cross laid upon her life and upon the Jewish victims of Nazi violence: "God had put a heavy hand upon His people, which was also my people." With these words the Carmelite Stein fused her Jewish identity and solidarity with Jews.[75]

Jesus's Jewishness was a key factor in Stein's Catholicism. She told her Jesuit confessor, Father Hirschmann, "You don't know what it means to me to be a daughter of the chosen people—to belong to Christ, not only spiritually, but according to the flesh."[76] For Stein, Jesus literally embodied the history of the Jewish people, past, present, and future, and thereby embodied the New Testament God's oneness with the suffering of Jews. One wonders whether Stein's emphasis on the body in her phenomenological analysis of personhood may reflect in part the importance to her of belonging to the Jewish people "according to the flesh."

Stein's effort to preserve various features of Judaism is evident in the appeal for her of Carmelite Catholicism. Although Stein did not know that Teresa of Avila was a *converso*, the Carmelite order that St. Teresa transformed appropriated and retained many Jewish religious and liturgical elements: Carmelites feel strong affinity with the Jewish Bible; they celebrate Elijah as the first Carmelite; and Carmelite friars and nuns regularly quote Elijah's "As the Lord lives, before whose face I stand," a phrase common in Jewish worship. Unique among Catholic orders, the Carmelites include the six-pointed star of David in their sacred art, and their worship begins with the Jewish declaration of monotheistic faith— *Schma Israel.*[77] In a letter following the death of her mother (September 14, 1936), Stein thanked her sister for sending her mother's prayer book to her: "Now I immediately opened it to the prayer for the dead and found in it the same faith that to us [meaning Carmelites] is so matter-of-fact and on which I now rely."[78] In response to the news of her mother's death, Stein asserted that her devout Jewish mother not only was in heaven but had saintly intercessory powers: "I have the firm conviction that my mother now has the power to help her children in these great afflictions."[79] Stein clearly felt quite free of pre–Vatican II doctrine that only Christians could be saved.

Still, various complexities and dilemmas enter into any understanding of Stein's desire to support the Jewish community. Granted that ethnic and religious identity are separable for many Jews today, such was not the general view in Stein's lifetime. Insofar as she abandoned Judaism as a religion, her ethnic pride could not be the same as for one whose religion was a key element. What does one make of her ambiguous remark in 1930 that her sister Rosa, who in 1936 converted to Catholicism, was enduring "almost unbearable" suffering from her niece Erika Tworoger's " increasingly pronounced Jewish leaning and her interference in running the household"?[80] Following Stein's conversion, her attitudes fluctuated concerning the conversion of Jews. In late 1930 she wrote to two Benedictine sisters of looking forward "with particular joy to the prospective baptism of a Jewess" that she had helped facilitate.[81] On the other hand, Stein's nephew Gerhard, a practicing Jew, claimed, "She never particularly stressed her religious convictions toward persons of another faith. She was no missionary."[82]

Along with her loss of faith as a teenager and conversion to Catholicism as an adult, both turns indicative of the limits of her regard for Judaism, Stein showed little interest in studying Jewish philosophy and theology. In fact, her scholarly interest in Judaism grew after her conversion and with her eagerness to gain command of Catholic thought. In light of Stein's dedication to objectivity, we can only wonder why she assumed uncritically that the Judaism of her Breslau experience was the full character of the religion.

Stein's eschewing serious study of Jewish thought as well as the particular nature of her Jewishness owes much to her experience as a woman. Just as discrimination against women and feminism shaped her Germanness, so too the sexism of Jewish philosophical, theological, and institutional history shaped her Jewishness. Since women were systematically excluded from the study of Jewish thought and erased from the histories of the Jewish people, Stein's opportunity to learn about the range and depth of Jewish religious history and thought was minimal. As a risk-taking and ambitious woman, she naturally was attracted to the figure of Esther, and, as noted above, her Esther identification strengthened her Jewishness; but apart from the exemplary daring, practical wisdom, and love of diverse Old Testament women, the Judaism that Stein knew and experienced lacked non-biblical historical female figures of inspiring prominence.

In Stein's time, Jewish women were also unable to participate fully in religious worship outside the home. Moreover, they were secondarily members of the Jewish community, since they were neither circumcised nor able to prepare for bar mitzvah. They could not become rabbis, and when they attended synagogue services they were forced to sit behind a screen *(mehitza)*. Rabbi Fuchs-Kreimer observed that if the young Franz Rosenzwieg, about to abandon Judaism, had been forced to sit behind a screen on the fateful Yom Kippur Eve that changed his mind, he would probably not have been newly awakened to the spiritual depth of his native religion.[83] (No wonder that the convent grille was not an alien fixture and that the absence of women in the priesthood posed no insuperable obstacle to Stein's converting.)

Although Catholicism, too, was rife with sexism, its history of distinguished female intellects, artists, abbesses, and saints as well as its validation of celibacy sharply differentiated it from both Lutheranism and Judaism. No figure in Jewish or Protestant history enjoyed the widespread admiration, if not reverence, of the woman who inspired Stein's conversion. St. Teresa of Avila combined business acumen, entrepreneurial derring-do, intellectual brilliance, mystic depth, and radical theological innovation. Though Stein was no radical or founder of a religious order, she did work to spread feminist ideas within Catholic thought and practice. Indeed, the major collection of her views on gender, *Die Frau (Essays on Woman)*, encouraged women to realize their talents fully, seek a complete education, claim independent time for spiritual and life contemplation, and consider all careers/professions. Stein intimates that even the priesthood should not be ruled out.[84]

Neither Judaism nor Lutheranism would have enabled Stein to live in a strictly female community with the time to combine both piety and intellectual work and to have her intellectual work esteemed and encouraged by both her convent sisters and a significant cadre of Catholic male intellectuals and priests. Given how powerful pronatalist rhetoric was throughout Europe during the interwar years, after the enormous loss of lives during World War I compounded by a widespread outbreak of fatal influenza, Stein's decision to pursue a career and later enter a convent would have struck many German Jews and Lutherans as grossly unpatriotic. If Stein's Jewishness curbed her obedience to the state, so, too, her feminism curbed her Jewish and German loyalty in a single stroke.

From Stein's singular meld of Germanness and Jewishness what do we learn about the German-Jewish symbiosis during the pre-Hitler era? Stein would surely have applauded the remark of Franz Rosenzwieg, a pathbreaker in early-twentieth-century adult Jewish education, philosophy, and theology: "Judaization made me not a worse but a better German."[85] Countless early-twentieth-century German Jews thought themselves as fully German and patriotic, if not nationalistic, as any other Germans. Many among these believed that German Gentiles thought similarly of them. For individuals determined to merge their Germanness and Jewishness, the Weimar Constitution embodied their hopes, one of the constitution's chief architects being Hugo Preuss, a left-leaning Jewish lawyer. During World War I and the 1920s, Jewish intellectuals, scientists, artists, lawyers, and doctors benefited from increased professional opportunities. But the war's devastation, along with progress in Jewish equality, unleashed a virulent anti-Semitism. Many Germans, groping with material and human loss, international humiliation, and internal political strife, needed ways to recover their self-esteem and to vent their grief and anger. The 1922 assassination of the Jewish industrialist Walter Rathenau, the brilliant wartime minister of national resources and later foreign minister, whose political ideas Stein admired highly, foreshadowed horrors ahead. While many Jews abandoned hope for a tolerant Germany, turned away from integration, and thus launched a Jewish-specific cultural renaissance or migrated to Palestine as part of the growing Zionist movement, others maintained their belief in the possibility of overcoming German anti-Semitism. Edith Stein belonged among the latter.

A study of the geography of this optimism would be most interesting. I anticipate that many such latter German Jews lived in cities like Breslau with traditions of positive German Christian and Jewish relations. In retrospect, the reluctance of Stein's entire family to leave Germany until the very late 1930s is astonishing. It is not as though Stein and her family were spared anti-Semitic reprisals. As early as 1933, when anti-Semitism enjoyed government approval, Stein reports that her family in Breslau were "very upset and depressed."[86] Her brother-in-law Hans Biberstein anticipated dismissal from his position as senior physician at the University of Breslau's dermatology department, a prelude to Stein's own dismissal from the University of Münster. Her relatives, unlike many of her Jewish friends, "seem inclined to remain in Germany as long as things are in any way bearable."[87] Even after Stein's mother died in 1936, her sisters Rosa and Frieda, who supported her mother in business and in the family home, determined to carry out their mother's wish that they continue to keep their Breslau house as a homestead for the entire family as long as possible.[88] They and their brother Paul died in the gas chambers.

Stein's letters chronicle the dispersal of the family, offspring often leaving ahead of parents, often to separate locations. Perpetually remarkable is the lateness of their departures. These were German Jews clearly loath to leave their beloved homeland, their beloved Breslau and family homestead, and anxious about their future in unknown countries. Stein fretted about the fate of her relatives abroad. As late as January 1937, when her brother Arno was arranging for himself and his family to emigrate to the United States, Stein feared that his situation would be worse for them there than in Germany.[89] The balance of her feelings shifted as 1938 advanced. Except for members of Arno's family, all of Stein's brothers and sisters were still in Germany. By summer 1938, Stein reported that Erna and Hans Biberstein "wanted to stay in Germany as long as possible, and to keep their children with them. But now they have to admit that it cannot go on any longer."[90] After Kristallnacht in November 1938, Stein's family realized their future in Germany was doomed. In December 1938, Stein wrote that Arno had left for the United States "on October 14, just in the nick of time"[91] and that her sister Erna's husband, Hans Biberstein, in the United States for several months, had recently received permission to remain there and for his family to join him immediately. Erna and her children were able to leave in early 1939. Stein's Hamburg relatives, her sister Else Gordon and her family, prepared to join their son in Colombia. At roughly this time, Stein began arrangements to shift to the Carmelite convent in Echt, Holland, where she arrived on New Year's Eve. A few months before the advent of World War II, Stein declared, "The family is scattered all over the world, but God knows the good of that."[92] The following year she was buoyed by good news from her family abroad, though she noted, "All of them are homesick for one another and worry about the ones who are still in Br.[Breslau]."[93] Following the Nazi edict in the Netherlands that all non-Aryan Germans were stateless and had to report for emigration by December 15, 1941, Stein and her sister complied lest they suffer "a severe penalty,"[94] but Stein immediately undertook two steps, one a petition for her and Rosa to remain in the Carmel of Echt and the other to seek alternatives, specifically a haven for both of them in a Carmelite convent in Switzerland. Toward the latter option, she sought the help of Hilde Vérène Borsinger, a jurist and editor of *The Swiss Woman*, whom she had met in 1930 through Erich Przywara, and who was indefatigable, though unsuccessful, in her efforts to fulfill Stein's request.[95]

Too many scholars attack Jewish optimism about their future in Germany and Jewish pride in their Germanness through a post-Holocaust lens. They fault these attitudes as stupidly and dangerously naïve and wishful thinking.[96] This ahistoric lens overlooks the virulent nature of anti-Semitism in France, England, and the United States and thus fails to consider the distinctive confluence and protean nature of economic, social, political, and cultural phenomena in interwar Germany. Given her life experience in Breslau and Göttingen as well as at Speyer and Münster, Edith Stein had no reason to conclude that German anti-Semitism represented more than the sickness and malice of a minority. Certainly, by late 1939, she was aware of her mistaken optimism. She began to revise her sense of the past. In one of her most important letters to Hans Biberstein, she reflected upon present and past: "You must find as I do that all the old war memories arise and one feels so strongly the contrast between now and then. And today it is not possible for us to follow events with undivided heart."[97] Although this statement clearly recalls Stein's easy loyalty to the state in 1914, it does not tell us specifically what she meant by a divided heart. For example, was her concern for the phenomenologist Hans Lipps, now fighting and eventually dying on the Eastern Front, intrinsic to what she had in mind? Stein's closest friend, Hedwig Conrad-Martius, believed Stein would have married Lipps had he proposed to her.[98]

What were Stein's remaining positive feelings toward the nation that prevented her from simply saying that this war was the polar opposite situation from 1914? Stein proceeded to compare Germany's situation with the Napoleonic era and wondered whether she and her family would live "to see the events of our days become 'history.'" Longing to see events "in the light of eternity," she asserts with stunning lucidity, "For one realizes ever more clearly how blind we are toward everything. One marvels at how mistakenly one viewed a lot of things before, and yet the very next moment one commits the blunder again of forming an opinion without having the necessary basis for it."[99] An opinion about what? Is this the quintessential Stein, the careful, rigorously rational phenomenologist, determined to have a thoroughly objective judgment of present events, or is this Stein, restraining her horror at her blindness, still clinging to shreds of optimism, still unwilling to abandon her love for Germany and its people? These comments appear in the same letter quoted in this essay's outset, as she urged her brother-in-law not to let his family become "totally alienated from their homeland." I am reminded of Stein's composition assignment to her students: "I am not a 'cleverly-designed book'; I am a human being with my contradictions."[100]

Even from the vantage point of the early twenty-first century, interwar Germany remains an immense and strenuously debated puzzle. The outcome of Stein's complex Germanness and Jewishness echoes the tragic fate of countless ethnic minorities in countless nations as they envision a national community in which they share cultural exchange and equality with all other constituents without loss of their cultural identity and traditions. To what extent was Stein's Germanness still flickering when she entered the gas chambers of Auschwitz? Her sense of the Jewish "we" is undeniable, but had she by 1942 become "totally alienated" from her homeland?

NOTES

1. Edith Stein to Roman Ingarden, February 9, 1917, in *Self-Portrait in Letters, 1916–1942*, ed. Lucy Gelber and Romaeus Leuven, OCD, trans. Josephine Koeppel, OCD, vol. 5 of *The Collected Works of Edith Stein* (Washington, DC: ICS Publications, 1993), 9–10. The Institute for Carmelite Studies, in Washington, D.C., began publishing English translations of Edith Stein's work in 1986 and as of 2004 has printed ten volumes. Stein's correspondence was published in *Selbstbildnis in Briefen*, pt. 1, *1916–1934*, and pt. 2, *1934–1942*, ed. Lucy Gelber and Michael Linssen, vols. 8 and 9, respectively, of *Edith Steins Werke* (Druten: De Maas und Waler; Freiburg: Herder, 1976, 1977). This letter appeared in pt. 1, *1916–1934*, 18–19. Stein's letters (*Selbstbildnis in Briefen*, pts. 1 and 2, and *Briefe an Roman Ingarden*) have also been published as vols. 2, 3, and 4, respectively (ed. Maria Amata Neyer, OCD, and Michael Linssen, OCD) of the new critical edition *Edith Stein Gesamtausgabe* (Freiburg: Herder, 2000, 2001). All English translations are problematic, as underscored by my e-mail correspondence with Edith Stein's niece Susanne M. Batzdorff, November 25, 1996. She describes Sr. Josephine Koeppel's translation "I am myself it" as "awkward" and favors "For I am myself an integral part of it."

2. Edith Stein to Hans Biberstein, November 17, 1939, in *Self-Portrait in Letters*, 315.

3. Edith Stein, *Life in a Jewish Family 1891–1916: Her Unfinished Autobiographical Account*, ed. Lucy Gelber and Romaeus Leuven, OCD, trans. Josephine Koeppel, OCD (Washington, DC: ICS Publications, 1986), 13. Originally published as *Aus dem Leben einer*

jüdischen Familie, Das Leben Edith Stein: Kindheit und Jugend, vol. 7 of *Edith Steins Werke* (Louvain: Archivum Carmelitanum Edith Stein, E. Nauwelaerts, 1965). Published in a new edition as *Aus dem Leben einer jüdischen Familie und weitere autobiographische Beiträge,* ed. Maria Amata Neyer and Hanna-Barbara Gerl-Falkovitz, vol. 1 of *Edith Stein Gesamtausgabe* (Freiburg: Herder, 2002).

4. Sander Gilman and Karen Remmler, introduction to *Reemerging Jewish Culture in Germany: Life and Literature since 1989* (New York: New York University Press, 1994), 5. Among the myriad and highly divergent approaches to the German-Jewish Symbiosis, the scholarship most influencing this study are George L. Mosse, "Jewish Emancipation: Between *Bildung* and Respectability," in *The Jewish Response to German Culture: From the Enlightenment to the Second World War,* ed. Jehuda Reinharz and Walter Schatzberg (Hanover, NH: University Press of New England, 1985); Marion A. Kaplan, "The German-Jewish Symbiosis Revisited," *New German Critique* 70 (Winter 1957): 183–90; Abraham Barkai, "Between Deutschtum and Judentum," in *In Search of Jewish Community: Jewish Identities in Germany and Austria, 1918–1933,* ed. Michael Brenner and Derek J. Penslar (Bloomington: Indiana University Press, 1998); Fritz Stern, *Einstein's German World* (Princeton, NJ: Princeton University Press, 1999); Paul Mendes-Flohr, *German Jews: A Dual Identity* (New Haven, CT: Yale University Press, 1999).

5. Stein, *Life,* 35. Stein wrote an additional memoir on December 18, 1938, "How I Came to Carmel," included in *Edith Stein: Selected Writings,* ed. Susanne M. Batzdorff (Springfield, IL: Templegate Publishers, 1990).

6. Ibid., 47. Stein's family's view that their homeland meant more than merely a territorial site was typical of many German Jews. See Donald Niewyck, *The Jews and Weimar Germany* (Baton Rouge: Louisiana State University Press, 1980).

7. Ibid., 406.

8. Ibid., 244.

9. Ibid., 242.

10. Edith Stein, *Beiträge zur philosophischen Begründung der Psychologie und Geisteswissenschaften: I. Psychische Kausalität, II. Individuum und Gemeinschaft,* in *Jahrbuch für Philosophie und phänomenologische Forschung,* vol. 5 (Tübingen: Max Niemeyer, 1922), 1–282. See summary of Stein's views on individual, community, and state in Mary Catharine Baseheart, SCN, *Person and the World: Introduction to the Philosophy of Edith Stein* (Dordrecht: Kluwer Academic Publishers, 1997), chap. 4. See, too, Marianne Sawicki's introduction to *Philosophy of Psychology and the Humanities,* by Edith Stein, ed. Marianne Sawicki, trans. Mary Catharine Baseheart and Marianne Sawicki, vol. 7 of *The Collected Works of Edith Stein* (Washington, DC: ICS Publications, 2000). Marianne Sawicki's translation of Stein's *Eine Untersuchung über den Staat,* originally published in *Jahrbuch für Philosophie und phänomenologische Forschung,* vol. 7 (Tübingen: Max Niemeyer, 1925), is forthcoming as vol. 7 of *Edith Stein Gesamtausgabe* (Freiburg: Herder).

11. Stein, *Life,* 68.

12. Ibid., 216.

13. Ibid., 172.

14. Ibid. Stein does not explain why she repudiated Wagner's operas.

15. Ibid., 191.

16. Ibid., 266.

17. See, e.g., Richard J. Evans, *Rereading German History from Unification to Reunification, 1800–1996* (London: Routledge, 1997).

18. Till van Rahden, "Words and Actions: Rethinking Social History of German Antisemitism, Breslau, 1870–1914," *German History* 18, no. 4 (2000): 413–38. Before 1933 Breslau was one of the three largest Jewish communities in Germany From 1870 to 1914, roughly one-quarter of the city's middle class and one-third of the voters were Jewish, though Jews constituted 4 to 7 percent of the total population of the city. Van Rahden belongs to the revisionist historians who maintain that Jewish-Gentile relations at the local level in imperial Germany were more prevalent and positive than has been supposed. He offers evidence for high levels of Jewish integration in the cities of Breslau, Berlin, Frankfurt, Hamburg, and Königsberg.

19. Stein, *Life*, 24.

20. Ibid., 299.

21. Edith Stein to Roman Ingarden, February 9, 1917, in *Self-Portrait in Letters*, 9–10.

22. Ibid.

23. Roman Ingarden, "Über die philosophischen Forschungen Edith Steins," *Freiburger Zeitschrift für Philosophie und Theologie* 26 (1979): 472–73.

24. Stein, *Life*, 168.

25. Ibid., 168–69.

26. Ibid., 190.

27. Ibid., 270–71.

28. Ibid., 229.

29. Edith Stein to Roman Ingarden, November 30, 1918, in *Briefe an Roman Ingarden* (Freiburg: Herder, 1991), 111–13.

30. Stein, *Life*, 150. For German women's secondary and higher education, see James C. Albisetti, *Schooling German Girls and Women: Secondary and Higher Education in the Nineteenth Century* (Princeton, NJ: Princeton University Press, 1999).

31. Ibid., 266.

32. For Stein's relationship with Erich Przywara, SJ, see Stein to Sr. Maria Ernst, OD, early 1937, in *Self-Portrait in Letters*, 245 n., and in the same collection, see Stein to Rev. Mother Callista, July 26, 1930, 67 n. Additional information in Waltraud Herbstrith, *Edith Stein: A Biography*, 2nd ed., trans. Father Bernard Bonowitz, OCSO (San Francisco: Ignatius Press, 1992), 17, 78, 89, 95, 141. For Przywara's relationship with Stein, see Thomas F. O'Meara, OP, *Erich Przywara, S.J.: His Theology and His World* (Notre Dame, IN: University of Notre Dame Press, 2002), 119–227. For further insight into this relationship as well as Stein's work on John Henry Cardinal Newman, see chap. 8 of this volume.

33. Stein, *Life*, 333–34.

34. George L. Mosse, *Nationalism and Sexuality: Respectability and Abnormal Sexuality in Modern Europe* (New York: Howard Fertig, 1985); Sander L. Gilman, *Inscribing the Other* (Lincoln: University of Nebraska Press, 1991); Omer Bartov, "Defining Enemies, Making Victims: Germans, Jews, and the Holocaust," *American Historical Review* 103 (June 1998): 771–816.

35. Stein, *Life*, 178.

36. Ibid., 191.

37. Ibid., 369.

38. Edith Stein to Mother Johanna van Weersth, OCD, October 13, 1941, in *Self-Portrait in Letters,* 336–37.

39. Edith Stein, *Eine Untersuchung,* 11–14, 42–45, 51–52, 340, 398.

40. Baseheart, *Person in the World,* 91, chap. 4.

41. Stein, *Life,* 271, 393.

42. Quoted by both Resi Posselt (Mother Teresia Renata de Spiritu Sancto), *Edith Stein,* trans. C. Hastings and Donald Nicholl (London: Sheed and Ward, 1952), 110–11, and Edith Stein herself, *Briefe an Hedwig Conrad-Martius* (Munich: Kösel-Verlag, 1960), 69–70.

43. David Novak, "Edith Stein, Apostate Saint," *First Things* 96 (October 1999): 15–17. See subsequent correspondence in *First Things* 99 (January 2000): 7–9. See various essays in Waltraud Herbstrith, OCD, ed., *Never Forget: Christian and Jewish Perspectives on Edith Stein,* trans. Susanne Batzdorff (Washington, DC: ICS Publications, 1998).

44. Susanne M. Batzdorff, *Aunt Edith: The Jewish Heritage of a Catholic Saint* (Springfield, IL: Templegate Publishers, 1998), passim.

45. Harriet Pass Friedenreich, "Gender Identity and Community: Jewish University Women in Germany and Austria," in Brenner and Penslar, *In Search,* 154–75.

46. Edith Stein, "Individual and Community," in *Philosophy of Psychology,* 156–57.

47. Friedenreich, "Gender Identity," 156–57.

48. Keith H. Pickus, *Constructing Modern Identities: Jewish University Students in Germany, 1815–1914* (Detroit: Wayne State University Press, 1999), 145.

49. Stein, *Life,* 23.

50. Ibid., 68–72, 236. Edith Stein to Sr. Callista Kopf, OP, October 4, 1936, in *Self-Portrait in Letters,* 238. According to Resi Posselt, prioress of Stein's convent in Cologne, Stein's family home featured an array of Jewish artifacts, such as religious engravings and biblical motifs carved onto cupboard chests. Posselt, *Edith Stein,* 3. Edith Stein's niece Susanne Batzdorff, in *Aunt Edith,* 95, disputes Posselt's account and claims that no such religious décor was evident.

51. Marion A. Kaplan, *The Making of the Jewish Middle Class: Women, Family, and Identity in Imperial Germany* (New York: Oxford University Press, 1991), 44, 138–50.

52. Ibid., 8–9, 54–63.

53. Edith Stein, "Sentient Causality," in *Philosophy of Psychology,* 55.

54. Fritz Kaufmann, "Review of Edith Stein, *Endliches und ewiges Sein,*" *Philosophy and Phenomenological Research* 12 (1952): 573.

55. Roman Ingarden, "Edith Stein on Her Activity as an Assistant of Edmund Husserl," *Philosophy and Phenomenological Research* 13, no. 2 (1962–63): 155–75, trans. P. Taranczewski from "Über die philosophischen Forschungen Edith Steins," *Freiburger Zeitschrift für Philosophie und Theologie* 26 (1979): 456–80.

56. Stein, *Life,* 85.

57. John Nota, "Edith Stein and Martin Heidegger," in *Edith Stein Symposium: Teresian Culture,* ed. John Sullivan, OCD, Carmelite Studies 4 (Washington, DC: ICS Publications, 1987), 51.

58. Josephine Koeppel, OCD, *Edith Stein: Philosopher and Mystic* (Collegeville, MN: Liturgical Press, 1990), 89.

59. Stein, *Life,* 85–86.

60. Ibid., 391.

61. Ibid., 229.

62. Edith Stein, "How I Came to Cologne Carmel," in *Selected Writings*, 18. See, too, Kenneth L. Woodward, *Making Saints* (New York: Simon and Schuster, 1990) 137–43.

63. Stein, *Life*, 127.

64. Ibid., 118.

65. Kaplan, *Making*, 8.

66. Ibid., 10.

67. Stein, *Life*, 147.

68. Posselt, *Edith Stein*, 66. She quotes a member of Stein's family who claimed to speak for the entire family's response to the shocking news of Stein's conversion.

69. Stein, *Life*, 34–35.

70. P.O. van Kempen, "Eyewitness in Westerbork," in Herbstrith, *Never Forget*, 275.

71. Stein, *Life*, 71.

72. Ibid., and Edith Stein to Sr. Adelgundis Jägerschmid, OSB, and Sr. Placida Laubhardt, OSB, December 10, 1930, in *Self-Portrait in Letters*, 76 n. 5.

73. Edith Stein to Hedwig Conrad-Martius and Theodor Conrad, end of June, 1933, in *Self-Portrait in Letters*, 147.

74. Edith Stein to Mother Petra Brüning, OSU, October, 31, 1938, in *Self-Portrait in Letters*, 291.

75. Stein, "How I Came," 16; Edith Stein, "Conversation at Night," in *The Hidden Life: Hagiographic Essays, Meditations, Spiritual Texts*, ed. Lucy Gelber and Michael Linssen, OCD, trans. Waltraut Stein (Washington, DC: ICS Publications, 1992), 128–13.

76. Quoted in Herbstrith, *Edith Stein*, 117.

77. Edith Stein, "The Prayer of the Church," in *Hidden Life*, 117.

78. Daniel Krochmalnik quotes Stein in his essay "Edith Stein: A Jew's Path to Catholicism," in Herbstrith, *Never Forget*, 70.

79. Edith Stein to Hedwig Dülberg, October 31, 1938, in *Self-Portrait in Letters*, 291. See similar sentiments in Edith Stein to Sr. Callista Kopf, OP, October 4, 1936, 238.

80. Edith Stein to Sr. Adelgundis Jägerschmid, OSB, and Sr. Placida Laubhardt, OSB, December 10, 1930, in *Self-Portrait in Letters*, 75.

81. Ibid.

82. Gerhard Stein, "My Experiences with My Aunt Edith," in Herbstrith, *Never Forget*, 55.

83. Nancy Fuchs-Kreimer, "Sister Edith Stein: A Rabbi Reacts," in Herbstrith, *Never Forget*, 162.

84. Edith Stein, *Essays on Woman*, ed. Lucy Gelber and Romaeus Leuven, OCD, trans. Freda Mary Oben (Washington, DC: ICS Publications, 1987), 83–84.

85. Quoted in Michael Brenner, *The Renaissance in Jewish Culture in Weimar Germany* (New Haven, CT: Yale University Press, 1996), 89.

86. Edith Stein to Hedwig Conrad-Martius, April 5, 1933, in *Self-Portrait in Letters*, 138.

87. Edith Stein to Fritz Kaufmann, October 17, 1933, in *Self-Portrait in Letters*, 161.

88. Edith Stein to Mother Petra Brüning, October 3, 1936, in *Self-Portrait in Letters*, 236.

89. Edith Stein to Hedwig Conrad-Martius, January 13, 1937, in *Self-Portrait in Letters*, 243.

90. Edith Stein to Sr. Callista Kopf, OP, August 1, 1938, in *Self-Portrait in Letters,* 284.
91. Edith Stein to Mother Petra Brüning, December 9, 1938, in *Self-Portrait in Letters,* 295.
92. Edith Stein to Uta von Bodman, January 22, 1939, in *Self-Portrait in Letters,* 301.
93. Edith Stein to Mother Petra Brüning, April 26, 1940, in *Self-Portrait in Letters,* 322.
94. Edith Stein to Hilde Vérène Bosinger, December 31, 1941, in *Self-Portrait in Letters,* 342.
95. Ibid., 343 n. 1.
96. Characteristic of this view is Ruth Gay, *The Jews of Germany: A Historical Portrait* (New Haven, CT: Yale University Press, 1992), 219. Brenner reviews the dominant negative view of German-Jewish attitudes in *Renaissance in Jewish Culture,* 1–2.
97. Edith Stein to Hans Biberstein, November 17, 1939, in *Self-Portrait in Letters,* 315.
98. Hedwig Conrad-Martius, translated excerpt, in Herbstrith, *Never Forget,* 265–66, from her letter to Msgr. John M. Österreicher. See *Christliche Innerlichkeit* 26 (1991): 189.
99. Edith Stein to Hans Biberstein, November 17, 1939, in *Self-Portrait in Letters,* 315.
100. Berta Hümpfer's recollection in Herbstrith, *Never Forget,* 214.

Part Two

"Every So-Called 'Masculine' Occupation May Be Exercised by Many Women"

Edith Stein's Feminism

Edith Stein

Essential Differences

LINDA LOPEZ McALISTER

Since Edith Stein was one of the first European women to earn a PhD in philosophy and since she was a feminist herself, one might think that feminist philosophers in the United States would have become very interested in her work, especially after her essays on woman became available in English translation in 1987. By and large, no such wave of interest has yet materialized among feminist philosophers.[1] The reason for this lack of interest, I would speculate, is largely a matter of timing; Stein's work on women appeared in English at a singularly inauspicious time. As a phenomenologist she is a philosopher engaged in the search for essences, yet her *Essays on Woman (Die Frau)* appeared exactly at the time when antiessentialism was reaching its peak among English-speaking feminist philosophers.

For those who are unfamiliar with this chapter in recent feminist philosophy, let me briefly outline the main issues. On the one side are those who, like Edith Stein, think that there is something—some characteristic or set of characteristics—that constitutes what it is to be a woman, something in virtue of which every woman is a woman, and this something, whatever it might be, is essential to her being a woman, it is her essence. As we'll see in a moment, not all essentialists agree on *what* this essence consists of, where it "resides," so to speak, or how it comes to be. But whatever it is, most essentialists are committed to the view that it is not just something that all women have as a contingent matter of fact but, logically speaking, something without which they would not be women. It is incontrovertible that Edith Stein fits into this essentialist category: she speaks repeatedly of man's nature and women's nature in addition to their common human nature.[2] She refers not only to humanity as a species but to the species man and the species woman.[3] In the context of asking whether the common core of the female soul can be found in literary depictions of several very different women's lives she says: "[Y]ou can compare as many types of women as you like, but I believe that as long as they are types of *women* you will always find this at the core" and then goes on to say what she believes the essence of woman consists in.[4]

For the last several years essentialist views such as Stein's have been under attack, and the critiques have been so vigorous and widespread that many feminist philosophers go to great lengths to avoid the dread "essentialist" label. One of the reasons feminists have been so leery of essentialist claims is that they sound so much like the patriarchal masculinism that has for so long branded women's nature as not just different but inferior to man's. *Feminist* essentialism does not, of course, make the inference from different to inferior. In fact, some feminist essentialists (Mary Daly comes to mind) may even go to the other extreme of inferring from different to superior! Nonetheless, many feminists are made extremely nervous by any talk of "woman's nature" in light of how this concept has been used throughout history to justify sexism and other oppressive practices.

A second critique of feminist essentialism emerges from the broader and more pervasive poststructuralist program of deconstructing and decentering everything that posits the existence of fixed, eternal, unchanging universal natures or verities and instead seeing everything as constructed, changing, and in flux. A third criticism, while not inconsistent with the poststructuralist program, is nonetheless more modest in its claims and more political and pragmatic in its motivation. This critique maintains that by focusing attention on characteristics that all women are supposed to have in common, essentialism glosses over the differences that exist between women, thereby rendering the specific socio-historical positioning of individual women invisible, with the result that women who are different from those doing the theorizing are ignored and marginalized. A good example of this attack on essentialism comes from Elizabeth Spelman in her aptly titled book *Inessential Woman*. She says:

> Positing an essential "womanness" has the effect of making women inessential in a variety of ways. First of all, if there is an essential womanness that

all women have and have always had, then we needn't know anything about any woman in particular. For the details of her situation and her experience are irrelevant to her being a woman. Thus if we want to understand what "being a woman" means, we needn't investigate her individual life or any other woman's individual life. All those particulars become inessential to her being and our understanding of her being a woman. . . .

Moreover, to think of "womanness" in this way obscures three related facts about the meaning of being a woman: first of all, that whatever similarities there are between Angela Davis and me, they exist in the context of differences between us; second, that there is ongoing debate about the effect such differences have on those similarities . . . ; third, not all participants in that debate get equal air time or are invested with equal authority. . . .

Essentialism invites me to take what I understand to be true of me "as a woman" for some golden nugget of womanness all women have as women; and it makes the participation of other women inessential to the production of the story. How lovely: the many turn out to be one, and the one that they are is me.[5]

Antiessentialists, whatever arguments they use, are firmly committed to the idea that who we are "as women" is socially constructed, and they are involved in the project of theorizing differences, something that, according to them, essentialists ignore or avoid. So anyone whose project seems, like Stein's, to involve the enumeration of the essential characteristics of woman would be very uncongenial to these theorists. It is for this reason, I believe, that Stein's work on women has been of so little interest to feminist philosophers to date, philosophers whom you might otherwise think would find her, as one of the first woman philosophers of our century, someone of intense interest.

Things are changing, however. Recently some sophisticated feminist philosophers have been doing some very interesting rethinking of essentialism and the antiessentialist critiques. Let me call your attention to four initiatives of this sort. First, people are taking a closer look at what essentialism is and seeing that it is not a single monolithic position but a variety of positions that need to be evaluated on their own merits. Second, people are arguing that it is impossible to function as feminist philosophers without retaining something akin to essentialism at some level because feminists have to be able to talk about women as a category. Third, people are suggesting that the antiessentialists' critiques are themselves implicated in essentialism. And fourth, people are looking more closely at specific essentialist accounts not so much to ask whether or not they are true as to see how they function. Let us consider an example of each of these four initiatives.

Elizabeth Grosz, in her essay "A Note on Essentialism and Difference,"[6] lays the groundwork for showing to what extent essentialism is not a single view but a variety of different positions, and she lays out some of the characteristics of its various subcategories. Among the subcategories of essentialism that Grosz identifies is "biologism," in which woman's essence is defined in terms of biological capacities, and, as Grosz remarks, "insofar as biology is assumed to constitute an unalterable bedrock of identity, the attribution of biologistic characteristics amounts to a permanent form of social containment for women."[7] A second version of essentialism, which Grosz calls "naturalism," differs from biologism in that it "may be asserted on theological or on ontological rather than on biological grounds. . . . It may be claimed that women's nature is derived from God-given attributes which are not explicable or observable simply in biological terms."[8] Finally, Grosz identifies a third variety, "universalism," which is "the attribution of invariant social categories, functions, and activities to which all women in all cultures are assigned."[9]

Grosz's essay also provides an example of the second initiative by pointing out the difficulties that antiessentialism poses for feminism both as a political theory and as a movement. She asks: "[I]f women cannot be characterized in any general way . . . then how can feminism be taken seriously? What justifies the assumption that women are oppressed as a sex? What, indeed, does it mean to talk about women as a category? If we are not justified in taking women as a category, then what political grounding does feminism have?"[10]

The third initiative is exemplified by Vicki Kirby in her article "Corporeal Habits: Addressing Essentialism Differently." She argues that those critics who think they escape essentialism themselves are deluded:

> Essentialism is not an entity that can be identified and dissolved by saying yes or no to it. . . .
> To put this in a way that better suggests that we are always already in the grip of essentialism's reflex, we might ask, where is the evidence for either essentialism's error or anti-essentialism's truth to be situated and of what does it consist? . . . If we assume that when we locate essentialism we identify it and corral its dangers the better to determine the virtue of our own practice, then we have merely embraced another of essentialism's many mutations and one that finds us right inside "the belly of the beast."[11]

Finally Kirby suggests that there may be some benefit for feminists in turning again to specific essentialist theories, not to deny their essentialism but to look at them in new ways. She says: "It is not so much the meaning of essentialism that requires further consideration but 'the how' of that meaning. How is 'essence' entailed, made proper, installed 'as such' and naturalized within our thought and our being? How does it congeal into an embodied reality?"[12]

These four initiatives signal that it may once again be safe for feminist philosophers to wade in essentialist waters. I propose that we at least get our feet wet by examining Edith Stein's essentialism in the light of these new initiatives and by asking the following questions: Just what kind of an essentialist position does Edith Stein hold? Is her essentialism the pernicious variety that ignores individual differences, homogenizes us into generic woman, limits our potential, and inhibits social change? Or is it the benign variety that is necessary for feminist theorizing? What insights can be won for feminist philosophy by looking at *how* Stein's essentialism functions and what it says about the interplay between essences and individuals?

Let's start by asking, in terms of Grosz's typology, what kind of an essentialist Edith Stein is. The most common form, historically, is biologism, but Stein does not believe that it is in the body that the essential differences between men and women reside. Whatever the essence or species of woman is, it is something that is fixed and unchanging.[13] But Stein does not think that male and female bodies constitute this kind of unchanging basis. She remarks that the idea that human bodies could undergo a transition from male to female "is not so absurd as it might seem at first glance."[14] She points out that while physical differences have been thought of as fixed and psychological differences as capable of wide variation, "certain facts, hermaphroditic forms, and intermediate forms can be cited as evidence against the immutability of physical differences."[15] (And clearly modern medical technological developments have proved Stein to be correct in this: through reconstructive surgery, hormone treatments, and gene splicing we can now transform male bodies into female ones, female into male.) But if that's the case, the essence of woman or of man cannot reside in the body. Nor, for Stein, does it reside in the mere fact of the ubiquitous assignment of invariant social categories, functions, and activities in all cultures to women. That is to say, she is not a universalist in Grosz's sense. No, Stein is clearly in the category of essentialist that Grosz calls naturalists, and she belongs in this category on two counts. She holds that women and men have differing essences or natures on both ontological and theological grounds—seeing this as a point at which the results of philosophy and theology converge.

That this is her view is nowhere expressed more clearly than in her essay "The Problems of Women's Education," where she says:

I am convinced that the species human being reveals itself to be a double species, man and woman, that the essence of the human being—from which no
essential characteristic can be missing—is imprinted by this duality, and that
its entire structure bears this specific stamp. It is not just a matter of [male
and female] bodies being differently constructed, it is not just individual physiological functions that are different; rather the entire physical life is different,
the relationship between body and soul is different, and within the soul the
relationship between the spirit and the senses is different, as are the relationships among the various spiritual powers. To the female species corresponds
unity and consistency of the total psycho-physical personality, and the development of one's powers in a harmonious way: to the male species corresponds the perfection of one's individual powers to the maximum level of
performance.[16]

In several of her essays on women Stein elaborates on what she takes these
differences between men's and women's nature to be. For example, in an essay
entitled "The Ethos of Women's Professions," she writes:

The woman is oriented toward the living/the personal and toward the whole.
Holding, protecting, and preserving, nurturing, and encouraging growth:
those are her natural, genuinely maternal aspirations. Lifeless things, objects
are of interest to her primarily insofar as they serve the living/the personal,
not so much for their own sakes. This is connected with the fact that abstraction in any sense is remote from her nature. The living/the personal toward
which her caring is directed is a concrete whole and needs to be protected and
supported as a whole—not one part at the expense of another, not the spirit
at the expense of the body or vice versa, and not one mental capability at the
expense of another. She can bear that neither in herself nor in others. And
to this practical orientation corresponds the theoretical: her natural way of
knowing is not so much conceptual and analytic as it is intuitive, experiential, and directed toward the concrete. This natural endowment enables the
woman to care for and raise her own children, but this fundamental attitude
of hers is directed not only toward them but toward her husband and all other
beings who come in contact with her as well.[17]

Some feminists will hear this and similar passages and think that Stein is making the old masculinist claim that women are by nature destined to be wives
and mothers, to be subservient and self-sacrificing to their husbands and families. She does say these things, but it would be a mistake simply to regard that as

her whole position (as I have heard people do). It is where she starts rather than where she finishes.

Others will hear in Stein's emphasis on wholeness, connection with other people, and concrete detail echoes of feminist theorists Carol Gilligan and Nel Noddings and the ethic of care, while Stein's talk of holding, preserving, and furthering growth recalls Sara Ruddick's analysis of the elements of maternal thinking. Yet no one calls these thinkers masculinist or questions their feminist credentials. Of course they, too, are accused of being essentialists. If they are, they are of the universalist variety—holding that these characteristics of women are largely socially constructed as a result of women's universal condition of subordination, rather than being God-given features of the female soul.

The next question I posed was whether Stein's essentialism is of the pernicious variety. Let's approach this first by asking whether Elizabeth Spelman's critiques of essentialism can gain any purchase against Stein's version of it. Spelman has argued that essentialists, in focusing on the features that women have in common, are likely to neglect individual features and differences and thus to render individual women, in their specific ways of being, inessential.

Here it seems to me that Stein's version of essentialism can serve as a powerful counterexample to Spelman's claim. Not only does Stein not neglect the question of individual differences, she has elaborately worked-out theories of individual differences and types that bear directly upon just those issues Spelman says essentialists ignore, namely the contention that similarities among women "exist in the context of differences" and "the ongoing debate about the effect such differences have on those similarities."

As I said earlier, Stein's elaboration of woman's essence is her starting point, not the end of what she has to say about women. We should remember the context in which Stein undertook her study of women: she had a very specific purpose in investigating women's nature, and it was an extremely concrete and practical one: she was teaching in a girls' secondary school. She came face to face with dozens of young women every day and attempted to teach them and assist in their formation. Her exploration of the fixed essence of woman was for the purpose of finding out the nature of the basic raw material, so to speak, that she had to work with, so she could know which features of these girls' identity and personality could be changed, guided, and developed through education and other environmental factors and which could not.

For that reason, if for no other, she could not be satisfied merely to identify essential features all women share—she also had to look at the broader picture of what elements were mutable. As she says: "The Nature of woman . . . is the material that girls' education has to reckon with. This material, as we experience it, is not uniform, it is differentiated according to types and individual differences. We have to investigate whether there is a unitary and unchanging core within these types that we can call the species Woman. If so then we must try to discover the factors that determine how types are formed, and we must clarify how and to what extent we can influence them in practice."[18]

What does she mean by *types?* They seem to be broad classifications of dispositional traits. Her examples, taken from Else Croner, include the maternal type, the erotic or strongly sexual type, the romantic, the sedate-sensible type, the intellectual type.[19] In contrast to woman's nature or essence, types can change. An individual can be one type for a while and become a different type over time as the result of environmental influences, experience, maturity, education, and so on. Different types will be typical of different age groups. Types are historically and culturally specific. They can vary from one decade or century to another, from one ethnic group to another, and so on. It appears that what type an individual is at any given point in time is—to put it in contemporary feminist language—a matter of socialization or social construction.

If I understand Stein correctly these type differences influence, not the existence of women's essential nature, but the manner in which that essential nature is expressed. For example, a maternal-type woman and an intellectual type will express their natural propensity to preserve, protect, and nurture in different ways. In the maternal type this may be expressed through the attentive care she shows for her children; in the intellectual type it may be something like the caring, respectful, almost interactive relationship that a biologist like Barbara McClintock has toward the corn she studies.[20] Already we can see that Stein is one essentialist who does pay attention to women's historical, cultural, geographical, and social positioning.

But she goes even further than this. Starting with her work on empathy and then in her philosophy of person in the *Beiträge*[21] and elsewhere, Stein elaborates a whole theory of the individual. As Sr. Mary Catharine Baseheart writes in her article "Edith Stein's Philosophy of Woman and Woman's Education" on this point: "Stein's phenomenology of woman is a good example of the way in which she takes Husserlian methodology of seeking knowledge of the essence of an entity under investigation and adapts it to the complexities of the entity as it exists and operates in the world of experience. Thus she attempts to implement Husserl's idea of a 'concrete essence' and avoids the tendency toward over-abstraction that can plague a philosophy of essence."[22]

It is Stein's emphasis on socially constructed types and individual differences that makes it untrue to say of her essentialism, as Grosz says of essentialism in general, that it "limits the possibilities of change and thus of social reorganizations."[23] Stein's view on women's careers and their participation in the public sphere bears this out. She believed there could be wide variation in individual characteristics, inclinations, talents, and abilities. She notes: "Men's and women's essences share the same basic human attributes, and this or that trait may come to the fore not only in one sex or the other but also in individuals. For that reason women can be very like the male nature and vice versa."[24]

This means that Stein sees, in principle, no limitation on the kinds of careers that women should be able to aspire to, no limitations on the kinds of life a woman can choose to lead. In a famous passage from "The Ethos of Women's Vocations" she says: "No woman is just woman; each one has her own individuality and talents just as men do, and these talents give women the capability to engage in any profession, whether it be in the arts, the sciences, or technical fields. In principle, one's individual talents may point to any field, including those that are a far cry from feminine nature."[25]

What Stein believed was that in a so-called "masculine profession" such as philosophy, women will bring to bear on the profession their particular way of expressing their essential nature as women. Perhaps their approach will typically be more synthesizing than analytic; it may seek constructive, supportive, and helpful approaches rather than agonistic, refutational ones; the subjects singled out for philosophical investigation may be different and more closely related to specific, concrete life experiences, for example. In offices and factories she saw women helping to humanize the workplace—their holistic/personal approach tempering men's tendency toward specialization and task orientation.

Such a position in 1930 was surely in the forefront of feminist social change. And while Stein does believe that women's and men's distinctive natures provide the limits within which change is possible, her theories of types and individual differences carve out an enormous range of variation in which social change can occur. I submit that it would be beneficial for feminist philosophers to pay serious attention to her suggestions as to how this interplay between similarities and differences operates.

Just as a group of philosophers met recently in Germany to ask whether Edith Stein's philosophy in general is worth studying, I have been asking in this essay whether her feminist philosophy is worth studying not merely for its historical interest but for what Stein can contribute to today's ongoing debates in feminist philosophy and theory. My conclusion is that it is and that it should be studied.

One of the things that puts off secular feminists is the intensely Catholic flavor of her writings on women and her tendency to interweave philosophical and theological arguments. However, as I have suggested above and as I believe this essay demonstrates, her religious arguments and her philosophical arguments are separable. They move on parallel but separable tracks and arrive at the same conclusions. So I believe Edith Stein's philosophy of women can be studied by secular feminist philosophers and that it has a potential contribution to make to their exploration of feminist philosophy. There is no essential difference—just differences in style, vocabulary, and point of departure—between Stein's efforts to understand the extent to which women are socially constructed and contemporary feminists' efforts to explore the same issues. While Stein herself believed that the religious dimension of the investigation was not something she could or would eschew, neither would she say that secular feminist philosophers cannot achieve important results. She might say of them as she said of others who did not share her Catholic faith, "They who seek the truth are seeking God whether they know it or not."[26]

NOTES

This chapter was originally presented as part of a symposium on the philosophy of Edith Stein at Spalding University, Louisville, Kentucky, October 12–13, 1991, on the occasion of the dedication of the Edith Stein Center for Study and Research. I thank Sr. Mary Catharine Baseheart, SCN, for inviting me to be one of the presenters at the symposium. Published under the same title in *Philosophy Today* (Spring 1993): 70–77, this essay has undergone only minor changes for this volume.

1. I note that there were two papers on Edith Stein on the program of the Fourth Symposium of the International Association of Women Philosophers held in Amsterdam on April 22–25, 1992, so perhaps European feminist philosophers are taking more of an interest in Stein's philosophy than American philosophers are.

2. Edith Stein, *Die Frau: lhre Aufgabe nach Natur and Gnade,* vol. 5 of *Edith Steins Werke* (Louvain: Nauwelaerts; Freiburg, Herder, 1959), 139.

3. Ibid., 138.

4. Ibid., 52 (italics in original).

5. Elizabeth V. Spelman, *Inessential Woman* (Boston: Beacon, 1988), 158–59.

6. Elizabeth Grosz, "A Note on Essentialism and Difference," in *Feminist Knowledge,* ed. Sneja Gunew (New York: Routledge, 1990).

7. Ibid., 334.

8. Ibid.

9. Ibid., 335.

10. Ibid., 341.

11. Vicki Kirby, "Corporeal Habits: Addressing Essentialism Differently," *Hypatia* 6, no. 3 (1991): 4–24.

12. Ibid., 9.

13. Stein, *Die Frau,* 120.

14. Ibid., 121.

15. Ibid.

16. Ibid., 138.

17. Ibid., 3.

18. Ibid., 109.

19. Ibid., 126.

20. For an account of the relationship between McClintock as researcher and the material she studies, see Evelyn Fox Keller, *A Feeling for the Organism* (San Francisco: John Wiley and Sons, 1983).

21. Edith Stein, *Beiträge zur philosophischen Begründung der Psychologie und der Geisteswissenschaften* (Tübingen: Niemeyer, 1970).

22. Mary Catharine Baseheart, "Edith Stein's Philosophy of Woman and Woman's Education," *Hypatia* 4, no. 1 (1989): 130.

23. Grosz, "A Note," 134.

24. Stein, *Die Frau,* 139.

25. Ibid., 7.

26. Edith Stein to Sr. Adelgundis Jaegerschmid, OSB, March 23, 1938, in *Selbstbildnis in Briefen,* pt. 2, *1934–1942,* vol. 9 of *Edith Steins Werke* (Freiburg: Herder, 1977), pp. 102–3.

Edith Stein

A Reading of Her Feminist Thought

RACHEL FELDHAY BRENNER

> *[The woman] craves for an unhampered development of her personality just as*
> *much as she does to help another toward the same goal.*
> —Edith Stein, *Essays on Woman*

Edith Stein's feminist vision emerges in the papers on women's education that she delivered prior to and during her tenure as a faculty member of the Catholic Pedagogical Institute in Münster. Stein's lectures, compiled in a volume of her collected works entitled *Essays on Woman,* present a theological-philosophical-psychological investigation of women's nature, a perspective on women's social vocation, and a proposal for a reform in women's education.

Stein's thought on women is rooted in the socio-political situation of Germany at the time. Her lectures on women's education constitute a response to Germany's catastrophic economic crisis and to the threatening rise to power of the National Socialist party, a situation that she calls "the beginning of a great cultural upheaval."[1] As Stein sees it, the coming rule of terror is based on a vision of society as "a mechanistically ordered structure . . . [determined] merely on a biological basis."[2] The threatening political climate thus contributes to "the breakdown of married and family life" and total moral dissolution.[3] Stein observes how Nazism has nullified the emancipatory "gains won during the last decades"[4] by limiting women's role to the biological function of "[bearing] babies of Aryan stock."[5] She therefore urges women to "remind themselves that the whole political situation depends on how they use their political rights," and admonishes them to get involved in matters of national and international welfare.[6]

Women should not, however, consider only political options for improving the situation. Their inherent qualities, natural inclinations, and social interests constitute their potential to redeem the collapsing civilization. Stein claims that "the development of the feminine nature can become a blessed counter-balance precisely here where everyone is in danger of becoming mechanized and losing its humanity."[7] This view places women over men as protectors and saviors of the endangered humanist tradition. Redemption is possible, and women are the potential source of the world's moral salvation.

Stein's notion of women's principal role in the world's moral rebirth evolves out of her phenomenological-theological orientation. She sees moral conduct as humankind's indelible need which can be re-validated through ethical re-education. The model of the pre-fall perfect balance, that is, the non-hierarchical, Edenic position of the man and the woman, serves as evidence that the lost humanist ethics can be re-established.

Stein's reading of the biblical story of creation with emphasis on Adam and Eve as equal counterparts constitutes the core of her feminist thinking. Both Adam and Eve were given three major duties: "[T]hey are to be in the image of God, bring forth posterity, and be masters over the earth." The fact that the creation of the woman succeeded that of the man does not imply women's inferiority. On the contrary, Eve was created as Adam's equal since "no helpmate corresponding to him was found for Adam" among God's creatures. Eve was destined as *Eser kenegdo,* which Stein interprets as "a helper as if vis-à-vis to him." The Edenic man and woman were counterparts. They were not identical but complementary, "as one hand [complements] another."[8] Indeed, as Stein explains, they were meant to become one: "It is not a question here of a sovereignty of man over woman. She is named as companion and helpmate, and it is said of her that he will cling to her and that both are to become one flesh. This signifies that we are to consider the life of the initial human pair as the most intimate community of love, that their faculties were in perfect harmony as within one single being."[9]

The fall terminated this harmony; it injected a new element that destroyed the perfect balance of the positions of men and women. It disclosed a different connection between the two sexes. As Stein argues, "Concupiscence had awakened in them," and therefore "they saw each other with different eyes than they had previously."[10] Consequently, "the relationship of the sexes . . . has become a brutal relationship of master and slave." In the post-fall situation "women's natural gifts . . . are no longer considered; rather, the man uses her as a means to achieve his own ends in the exercise of his work or in pacifying his own lust." But while the woman is subservient to the man's lust, the man "becomes a slave to his lust." The Edenic relations of freedom and harmony are totally distorted when the man eventually becomes "a slave of the slave who must satisfy him."[11]

A juxtaposition of Stein's reading of the story of creation and fall with that of Phyllis Trible, a contemporary feminist theologian, reveals similarities which validate the claim for Stein's prescience regarding the feminine condition. Trible's view of *Eser kenegdo* as "a helper who is counterpart" and her conclusion that "woman is the helper equal to man"[12] are similar to Stein's perception of the initial harmoniously balanced relationship between men and women. Even closer to Stein's position is Trible's contention that the post-fall male supremacy distorts the ideal order of creation. Trible maintains that "Subjugation and supremacy are perversions of creation. Through disobedience, the woman has become a slave. . . . The man is corrupted also, for he has become master, ruling over the one who is God-given equal. . . . The suffering and oppression we women and men know now are marks of our fall, not of our creation."[13]

Trible ends her exegesis stating that the feminist interpretation which tells us that we have become "creatures of oppression . . . opens possibilities for change, for a return to our true liberation under God."[14] Similarly Stein not only sees the biblical narrative as a liberating text but actually uses it as such in her attempt to illuminate the sources of social evil.

Furthermore, Stein's "liberating" view of creation helps her to reconsider some of the mispresentations of women in the New Testament, especially in the letters of Paul. While her perception reflects to a degree the traditional view of women in her day, she departs in radical ways from accepted beliefs and concepts pertaining to women. She sees Paul's tenacious view of women's inferiority as a reflection of the fallen state of humanity. Rather than strive to restore the "original and redemptive order," which emphasizes the direct contact between God and all creation, the Apostle insists on "man's role as mediator between the Redeemer and woman," asserting that a woman is to her husband as the Church is to Christ and therefore that "the woman should stand in awe of her husband." Stein argues that the connection of Christ and the Church "is a matter of symbolic relationship" and that "[t]he husband is *not* Christ."

The relationship between husband and wife should assume a different mode, whereby the husband, who is not perfect, should "permit the gifts of the other members to compensate for his defects, just as it could be the highest political wisdom of the sovereign to allow a judicious minister to rule." In her consideration of the relationship between husband and wife, Stein maintains the traditional view of marriage headed by the male spouse. Indeed, her metaphorical representation of the marriage relationship resorts to the images of the head and the body. The man who rules over the wife, as the head rules over the body, must prove a magnanimous ruler and allow the woman to develop her gifts and talents in order to contribute to the salvation of the marriage.[15]

Against Paul's view of women's inferiority, Stein offers three counter-arguments: Jesus's disallowing divorce, the ideal of Virgin-Mother, and the fact that women were among Jesus' closest and most trusted companions.[16] These counter-arguments vacillate between the desire to see women in a position equal to that of men and adherence to the notion of women's secondary position in terms of the religious dogma.

In forbidding divorce Jesus invokes the pre-fall "two in one flesh" coexistence of man and woman. Thus, he advances the notion of redemptive equality which would reconstruct, to an extent, Edenic equality between men and women. The traditional aspect of Stein's thought emerges here in the omission of the notion of divorce, which enables each spouse to exit a relationship that has not proven "Edenic."

The concept of Virgin-Mother advances the position of woman as a mediator, rather than equal partner, in Redemption. The Virgin Mary is "the gateway through which God found entrance to humankind."[17] While the Virgin Mary is "co-redeemer by the side of the Redeemer,"[18] her example becomes a model, nevertheless, whereby the woman "should honor the image of Christ in her husband. . . . [The woman] herself is to be the image of God's mother. . . . [S]he is to be Christ's image."[19] In Stein's perception, the Virgin Mary, though instrumental in the redemption process, remains precisely that, an instrument or a vehicle which facilitated the appearance of the Redeemer. Consequently, the woman reflects the image of the Redeemer indirectly, through her identification with the Redeemer's mother.

Women's close companionship with Jesus is a proof that "salvation admits of no differences between the sexes."[20] The sense of oneness with Jesus is equally possible for men and women; the duty of emulating the Lord is incumbent upon man and woman alike. Stein points to St. Paul's self-contradiction in terms of his consideration of women's position vis-à-vis men when she invokes his famous letter to the Galatians, "There is neither Jew nor Greek, slave nor freeman; *there is neither male nor female.* For you are all one in Christ Jesus."[21]

Stein's contention about Jesus' female followers is similar to the conclusion reached by Elisabeth Schüssler Fiorenza: "[I]t cannot be justifiably argued that Jesus as a Jew of the first century could not have women disciples." All four

Gospels not only mention women in the fellowship of Jesus but single them out as the most courageous of his disciples. Like Stein, Fiorenza refers to Paul's letter to the Galatians, but she goes further than Stein by inferring that "[w]omen were not marginal figures in this community but exercised leadership as apostles, prophets, and missionaries."[22]

Stein does not elaborate on the functions fulfilled by the women in Jesus' entourage. At the same time, she associates the discussion of women as Jesus' followers and emissaries with the contemporary problem of women's position in the Church. Here she adopts a conservative position, maintaining that although "women were among His disciples and most intimate confidants . . . [Jesus] did not grant them the priesthood" and therefore that "the actual priestly work is reserved for men." Stein, however, makes an accurate prediction that "it may well be that one day attention will be given to the demand" of the recognition of women's services to the Church. Though refraining from supporting female priesthood, Stein nevertheless admits that such reform "cannot be forbidden by dogma."[23]

Her espousal of the conservative view of women's position in the Church should not be understood merely as a reflection of her traditionalism. Rather, it seems to reaffirm Stein's view of women's particular social destiny. Women's social objective, as Stein sees it, should not amount to sharing religious functions with men but to actualizing their particular feminine singularity. Stein's feminist thought focuses on women's "*intrinsic feminine value*" and on its redemptive potential in the context of family and society at large.[24]

The social position and role that Stein assigns to women seem rooted in her theological conviction that men and women were created equal, yet distinct from each other. Each sex, therefore, represents its singular potential in terms of its social function, a potential which needs to be actualized through an adequate education. An educator and feminist, Stein was particularly interested in female characteristics and their promise in respect to society's moral welfare.

She thus ponders the issue of gender distinctions and their treatment in the framework of an educational system. Undoubtedly, gender differentiation affects the mind. Should education strive to blur the differences between the sexes, or, rather, should the intrinsic characteristics of each sex be developed? In other words, should intellect be considered inseparable from the total human being and thus developed in accordance with the inherent particularity of the sex?[25]

These questions direct Stein toward a philosophical consideration of the human ability to distinguish between the notions of individual and type. Our cognition endows us with the perception which "confers on a concrete subject its universal structure."[26] In other words, we have the ability to identify the individual according to his or her particular characteristics and qualities, and, at the same time, we are able to define the individual in the abstract terms of typology. Each individual is unrepeatable and therefore unique, and, in that sense, he or she resists abstraction, but since every individual is a representative of the human species and one of the sexes, "every description of an individual also deals with the concept of his type."[27] Psychology helps us understand the typology of human behavior—that is, patterns of responses to motivation and circumstances predicated upon typological common denominators.

Gender typology delineates such responses, as they are determined by the male-female characteristics not only in body structure and in particular physiological functions but in the entire corporeal life[28]—that is, by characteristics which are not subject to change.

Stein's phenomenological investigation of "the essence of woman" does not contradict her theological perspective. On the contrary, she claims that the "differentiation of the species as presented by philosophy corresponds to the destiny of the sexes as shown to us by theology."[29] The male and female social functions of, respectively, protector and nurturer, as defined in the biblical story, are reaffirmed by the philosophical inference of the indivisibility of body and soul, of physiology and mind. "The relationship of soul and body is different in man and woman,"[30] postulates Stein, and this differentiation allows us to speak about the feminine typology. If body and soul have an effect upon each other, woman's typology shows that her psychological make-up is to a great extent determined by the biological function of reproduction. The function of motherhood structures a typology informed by the sense of self in relation to others. Stein's emphasis on the notion of reproduction as an indelible factor in women's relations with the world presages a contemporary trend in feminist thought perhaps best represented by the work of Nancy Chodorow.

In *The Reproduction of Mothering*, Chodorow demonstrates how the female gender fosters "attachment . . . and the fusion of identification with object of choice." The mother who brings into the relationship with her daughter "her own internalized early relationship with her mother"[31] provides a model which emphasizes correctness, continuity, and the recognition of the other. The early consciousness of the world—that is, the "social ascription of sex that begins at birth," as Chodorow terms it—explains the unity between mother and child which accounts for the mother's ambivalent "desire both to keep daughters close and to push them to adulthood," and for the daughter's tendency to act upon "her feelings of dependence on and primary identification with this mother."[32]

Stein's discussion of mother-daughter relationships seems to prefigure Chodorow's assessments. The interaction between mother and daughter is underscored by the sense of connectedness, caring, and guidance. On the one hand, a mother's commitment to her child is "her first duty";[33] on the other hand, for her daughter, she "embodies authentic womanhood." The relationship, based on "caring love," creates "vital solidarity between mother and daughter . . . a spiritual-intellectual tie scarcely to be severed."[34] Like Chodorow, Stein recognizes the ambivalent mother-daughter relationships which develop at the time of puberty. At the age when the daughter wishes to assert her independence, "yet longs for understanding and guidance," the mother must realize that "the child is no longer a child" and offer "example and judgment [which] will be the child's guiding principle"[35] in her future role of mother.

Chodorow asserts that identification with the mother accounts for the emergence of the sentiment of empathy in the daughter's "primary definition of self."[36] This observation has been further expounded by contemporary feminist thinkers. For instance, in the philosophical study *Caring,* Nell Noddings postulates that "the ethical self can emerge only from caring for others"[37] and that caring is possible thanks to the value of empathic receptivity, whereby "I receive the other into myself, and I see and feel with the other."[38]

The emphasis on empathy in contemporary feminist thought invokes Stein's deep interest in the phenomenon of empathy. In fact, she explores the phenomenology of empathy in her doctoral thesis *On the Problem of Empathy,* completed in 1916. In her dissertation, Stein defines empathy as "the basis of intersubjective experience":[39] the other "is other than 'I' . . . it is 'you.' But, since it experiences itself as I experience myself, the 'you' is another 'I.'"[40] The other will never become me; neither shall I become the other. It is, however, possible to approximate his or her experience through empathy which communicates that the other responds to the world as I do. The capacity to gain an insight into the other's world enables me to act empathically toward my fellow human beings. The capacity to gain an insight into the other's empathic experience of me teaches me about myself through the other. As Stein observes, "By empathy with differently composed personal structures we become clear on what we are not, and what we are . . . to others. Thus together with self knowledge, we also have an important aid to self evaluation."[41]

This dynamic of empathic response to the world and to oneself, whereby "only he who experiences himself as a person, as a meaningful whole, can understand other persons,"[42] informs Stein's concept of education. More specifically, Stein's consideration of the social ramifications of empathic behavior underscores her thought on women's function in society. In contrast with man, woman, whose primary function is maternal, "has a more sensitive faculty of empathy."[43] It seems important to note that Stein sees maternity in a larger sense than a characteristic related to the function of reproduction. Like many later feminist thinkers, Stein claims that woman's empathy is by no means limited to her children; rather, it enables her to understand "the special, individual destiny of every living being"[44] and relate to humanity at large. In Stein's *Weltanschauung*, motherhood as a social concept assumes twofold signification. It assigns woman the concrete tasks of the nurturer-educator of her biological offspring. At the same time, motherhood also typifies woman as a universal nurturer and teacher of humankind.

Such global understanding of motherhood liberates women in terms of their choice of profession. The importance of women as educators of humanity disallows the distribution of professions according to gender differentiation. Women are needed, claims Stein, wherever the "true feminine qualities . . . of feeling, intuition, empathy, and adaptability come into play." Whenever her profession "involves the total person in caring for, cultivating, helping, understanding, and in encouraging the gifts of the other," woman's choice of vocation is justified.[45] Moreover, the feminine empathic inclination, which can be actualized in practically every profession, highlights the symbolic significance of mother as the agent for the world's moral recovery, as the healer of the diseased civilization.

Stein's consideration of motherhood in terms of its universalist notion presages Sara Ruddick's concept of "maternal thinking." Like Stein, Ruddick sees woman's mode of thought, the "maternal," coming from concrete child-caring, biological situations. At the same time, like Stein, she by no means attributes the maternal attitude to the biological factor. Maternal thinking, claims Ruddick, is inherently feminine "because we are all daughters." Maternal thinking, however, does not separate "intellectual activities" from the "disciplines of feeling." Woman's thought, as Ruddick defines it, is "a unity of reflection, judgment, and emotion."[46] If maternal thinking is governed by the values of "capacity of attention" and "virtue of love," rather than by the desire to shape the child's "acceptability" to the dominant culture, it will produce an educational discourse "of general intellectual and moral benefit." Maternal thinking, claims Ruddick, transcends a mother's interest in her own children and makes the interest of all children her own. It involves self-education, since attention "requires effort and self-training," and love signifies attachment, but "also a detachment, a giving up" in order to allow the child to grow. And so, Ruddick notes, "Many mothers also train themselves in the looking, self-restraining, and *empathy that is loving attention.*"[47]

Ruddick's notion of "empathy as loving attention" reiterates Stein's notion of empathy as the faculty through which we both reach to the other and gain self-knowledge. Stein's study of the phenomenology of the human constitution led her to a definition of empathic education which encompasses the student's emotional as well as intellectual needs in pursuit of self-improvement. The purpose of education "is not an external possession of learning but rather "the *gestalt which the human personality assumes under the influence of manifold external forces*"; it is the confluence of "the inherited physical-psychic disposition" and of "the formative materials" that produces the educated human being. Education cannot "make something which is not by nature"; it only "helps the soul reach its intended gestalt."[48] Since the educational process involves the whole human being, it cannot be limited to the development of the intellect only; it must also apply itself to the development of the child's emotional potential.[49] To define Stein's position in Ruddick's terms: maternal thinking, as an educational means, must direct its empathic loving attention to the inherent needs of the child and to its potential, rather than shape it according to the rules of social acceptability.

What, then, are the social needs that educational reform, as Stein sees it, must address? We have already noted that, thanks to her vocation as mother, woman's empathic nature sets her on the mission to bring forth the ethical and emotional actualization of those who surround her. This mission, however, cannot be accomplished before the woman's wholeness as a person is achieved. Only a lucid, critical self-evaluation will bring forth an adequate level of maturation to lead others toward self-improvement.

The main weakness which hinders women's "true humanity," as Stein sees it, lies in their "excessive interest in others." This flaw is deeply rooted in a woman's tendency to assert her identity through others. The woman's sense of self-importance draws upon an unrealistically perfected view of her family, while her inordinate interest in others reveals the desire to lose her own personality.[50]

Stein explains women's psychological weaknesses in the framework of their theological thought. After the fall, "[t]he specific degeneracy of woman is seen in her servile dependency on man and in the decline of her spiritual life into a predominantly sensual one."[51] Ironically, the "punishment" of the fallen woman is, in fact, subversion of empathy through excess of identification with others. Instead of striving to comprehend the other, she tries to become the other.

In the essay "The Human Situation," the feminist theologian Valerie Saiving echoes Stein's observations of female predicament: "[Woman's] receptivity to the moods and feelings of others and her tendency to merge her selfhood in the joys, sorrows, hopes, and problems of those around her are the positive expressions of an aspect of the feminine character which may also take the negative forms of gossipy sociability, dependence on others (such as husband or children) for the definition of her values, or a refusal to respect another's right to privacy."[52] Like Stein, Saiving believes that the woman's self-affirmation of her feminine uniqueness and value, her self-acceptance "with joy," will enable her "to be a source of strength and refreshment to her husband, her children, the wider community."[53] Stein, believes, however, that women's self-reaffirmation is the goal of appropriate training, which will raise the consciousness of women's position in society by developing feminine self-awareness. Stein thus designs a curriculum which will train the "ability to discriminate," as well as develop feminine inherent qualities. Thus, she recommends that emotional faculties be developed through the study of languages, history, and religion; that the mind be trained through mathematics, natural sciences and the classics; that the intellectual receptivity be encouraged through emphasis on spontaneity;[54] and that clear thought be enhanced through the study of language.

Stein designs a curriculum intended to produce a well-rounded, knowledgeable woman. It is, especially, the study of language "to make the right use of speech" that highlights woman's mission as the empathic teacher of humanity: "Whoever is unable to express himself is imprisoned in his own soul; he is unable to liberate himself and cannot relate to others. . . . To be able to express oneself appropriately is thus something which belongs essentially to perfected humanity."[55]

As a teacher, the woman must convey the notion of one's accountability for one's words. She must instill the consciousness that expression liberates self-knowledge that allows us to connect meaningfully with others. The ability "to clothe inward thoughts with outward speech"[56] establishes an empathic bridge which helps to relate to others while preserving independent, self-conscious individuality. Clear articulation of thoughts helps communicate the individual's position vis-à-vis the world, a position that Carol Gilligan defines as "the paradoxical truths of human experience that we know ourselves as separate only insofar as we live in connection with others, and that we experience relationship only insofar as we differentiate other from self."[57] In other words, self-knowledge can be reached only within the framework of communal life. Relationships help us understand the uniqueness of every individual and, at the same time, elucidate the extent to which social environment shapes individuality.

Self-knowledge, which allows for independent, not servile, relationships, leads to a new understanding of the concept of objectivity. Cultivating the illusion that a totally detached, impartial point of view is possible signifies, in fact, women's desire to attain merely "an analogy to the masculine species." A different concept of objectivity must be assimilated, whereby the notion of intersubjectivity—that is, the recognition that each of us has a particular point of view—leads to truly objective self-knowledge. Stein suggests that "[w]e must advance further from the objective outlook to the proper personal one, which is also the attitude that is actually most highly objective. But relevant to this personal outlook is a realization of true humanity, i.e., of its ideal image, and a perception of the predisposition towards it as well as departures from it within ourselves and in others, a freedom of insight, an autonomy within ourselves and in others."[58] The ability to see oneself as an imperfect human being, striving to approach the idea of true humanity, endows one with an objective, lucid, yet empathic perception of the other. The acceptance of the relativity, instability, and contextuality that characterizes human existence leads to the understanding that intersubjectivity is the only avenue to attain objectivity.

It is important to note that the phenomenology of "objective subjectivity" has informed the educational concept of "connected knowledge," defined as "seeing the other, the student, in the student's own terms."[59] Many educators today practice "disciplined subjectivity" when, aware of their own biases, they try to connect—that is, to enter the student's perspective.[60] Stephen Wilson demonstrates the phenomenological basis of such an approach in scientific research. Wilson states that "[p]henomenology . . . offers an alternative view of objectivity . . . for studying human behavior. . . . [T]his tradition assert[s] that [we] *cannot understand human behavior without understanding the framework within which the subjects interpret their thoughts, feelings, and actions.*"[61] "Through the technique of "disciplined subjectivity" the educator "must learn to systematically empathize with the participants."[62]

Stein examines the issue of professions for women from the point of view of the woman's contribution to social and ethical reform. Whatever the profession, it must focus on the emotional and intellectual totality of the human being. Whether physician, scholar, or politician, woman has undertaken an essentially empathic mission: "to save, to heal endangered or demoralized humanity, to steer it into healthy ways."[63]

This vision does not remain in the sphere of abstraction; it is meant to be implemented. By devising an educational system for women, Stein consciously displaces the old order and implements new concepts by way of new formative experiences for girls. In view of today's empathic approach to education, it is important to mention that, as Stein sees it, "[t]he crux of the matter" is that "the educational system for girls . . . was exclusively conducted by men and [its] purpose and method were determined by men."[64] The system which she devises advances a method adapted to "feminine spirituality and the individual nature of pupils."[65] The exclusivity of this system in terms of its feminist orientation is even further highlighted by Stein's astute observation that "for women to be shaped in accordance with their authentic nature and destiny, they must be edu-

cated by authentic women."[66] While established by women for women, the social implications of the program are global, they affect society at large and "[in-
volve] . . . the entire range of educational reform."[67]

Stein's extraordinary anticipation of contemporary feminist thought must
be considered in the socio-political context of her time. Let us remember the
particular circumstances under which Stein was presenting her ideas and recognize that her educational project was a direct response to a regime of terror
which she openly abhorred. Edith Stein's intellectual undertaking to empower
women deserves particular attention. As a woman in imminent danger of annihilation asserting the vitality of women's position in society, Stein represents
an exemplary feminist. Her plan to heal humanity, consciously undertaken at
the time when the world around her was collapsing, presents Edith Stein as a
courageous and self-aware woman whose act inspires faith in her thought.

NOTES

This essay appeared originally in *Studies in Religion/Sciences Religieuses* 23, no. 1 (1994):
43–56.

1. Edith Stein, *Essays on Woman*, trans. Freda Mary Oben (Washington, DC: ICS
Publications, 1987), 140.
2. Ibid., 197.
3. Ibid., 136.
4. For a detailed discussion of German women's economic, political, and cultural
achievements, see Mary Nolan, " 'Housework Made Easy': The Taylorized Housewife in
Weimar Germany's Rationalized Economy," *Feminist Studies* 16, no. 3 (1990): 579–606.
5. Stein, *Essays on Woman*, 145.
6. Ibid., 141–42.
7. Ibid., 48.
8. Ibid., 59.
9. Ibid., 60.
10. Ibid., 61–62.
11. Ibid., 71.
12. Phyllis Trible, "Eve and Adam: Genesis 2–3," in *Womanspirit Rising*, ed. Carol P.
Christ and Judith Plaskow (San Francisco: Harper and Row, 1979), 75.
13. Ibid., 80–81.
14. Ibid., 81.
15. Stein, *Essays on Woman*, 65–67.
16. Ibid., 66–68.
17. Ibid., 69.
18. Ibid., 189.
19. Ibid., 69.
20. Ibid., 75.

21. Ibid., 68.

22. Elisabeth Schüssler Fiorenza, "Women in the Early Christian Movement," in Christ and Plaskow, *Womanspirit Rising*, 87–89.

23. Stein, *Essays on Woman*, 83–84.

24. Ibid., 247.

25. Ibid., 172–73.

26. Ibid., 168.

27. Ibid., 166.

28. Ibid., 177.

29. Ibid., 178.

30. Ibid., 177.

31. Nancy Chodorow, *The Reproduction of Mothering: Psychoanalysis and the Sociology of Gender* (Berkeley: University of California Press, 1978), 166–67.

32. Ibid., 135.

33. Stein, *Essays on Woman*, 178.

34. Ibid., 214.

35. Ibid.

36. Chodorow, *Reproduction of Mothering*, 167.

37. Nell Noddings, *Caring: A Feminine Approach to Ethics and Moral Education* (Berkeley: University of California Press, 1984), 14.

38. Ibid., 31.

39. Edith Stein, *On the Problem of Empathy* (Washington, DC: ICS Publications, 1987), 64.

40. Ibid., 38.

41. Ibid., 116.

42. Ibid.

43. Stein, *Essays on Woman*, 207.

44. Ibid., 73.

45. Ibid., 81–82.

46. Sara Ruddick, "Maternal Thinking," in *Philosophy, Children and the Family*, ed. Albert C. Cagfagna, Richard T. Peterson, and Craig A. Staundenbaur (New York: Plenum Press, 1982), 105–6.

47. Ibid., 116–19 (emphasis mine).

48. Stein, *Essays on Woman*, 116–17.

49. Ibid., 123.

50. Ibid., 250.

51. Ibid., 180.

52. Valerie Saiving, "The Human Situation: A Feminine View," in Christ and Plaskow, *Womanspirit Rising*, 38.

53. Ibid.

54. Stein, *Essays on Woman*, 103–5.

55. Ibid., 225.

56. Ibid., 224.

57. Carol Gilligan, *In a Different Voice: Psychological Theory and Women's Development* (Cambridge, MA: Harvard University Press, 1982), 63.

58. Stein, *Essays on Woman*, 251.

59. Mary Field Belenky, Blythe McVicker Clinchy, Nancy Rule Goldberger, and Jill Mattuck Tarule, *Women's Ways of Knowing: The Development of Self, Voice and Mind* (New York: Basic Books, 1986), 224.

60. Ibid., 226.

61. Stephen Wilson, "The Use of Ethnographic Techniques in Educational Research," *Review of Educational Research*, 47, no. 1 (1977): 249.

62. Ibid., 258.

63. Stein, *Essays on Woman*, 157.

64. Ibid., 152.

65. Ibid., 99.

66. Ibid., 107.

67. Ibid., 115.

Chapter 12

Edith Stein's Philosophy of "Liberal" Education

LISA M. DOLLING

It may come as a surprise to those more familiar with the speculative philosophy of Edith Stein to learn that some of her most committed work in the form of both essays and lectures centers on the philosophy of women and of education. This last concern was driven primarily by a combination of her personal situation (e.g., Stein's many experiences as educator) and the existing state of affairs in Germany during the time Stein wrote. In fact, in one of her essays on women's education,[1] Stein describes the situation of her day as a state of crisis, requiring total reconstruction from the ground up. Her suggestions for bringing about such radical pedagogical reform articulate a sophisticated philosophy of liberal education that provides valuable, often inspiring, advice for both students concerned with their own educational development and educators responding to the call to teach. Moreover—and perhaps most significantly—Stein's writings on education contain not only relevant advice for addressing some of the more traditional issues found within the philosophy of education but also some suggestions pertinent to some of today's debates regarding the future of educational reform. It is the aim of this chapter to highlight some of the ideas found in Stein's writings on education and show how they might be of use in contributing to today's discussion of the aim and purpose of education, especially its role in shaping a tolerant, intelligent, and compassionate human being.

Upon closer study, it becomes apparent that there are striking similarities between Stein's liberal philosophy of education and that of other pathbreaking thinkers who also tend to see education as central to both the development of the person and an overall enrichment of what it means to be human. These include such varied thinkers as the late-eighteenth-/early-nineteenth-century German humanist Wilhelm von Humboldt and several twentieth-century theorists: the existential philosopher Martin Buber, the German philosopher Hans-Georg Gadamer, the philosopher of education Nel Noddings, and, finally, the philosopher/classicist Martha Nussbaum. Their common views structure this essay.

The principal source for Edith Stein's writings on education (as well as on women) is a collection of papers that has been published as volume 2 of the English translation of *Edith Steins Werke (The Collected Works of Edith Stein).*[2] This volume, *Essays on Woman (Die Frau),* focuses on Stein's concern for educating women and elucidates—and indeed celebrates—what she viewed as the true nature of women. In these essays Stein discusses women in terms of not only their essence, their spirituality, their humanity, and their vocation but also, and perhaps most importantly, their educational needs. The essays, spurred by Stein's view that Germany's educational system was in "shambles," were originally lectures that Stein delivered to various educational groups while on a tour between 1928 and 1932. During these talks, Stein made ardent pleas for significant pedagogical reform throughout Germany's educational system, with special attention directed toward the needs of women. While it was true that great strides had already been made in Germany toward achieving sexual parity in education, nevertheless, as Stein often noted, much still needed to be done to guarantee women their educational due.

Education was a topic dear to Edith Stein, given her passion not only for her own educational development but also for the profession of teaching, which she practiced with great commitment and enthusiasm—bordering on religious fervor. Indeed, she often described her chosen career as a sacred "calling."[3] Moreover, since for Stein proper education was a propaedeutic to grace—something she viewed as crucial for the full realization of a person's potential—one can imagine the powerful role she would give to both the educational process and the educator who helps bring it about. While much of Stein's philosophy of education is entwined with her Catholic religious beliefs about knowledge of God, it is still possible, as this essay attempts, to look exclusively at the philosophical import of her educational ideas apart from their religious implications.

According to Edith Stein, education is defined simply as the formation of the human person. It is a process of bringing to fruition what is there by nature; a bringing to actuality what is there potentially. Stein describes this as a threefold process, taking place on three different levels: the development of the person in terms of his or her *humanity, gender,*[4] and, finally, *individuality.* This last level pays special attention to the uniqueness of the pupil—his or her natural endowments and abilities as well as limitations. Stein is quick to point out, however, that these are not three separate goals, since the nature of a particular human individual is not divided into three parts but is *one.* These represent three ways of achieving the same goal, which remains the integrated development of the whole person. In other words, Stein emphasizes that these three aims—when pursued properly—can never be at cross-purposes, since they all have as their guiding principle the development of the person's full humanity. In that respect, while the three goals pursued in the education of the individual can be separated by way of analysis, practically, one can never exist apart from the others.

To educate most effectively, according to Stein, the educator must remain ever mindful of this threefold goal of education. Though concerned at all times with the three levels of the student's development, the teacher should focus especially on the student's distinct individuality. It is precisely this concern for the uniqueness of the individual that Stein believed was sorely lacking in the educational system of her day. In her essay entitled "Fundamental Principles of Women's Education," Stein criticizes the prevailing approach, or "old system"—something she characterizes as a "child of the Enlightenment"—in which the ideal, instead of a concern for the particularity of the student, becomes the accumulation of facts with the aim that the student gain encyclopedic knowledge. This philosophy regards the mind of the student as a tabula rasa that receives as many impressions as possible. Such a view leads to a mechanical and technical approach to education that regards the student's mind as primarily passive. Stein asserts that the goal of education, rather than being a student's external possession of learning, is "the gestalt which the human personality assumes under the guidance of manifold external forces."[5]

Foremost among these "external forces," of course, is the educator, whose primary responsibility is to identify the personality of the student so as to help bring about this gestalt. Throughout her work Stein describes this individual gestalt in terms of the person's "inner form" or seed of nature that God has implanted. In another address, entitled "Problems of Women's Education,"[6] Stein acknowledges the "heavy" task given to the educator who must identify this inner form. Here she notes that the educator needs to have knowledge of the human personality, of its structure and development, in addition to an understanding of the uniqueness of the person and the person's needs. Further, Stein asserts, the educator must have knowledge of and introduce students to cultural traditions that include the norms suitable for the intellectual and spiritual life. With all this in mind as well as the goal of developing a student's sense of humanity, the educator should foster a student's harmonious growth in wholeness and balance of personality.

Moreover, in promoting a student's sense of humanity, the educator is responsible not only to set the student on this course but, perhaps more importantly, to do the same for him- or herself. As Stein is wont to remind the educator, "[O]ne can only teach what one practices oneself."[7] This is precisely why Stein maintains the paramount importance of the moral integrity of the educator. Setting forth what would be a decidedly unpopular position today, Stein holds that the rectitude of the educator is of great consequence to the student, since the teacher's views and principles cannot but influence the manner of teaching. Stein maintains that teachers can never carry out the educational process indifferently—that is, separated from their personal views and principles. As Lucy Gelber states in the Editor's Introduction to Stein's *Essays on Woman,* "Whether or not they are acknowledged, the teacher's moral views and principles influence his reasoning and conduct. If these views and principles are lacking, then the teacher stands, as it were, before the anvil without a hammer. Perhaps he can make the iron red-hot, but he cannot forge it."[8]

Stein's emphasis upon the teacher as moral model would surely raise a good deal of ire today, when so many try to separate the private lives of educators from their work. But we must bear in mind that since Stein views teaching as a religious calling, it carries the gravest of responsibilities. As she often reminds educators, students "do not need merely what we have but rather what we are."[9]

Stein, however, insists that for the educator to perform this task for students successfully, students must acknowledge their need for external assistance. The threefold process of education is not something students can effect on their own. This makes proper formal education imperative. In short, a certain humility on the part of the student is necessary. (Ultimately, Stein believes, the student and teacher must recognize that the individual needs not only the natural assistance of the educational process but the supernatural assistance of grace as well. Again, a comprehensive discussion of the importance of grace and its role in "perfecting nature" is more appropriate to a theological treatment of Stein's theory of education than to the present philosophical one.) Additionally, the success of this threefold educational process requires not only a student's willingness to submit to this formative process—to be molded and guided by the educator—but also a profound openness and sense of trust on the part of the student toward the educator and the educative process. (Such trust is at the heart of the philosopher Nel Noddings's incorporation of an ethics of care into her educational theory and will be returned to below.)

In describing the ways an educator fosters student development of the person, Stein uses the metaphor of an artist setting out to create a statue. She tells us that "[t]he small child with its physical-psychic disposition and its innate singleness of purpose is delivered into the hands of human sculptors, given over to the educator's 'forming hand.'"[10] The educator shapes and molds the student, always aware of the limitations of the material at hand, in terms of both nature and individuality. It is most essential that educators familiarize themselves with these limitations, since, according to Stein, they are consonant with God's intentions, the so-called seed that God has implanted in each of us. Here, along with the metaphor of sculptor and clay, Stein invokes the image of educator as sower and cultivator of seeds. And, most importantly, in describing the seed that is the individual's humanity, Stein points out that it is God's seed of himself that he has planted.

Aside from their profound poetic import, these metaphors provide a model for understanding the student's eventual self-development. It is essential for Stein that we recognize that as vital and effective as educators are to the educational process, their role in the formation of the student remains indirect. Educators are always limited to having an extraneous influence, as they allow the student's true nature and individuality to dictate the course of the development. In short, educators must constantly bear in mind that all development is self-development; eventually the student must take over as self-sculptor. As Stein describes it, "The small child is put into the hands of human educators but the maturing person awakening to spiritual freedom is given into his own hand. He himself can work for his growth through the faculty of free will: he can discover and develop his faculties; he can open himself up to the formative influences or cut himself off from them. He, too, is bound by the material given to him and the primary formative principle acting within: nobody can make of himself something which he is not by nature."[11]

Since students must acquire knowledge of their strengths as well as weaknesses and a commitment to self-development within those parameters, Stein's outlook requires of students both profound self-knowledge and a Stoic sense of humility. A similar observation regarding the educational process can be found in Martin Buber's essay "The Education of Character": "Education worthy of the name is essentially education of character. For the genuine educator does not merely consider the pupil's individual functions, teaching the pupil only to know and be capable of certain definite things; but the educator's concern is always the pupil as a whole, both in the actuality in which the pupil lives before you now and in his/her possibilities, what s/he can become."[12]

Indeed, for Buber, to assist in the molding of character is the educator's greatest task. As Buber also underscores, there are *limits* regarding the degree of influence an educator can have. Above all, for both Buber and Stein, the educative process involves an *ongoing* effort at molding and sculpting the material one is given. One must never be led to believe that the project is complete, as one can always rise to a higher level of development and, thereby, a keener sense of judgment.[13] Education is best understood as a continual effort toward intellectual and moral cultivation, yielding an ever refined sense of value formation and deeper insight into a conception of the good in the Platonic-Aristotelian sense of the term.[14]

Interestingly, we find a similar use of the metaphor of sculpting one's soul to achieve a sense of virtue and concern for the good in the thought of the ancient/medieval philosopher Plotinus. In the discussion of beauty found in *Ennead* I.6, Plotinus tells us that before we can behold true beauty, we must be able to see it within ourselves. If we cannot yet find it, we must look upon ourselves as a statue to be carved. To find the beauty of a virtuous soul within us, Plotinus exhorts,

> Withdraw into yourself and look. And if you do not find yourself beautiful yet, act as does the creator of a statue that is to be made beautiful: he cuts away here, he smoothes there, he makes this line lighter, this other purer, until a lovely face has grown upon his work. So do you also: cut away all that is excessive, straighten all that is crooked, bring light to all that is overcast, labour to make all one glow of beauty and never cease chiseling your statue, until there shall shine out on you from it the godlike splendour of virtue, until you shall see the perfect goodness surely established in the stainless shrine.[15]

For Plotinus, one cannot recognize beauty or goodness or a virtuous soul until one sees it within oneself. If it is not yet there, one must create it. And most important of all, one never rests content with the end product. This is precisely the process of education as Stein describes it: forming one's soul to see the good, honing one's skills at valuation and discrimination. In her essay "Edith Stein's Philosophy of Woman," Mary Catharine Baseheart tells us that Stein's view of the purpose of education is to assist students, through a combination of actions, "feeling-forming, choice, and decision,"[16] to change faulty values and rise to higher ones. In describing the goal of the proper educational process, Stein points out that "[i]n order that the soul be rightly formed and not malformed, it must be able to compare and discriminate, weigh and measure . . . and it must attain fine perception and sharp judgment."[17] For Stein, this process is the function of practical wisdom, properly cultivated. In fact, throughout her writings on education one finds Stein emphasizing the practical over the merely speculative. She warns that the educator must remember that there is not merely a speculative intellect but a practical intellect as well and that the abstract activity of the intellect and the concrete application should go hand in hand.

We can further understand Stein's emphasis on teaching value formation through an examination of the philosophical hermeneutics of Hans-Georg Gadamer. (Of course, this is not surprising given the common origin of both Stein and Gadamer in the tradition of Husserlian phenomenology.) What is important according to Gadamer is not a possession of facts (what Stein referred to as the "old system of education") but rather one's own personal development, a cultivation of practical knowledge—or Aristotelian *phronesis,* as Gadamer often refers to it. This yields knowledge of how to discriminate between good and bad, right and wrong, important and unimportant. As Gadamer puts it, "Whosoever has a sound judgment is not thereby enabled to judge particulars under universal viewpoints, but he knows what is important, i.e. he sees things from right and sound points of view."[18]

Returning to Stein's use of the metaphor of sculpting oneself to describe the process of self-development, Stein suggests for the individual not only a much more aesthetic and creative role in self-formation but also a greater degree of freedom and responsibility. While we are indeed limited by our abilities and natures (what Stein refers to as the potential of our inner form), what is done with that potential is up to us. And while submission to educators and other external forces is necessary, those external influences we choose to submit ourselves to are of decisive importance. In fact, according to Stein, external influences are not limited to the context of the formal educational setting. The formative effect of molding an individual can take place in a variety of arenas and ways. Here Stein mentions political parties, the youth movement, and the feminist movement of her day as essential in either continuing this formative process or, more importantly, compensating for where more conventional attempts at education have failed. In fact, our ability to both influence and be influenced in a formative way is extended to everyone and anyone with whom we come into contact. As Stein puts it, "Everything that is truly absorbed into the depths of the soul educates and forms the whole person. Consequently, every human contact can have its educational effect."[19] Thus, for Stein, an "educator" need not be one formally designated as such. Indeed, one finds potential educators nearly everywhere one looks.

Such a broadening of the educative process to include almost every individual and situation one encounters is at the heart of remarks about education found in the late-eighteenth-/early-nineteenth-century writings of Wilhelm von Humboldt, in many ways the primary advocate of liberal education in Germany. In commenting on the wide range of opportunity for educational experiences, he asserts that "[t]o form and educate and organize human beings is not only a task meant for teachers, religious advisors, and lawgivers. As a man always remains a human being in addition to everything else he may become, he always has the duty no matter what business he may engage in, to take practical consideration of his own and others' intellectual and moral education."[20] Such a broad and inclusive conception of the educational process anticipated Stein's work. Stein reminded us of the possible effects our activities can have not only on those immediately around us but, perhaps equally important, on the society in which we live. Whether we accept it or not, our actions are of great consequence to the development of humanity in general. Recognition of this fact should be at the heart of an educational system that is properly conceived. As Humboldt acutely notes,

> Man stands in such close contact with his whole environment that many of his actions exert a great and visible, and all of his actions some, even if weak, influence on the remotest corners of human activity. He cannot loosen the bonds that connect him with all his fellow creatures; he cannot prevent the seismic impulses that his actions impart to the body of mankind. Whatever his objections, his sphere of influence is infinite; even if the active part of his existence should finally pass away, just as a stone thrown in water forms visible circles up to a certain point, yet he can never calculate the point of his disappearance and, to avoid dangerous error, must assume himself to form much wider circles than he thinks.[21]

Since for Humboldt—as well as for Stein—one's environment does contain such potential influence, the concept of self-knowledge required for a successful educational process runs much deeper than awareness only of one's strengths and limitations. It involves an acute knowledge of the nature and history of one's society and culture. As Humboldt describes it, "In order for an individual to extend and individuate his character (and this is what all character building comes down to), he must first know himself in the fullest sense of the word. And because of his intimate contact with all his environment, not only know himself but also his fellow citizens, his situation, his era."[22]

Correspondingly, Stein emphasizes the need of the student for experience with a variety of individuals. She observes that "[a]mong other things, this [personal development] can be accomplished through discussion with different kinds of people, perhaps with contrasting personalities."[23] Similarly, she stresses that ample encounter with a variety of cultural forms is essential. "Intellectual life does not depend only on contact with intellectual people. It also depends on discovering impersonal forms of intellectuality which we might call works of the objective mind, that is to say, culture. The human mind is designed to understand and to enjoy works of culture. It cannot be developed fully if it does not come into contact with a multiplicity of cultural disciplines."[24] She goes on to define *objective mind* as "all impersonal objects or manifestations which potentially contain mind; this mind is actualized in contact with persons who are intellectually open and interested."[25]

Stein understands such an education as a lifelong process, noting that in addition to those responsible for the education of youth, some "remain responsible for mature persons as well—for their understanding, freedom, and development. This can be accepted because humanity shares a common responsibility and because the individual is a member of this most comprehensive oneness and also of the concrete communities in which this oneness is structured."[26] Stein would agree with Humboldt that "[t]he single human individual is ever connected with a whole—with his nation, the race to which it belongs, the human race itself. His life, regardless of what aspect one looks at, is necessarily bound to sociality."[27]

This view of education clearly places an immense burden of responsibility on society at large for the development of the individual person. While this might be a duty that many today would try to shirk, Stein highlights the importance of society's commitment to foster a sense of solidarity with all human beings.[28]

Stein upheld an ideal of education, defined as *Bildung,* first enunciated by Humboldt and later adopted by many German educational theorists. As Humboldt describes it, "[W]hen we say *Bildung* in German, we mean something at once higher and more inward, namely, the disposition which harmoniously imparts itself to feelings and character and which stems from insights into and feeling for man's whole spiritual and moral striving."[29] But Humboldt and Stein's understanding of *Bildung* further involved a moral education premised upon tolerance and mutual respect for all human beings. As Humboldt contended,

> Civilization and culture gradually cancel out the glaring contrasts between peoples, and even more successful is the striving for more universal moral forms on the part of a deep, refined feeling for education. The advances of science and art, too, fall in with this, for they strive toward ever more universal ideals, unfettered by national prejudice. But though we seek for equality, we can attain it only each in his way, and the diversity with which human in-

dividuality, without falling into one-sidedness, can express itself reaches infinite proportions. And it is just this diversity upon which the successful striving for universals solely depends. A nation therefore intervenes most fruitfully and powerfully in the course of universal culture not only by succeeding in various particular scientific endeavors, but especially by a total exertion of that which makes out the center of human nature.[30]

Since for Humboldt and Stein *Bildung* should focus on what all human beings share — the cultivation of a sense of shared humanity — moral education, especially one that leads to tolerance and mutual respect, is central to both their outlooks. Indeed, a crucial feature of *Bildung* involves the learner's confrontation with diverse works of art, literature, and other embodiments of culture. In confronting other cultures' forms and conceptions of the good, the student learns to understand and develop values and skills necessary for the good life.

When one examines the philosophy of education found in Stein's essays, one finds, above all, her earlier mentioned concern for the uniqueness of the individual. This emphasis is certainly at odds with current trends of education reform that aim at standardizing the educational process. She would undoubtedly oppose those who promote curricular reform in terms of standardized testing over individual development. This latter approach is typified in Mortimer Adler's *Paideia Proposal*.[31] Adler recommends that all students should have the same curriculum at least through grade 12. Representing a Stein-like perspective, Nel Noddings in her *Philosophy of Education* criticizes such an approach as being especially blind to the individual interests of students. Appealing to the educational theory of John Dewey for support, Noddings argues that since "the context of study is not nearly so important as the method of inquiry and the level of thought involved in its pursuit . . . [m]ind is entirely a dynamic affair, and intelligence should be applied to *doings*, not to some unseen and stable capacity."[32] Indeed, Noddings goes on to reject a model of reform that most often has a "national curriculum" as its goal, and in its place she suggests a "multiple of ideals of what it means to be educated."[33]

Sharing with Stein the more phenomenological approach to the philosophy of education, Noddings develops a theory of education based on and incorporating an ethics of care, an alternative she sets forth as follows:

[T]he ethic of care recognizes the contribution of the student to the teaching relation. The odd notion that establishing national goals will make teachers work harder and more effectively, thereby making students work harder and more effectively, is part of a long, long tradition that assumes an autonomous agent can logically plot a course of action and, through personal competence, somehow carry it out, even if others are intimately involved. The ethic of care rejects the notion of a truly autonomous moral agent and accepts the reality of moral interdependence. Our goodness and our growth are inextricably bound to that of others we encounter. As teachers, we are as dependent on our students as they are on us.[34]

Such an approach, in harmony with Stein's, integrates into the educational process the ideals of a moral education based upon four components: *modeling, dialogue, practice, confirmation.*[35] Very briefly stated, for Noddings, *modeling* involves the willingness on the part of the educator to serve as a role model for properly developing one's capacity for caring; *dialogue* involves the ongoing exchange and discussion of ideas in a mutually open and authentic manner; *practice* involves the application of caring skills acquired; and *confirmation* involves a sense of trust and continuity that allows one to be morally critical and aware. While all four are affirmed in Stein's writings on education, the last echoes Stein's and Gadamer's concern for the development of value formation skills described earlier in this chapter.

Throughout her writings on education, Stein, like Noddings, asserts that those best able to cultivate the trust between student and teacher essential to moral development tend to be women. Women's natural tendencies toward compassion, care, and wholeness are crucial to a successful educative process.[36] While there continues to be much debate today regarding whether an ethic of care can be properly called a "feminist" ethic, it is clear that here as well Stein would have much to contribute to the conversation.

Finally, such an approach to education, emphasizing mutual respect, caring, and open dialogue, can be extended to thinking about multicultural dialogue. Consonant with Stein's emphasis upon understanding of diverse peoples and cultural forms, Noddings holds that one of the virtues of education modeled on care is that "[i]nstead of encouraging an atmosphere in which subgroups compete for time in the curriculum and space for sharply political action, we invite dialogue and genuine meetings. [This perspective] calls for reciprocity of understanding, co-exploration and coenjoyment."[37]

In addition, Stein would certainly endorse Martha Nussbaum's brilliant advocacy of multicultural education. In her recent work *Cultivating Humanity: A Classical Defense of Reform in Liberal Education*,[38] Nussbaum points to three capacities she believes essential to the cultivation of humanity and at the heart of a liberal education: (1) the capacity for critical examination of oneself and one's traditions; (2) an ability to see oneself most simply as a citizen of some local group or region but also, and above all, as a human being bound to all other human beings by ties of recognition and concern; and (3) narrative imagination, understood as the ability to think what it might be like to be in the shoes of a person different from oneself, or to be an intelligent reader of that person's story. When these three capacities are brought to fruition, what one gains is an approach to new knowledge that is much more empathetic in nature. These three capacities formed the core of Stein's phenomenological research on individuals, community, and education. Given Stein's dissertation on empathy and her lifelong exploration of this human capacity, Stein's and Nussbaum's theories of education dovetail remarkably. In fact, an encounter between the two theories of education might allow us to revise the title of Nussbaum's work to read *Cultivating Humanity's Capacity for Empathy: A Classical Defense of Reform in Liberal Education.*

In conclusion, Edith Stein is an advocate of liberal education—an education that liberates the mind from the bondage of habit and custom and, in Nussbaum's words, "a higher education that is a cultivation of the whole human being for the functions of citizenship and life generally."[39] Edith Stein would no doubt concur with this definition of liberal education as well as Nussbaum's assertion that becoming an educated citizen "means learning how to be a human being capable of love and imagination."[40]

NOTES

1. Edith Stein, "Fundamental Principles of Women's Education," in *Essays on Woman*, trans. Freda Mary Oben, vol. 2 of *The Collected Works of Edith Stein* (Washington, DC: ICS Publications, 1996), 129–45.

2. Ibid.

3. See especially Edith Stein, *Life in a Jewish Family: Her Unfinished Autobiographical Account* (Washington, DC: ICS Publications, 1986), as well as Waltraud Herbstrith, *Edith Stein: The Untold Story of the Philosopher and Mystic Who Lost Her Life in the Death Camps of Auschwitz* (San Francisco: Ignatius Press, 1992), and Freda Mary Oben, *The Life and Thought of St. Edith Stein* (New York: Alba House, 2001), for more biographical accounts of Stein's attitude toward her chosen profession.

4. Here, of course, Stein emphasizes the development of womanhood.

5. Stein, "Fundamental Principles," 130.

6. Edith Stein, "Problems of Women's Education," chap. 5 of *Essays on Woman*, 147–235.

7. See especially Editor's Introduction to Stein, *Essays on Woman*. There Lucy Gelber refers to the pedagogical essays in Edith Stein, *Ganzheitliches Leben: Schriften zur religiösen Bildung*, vol. 12 of *Edith Steins Werke* (Freiburg: Herder, 1991).

8. Ibid., 7.

9. Ibid., 9.

10. Stein, "Fundamental Principles," 130.

11. Ibid., 131.

12. Martin Buber, "The Education of Character," in *Between Man and Man* (New York: Macmillan, 1978).

13. See especially Stein, "Fundamental Principles."

14. For present purposes, this is understood primarily in terms of a concern for *arete* in the classical sense, especially as developed in Hans-Georg Gadamer, *The Idea of the Good in Platonic-Aristotelian Philosophy,* ed. and trans. P. Christopher Smith (New Haven, CT: Yale University Press, 1986).

15. Plotinus, *Ennead* I.6, quoted in Albert Hofstadter and Richard Kuhns, eds., *Philosophies of Art and Beauty: Selected Readings in Aesthetics from Plato to Heidegger* (Chicago: University of Chicago Press, 1964), 150.

16. Mary Catharine Baseheart, "Edith Stein's Philosophy of Woman," in *Hypatia's Daughters: Fifteen Hundred Years of Women Philosophers,* ed. Linda Lopez McAlister (Bloomington: Indiana University Press, 1996), 267–79, esp. 276.

17. Stein, "Fundamental Principles," 136.

18. Hans-Georg Gadamer, *Truth and Method* (New York: Seabury Press, 1975), 21. Gadamer explores this notion of *Bildung* in the section of *Truth and Method* entitled "The Significance of the Humanist Tradition."

19. Stein, "Problems of Women's Education," 212.

20. Wilhelm von Humboldt, *Humanist without Portfolio: An Anthology of the Writings of Wilhelm von Humboldt,* ed. and trans. Marianne Cowan (Detroit: Wayne State University Press, 1963), 125.

21. Ibid., 24–25.

22. Ibid., 124–25.

23. Stein, "Problems of Women's Education," 214.

24. Ibid., 217.

25. Ibid.

26. Ibid., 207.

27. Humboldt, *Humanist without Portfolio,* 271.

28. While it is important to note that here Edith Stein is expounding the encyclical on education by Pope Pius XI entitled *Representanti,* especially the papal assertion that "[e]ducation is necessarily the work of a community," it is likewise the case that such a call for more of a societal or communal responsibility for education continues to be both widely advanced as well as contested today. The debate involves everything from complaints about taxation for public education that may not be utilized by the individual taxpayer, to the disavowing of a sense of responsibility for private morality and behavior on the part of role models in sports and entertainment, finally to a general refusal on the part of many today to consider the influence of one's private actions on other individuals and the public good. Moreover, one need only consider the recent storm of controversy over the former American First Lady's suggestion that "it takes a village to raise a child."

29. Humboldt, *Humanist without Portfolio,* 266.

30. Ibid., 272.

31. Mortimer J. Adler, *The Paideia Proposal* (New York: Macmillan, 1982).

32. Nel Noddings, *The Philosophy of Education* (Boulder, CO: Westview Press, 1998), 174–75.

33. Ibid., 196.

34. Ibid.

35. Ibid. Developed in chap. 10, "Feminism, Philosophy, and Education."

36. This sentiment is expressed throughout Stein's *Essays on Woman*, but most especially in "The Ethos of Women's Professions" and "Women's Value in National Life," 261 ff.

37. Noddings, *Philosophy of Education*, 193. Here Noddings is expounding the work of Ann Diller in "Pluralisms for Education: An Ethics of Care Perspective," in *Philosophy of Education*, ed. H.A. Alexander (Champagne, IL: Philosophy of Education Society, 1993).

38. Martha C. Nussbaum, *Cultivating Humanity: A Classical Defense of Reform in Liberal Education* (Cambridge, MA: Harvard University Press, 1997).

39. Ibid., 9.

40. Ibid., 14.

Part Three

---

*"Without Personally Having Done Such Creative Philosophical Work
a Person Cannot Possibly Imagine What It Demanded of Me"*

Stein the Philosopher

Chapter 13

Assistant and/or Collaborator?

Edith Stein's Relationship to Edmund Husserl's Ideen II

ANTONIO CALCAGNO

for Edit Nagy-Bakos—amica

The relationship between Edith Stein and Edmund Husserl has been traditionally characterized as that of teacher and student, master and disciple. Stein was Husserl's first assistant from 1916 to 1918 and was responsible for preparing and editing early drafts of *Ideas II* and *III, The Phenomenology of Inner Time-Consciousness,* and early arrangements of Husserl's 1907 lectures entitled *Thing and Space.* As Husserl's assistant, Stein was responsible for transcribing many of Husserl's stenographic notes into longhand. Furthermore, she arranged and edited many of Husserl's countless "scraps of paper" to form more or less consistent texts. In the Translators' Introduction to Husserl's *Ideas II,* Rojcewicz and Schuwer note, "In 1918, Stein completed her second redaction. This time her work involved much more than merely transcribing. By incorporating into the text writings of the H-folio and others from the war years, the main text of *Ideas II* began to take its present form."[1] Stein is credited with doing "much more" than transcribing insofar as she established the primary form of *Ideas II* and *III.* What does the aforementioned doing "much more" mean? This question compels one to inquire about the specific nature of the relationship between Husserl and Stein within the framework of master and assistant. The role and impact of Edith Stein's efforts in the structuring, editing, and composition of Husserl's *Ideas II* and *III* have never ceased to be a source of controversy and investigation for scholars.[2]

This essay will argue that Edith Stein was not only Husserl's secretary and editor; rather, her assistantship became one of "collaboration" with Husserl, a collaboration that was given full recognition neither by Husserl nor by his later assistants. In essence, I shall show that the nature of Stein's assistantship was much like that of Husserl's other assistants such as Landgrebe and Fink—characterized not only by editing but by philosophical dialogue.

Background

In 1913, Husserl was *Professor extraordinarius* (a full professor without tenure, as distinct from a *Professor ordinarius*, a full professor with tenure) at the University of Göttingen. By the time Stein had arrived in Göttingen, Husserl had just published his "Ideen zu einer reinen Phänomenologie und phänomenologischen Philosophie" as the opening article in the *Jahrbuch*.[3] In the summer semester of 1913, Husserl delivered his lectures *Natur und Geist (Nature and Spirit).*[4] Prior to attending the seminar, new students, at Husserl's request, met in the philosophy seminar room to have a preliminary discussion. Stein, being a new student, duly presented herself. She recounts her first impressions upon meeting the "Master."

> Here, then, for the first time, I *did* see: "Husserl, as real as he can be." Neither striking nor overwhelming, his external appearance was rather of an elegant professional type. His height was average; his bearing dignified; his head, handsome and impressive. His speech at once betrayed his Austrian birth: he came from Moravia and had studied in Vienna. His serene amiability also had something of old Vienna about it. He had just completed his fifty-fourth year.

> After the general discussion, he called the new students to come up to him one by one. When I mentioned my name, he said, "Dr. Reinach has spoken to me about you. How much of my work have you read?"

> "The *Logische Untersuchungen.*" "All of the *Logische Untersuchungen*?" he asked me. "Volume Two—all of it." "All of Volume Two? Why, that's a heroic achievement!" he said, smiling. With that I was accepted.[5]

Under Husserl's auspices, Stein followed various lectures. The summer semester lectures of 1913 revolving around the themes of nature and spirit were punctuated by a two-week visit by Max Scheler to the Philosophical Circle at Göttingen in which he delivered a series of lectures. In the winter semester of 1913–14, Stein attended Husserl's lectures and small tutorials geared to introductory exercises in philosophy, including his course entitled "Allgemeine Geschichte der Pädagogik" (general history of pedagogy). Stein participated in Husserl's seminar on Kant's *Critique of Practical Reason* and *Groundwork for the Metaphysics of Morals.*[6] In the summer semester of 1914, Stein heard Husserl speak about certain problems in phenomenology. Husserl also continued some of his smaller tutorials on problems in Kant's philosophy. The winter semester of 1915 was devoted to a lecture course entitled "Logik als Erkenntnistheorie" (logic as theory of knowledge).[7] While Stein continued to study under Husserl she also followed courses in psychology at the Psychological Institute.[8]

It was while following Husserl's lectures on nature and spirit in 1913 that Edith Stein began worrying about a topic for her dissertation.[9] Stein saw her dissertation on the theme of empathy to be filling in a perceived gap that Husserl had not immediately addressed in his lectures. Moreover, Husserl had a vested interest in the topic of empathy because he was developing his own theory of empathy, and Stein's research could be used to give Husserl an overall history of the problem. Hence, Husserl insisted that Stein cover the history of the problem of empathy, especially in the works of Theodor Lipps.[10] In fact, a large part of Stein's dissertation was devoted to the history of empathy, but this part of the dissertation is no longer extant. While researching and writing her dissertation, Stein admits that the overwhelming nature of the work combined with the loneliness of her enterprise rendered her solitary battle very difficult.[11] Moreover, Husserl would expect progress reports throughout the semester of 1913–14, and Stein always felt that she never had a firm grasp of all the material before her. These meetings were a source of added anxiety for Stein. She took consolation in attending Reinach's introductory seminar on phenomenology and in the meetings of the Philosophical Society. Between 1913 and 1914, Edith Stein began to prepare for her state board examinations.[12] Part of the work she was preparing on empathy was to serve as part of the examination. Stein was so unsure as to what she had written that she asked Reinach to help her. He encouraged Stein to continue with her work and try to condense all of her research into a more precise format. Stein requested to be examined in both philosophy and German. Husserl was appointed state examiner for philosophy. With Reinach's encouragement, Stein managed to "refresh" herself and prepared herself to stand before Husserl on January 15, 1915, at 11 a.m.

Husserl's comments on Stein's examination are preserved in the Husserl Archives.[13] Stein passed the examination, but what is interesting in Husserl's analysis of her examination is the close attention he paid to Stein's critique of others' philosophical work. Husserl concentrates his comments on the role of expression, symbol, and speech as transmitting some knowledge of the other. He seriously engaged the work of Theodor Lipps, Max Scheler,[14] and Moritz Geiger.[15] Husserl expanded his own reading on the topic of *Einfühlung* through Stein's research.

Of considerable importance in the deepening accord between Stein and Husserl was Stein's extensive World War I experience as a Red Cross nurse, out of which grew her analyses of death, especially in the *Beiträge* and in Stein's *Martin Heideggers Existentialphilosophie*.[16] During the First World War, Husserl not only missed his students who were serving their country but also saw his colleagues and students die or become wounded.[17] Even more shattering was his own son's death. Wolfgang Husserl was mortally wounded in Flanders while working as a volunteer. He was only seventeen years old.

After completing her service in Austria in 1915, Stein returned to completing her studies and writing her dissertation. She resided in Breslau while making occasional visits to Husserl in Göttingen. It was while Husserl was researching and writing in Göttingen in 1916 that Stein learned that Husserl had been named professor at Freiburg. He was scheduled to take over the chair of Rickert, who had been named to the chair in Heidelberg. Stein, having taken for granted that she would be completing her doctoral examination under Husserl, was both shocked and elated for Husserl. Plans were made such that Stein would transfer to Freiburg and complete her doctorate under Husserl's direction there. While in Breslau, Stein substituted for an ill teacher at her old *Oberschule*. After completing her teaching duties in 1916, she reported to Freiburg.

In the summer of 1916, Stein made arrangements for the *Rigorosum*, the final series of comprehensive examinations designed to test a student's competence in a series of given subjects. She was to stand for the examinations in history, literature, and philosophy. Husserl was assigned to be the examiner in philosophy. Stein recounts how Husserl spent a lot of time reading her thesis and deemed it original.[18] Some of the themes corresponded to themes he was working on in the second volume of his *Ideen*. Prior to her examination, Stein learned from her friend and fellow student that Husserl needed someone to help him with his work. Stein thought that she could be of service to Husserl and proposed her services to the "Master."

"I am only deliberating whether it will be possible to put this work in the *Yearbook* along with the *Ideas*. I have an impression that in your work you forestall some material that is in my second part of *Ideas*." His words gave me a jolt! Surely this was the moment to ask him. Seize the opportunity by the scruff of the neck! "If this is really so, Professor, then there's a question I have been meaning to ask you. Fräulein Gothe told me of your need for an assistant. Do you think I might be able to help you?" At that point we were just crossing over the Dreisam. The Master stood stock still in the middle of the *Friedrichsbrücke* and exclaimed in delighted surprise: "You want to help me? Yes! With you, I would enjoy working!" I do not know which one of us was more elated. We were like a young couple at the moment of their betrothal. In the Lorettostraße, Frau Husserl and Erike stood watching us. Husserl said to his wife: "Think of it! Fräulein Stein wants to come to be my assistant." Erika looked at me. We needed no exchange of words to reach an understanding. Her deep-set, dark eyes were alight with intense joy.[19]

On August 3, 1916, Stein sat before the doctoral commission to undergo the doctoral examination, which she passed with the highest distinction. Husserl's written judgment of Stein's dissertation stresses that Stein provided a good understanding of the historical background of the problem of empathy while also contributing some significant insights to the actual phenomenology of empathy. Husserl credits Stein with interesting phenomenological analyses of the ideas of the body *(Leib)*, soul, individual, spiritual personality, the social community, and the structure of the community.[20] Stein's dissertation has been lost. A portion of the dissertation is extant as it was published in 1917, *Zum Problem der Einfühlung (On the Problem of Empathy)*.[21] The semester having come to an end and the *Rigorosum* complete, Stein returned to Breslau for a quick holiday. She would return in the fall of 1916 to take up her new assistant duties.

The second major period that covers the relationship between Husserl and Stein is characterized by the transition of Edith Stein from student to assistant. The relationship between the two philosophers became more professional. For Stein to have access to Husserl's thought and works, she had to undertake the learning of Gabelsberger shorthand, the type of shorthand in which Husserl wrote. One of Stein's principal tasks as Husserl's assistant was to collate, transcribe, and edit his manuscripts, which consisted of barely legible, scribbled bundles of notes. Roman Ingarden notes that Edith Stein's task was not only one of editing, transcription, and collation, for Stein was also charged with making necessary changes in content and form to better clarify the texts at hand. Husserl and Stein would discuss changes, and Husserl was supposed to read more complete versions of texts as they came together in a more or less final form—a task Husserl kept postponing, as he was always dissatisfied with his older writings and insights.[22] Ingarden also maintains that Husserl wrote as a way of thinking and that the bundles of paper that Edith Stein received were unpublishable in their given form. An assistant was necessary to render them more intelligible and communicable to a larger audience.

Clearly, more than simple translation was required, which raises the central question: What exactly was the nature of Edith Stein's assistantship? In other words, what did Edith Stein contribute, if anything, to Husserl's philosophy during the time she was Husserl's assistant? Scholarship has tended to attribute important contributions to Husserl's other assistants, namely, Eugen Fink, Ludwig Landgrebe, and Martin Heidegger. Landgrebe helped Husserl with later revisions of *Ideas II* and *Formal and Transcendental Logic*. Fink was known for his elaborations and reworking of the *Cartesian Meditations* and the *Crisis of the European Sciences*, whereas Heidegger gave himself credit for editing *The Phenomenology of Inner Time-Consciousness*, even though the text Heidegger submitted was Stein's own elaboration of the text virtually unaltered. Stein was never given full credit. She was merely thanked.[23] Stein seems never to be credited with much except the transcription and piecing together of texts. Husserl, in his *Briefwechsel*, refers to Stein as his assistant in describing her preparation of the text of the *Ideas*.[24] He further mentions Stein in reference to her own works, including Stein's "Psychische Kausalität," which Husserl accepted for publication in his *Jahrbuch*.[25]

This essay will explore the philosophical nature of Stein's assistantship in the following manner. After offering some background comments on the editing and publication of Husserl's *Ideas II* and *III*, I will focus on a Steinian text written between 1917 and 1932 entitled *Einführung in die Philosophie (Introduction to Philosophy)*.[26] In this text, Stein attempts to rework her doctoral dissertation in addition to laying down the groundwork for her two phenomenological works published in Husserl's *Jahrbuch*, *Beiträge zur philosophischen Begründung der Psychologie und der Geisteswissenschaften (Contributions toward the Philosophical Grounding of Psychology and the Human Sciences)* and *Über den Staat (On the State)*.[27] *Einführung in die Philosophie (Introduction to Philosophy)* was to serve as a preparatory part of Edith Stein's projected *Habilitation*.[28] This text was not published until 1991 by the Archivum Carmelitanum Edith Stein as Volume 13 of *Edith Steins Werke*.

Introduction to Philosophy is a remarkable text, for its structure and content very much parallel the structure and content of Husserl's *Ideas II* and *III*. A large part of *Introduction to Philosophy* was written simultaneously with Stein's elaboration of *Ideas II*. By referring to Stein's letters to various individuals during and after the period in which she was Husserl's assistant and by citing passages in Stein's *Introduction to Philosophy,* I will demonstrate how Stein tried to change Husserl's mind on certain philosophical insights central to *Ideas II.* Stein's *Introduction to Philosophy* is to be read as more than background work for her future philosophical writings—it is to be read also as a commentary on and dialogue with Husserl's *Ideas.* Hence, I will devote the next section of this essay to demonstrating how Husserl and Stein converged and diverged upon issues of philosophical import discussed within the framework of the *Ideas.* In doing so, I hope to demonstrate the exact nature of the philosophical "collaboration" that took place between Husserl and Stein. The last part of this essay will be devoted to the question concerning both Husserlian and Steinian scholars' neglect of the contributions of Stein's assistantship.

The Question of Collaboration between Stein and Husserl

In 1952, the Husserl Archives at Louvain published in the Husserliana series *(Edmund Husserl: Gesammelte Werke)* two posthumous texts of Husserl entitled *Ideen zu einer reinen Phänomenologie und phänomenologischen Philosophie—Zweites Buch: Phänomenologische Untersuchungen zur Konstitution (Ideas II)* and *Drittes Buch: Die Phänomenologie und die Fundamente der Wissenschaften (Ideas III).*[29] These books were to serve as a continuation of Husserl's project as announced in *Ideen I, Erstes Buch: Allgemeine Einführung in die reine Phänomenologie (Ideas I).*[30] This first book was the only one of the aforementioned books that was published in Husserl's lifetime.

Preliminary and preparatory work on the *Ideas* was completed by Husserl between May and September of 1912. These initial sketches are known as the "ink manuscripts." In the fall of 1912, within a six-week period from September to October 1912, Husserl completed a more comprehensive manuscript of the *Ideas* known as the "pencil manuscript."[31] Work on the so-called "pencil manuscript" continued up until December of 1912. The earlier part of the manuscript written in a six-week stretch forms a more or less consistent whole and was later published in 1913 as *Ideas I.* Stein brought *Ideas I* to the lazaretto where she worked as a nurse during World War I.[32] In this work, Husserl tries to establish the groundwork for a pure, transcendental phenomenology. He maintains that phenomenology is a foundational science that is to be viewed as different from a mere descriptive psychology. In the so-called "pencil manuscripts" Husserl conceived the first and second books of the *Ideas* as forming a whole.[33] The second book was to show the application of phenomenology to various problems and areas of philosophy. It was also conceived as addressing concerns raised by the sciences.

Only during the printing of *Ideas I* did Husserl return to the later portions of the "pencil manuscript" to elaborate further certain ideas with regard to the relation of phenomenology to psychology and to other sciences. Husserl continued to add to the manuscript various reflections and lecture notes up until 1917. In 1916, Edith Stein received from Husserl a large manuscript that included the "pencil manuscript." She was charged with bringing some order to Husserl's notes written in Husserl's barely decipherable script. Among the writings she concentrated on were "Nature and Spirit" and Husserl's notes entitled "Concerning the Constitution of the Spiritual World." Since the redactions produced by Stein's efforts were too numerous to be placed in one volume, Stein decided to eliminate from *Ideas II* Husserl's notes on "explanations on the theory of science." She placed the notes in another folder labeled *Ideas III*.[34] By 1918, Stein had completed what she thought was a more or less adequate form of *Ideas II*.[35] Edith Stein had a hard time convincing Husserl to examine the texts, for he had a habit of picking up new trains of thought and abandoning older ones. He was always beginning and thinking anew. Stein found Husserl's unwillingness to read her elaboration of his work immensely frustrating. Husserl was reluctant to read the manuscript because he was distracted by new projects and thoughts, such as the revision of various parts of already extant manuscripts, including *Ideas I* and the *Logical Investigations*.

> He keeps occupying himself with individual questions about which he dutifully informs me, but he cannot be moved, even once, to look at the draft I am making for him out of his old material to enable him to regain the overview of the whole that he has lost. As long as that cannot be achieved it is obviously impossible to think of composing a definitive draft.[36]

> I am now determined that, independent of the dear Master's sudden and variable fancies and as speedily as other assignments will permit, I will put the material I have into a form in which it will be available to others also. When I have accomplished that, and if by then he is still not resolved to go through it systematically, then I will attempt on my own to clarify the cloudy points.[37]

This frustration was one of the reasons why Stein could no longer continue as Husserl's assistant. Stein was also frustrated by Husserl's failure to see her assistantship as one of collaboration between the two philosophers. In a letter to Roman Ingarden she states,

Basically, it is the thought of being at someone's disposition that I cannot bear. I can place myself at the service of something, and I can do all manner of things for the love of someone, but to be at the service of a person, in short— to obey, is something I cannot do. And if Husserl will not accustom himself once more to treat me as a collaborator in the work—as I have always considered our situation to be and he, in theory, did likewise—then we shall have to part company. I would regret that, for I believe there would be even less hope of connection between himself and "youth."[38]

Stein wrote to Ingarden in February 1918 near the end of her assistantship with Husserl. This letter reveals something very interesting about the nature of the relationship between Husserl and Stein. Stein feels like a servant, someone who has to "obey." She is not being treated like a "collaborator." According to Stein, Husserl had agreed "in theory" to treat Stein as a "collaborator" but had failed to do so. This failure on the part of Husserl explains the tone of frustration, anger, and even bitterness in Stein's letter. After Stein's resignation, the manuscript was not looked at much until Ludwig Landgrebe, Husserl's new assistant, took up the text between 1924 and 1925. Husserl again suggested changes, but he could not bring himself to publish the text. Both *Ideas II* and *III* were published posthumously in 1952.

While Edith Stein carried out her work for Husserl, she was also making plans for *Habilitation*. Just after her resignation, Stein nursed Husserl back to health after a bad case of influenza. Between 1918 and 1922, Stein tried several times to obtain *Habilitation* and failed. By 1920, and after much struggle, women were technically allowed to habilitate, but the practice of women habilitating in philosophy was not actively promoted by the male-dominated German academic hierarchy. Stein petitioned and lobbied the Ministry of Education to allow women to habilitate in philosophy, especially since women were allowed to habilitate in mathematics. To this end, Husserl wrote Stein a recommendation letter, but even he limited his recommendation, for he concluded his letter by saying, "If academic careers should ever be opened up for women, I would warmly recommend Stein for *Habilitation*."[39] From 1918 to 1921 Stein tried in vain to habilitate at Göttingen, Kiel, Hamburg, and Breslau. She began to give private lectures in her home at Breslau, which attracted a wide and interested public.[40] Stein prepared two large works that were published in Husserl's *Jahrbuch*, namely, the *Beiträge* and a work devoted to a phenomenology of the state. All of these works drew heavily on Stein's encounter with Husserl's manuscripts while she had been his assistant in Freiburg. Stein remained in contact with Husserl while carrying out her private research activities aimed at *Habilitation*. Preparing the *Ideas* for publication was not a purely philosophical enterprise for Stein. It was to be a stepping-stone to *Habilitation*. Stein wanted Husserl to accept her draft in order to assert her own role within the new and developing school of phenomenology. If the text had been published, Stein would have been seen in another light, just as later assistants of Husserl were viewed as up-and-coming professors. Moreover, Stein needed the analyses of the *Ideas* to promote her own work as carried out in the *Beiträge*. If the *Ideas* were published, then Stein's work would be viewed much more favorably and within a much more established context, namely, that of Husserl's philosophy. Stein's assistantship was marked not only by philosophical dialogue but also by her deep personal ambitions to establish herself within German academe. Stein's collaboration, then, must be seen as mixed, a collaboration of genuine philosophical exchange that was also aimed at personal gain. Even after resigning from her position as Husserl's assistant, Stein remained convinced of the validity of phenomenology, as evidenced by her use of phenomenology in her later writings. The relationship between the two philosophers continued, and Stein always informed herself, through friends, about Husserl's well-being even after she entered the Carmel at Cologne in 1933. Husserl also regarded Stein with great affection, as witnessed by the fact that of the few people invited back to the intimate dinner for Husserl's seventieth birthday in April 1929, "Fräulein Stein" was included among the select company.

Having this background information, let us turn to Stein's *Introduction to Philosophy*, which was begun in 1917.[41] The texts contained in the volume can be viewed within the framework of three principal objectives: first, a reworking of themes presented in Stein's earlier 1916 doctoral dissertation on empathy; second, preparatory notes for her *Beiträge* that were to serve as part of her projected *Habilitation*; and finally, a serious study of Husserl's *Ideas II*. Stein very much appreciated the originality and penetration of Husserl's text.[42] Stein augmented her *Introduction* in scope over time.

Edith Stein viewed the manuscript now called *Introduction to Philosophy* as significant, for it was one of the few manuscripts she took with her to the Carmel at Echt in Holland when she had to flee Nazi persecution in Germany. The manuscript upon which the critical edition of the *Introduction* was based was found after the war in the Carmel at Herkenbosch, where it was saved from the rubble of the bombed cloister by Stein's Carmelite sisters. The manuscript was in no way conserved as a whole but was found by Stein's fellow religious in parts among scattered papers. Lucy Gelber, the archivist of *Edith Steins Werke*, managed to piece together the manuscript through time as more and more of Stein's *Nachlass* (literary legacy) became organized and catalogued.[43] The text was never conceived of being published in its present form. Rather, it was a kind of reference material. Stein mentions the work in various letters, but she never speaks of publishing the text.[44] The material collected in the text, given its similarity to Husserl's *Ideas*, could have also been used by Stein to prepare Husserl's students for his advanced classes. In addition to editing Husserl's manuscripts, Stein, like Reinach before her, assumed some of Husserl's teaching duties by preparing neophytes in phenomenology for more advanced courses in Husserlian phenomenology. Stein amusingly referred to her classes as a "philosophical kindergarten."[45] Gelber, however, never mentions the relation of Stein's text to Husserl's *Ideas*.

Hanna-Barbara Gerl-Falkovitz's postscript to Stein's *Introduction,* included in the volume containing Stein's *Introduction,* does examine the connection between Husserl's thought and Edith Stein's elaboration of his thought, but her analysis is flawed. Although Gerl-Falkovitz makes the connection between Stein and Husserl, she fails to provide an adequate analysis of the Husserlian position as developed in *Ideas II* and *III.* She bases her criticism of Husserl on Stein's analyses and letters concerning Husserl's thought in *Ideas II,* but she never bothers to go back to the *Ideas* to see whether Stein's analyses hold true given the development of Husserl's thought. We are not sure who exactly inspired a change in Husserl's thought, for Husserl rarely cited his philosophical sources. We know from the *Briefwechsel,* however, that Edith Stein was not the only Husserlian critic. Members of the Göttingen circle, including Theodor Conrad, Hedwig Conrad-Martius, and Max Scheler, as well as the Munich *Real*ontologist Alexander Pfänder,[46] were quick to criticize Husserl. And since Gerl-Falkovitz renders the developments in Husserl's thought invisible, Edith Stein becomes outdated in her critiques, for they have already been addressed by Husserl. For example, Gerl-Falkovitz remarks that according to Stein nature and consciousness are related but independent from one another. One does not derive from the other. Reading Husserl as saying that all is constituted in consciousness, including the world, she views Husserl as an idealist in the Kantian sense of the transcendental ego.[47] In fact, however, Husserl does not deny the existence of the real world, for he describes the world as a given—a givenness to which we are fundamentally related.[48] A second example of Gerl-Falkovitz's misrepresentation of Husserl pivots on his analysis of person. She sees Stein as differing from Husserl in that Stein emphasizes the structure of the human person in her text whereas Husserl does not.[49] One of the texts Edith Stein busied herself with while preparing the *Ideas* was the section entitled "The Constitution of the Spiritual World." This section forms a good third of *Ideas II* and is a profound meditation on the person. Husserl writes about the personal ego, empathy, and the person as a subject of acts of reason and as a free ego. In fact, Stein draws heavily on Husserl's analyses.

A common myth about Edith Stein's work claims that Edith Stein's personalist[50] philosophy, as expressed in her later works like *Finite and Eternal Being*[51] and her Münster lectures,[52] developed exclusively as a result of her conversion to Catholicism.[53] This is false. Edith Stein's interest in the philosophy of the human person stemmed from Husserl and other philosophers like Scheler and was developed throughout the rest of her life, including her Catholic period. Stein's encounter with Catholicism was not exclusively responsible for her interest in the philosophy of the human person. For example, her phenomenological analyses of the ego and the pure ego in *Finite and Eternal Being*, a later work often regarded as a personalist work, amply reveal Husserl's influence.

Although Husserl addressed some of Stein's major critiques of his thought, attention to several points of divergence and convergence between the two thinkers shows the originality that characterized Stein's *Introduction to Philosophy*. Within this framework of dialogue marked by such convergence and divergence, Edith Stein saw herself not merely as a secretary to Husserl but as a "collaborator" engaged in serious philosophical (scientific) research.

Introduction to Philosophy serves as proof of Stein's conviction that she was collaborating with Husserl.[54] The text is structured similarly to *Ideas II* and *III* and contains many similar, almost verbatim, philosophical insights. Stein was not only copying Husserl but also trying to understand the richness and complexity of his thought. Perhaps Stein's *Introduction* could be read as her own elaboration and development of *Ideas II* and *III*—a sort of running commentary through which she attempted to better understand and rethink certain elements in Husserl's thoughts as well as develop her own insights, which ultimately would both relate to and distinguish her from Husserl.

The similarities between Stein's *Introduction* and Husserl's *Ideas II* and *III* are striking, especially in terms of structure. Stein begins her work by outlining both the task of philosophy and the method she will employ to achieve that task. The ultimate goal of philosophy is to better understand the world.[55] Like Husserl, Stein emphasizes consciousness as the key to better understanding the world. Phenomenology is to be Stein's method. She will follow Husserl's *Wesenswissenschaft*[56] to arrive at a better understanding of things in the world.

Stein begins her text, like Husserl's *Ideas II*, with a meditation on nature and natural philosophy. Husserl and Stein offer similar readings of materiality, space, and movement. Both discuss substance and physicalist views of nature. The second section of *Ideas II*, "The Constitution of Animal Nature," is devoted to the topics of the pure ego, psychic reality, the constitution of psychic reality through the body, and the constitution of psychic reality in empathy. Stein in the first portion (sections a, b, and c) of the second part of her *Introduction*, entitled "The

Problem of Subjectivity," follows the order of Husserl's *Ideas II*. She begins with a consideration of consciousness and one's knowledge of consciousness by writing about the pure ego. Stein then switches the order but not the content followed in section 2 of *Ideas II*. She offers some reflections first on the body and then on the psyche. Both Husserl and Stein view the body as the organ of the will and as the center of free movement. Stein concludes the first portion on subjectivity as Husserl concludes the second section of *Ideas II*, by considering the themes of intersubjectivity and empathy. Section 3 of *Ideas II* is devoted to an investigation of the constitution of the spiritual world. Again, Husserl takes up the themes of the opposition between the naturalistic and personal worlds and of motivation as the fundamental law of the spiritual world. The first chapter of this section tries to develop the difference between the naturalistic and the personalistic attitudes. Temporality, personal relations, and the theme of the person and the surrounding world are examined. Stein also follows similar discussions of Husserl, but she incorporates these discussions in Part I and in the first portion of Part II (sections a, b, and c). She does not place these questions in a separate section, as does Husserl. Curiously, Stein does not provide an analysis of motivation, association, and causality in the *Introduction*. These she will explicate in her *Beiträge*. Stein's *Introduction* ends with a meditation on the sciences concerned with subjectivity. She discusses psychology, psychophysics, and human sciences like history and philology. Again, this section will be seminal for her later work in the *Beiträge*. Stein, like Husserl in *Ideas III*, meditates on the connection between psychology and phenomenology. Husserl does not here develop the role of subjectivity to the human and social sciences as does Stein. Overall, the striking structural similarities between Stein's *Introduction* and Husserl's *Ideas II* and *III*, as confirmed by both Stein's and Husserl's reflections on nature, natural science, the ego, intersubjectivity, the person, and the sciences, reveal an intimate relationship between the ideas of the two thinkers.

Besides these structural parallels, Stein follows Husserl very closely on certain key insights. I would like to focus on two principal insights, namely, the notion of person and the theme of the body *(Leib)*, to demonstrate how the two authors further converge on similar themes. Stein characterizes the person as a center from which radiate all lived experiences.[57] The person is considered the point where one actually lives through certain experiences that occur in life as experienced in consciousness. Stein characterizes the person as a bearer *(Träger)* of certain qualities and formative experiences. Husserl shares this conviction insofar as he also conceives the person as a bearer of relations.[58] Moreover, Stein characterizes the personal ego as the core that actually lives through experiences insofar as the person is the center of the surrounding world.[59] One distinguishing point of the person is his or her ability to initiate certain free acts that originate within the freedom of the free, personal ego.[60] Freedom, rationality, and the "I can" are key qualities describing the personal ego for both Husserl and Stein.[61] Stein, following Husserl, affirms the centrality of freedom as definitive or constitutive for the life of the person. Freedom is about making certain willed choices or taking certain willed stands. Such stands must be original in that they must originate in the soul of the individual. They do not originate with others, for they are original to the individual person's soul and bear the personal stamp, quality, or characteristic of the person from which such willed stands originate.

A second, pronounced similarity occurs in the two authors' views of the significant role of the body *(Leib)* as constitutive of the person. For Stein as for Husserl, the body is the locus of sensations.[62] Moreover, the body is seen as intimately related to the psychic and spiritual elements of the person, as evidenced by both authors' views of the body as organ of the will. It concretizes the will's motivations, desires, volitions, and so forth.[63] The will in itself moves spontaneously, but the body as organ of the will moves things secondarily through the will; hence, both Husserl and Stein speak of mechanical movement. Many more similarities exist between the two works in question, including Husserl's and Stein's analyses of empathy, the role of bodily and linguistic expression, and the experience of the other in ego consciousness. Space limitations preclude discussion of these topics here.

Shifting to Stein's direct critiques of Husserl as found both in Stein's *Introduction* and in her letters written at the same time as her *Introduction,* I find evidence that Husserl changed his views and also that Stein may have misinterpreted Husserl's position. Stein accuses Husserl of committing three basic philosophic faults. Her critiques of Husserl revolve around the themes of idealism, nature, and the body. All of these critiques are based on Stein's early reading of *Ideas I,* a work that was modified by Husserl himself, as indicated in the introduction.[64] Husserl intended to add to Boyce Gibson's English translation of *Ideas I,* as well as Stein's work on the manuscripts that formed the basis for *Ideas II* and *III.*

In another letter to Ingarden, Stein describes the nature of her work for Husserl. She tells Ingarden that she is trying to establish a unified draft of the *Ideen.* The letter also contains a critique of Husserl's project by Stein. "Besides, as a consequence [of the discussion] I have experienced a breakthrough. Now I imagine I know pretty well what 'constitution' is—but with a break from Idealism. An absolutely existing physical nature on the one hand, a distinctly structured subjectivity on the other, seem to me to be prerequisites before an intuiting nature can constitute itself. I have not yet had the chance to confess my heresy to the Master."[65] This small excerpt is extremely telling, for one sees both a critique of Husserl and a crucial point for Stein's thought. Concerning the latter, the distinction Stein makes between nature and subjectivity is the same distinction that divides the two parts of her *Introduction,* the first part being devoted to the problems of a philosophy of nature and the second focusing on the structure of subjectivity. Stein criticizes Husserl for his idealism in that she thinks of "constitution" apart from idealism. She jokingly refers to her breakthrough as a "heresy."

The idealism for which Stein attacks Husserl stems not so much from the texts of *Ideas II* as from Husserl's 1913 published version of *Ideas I.* Husserl placed much emphasis on the eidetic and the absoluteness of the eidetic.[66] The "natural" world seems to have been given a secondary place; hence the need for a clarification of the constitution of the world as planned in *Ideas II.* In his proposed introduction to Boyce Gibson's translation of *Ideas I,* Husserl claims that people have misunderstood what he meant by "idea."[67] Husserl is not calling for a sort of idealism that marked the modern philosophies of Kant and Hegel. Rather, Husserl sees idea as objective, incarnate in the world. It lacks the absolute totality claimed by Hegel. The second printing (1922) of *Ideas I* included revisions as documented in the Husserliana version of the text. Husserl tones down his earlier emphasis on the absoluteness of the eidetic as thought apart or suspended (Husserlian epoché) from the natural world.[68] In fact, his later writings, including the *Cartesian Meditations* and the *Crisis,* try to connect Husserl's "idea" to the pregivenness of the world. The world is viewed as significant for constitution, much in the same light as the world is viewed in *Ideas II.* One can maintain that Stein argued with Husserl over the question of idealism for reasons of consistency.

> Recently I laid before the Master (Husserl), most solemnly, my reservations against idealism. It was not at all (as you had feared) a "painful situation." I was deposited in a corner of the dear old leather sofa, and then for two hours there was a heated debate—naturally without either side persuading the other. The Master is of the opinion that he is not at all disinclined to change his viewpoint if one demonstrates to him such a necessity. I have, however, never yet managed to do that. In any case, he is now aware that he has to think this point through once more, thoroughly, even though, for the moment, he has postponed that.[69]

Stein wanted to convince Husserl that a science based on the ego as described in *Ideas I* (1913 version) could not properly function as a science unless it accounted for things to which the ego was fundamentally related—to the world, the psyche, and other persons. A pure ego laying the foundations of an eidetic science without reference to a suspended natural world was impossible, for that very ego's existence was dependent upon the world prior to its having consciousness of itself and consciousness of the "idea" of the world—Husserl had to account for the pregivens that enabled his ego to analyze the content of its "ideas." In 1917, Husserl did not see this immediately, but by 1920 he had begun to listen to his critics and tried to connect the idealism of his earlier phenomenology with a broader notion of transcendental subjectivity that contained within its framework a broader vision of the ego and its relation to the world, to nature, and to others. Stein's critique of idealism is fair, but only if one restricts Husserl to the 1913 version of his *Ideas*. Later revisions of *Ideas I* and writings from the *Nachlass* reveal a Husserl who is trying to connect more intimately the purity of the "idea" with the natural surrounding world.

Another critique that stems from our earlier citation of Stein's letter to Ingarden revolves around the question of nature. Stein believes that one must have an absolutely existing physical nature on the one hand and a distinctly structured subjectivity on the other hand as preconditions before an intuiting nature can constitute itself. Stein, as seen from the texts on nature in the *Introduction,* views subjectivity as fundamentally related to yet distinct from nature.[70] In other words, the ego is not absolutely self-constituting and, hence, constitutive of the surrounding world. Again, Stein is reading from certain key assumptions found in *Ideas I*—an idealism of sorts where primacy of place is given to the pure ego as the locus of intentional consciousness. Nature, ultimately, is to be suspended (bracketed) in the phenomenological reduction. For Stein, on the other hand, nature, like certain subjective structures, is fundamental for the pure ego to become aware of its surroundings and aware of itself.

Husserl is aware of this difficulty, and nature becomes something more connected to the life of the ego in *Ideas II* and in his subsequent works in that subjects find themselves as pregiven intersubjectively in the world.[71] Husserl affirms the necessity of a pregivenness of the natural world and the community (a structure of subjectivity) as vital for understanding the theoretical and, therefore, scientific structures of human existents, the world, and other animalia. Stein's critique of Husserl may be obsolete now, but it is a fair critique that Husserl took into consideration when he went on to develop his phenomenology further in his later works.

A final, significant critique made by Stein deals with the role of the body *(Leib).* For Stein and Husserl, body and soul are not separate entities of the human person; rather, they are inextricably intertwined. In a section entitled "Gaps in the Experience Proper to the Person," Edith Stein connects not only body to soul but body to a proper sense of the I, the personal ego.[72] In other words, the I cannot be an I without a body. This connection for Stein of the body to the personal ego is significant in that she frames the discussion within the context of empathy. The body, then, if intimately connected to the interiority of the person, not only signifies the presence of another person but also allows us to have a deeper consciousness of the interiority of the other person: "The body *(Leib)* of the other person appears in its spatial bodiliness as a thing like all other things. Its innerness (in different possible meanings) is closed within the body, and bodily expression is the 'mirror' of the person's psycho-spiritual being and life. The body is the gate through which we can enter into the other. Only when we constitute the actual [*eigene*] person as an analogon of the other, then, only at that moment, are we able to bring to givenness a full re-presentation."[73] Because there is an intimate link between not only the body and the spirit but also the body and the person and therefore the personal ego, the body as an experience of something external not only permits us to see and know the activity of the body but also allows us to know or be conscious of the interior life of another person. The body reveals something of the uniquely personal. It gives us insight into the personal qualities that distinguish one person from another. Husserl, in Supplement VIII of *Ideas II,* writes beautifully of the relation between body and spirit, speaking of the body as the articulation of the spirit. Stein sees her connection of the body to the personal ego as filling in some "gap" in the analysis of consciousness of external experiences, namely, those of other persons, implying that Husserl has not addressed this concern.[74]

Husserl's notion of body is given a central place in *Ideas II,* for it is conceived as a point of orientation.[75] Husserl views the body as a "passageway" to understanding the motivations of another subject.[76] He does not explicitly attribute to the body the deeply personal attachment that Stein does. Stein speaks of the body as enclosing interiority and as a gateway to interiority, both the psychospiritual and the personal. Husserl, does, however, implicitly connect the body to the uniquely personal in that every subject and therefore every body is personal. Stein views the body as a mirror of the person's psycho-spiritual being. She would have us accept a more intimate connection between person and body, but her description of the body as a "mirror" compels one to ask whether such a description weakens the intimacy that Stein calls for in that the body becomes merely a reflecting agent giving us what every mirror does, namely, a static, reproductive image. The body itself, then, does not seem to have a formative role in the psycho-spiritual life of the person, for it merely reflects or is informed by the psycho-spiritual; the body is affected but does not affect. Husserl's description, however, may be viewed as somewhat more intimate than Stein's in that he speaks of a deepening sense of subjectivity and intersubjectivity. A passageway suggests a pathway to be traveled along, ultimately leading to a deeper sense of the alterity of the other. Husserl, however, here describes the body as a localizing point in that it serves as a nexus for motivations. Stein wants to see the body not only in terms of orientation and localization of the psycho-spiritual but as a reflection of the person's interiority *(Persönlichkeitskern)*. Ultimately, I see Stein and Husserl affirming the same thing—the body as a keyhole to one's personal interiority. The question that remains is that of degree: How much can the body reveal? To what degree does the body affect the psycho-spiritual life of the individual? It would appear that Stein wants the body to reveal much more than Husserl is prepared to concede in *Ideas II* and *III*.

Stein's distinctive insights that are not dealt with by *Ideas II* and *III* include her ideas on character, value, and the relation between the soul and depth. These Steinian insights may be viewed as broadening themes discussed in *Ideas II*, especially concerning the nature of the constitution of the human person.

Prior to following Husserl to Göttingen, Stein had studied psychology at the University of Breslau. Both Husserl and Stein dismissed empirical psychology's attempt to reduce the psycho-spiritual life of the individual to mere empirically quantifiable psychic mechanisms (psychologism). They saw their work as an attempt to combat the psychologism prevalent within the German academy while at the same time offering a broader view of human psycho-spiritual life than that commonly espoused by psychologists of the behaviorist and determinist schools. Stein's interest in psychology and Husserl's attempt to ground psychology in phenomenology left their mark on her work. In the *Introduction*, Stein sees character, understood in the psychological sense, as significant when considering the ontic structure of the subject. One's character and the characteristics one possesses delimit the spirit of a person.[77] In other words, one's characteristics lend definition to one's person. Character is that which individualizes each person by allowing him or her to be viewed as person but also as unique. Husserl, though he speaks of personal qualities much as Stein speaks of character, still speaks in universal terms.[78] Stein would not want to negate the universality implicit in Husserl's analysis, but she also wants to maintain that when we speak of personhood and persons, we must not fall into the trap of forgetting that each person is a unique individual. Stein calls this uniqueness of the individual the personal *Kern* or kernel. The kernel or unique individuality of the person unfolds through character.[79] Though the kernel of the person is a universal phenomenon, shared by all human beings, its content is uniquely individualized, thereby distinguishing one person from the next.

Within the framework of character and the uniqueness of the individual person, Stein maintains that the person is also the seat of values *(Werte)*. When discussing values and the formative influence of values on individual persons and how they may condition our experience of others, Stein tries to incorporate into her *Introduction* some of Scheler's insights regarding the objective nature of values.[80] She is also continuing a line of thinking that she initiated in her doctoral dissertation on empathy. The last section of her dissertation is devoted to the question of value, and the theme of value will also appear in other texts like the *Beiträge* and her writings on the state. The values we ascribe to things as well as the values we encounter in society shape the person, they are formative. This is not to say that they are absolutely relative. On the contrary, they are concrete objectivities that relate to us and to which we relate, whether they are social, political, and/or aesthetic.[81] Stein believes that certain objective values may be so strong that one's character, indeed personality, may become deeply marked by them.[82] As exemplified in Stein's work on the state, certain religious values may cause one to oppose certain principles of the state. Conflicts may arise in such a situation, and the state must have a mechanism in place to deal with them if and when they arise. When addressing the question of constitution in the *Ideas*, Husserl does not explicitly engage the themes of values and the role they play in shaping our existence and the existence of the world. This discussion is carried out in Husserl's ethical writings. Value is mentioned in the *Ideas*, but not in the same context as in Stein's *Introduction*. Husserl focuses more on value theory and judgments.

In the *Introduction*, Stein describes the peculiar quality of the soul of the human person as depth *(die Tiefe)*. What does Stein intend by the word *depth*? I think the word must be understood in its root sense insofar as the soul is conceived as created and literally "stamped" *(geprägt)* by an infinite God and, therefore, is called to share in the infinite life of God. Depth is that human and personal relationship that we are invited to have with God the Creator. In its relationship with God, the soul becomes infinitely open to possibilities and transformations that ultimately will mark the character and personal core of the individual. Insofar as the soul stands in an infinite relation with God, the soul becomes deep, it becomes a depth—that is, it extends its limited human capacities through its relationship with an infinite, eternal being, namely, God. *Depth*, then, refers to that profundity of soul that becomes infinitely open when one enters more intimately into a relationship with the infinite God as a creature of God. Because the soul is connected to the body, the body also participates in such depth. By implication, then, the person is marked by depth, as qualities of the soul also determine one's personhood. This description of the soul is telling, for it suggests an infinity or potentiality of the soul that lies open—an open-endedness. This depth is what holds together the personal kernel, the soul and the character of the person.[83] *Depth* is also employed to describe the relationship between the soul and feelings and the life of the will. The will and feelings are situated in the soul, but they originate out of the depth of personal existence. Though every person can experience the depths of the soul, each person's experience may be different. Stein wishes to emphasize both the particularity and universality of such a depth. *Depth* is used to suggest the groundedness of both the will and the feelings we experience. *Depth* is also used to speak of values that take root in the soul. Will, feeling, and value permeate and color our existence, and they have objective meaning for our existence as individuals and in community. The description of depth is interesting, for it reveals something about human existence, namely, its mystery. It points to the deep-seated wellsprings from which many of our fundamental life experiences and personal life structures like will, feelings, and emotions originate. Human beings cannot be entirely quantified, for there is something in our very nature that defies strict empirical analysis, a transcendence of sorts that Stein calls depth. What is also interesting about Stein's notion of depth is what she will do with it in her later philosophy. Depth will become a specifically human and personal way to describe the relationships that exist between self and self, self and others, and ultimately self and God.[84] Depth becomes not only a way of describing the nature of certain relationships, in that depth is viewed as a *quale* of the soul, a quality of the nature of its existence, but also a place—a place of poignant encounter. The soul also becomes depth, an infinite space where the human person can encounter the divine persons.

Stein's *Introduction* attests to Stein's project of collaboration. She did not merely transcribe Husserl's bundled notes of shorthand. She was responsible for giving them shape, and in doing so she articulated what a Husserlian phenomenology would look like—a phenomenology that would have tempered the transcendental and idealistic turns of *Ideas I* and a philosophy that would not have been so radically transcendental as later Husserlian writings. The fact that Stein's *Introduction* and Husserl's *Ideas II* parallel one another in structure reveals that Stein had her own vision of how *Ideas II* should look. The points of convergence and divergence between the two thinkers' texts demonstrate exactly where they came together and where they differed. In short, the *Introduction* can be read as a living testament documenting the collaboration of Edith Stein and Edmund Husserl.

Scholarly Neglect of Stein's Philosophical Influence

One of the principal reasons why Stein was never viewed as a collaborator is historically rooted. Stein was Husserl's first assistant. Many assistants followed after Stein. Husserl continued to write and produce a great amount of work after Stein had left him. His thought evolved and became more established. Those interested in Husserl's thought studied the whole corpus, while Stein had access to only a small portion of Husserl's work. Hence, her work for Husserl was seen as transitional, for Husserl's thought on the *Ideas* had changed and developed over time, thereby rendering her work "obsolete." Other assistants began to work on the *Ideas*. What Stein knew of Husserl while she was his assistant between 1916 and 1918 was not the whole picture. Moreover, the Husserl Archives possess only Stein's *Ausarbeitung* of Husserl's text. Stein's own reaction to the *Ideas* can be seen in her *Introduction to Philosophy*, which was published only in 1991.

A second reason why Stein's project of collaboration was never recognized stems from Steinian scholarship itself. Steinian scholarship has been heavily focused on Stein's biography, religious writings, and writings on education. Only recently have her philosophy, and indeed her phenomenology, been given the attention they deserve, especially given that a vast part of Stein's corpus is philosophical.[85] This predilection for Stein's religious writings is connected with newfound interest in her thought since her beatification and her more recent canonization. Hence, Stein scholars have overlooked her project of philosophical "collaboration" with Husserl because not all Stein scholars are familiar with Husserl's corpus, although Angela Ales Bello, Marianne Sawicki, and Mary Catharine Baseheart have played pivotal roles in showing the phenomenological legacy of Husserl within Stein's work. Stein, it should be noted, saw an intimate connection between her religious writings and her phenomenology, as evidenced by her introduction to *Endliches und ewiges Sein*.

Finally, sexism undoubtedly played a role in the view of Stein's assistantship as merely one of transcription and redaction. *Habilitation* was denied to Edith Stein because she was a woman. Philosophy had no women professors at the time in Germany. Stein did not appreciate being treated as someone who should only take orders, a secretary of sorts. One can infer from her frustration with Husserl and the situation in Germany with regard to female *Habilitation* that her contributions may have been minimized or looked upon as merely secondary. Even Husserl was opposed to the *Habilitation* of women in philosophy, as evidenced in his recommendation letter for Stein, where he says that if women should ever be allowed to habilitate, Fräulein Stein certainly would be an exemplary choice—a point of great pain for Stein. If Husserl was opposed to Stein's *Habilitation,* and if Husserl was not opposed to the *Habilitation* of his male assistants, one can only wonder whether Husserl did not fully recognize Stein's full potential simply because he was blinded by her being a woman.

It should also be remarked that Husserl scholars and phenomenologists in general devote little attention to Stein and other women phenomenologists, such as Hedwig Conrad-Martius[86] and Gerda Walther.[87] Angela Ales Bello has done considerable work in bringing to light the contributions of these women philosophers and students of Husserl.[88] Considering that Edith Stein studied and worked with Husserl during a very formative time for both Husserl and Stein, it is rather disheartening to see how Edith Stein has been marginalized. Examining Edith Stein's early phenomenology provides valuable clues for better understanding Husserl's thought and what he understood phenomenology to be, especially given his later writings, where he tries to reconcile his world-bracketing idealism with a philosophy of worldly experience. More importantly, however, Stein's writings provide invaluable phenomenological contributions to philosophy. First, her writings demonstrate the possibility and validity of a descriptive phenomenology of experience, despite claims of its perfunctory nature by Husserl and charges of its impossibility by Husserlian scholars. Stein's phenomenological descriptions bear witness to the possibility of a universal philosophy of human experience rooted in both reason and accessibility. Second, Stein delivers a unique and powerful philosophy of the human person, mindful of the realities of the radically individual and communal frameworks that help structure the being of the human person. Finally, Stein's phenomenology works out what intersubjectivity consists of in phenomenological terms. Moreover, one can read Stein's later phenomenology within the above-mentioned context, always mindful that Stein did not see phenomena of faith and belief as automatically excluded from the purview of the phenomenologist. Much work has to be done to uncover what has been ignored and marginalized by Husserl scholars and phenomenologists in general. Regardless of the reasons for scholarly neglect of Stein-Husserl collaboration, the importance of their collaboration can no longer be overlooked. It is central to our understanding of the life and work of Edith Stein and Edmund Husserl.

NOTES

I would like to acknowledge and thank the Social Sciences and Humanities Research Council of Canada for its generous support.

1. Edmund Husserl, *Ideas Pertaining to a Pure Phenomenology and to a Phenomeno-logical Philosophy—Second Book,* trans. R. Rojcewicz and A. Schuwer (Boston: Kluwer, 1989), xii–xiii. Hereafter referred to as *Ideas II.*

2. See Marly Biemel's introduction to Husserl's *Ideen zu einer reinen Phänomenologie und phänomenologischen Philosophie—Zweites Buch: Phänomenologische Untersuchungen zur Konstitution,* Husserliana 4 (The Hague: Martinus Nijhoff, 1952). See also Karl Schuh-mann's introduction to his edition (The Hague: Martinus Nijhoff, 1976). Other works of interest include Angela Ales Bello, *Fenomenologia dell'essere umano: Lineamenti di una filosofia al feminile* (Rome: Città Nuova Editrice, 1992); T. Nenon and L. Embree, eds., *Issues in Husserl's Ideas II* (Dordrecht: Kluwer, 1996); B. Imhof, *Edith Steins philosophische Ent-wicklung* (Basel: Birkhaüser, 1987); Mary Catharine Baseheart, *Person in the World: Intro-duction to the Philosophy of Edith Stein* (Dordrecht: Kluwer, 1997); Marianne Sawicki, *Body, Text, and Science: The Literacy of Investigative Practices and the Phenomenology of Edith Stein* (Dordrecht: Kluwer, 1997).

3. Karl Schuhmann, *Husserl-Chronik: Denk und Lebensweg Edmund Husserls* (The Hague: Martinus Nijhoff, 1977), 177.

4. Ibid., 178–83.

5. Edith Stein, *Life in a Jewish Family, 1891–1916: Her Unfinished Account,* ed. Lucy Gelber and Romaeus Leuven, OCD, trans. Josephine Koeppel, OCD, vol. 1 of *The Col-lected Works of Edith Stein* (Washington, DC: ICS Publications, 1986), 249–50.

6. Ibid., 186–87.

7. Ibid., 190.

8. Ibid., 264–65.

9. "Now the question needed to be settled: what did I want to work on? I had no difficulty on this. In his course on nature and spirit, Husserl had said that an objective outer world could only be experienced intersubjectively, i.e., through a plurality of per-ceiving individuals who relate in a mutual exchange of information. Accordingly, an ex-perience of other individuals is a prerequisite. To the experience, an application of the work of Theodor Lipps, Husserl gave the name *Einfühlung* [empathy]. What it consists of, however, he nowhere detailed. Here was a lacuna to be filled; therefore, I wished to examine what empathy might be. The Master found this suggestion not bad at all. However, almost immediately, I was given another bitter pill to swallow: he required that, as format for the dissertation, I use that of an analytical dialogue with Theodor Lipps. He liked to have his students clarify, in their assignments, the relation of phe-nomenology to the other significant directions current in philosophy. This was not his forte." Ibid., 269.

10. Theodor Lipps (1851–1914) was an influential philosopher and psychologist. Lipps's work on empathy had a profound impact on Husserl and Stein. Lipps is credited with de-veloping a theory of empathy characterized by a feeling of oneness or identity between per-sons. Lipps supports his theory by appealing to so-called aesthetic events in which a mutual feeling of oneness between persons is typical.

11. Stein, *Life,* 278.

12. State board examinations were examinations designed, administered, and carried out by a university, in the name of the Ministry of Education, to ensure the competency of a graduating candidate in certain declared fields.

13. Preserved as pp. 83–87 of the Manuskriptkonvolut, Husserl Archives (Louvain), E I 3 I. Karl Schuhmann has provided an edited version of the manuscript in "Textuitgave: Husserl's Exzerpt aus der Staatsexamensarbeit von Edith Stein," *Tijdschrift voor Filosofie* 53, no. 4 (1991): 686–99.

14. Max Scheler (1874–1928) was one of the founders of phenomenology in Germany. His works were seminal, and he had a marked influence on many philosophers, psychologists, and sociologists. His great works include *Formalism in Ethics and Non-Formal Ethics of Values* and *Resentiment*.

15. Geiger was originally a student of Lipps who came to Göttingen to study with Husserl. He was a friend of Reinach.

16. Edith Stein, "Martin Heideggers Existentialphilosophie," in *Welt und Person*, vol. 6 of *Edith Steins Werke*, ed. Lucy Gelber and Romaeus Leuven (Louvain: Editions Nauwelaerts, 1962).

17. Stein, *Life*, 316–17.

18. Edmund Husserl, "Husserl's Gutachten über Steins Dissertation, 29. VII. 1916," appendix to *Briefwechsel*, ed. Karl Schuhmann (Dordrecht: Kluwer, 1993), 3:548.

19. Stein, *Life*, 411.

20. Husserl, "Husserl's Gutachten," 548.

21. Edith Stein, *Zum Problem der Einfühlung* (Munich: Kaffke, 1917, 1980).

22. Roman Ingarden, "Edith Stein on Her Activity as an Assistant of Edmund Husserl," *Philosophy and Phenomenological Research* 23, no. 2 (1962): 157.

23. See Husserl's introduction to *Zur Phänomenologie des inneren Zeitbewusstseins*, Husserliana 10 (The Hague: Martinus Nijhoff, 1966).

24. Husserl to Roman Ingarden, June 20, 1917, in *Briefwechsel* 3:181–82.

25. Husserl to Roman Ingarden, March 12, 1920, in *Briefwechsel*, 3:203.

26. Edith Stein, *Einführung in die Philosophie*, vol. 13 of *Edith Steins Werke* (Freiburg: Herder, 1991).

27. Edith Stein, *Beiträge zur philosophischen Begründung der Psychologie und der Geisteswissenschaften*, in *Jahrbuch für Philosophie und phänomenologische Forschung*, vol. 5, ed. Edmund Husserl (Halle: Max Niemeyer, 1922), vol. 5, and *Eine Untersuchung über den Staat* in *Jahrbuch für Philosophie und phänomenologische Forschung*, vol. 7, ed. Edmund Husserl (Halle: Max Niemeyer, 1925). These two works have been published together as *Beiträge zur philosophischen Begründung der Psychologie und der Geisteswissenschaften. Eine Untersuchung über den Staat* (Tübingen: Max Niemeyer, 1970).

28. *Habilitation* was the process whereby a recent PhD graduate would submit another more substantial dissertation in order to qualify for an appointment to a university faculty. The state would decide how many new positions needed to be filled and, hence, who could habilitate. Though *Habilitation* finally became a possibility for women in the university system by the mid-1920s, it was still pragmatically difficult to enter a male-oriented university system. Stein fought this form of discrimination attempting to acquire *Habilitation*. Each attempt failed.

29. Edmund Husserl, *Ideen zu einer reinen Phänomenologie und phänomenologischen Philosophie. Drittes Buch. Die Phänomenologie und die Fundamente der Wissenschaften*, ed. Marly Biemel, Husserliana 5 (The Hague: Martinus Nijhoff, 1952).

30. Edmund Husserl, *Ideen zu einer reinen Phänomenologie und phänomenologischen Philosophie. Erstes Buch. Allgemeine Einführung in die reine Phänomenologie*, ed. Walter

Biemel, Husserliana 3 (The Hague: Martinus Nijhoff, 1952). There is also a more recent edition ed. Karl Schuhmann, Husserliana 3/1 and 3/2 (The Hague: Martinus Nijhoff, 1976).

31. Preserved in the Husserl Archives as MS K IX 1.

32. Stein, *Life*, 347.

33. See Guy Van Kerckhoven's "Historico-Critical Foreword" in *Ideas III: Phenomenology and the Foundations of the Sciences*, trans. T. E. Klein and W. E. Pohl (The Hague: Martinus Nijhoff, 1980), xv.

34. Preserved in the Husserl Archives as MS. M III 1 I 7/1.

35. This version is known as Edith Stein's second *Ausarbeitung*. It is preserved in the Husserl Archives as MS. M III 1 I 1, MS. M. III 1 I 2.

36. Edith Stein to Fritz Kaufmann, January 12, 1917, in *Self-Portrait in Letters 1916–1942*, ed. Lucy Gelber and Romaeus Leuven, OCD, trans. Josephine Koeppel, OCD (Washington, DC: ICS Publications, 1993), 4.

37. Stein to Roman Ingarden, January 5, 1917, in *Self-Portrait in Letters*, 3.

38. Stein to Roman Ingarden, February 19, 1918, in *Self-Portrait in Letters*, 19.

39. Husserl, "Empfehlungsschreiben Husserls für Stein, 6.II. 1919," in *Briefwechsel*, 3:549.

40. Lucy Gelber documents both Stein's attempts to habilitate and her private lectures in Breslau in her introduction to Stein's *Einführung*.

41. "The Master is still in Bernau and is thinking of remaining there until the middle of September. So nothing will come of the longed-for *joint work*. I have now taken up his notes on the constitution of space and will see what can be done with them. In between, I am occupying myself somewhat with my own work and am supplementing it by writing down what has occurred to me, partially in connection with the *Ideas*" (emphasis mine). Stein to Roman Ingarden, August 28, 1917, in *Self-Portrait in Letters*, 17.

42. Stein to Fritz Kaufmann, November 22, 1919, in *Self-Portrait in Letters*, 32.

43. The manuscript consists now of some 756 pages written in Edith Stein's hand in two different styles of handwriting: 299 pages in what was then-called *Kurrentschrift*, the handwriting common in Germany between 1900 and 1925; 419 pages in Latinscript, a handwriting that became popular after the First World War; and 38 pages in *Kurrentschrift* with redactions in Stein's own hand in Latinscript. The rupture in the styles of handwriting suggests that Edith Stein returned to the text at various times to develop or edit the text. See Lucy Gelber, introduction to Stein, *Einführung*, 7–14.

44. Ibid., 11–12. See also Stein to Fritz Kaufmann, March 10, 1918, in *Self-Portrait in Letters*, 21.

45. Stein to Roman Ingarden, May 31, 1917, in *Self-Portrait in Letters*, 14.

46. Alexander Pfänder is credited with being one of the founders of phenomenology. He worked in Munich, and his students often went to attend Husserl's lectures and vice versa. He is credited with developing *Realontologie*, an approach to philosophy that maintained that life experiences can yield knowledge about the nature of things in the world.

47. See Hanna-Barbara Gerl, postscript to Stein, *Einführung*, 272.

48. "This Ego of intentionality is related in the cogito to its surrounding world and especially to its real surrounding world, e.g., to the things and the people it experiences. This relation is not immediately a real relation but an intentional relation to something real." Husserl, *Ideas II*, 226–27.

49. Gerl, postscript to Stein, *Einführung*, 273–74.

50. Personalism or personalist philosophy was a philosophical movement that took root in continental Europe, especially France, Italy, and Germany. Drawing on the tradition of seminal thinkers like Augustine, Aquinas, and Schleiermacher, personalists tried to place the human person at the center of philosophical inquiry, often resulting in philosophical anthropologies that were rooted in the Christian theological tradition and Christian metaphysics. The principal representative of contemporary personalism was Emmanuel Mounier (1905–50). His thought, especially in his manifesto *Le personalisme* (1938), had a profound impact on continental philosophy of the twentieth century.

51. Edith Stein, *Endliches und ewiges Sein*, ed. Lucy Gelber and Romaeus Leuven, OCD, vol. 2 of *Edith Steins Werke* (Freiburg: Herder, 1986).

52. Edith Stein, *Der Aufbau der menschlichen Person*, ed. Michael Linssen, OCD, vol. 16 of *Edith Steins Werke* (Freiburg: Herder, 1994), and *Was ist der Mensch? Eine theologische Anthropologie*, ed. Michael Linssen, OCD, vol. 17 of *Edith Steins Werke* (Freiburg: Herder, 1994).

53. See Reuben Guilead, *De la phénoménologie à la science de la croix: L'itinéraire philosophique d'Edith Stein* (Louvain: Nauwelaerts, 1974), 109.

54. See Stein to Roman Ingarden, August 28, 1917, in *Self-Portrait in Letters*, 17. Here, Stein speaks of a "joint effort" with Husserl.

55. Stein, *Einführung*, 29.

56. Science of essences. Phenomenology claims that it can bring to givenness in consciousness the essential structures of things in the world.

57. Stein, *Einführung*, 142.

58. Husserl, *Ideas II*, 192.

59. Ibid., § 50.

60. Ibid., 143, 160–61.

61. "Above all, however, it is against the empirical subject, in its generality and its unity, that the 'person' is to be defined in the specific sense: the subject of acts that are to be judged from the standpoint of reason, the subject that is 'self-responsible'" (Ibid., 269). "Therefore the autonomy of reason, the 'freedom' of the personal subject, consists in the fact that I do not yield passively to the influence of others but instead decide for myself. Or again, it consists in this, that I do not let myself be 'drawn' by any other inclinations and drives but instead act freely and do so in the mode of reason" (Ibid., 282). "Where [the] freedom of self-determination does not exist, where one cannot be held responsible for his or her acts, there one finds that one's personhood has been canceled. Undoubtedly, freedom is constitutive of the person. The 'life of the will' [*Willensleben*] has a natural share in [determining] a 'personal quality.' Freedom comes to every person in the same way, namely, through taking willed stands [*Willensstellungnahmen*]. However, taking such a willed stand is motivated by taking certain emotional stands [*Gefühlsstellungnahmen*] and is not produced intentionally [or premeditatively]; they [willed stands] originate vividly in the soul, and they bear the stamp of their own qualities" (Stein, *Einführung*, 161). Translations mine unless otherwise stated.

62. Husserl, *Ideas II*, 161 ff.; Stein, *Einführung*, 136–37.

63. "The distinctive feature of the body as a field of localization is the presupposition for its further distinctive features setting it off from all material things. In particular, it is the precondition for the fact that it, already taken as body (namely, as the thing that has a stratum of localized sensations) is an organ of the will, the one and only object that, for the

will of my pure ego, is movable immediately and spontaneously and is a means for producing a mediate spontaneous movement in other things—in, for example, things struck by my immediately spontaneously moved hand, grasped by it, lifted, and so forth. Sheer material things are movable only mechanically and partake of spontaneous movement only in a mediate way" (Husserl, *Ideas II*, 159). "Because of the double nature of the body [*Leibes*], [one can deduce that] the life of the subject is dependent on the outside world. [This dependence] makes possible the understanding of the subject in relation to his or her external becoming. To the free act, of which the I is capable, belongs the movement of the body (the whole as well as the individual members). These movements are likewise mechanical events and bear consequences in material nature. Hence, the subject, who possesses a body, thanks to its capacities, and whose body is an organ of the will, is able to carry out the effects [of the will] on the things of the outside world, to create new things and have them ready at hand" (Stein, *Einführung*, 144).

64. This introduction appears as the epilogue in Husserl, *Ideas II*, and is reproduced in English translation at the end of *Ideas II*, 403–30.

65. Stein to Roman Ingarden, February 3, 1917, in *Self-Portrait in Letters*, 6.

66. The eidetic, for Husserl, is the objective idea of an object as it appears essentially or as it really is in consciousness. The eidetic, then, is the "thing in itself" as it comes to be given in consciousness.

67. "For me, philosophy, as an idea, means universal, and in a radical sense, 'rigorous' science. As such, it is a science built on an ultimate foundation, or, what comes down to the same thing, a science based on ultimate self-responsibility, in which, hence, nothing held to be obvious, either predicatively or pre-predicatively, can pass, unquestioned as a basis for knowledge. It is, I emphasize, an *idea*, which, as the further meditative interpretation will show, is to be realized only by way of relative and temporary validities and in an ultimate historical process—but in this way it is, in fact, realizable" (Husserl, epilogue to *Ideas II*, 406).

68. Husserl's epoché is the literal bracketing of natural, prejudicial assumptions or attitudes toward things or states of affairs. One brackets one's natural prejudices in order to allow an object or a state of affairs to come to givenness in consciousness in a more adequate or clear form.

69. Stein to Roman Ingarden, February 20, 1917, in *Self-Portrait in Letters*, 8.

70. Stein, *Einführung*, 39–40.

71. "For we see an uncomfortable difficulty here, a certain tension between the nature that stood at the beginning and the nature that has now arisen for us out of the context of the community. Our point of departure was the naturalistic (natural-scientific) attitude, in which nature comes to givenness and to theoretical cognition as physical, bodily, and psychic nature. This naturalistically considered world is of course not *the* world. Rather, the everyday world is pregiven, and within this arises man's theoretical interest in the sciences related to the world, among which is natural science under the ideal of truths in themselves. This pregiven world is investigated first with respect to nature. Then animalia have their turn, human beings before all others. And this is precisely the first task: to investigate them as ego-subjects" (Husserl, *Ideas II*, 219).

72. Stein, *Einführung*, 224.

73. Ibid., 224–25.

74. Stein to Roman Ingarden, March 20, 1917, in *Self-Portrait in Letters*, 11.

75. See § 41 of Husserl, *Ideas II*.

76. "The other's body is for me a passageway (in 'expression,' in intimation, etc.) to-ward the understanding of the ego there, the 'he': he moves his hand, he reaches for this or that, he strikes, he considers, he is motivated by this or that. He is the center of a sur-rounding world appearing to him, presentified to him in memory, thought about, etc., and included in it is a corporeal surrounding world, which to a great extent he has in common with me and with others. The human being appears, but I am focused on the human subject and on the subjectivity in its subjective comportments, in its nexus of motivation" (Ibid., 359, suppl. 5).

77. Stein, *Einführung*, 149–52.

78. Husserl, *Ideas II*, 129, 283.

79. Stein, *Einführung*, § 3 on the personal ego.

80. Max Scheler, *Der Formalismus in der Ethik und die materiale Wertethik* (Bern: Francke, 1966), § II, B.

81. Stein, *Einführung*, 153–61.

82. Ibid., 154.

83. Ibid., 159.

84. See Stein, *Endliches und ewiges Sein* and *Der Aufbau der menschlichen Person*.

85. Mary Catharine Baseheart, *Person in the World: Introduction to the Philosophy of Edith Stein* (Dordrecht: Kluwer, 1997); Angela Ales Bello, "Soggetto, persona e comunità: Analisi fenomenologica," *Aquinas* 40, no. 3 (1997): 441–51; Linda L. McAlister, "Essential Differences," *Philosophy Today* 37, no. 1 (1993): 70–77.

86. Hedwig Conrad-Martius (1888–1966) was a student of both Husserl and Pfänder. As one of Edith Stein's best friends and as a fellow philosopher, Conrad-Martius had a profound influence on Stein's philosophy, especially concerning time. She was interested in many different fields, especially the natural sciences. She was a prolific writer and wrote on themes in metaphysics, biology, perception, psychology, and time.

87. Gerda Walther (1897–1977) wrote interesting texts on different aspects of the social world, including her work on the nature of community and social relationships. Her later works are devoted to a study of the paranormal.

88. See Ales Bello, *Fenomenologia*.

Chapter 14

Ontology, Metaphysics, and Life in Edith Stein

ANGELA ALES BELLO

translated by Antonio Calcagno

Of all of Husserl's students at Göttingen, Edith Stein was the one who completed her philosophical formation most directly under Edmund Husserl's guidance. She transferred from the University of Breslau, her native city, where she studied psychology and German, to Göttingen in 1913 in order to complete her studies in philosophy and carry out her doctoral dissertation on empathy.[1] From the very beginning of her dissertation, in a clear, brief and effective manner, the young Edith Stein employs the fundamental concepts of the phenomenological method, which shapes the entire corpus of her philosophical writing. She explains the preliminary operation of the epoché[2] and clarifies the significance of suspending the belief in one's "position of being" with its preconceptions and inherited prejudices. She notes that there is a difficulty in understanding how it is possible to suspend the act of positing being while simultaneously preserving the significance of the perception in its fullness. She overcomes this difficulty by using the example of a hallucination, which remains valid as a perception even though it is not filled with the real existence of the object perceived. Thus it is possible to "suspend" judgment on the existence of the world, as Husserl conceded to Descartes, in order to illuminate more clearly the phenomena that permit us to know the world. Among these fundamental phenomena is the particular lived experience, which Husserl had already articulated and which Stein acutely examines, constituted by the experience of the other, namely, empathy.

In every case, there is always a consideration of essence: "Each phenomenon forms an exemplary basis for the consideration of its essence."[3] One must also consider the phenomenon from the standpoint of the person analyzing the phenomenon. The empirical and psychological subject can and must be bracketed, but it always remains the subject of the lived experience. I am the one "who considers the world and my person as phenomena, and, therefore, it is impossible that one can doubt either the 'I' or the very same experience the 'I' is experiencing."[4] In such a fashion, Edith Stein the phenomenologist analyzes and clarifies in a unique way the relationship between the world, the question of its existence, and the subject.

The Theme of Being

Though a faithful adherent to the Husserlian phenomenological method in her works written between 1922 and 1925, Stein had already begun to display her self-described "heresies"[5] in 1917. These concerned certain Husserlian positions that revolved not so much around Husserl's analysis of subjectivity as around the constitution of nature. She maintained that the premises for such a constitution of nature are found, on one hand, in a physical nature that is absolutely existing and, on the other hand, in a subjectivity with determined structures.

Stein's realist position becomes more layered with her encounter with the philosophy of Thomas Aquinas and with the significant thinkers of ancient and medieval philosophy. Her intent is to bring the theories of contemporary thought into a face-to-face encounter with medieval and ancient thought, not to force a conflict of ideas to arise but to facilitate understanding possible and useful ways of comprehending reality.[6] Thus Edith Stein does not repudiate her phenomenological formation. Rather, she employs it to launch a more ample investigation of what, in her opinion, Husserl achieved. In fact, she feels an urgency about confronting the traditional questions of metaphysics that Husserl thematized, even though he felt compelled to perfect his method as an essentially cognitive instrument.[7]

Edith Stein proposes certain fundamental theses, which were already anticipated in the work of her friend and philosophical comrade Hedwig Conrad-Martius, including the prior nature of the reduction to essence, the reclaiming of the theme of existence, and the question of idealism. Stein developed these theses from her own perspective; she not only gave her own form to various objections but also added her own substance to the various theses. It should be remarked, however, that Conrad-Martius had some reservations and difficulties about Stein's appropriation of some of her insights.

Turning briefly to the above-mentioned themes, one can certainly see the influence of Hedwig Conrad-Martius on Stein's *Finite and Eternal Being (Endliches und ewiges Sein)*.[8] Stein acknowledges Conrad-Martius's influence in the preface to her work. At this point, it would be noteworthy to mention some substantial distinctions in Stein's work. Stein maintains the double essence of essence. This consists of, on one hand, the relationship between essence and essential being. That is, there is a relationship between essence and the essential *(le essenzialità)* such that the unique essence is the essential one. On the other hand, there is a relationship of essence with the actual-real being of the objects that determines the *quid* of the object. This doubleness of essence is clarified through a deepening of the analyses of essence as originally developed by the Alsatian philosopher and theologian Jean Hering,[9] who believed that essence occupies an intermediate position between essentiality (whose unique being is essential being) and the actual-real world. Stein directs her attention to the actual-real dimension. She argues against Hering's interpretation that "*ousia* (essence), understood in the proper and most restricted sense, as understood by Aristotle, is a substance, that is, a real thing that is founded in itself and that contains itself its proper essence and develops it."[10] Contrarily, for Husserl, according to Edith Stein, essence is primary and the connection to the actual-real moment is not sufficiently recognized, and it is on this point that Husserl's idealism begins to define itself.

One can observe that Stein sees Husserl's idealism as upheld by neo-Kantian[11] underpinnings—for example, those of Paul Natorp[12]—rather than the more classic formulations of Johann Fichte.[13] In fact, Stein centers Husserlian idealism more in the insistent treatment of the ideality of the noetic content[14] than in the centrality of the "I." The ego, however, as developed in Stein's investigations of *Finite and Eternal Being,* employs the fundamental specifications laid out by Husserl. The entire flow of lived experiences belongs to the "I," and it is in this flow that one's life consists. The "I's" "living" is in time in the sense that its living flows moment to moment.

Temporality and Stein's analyses of Husserl's thought lead her to posit the finitude of the "I." The finitude of the "I," therefore, serves as a valid starting point to examine the "I" itself with respect to its existence. *Finite and Eternal Being* opens not with contrasts but with continuity, the metaphysical question concerning the origin of the "I," which Husserl did not ignore but which he dealt with only cursorily. One notes in Stein's development of the problem an affinity with the thought of Saint Augustine. It also should be noted that Stein reminds her readers that Martin Heidegger, in *Being and Time,* excellently describes the "I" as "thrown into *Dasein.*" Heidegger fails, however, to confront the question of origins that "always returns to be asked in an undeniable fashion." The specificity of the being of human kind is such, Stein maintains, that it "demands that there be a Being that throws the thrown *Dasein* into being."[15]

Stein anchors her theoretical observations concerning the pervasive concept of essence as well as her phenomenological analyses concerning subjectivity in the metaphysical framework of being. This move does not strictly allow her to remain in the Husserlian phenomenological camp but nonetheless does not force her to abandon her phenomenological perspective. In fact, Stein's analyses grant certain conclusions that can be inserted into a larger context.

Insofar as Stein's project consists of understanding the sense of being, a project that shows the originality of Stein's thought with respect to the philosophical theme of being, it is useful to accept the analysis of essence that Husserl proposed. But the analysis carried out on being cannot be reduced to pure investigation exclusively focused on the noetic realm. At this point one finds a major point of convergence and divergence between Husserl and Stein. For Stein, essences, or better still the essentialities, have an existence; ontology roots itself not only in questions of essentialities but also in questions of being. The being of the essentialities and quiddities does not have to be thought of as something autonomous. "That which gives being to me and at the same time fills the sense of this being must be not only the master of being but also the master of the sense of being. The fullness of sense is contained in eternal being, and eternal being cannot attain its own sense, a sense that fills every creature, except through itself. Every creature endowed with this sense is called into existence."[16] A hierarchy is delineated. At the lowest level of the hierarchy, one observes the actual-real being of an object, which becomes actual-real through its essence. And this last step renders back to the being of the object its essentialities, which constitute the simple element and archetype of the highest form. These essentialities, in their highest form, rest in Eternal Being. In delineating such a hierarchy, Stein retraces the fundamental stages of the development of ancient Greek thought. She pauses and considers Plato and Aristotle and the more salient moments in medieval philosophy, bringing into dialogue the Aristotelian-Thomist tradition with what Stein defines as the neo-Platonic-Augustinian-Franciscan tradition.

Stein's rediscovery of the theme of being, then, in the phenomenological tradition comes about through an examination of the importance Husserl attributed to essence. An analysis of essence, if conducted in such a fashion as to respect all of its various profiles and articulations and its relationship to the actual-real moment, leads to the question of being and enables phenomenologists such as Hering and Conrad-Martius to establish a connection between contemporary philosophy and ancient Greek philosophy. Similarly, Edith Stein can establish a bridge between contemporary philosophy and medieval philosophy, attempting, as mentioned above, to respond to the ultimate questions of metaphysics by employing all of the suggestions coming from contemporary Western thought in order to clarify that "thing" *(Sache)* called "Being."

Stein's work, then, must be seen not as a kind of eclecticism but rather as a work of understanding that bonds, beyond all temporal differences, all those who worked tirelessly on the aforementioned theme and who are called upon to clarify, with their various positions, important aspects that progressively come to be evidenced.[17] The decision on the validity of such thinkers' claims is linked not to a merely subjective judgment but to a capacity to "demonstrate" to our minds, ever more clearly, the significance of the object of research in question, namely, the sense of being. This uncovering of the sense of being, through the use and application of the inherited Husserlian phenomenological method, Stein undertook as her object of research, ultimately delivering original results.

The Theme of Life

In 1918, Stein, who was then assistant to Edmund Husserl, transcribed and prepared the second volume of Husserl's *Ideas Pertaining to a Pure Phenomenology and to a Phenomenological Philosophy*. Husserl writes in *Ideas II* that in the reflection on the "I," one remarks that originarily, "I am the subject of my life, and living, the subject develops itself; primarily the subject does not experience itself, albeit it constitutes natural objects, things of value, instruments, etc. In so far as it is active, it does not mold itself although it forms and molds things as works. The 'I' is not given originarily to itself in experience but more through life (It is what it is, not through the 'I': it is the 'I')."[18]

Having already analyzed in her doctoral dissertation on empathy the significance of the *Erlebnis* (lived experience) of empathy as an act and as a lived experience of intersubjectivity, Stein sets as her task at the beginning of the 1920s the examination of the deep structures of the human person. Following the insights of Husserl and led by the philosophical tradition, Stein begins to explore what it means to affirm that a human person is formed of body and soul. Stein does not wish to accept blindly the assumption that we are formed as body and soul. Rather, she wishes to confirm that the human person is constituted as body and soul by placing this affirmation in question only to verify its validity on diverse philosophical grounds.

In her first work, Stein had already examined the human being in its corporeal constitution and in its psychological dimensions and had prepared the way for a consideration of the spiritual life. If we read in a parallel fashion the analyses contained in the *Ideas II* of Husserl and in Stein's *Philosophy of Psychology and the Humanities,* we find considerable similarities in the development of Stein's and Husserl's investigations. Stein is conscious of these similarities and remarks in her introduction to her work that she is not able to distinguish what she has assimilated through her work with and for Husserl from her own research.

In *Philosophy of Psychology and the Humanities,* Stein, focusing on the psyche and its mechanisms, completes and integrates the insights of Husserl, demonstrating her extraordinary analytical capacity. She gives credence to the intuitions of Husserl developed in *Ideas II.* The centrality of life is most evident in the psychological dimension, which, in conjunction with the physical-corporeal elements, permits phenomenologists to claim that we all have a living body *(Leib).* Stein dedicates most of her philosophical attention to the sections devoted to the phenomenon of the psychological.

She begins with a recurring question in the history of philosophy, which took on greater prominence in positivistic philosophical circles. Stein asks if and in what measure the human being is to be linked with relations of causality, relations that also occur in nature. Revolving around such a theme, one finds both determinist and nondeterminist positions, and hence the insistence upon necessity or freedom and upon the preeminence of that which is physical or that which is psychological. To resolve such contrasts and conflicts of opinion, Stein undertook a systematic study of psychological causality. Assuming that phenomenology was a call to "return to things themselves"—that is, to phenomena as they present themselves—Stein examined the phenomena of "psyche" and "causality."[19]

The analysis begins from a common experience: I feel cold, but I can mistake the content of this particular sensation that I indicate as "cold." I can also be mistaken about my consciousness of this lived experience. Certainly, I feel when I am aware of the sensation, and I feel cold and nothing else when, of course, I have this sensation. It is possible, however, to feel cold without the conditions for coldness really being present, and I can subsequently become conscious of this. Whether in the case of sensations concerning myself *(Gefühle),* like that of feeling cold, or sensations relative to an external property *(Empfindungen)*—for example, the sensations of color relative to a colored thing—an external condition (the cold) and an internal property or capacity come to the fore. The internal property or capacity may also be defined as the "life force" *(Lebenskraft)*, which should not be confused with the structure of consciousness—that is, with the pure ego and its lived experiences.[20]

The above-mentioned distinction between the internal and external is the same distinction that allows one to distinguish phenomenology from psychology and aids one in clarifying the relationship between psyche and consciousness. If one investigates the causes that affect the life of the psyche, one ought to investigate the modes in which the life force manifests itself, always articulating itself in life feelings *(Lebensgefühle).*

Changes in life conditions indicate a major or minor life force. This means that causality is not necessarily concerned with the sphere of lived experiences. No pure lived experience can happen causally. Rather, causality is concerned with the life force. Moreover, psychological causality is distinguished from physical causality, and the psyche of an individual has its own mode of being, just like material nature. It should be noted that even force manifests itself differently in the two cases. In physical nature, force articulates itself in a happening, whereas in the psychological sphere, force is cultivated in its modes of lived experiences.[21]

Stein insists on the difference between the sphere of consciousness and the flow of its lived experiences from the sphere of life feelings. The former lacks life feelings and consists of a flow of data of diverse species, quality, and intensity but without any "coloration" or tension. Coloration and intensity belong to the sphere of life feelings. Life feelings have their own characteristics, but they "color" every datum of the flow of consciousness, and such a flow is unstoppable.[22]

At this point, it is useful to remark that there is an undeniable relationship between the thought of Stein and that of the French philosopher Henri Bergson.[23] Stein maintains that the psyche is a qualitative continuity, and this is why she is in agreement with Bergson concerning the evaluation of the moments of the life of the psyche, which are to be attributed to differences of intensity. However, Stein differs from Bergson insofar as she maintains that it is possible to individuate the parts of this continuity and the place they occupy; though it is difficult to distinguish the various shades of red, it still is possible to distinguish red from blue. Hence, it is possible to point out life feelings of one quality or another. In this distinction between the qualities resides the possibility of tracing a law of causality, and in this regard Edith Stein distances herself from the thought of Bergson.[24] In any case, the causality that Stein tries to individuate in her investigations differs greatly from that of the more traditional scientific model. Stein's analyses do not pretend to sketch an "exact" science of causality that lies at the basis of all physical sciences. Rather, Stein is attempting to articulate a "prescientific" causality that presents itself in experience. Examples of causal connections that are found internally in the life of the psyche and that are still related to experiencing events of nature include "I am so tired that I am unable to read a book that engages me intellectually" and "Today it is so clear outside that it is possible to have good visibility." Certainly, these connections are not determinable in a rigid way. Rather, they are more or less vague, and they have a purely empirical value. But this does not mean that they do not express a sort of "necessity."

According to Stein, there is no determinism in the life of the psyche, even if we discover connections and, therefore, causal relations. Moreover, every quantitative determination of psychological states is unsustainable because we are in front of a flow of qualitative states, and they can be individuated according to their essential structure. This last point distinguishes the phenomenological reading of the psyche from the analysis of Bergson.

I have paused to consider Edith Stein's interpretation concerning the life of the psyche because her original contribution, even with respect to the results obtained by Husserl in his analyses, consists in the individuation of the life force that is the propulsive center of the human being. It should be remarked that she does not end her study with the psychological dimension. She also acutely analyzes the life of the spirit, characterized by motivation and freedom.

Rather than lingering over this last aspect, I prefer to see "life" and the "life of the spirit" at work in a new philosophical consideration that Stein presents in her most important book, *Finite and Eternal Being*, completed between 1935 and 1936 while Stein lived in the Carmel at Cologne. In this work, Stein clarifies with profundity Husserl's analysis of the centrality of the subject relative to our own experience of the subject, but also the subject opening unto "the other" and therefore to others, the world, and God.

Let us follow Stein's analyses in this regard, focusing on the centrality of the life of the "I." Following Husserl, she distinguishes corporeality from the psychological sphere of consciousness, which is the ground that affords one immediate awareness of one's living. Husserl calls this ground the pure "I." According to Stein, this term means that the "I" lives in every lived experience and therefore can never be eliminated. Not only is a life force existing on the psychological level traceable, but also life characterizes the whole "I." Concretely, "This means that the 'I' lives in every 'I perceive,' 'I think,' 'I draw conclusions,' 'I enjoy,' 'I desire,' et cetera, and is turned in this or that particular way toward that which is perceived, thought, desired, and so on."[25] The "I" is inseparable from all content of a lived experience in the sense that all content belongs to it. "The 'I' is that which lives in each one of these lived experiences; its life is the flow in which they proceed, always forming new unities of lived experiences. This means more, however, than the simple fact that some contents of lived experiences belong to it. The 'I' *lives,* and life is its being. It lives now in joy, in a few moments in desire, then in reflection (many times the 'I' lives in these distinct unities of lived experience); joy dissipates, desire subsides, thought ceases, but the 'I' is never diminished, does not cease, it lives in every instant."[26]

It can be said, therefore, that "I" lives and that life is its being. But how should one metaphysically interpret this observation? What is the relationship between life and being? On this matter, Stein is most explicit.[27] She realizes that her arguments are very similar to those of Augustine, Descartes, and Husserl. What remains hidden in the reflections of the philosophers just mentioned is, in Stein's opinion, the undeniable fact that "I am." The certainty of one's own being is not extracted or deduced from thought, and this is the argument made against Descartes. This is the most originary form of knowledge, which is much in line with the thought of Augustine and Husserl. It is not, however, the first knowledge that one acquires in the temporal order, because the natural disposition of human beings is turned first and foremost toward the external world. Husserl already showed this in the above-mentioned sections of his *Ideas II,* and such a disposition toward the external world arises well before self-awareness. Yet this originary knowledge of the certainty of the "I am" is the most intimate and most essential fact of our existence, and it is placed before every reflection.

When reflection intervenes—that is, when the spirit immerses itself in itself in order to contemplate itself—the spirit recognizes that this contemplation is inseparable from temporality. But this being immersed in time does not mean a simple flowing and diffusion of time. In this regard, Stein uses certain suggestions of Hedwig Conrad-Martius concerning the nature of time.[28] Stein individuates actuality as emerging in a point from contact with being, thereby sustaining the existence of a continual flowing of points of contact. Hence, the pivotal hinge to understanding the temporality of being is the present that flows.

These affirmations lead Stein to consider the opposition between actuality and potency in the life of our "I." In fact, our actuality is not pure because we are not equally in all that we are at this very instant. To understand this, we must posit a being in whom potency and act are united in the manner currently indicated against another being in which these differences between potency and act are removed—that is, God understood as pure act *(purus actus).* Only infinite being is and, in fact, exists as purely actual.

The reflection on life, therefore, leads one back to being understood as participative and as a purely actual being. This understanding permits one to give a new significance to the relationship between the "I" and the contents of consciousness. The contents of consciousness cannot realize their own being by themselves. Rather, they participate solely through the "I," in whose life they enter, entering into its being. For this reason, the "I" is a being in an immanent sense.[29] The "I," therefore, is, but it cannot be without being a living being.

At this point, Stein posits an objection to her own analyses that permits her to overcome a purely vitalistic vision of being—that is, an absolutization of life. If the "I" is a source of life, does this mean that life has the same being as its "I"? Experience of one's own being leads one to affirm that something is living and exists in the present but that it comes from a past and is anticipated *(proteso)* in the future. Our being is, to borrow an expression from Heidegger, "thrown into being-there *[Dasein]*." That is, one discovers one's being as a being that does not have its origins in itself. "Being cannot stop itself because it flows 'unceasingly.' Thus it can never possess itself fully and truly."[30] One must conclude, therefore, that we are constrained to define the being of the "I" as received. "It is placed in its being-there *[Dasein]*, and it is maintained there moment to moment. In such a fashion, it is possible, therefore, to speak about its beginning, its end, and even a fracturing of its being."[31]

Accepting Heidegger's insight regarding the "thrownness" of our being-there, Stein draws metaphysical conclusions that distance her from Heidegger and permit her to recover the insights of certain ancient and medieval thinkers. This return to the ancients and the medievals permits Stein, always drawing upon a rational reflection on the First Being, who is the Creator of every being, to draw such conclusions. And the First Being, the divine Spirit, is viewed as life and living understanding. In this way, God, insofar as he is pure act, is considered to be immutable vitality. And this opens the way to a philosophical and theological consideration of creation.

NOTES

This essay has appeared as "Edith Stein—Ontologia Metafisica Vita," in *Il Faro (sofare) di Arianna: Percorsi del pensiero feminile nel Novecento,* ed. A. Ales Bello and F. Brezzi (Milan: Mimesis, 2001), 31–42.

1. Edith Stein, *On the Problem of Empathy,* trans. Waltraut Stein (Washington, DC: ICS Publications, 1989).

2. The Husserlian epoché is the methodological bracketing of one's belief in the existence of the world or the bracketing of one's belief in the natural world. By bracketing one's belief in the natural world one is, according to Husserl, able to focus phenomenologically on the transcendental structures of consciousness and the objects contained therein.

3. Stein, *On the Problem of Empathy,* 4.

4. Ibid.

5. Edith Stein to Roman Ingarden, March 20, 1917, in *Briefe an Roman Ingarden*, vol. 14 of *Edith Steins Werke* (Freiburg: Herder, 1991).

6. The phenomenological trilogy written by Edith Stein consists of *On The Problem of Empathy; Philosophy of Psychology and the Humanities*, trans. Mary Catharine Baseheart and Marianne A. Sawicki (Washington, DC: ICS Publications, 2000); and *On the State*, originally published in German as *Über den Staat* (Tübingen: Max Niemeyer, 1971).

7. For a more specific treatment of this theme, see Angela Ales Bello, "Fenomenologia e metafisica: Seconda navigazione," in *Annuario di Filosofia* (Milan: Arnoldo Monditori, 2000).

8. Edith Stein, *Endliches und ewiges Sein*, ed. Lucy Gelber and Romaeus Leuven, vol. 2 of *Edith Steins Werke* (Freiburg: Herder, 1986).

9. Jean (Johannes) Hering (1891–1966) was an Alsatian philosopher who was a member of the Göttingen Philosophical Society, of which Edith Stein was a member. Hering was considered more a supporter of the "real ontology" developments of phenomenology, which emphasized a real and concrete relation between the essence of an object and its relation to the real world. Of great importance for Stein was Hering's work entitled "Bemerkungen über das Wesen, die Wesenheit und die Idee," *Jahrbuch für Philosophie und phänomenologische Forschung* 4 (1921): 495 ff. This work is cited frequently in Stein's *Endliches und ewiges Sein*.

10. Stein, *Endliches und ewiges Sein*, 255–56.

11. Neo-Kantianism was a school of thought, founded at the University of Marburg, that dominated German universities at the turn of the twentieth century. Prominent neo-Kantians included Ernst Cassirer and Hermann Cohen. A great interest resurfaced in the writings of Kant, especially as Kant's critical philosophy was seen as a means of guaranteeing scientific rigor and scientific objectivity. Given that this Kantian framework dominated science, one could see why Husserl would wish to appeal to the then-scientific model by drawing on Kantian idealism.

12. Paul Natorp (1854–1924) was a German philosopher and composer. He cofounded, with Hermann Cohen (1842–1918), the Marburg neo-Kantian movement. Natorp is often addressed in Husserl's writing. Natorp's logical writings made a profound impact on Husserl. Natorp was also a specialist in the development of social pedagogy.

13. Johann Gottlieb Fichte (1762–1814) was an eminent German idealist. Fichte saw himself as completing Kant's project. One of Fichte's greatest contributions is his explanation of the ego as self-positing, which can be read as relevant to contemporary phenomenological discussions of auto-affection. *Wissenschaftslehre* and the *Vocation of Man* are some of Fichte's more prominent works.

14. *Noetic* is the term Husserl employs to describe the transcendental structure of consciousness. *Noetic* stems from the Greek root of the verb "to know." Noetic content is that content of one's phenomenological knowledge of a certain act, object, or state of affairs.

15. Edith Stein, *Martin Heideggers Existentialphilosophie*, in *Welt und Person: Beitrag zum christlichen Wahrheitsstreben*, vol. 6 of *Edith Steins Werke* (Louvain: Éditions Nauwelaerts, 1962).

16. Stein, *Endliches und ewiges Sein*, 102–3.

17. From the Italian *evidenziati*. I have kept the root sense of this term, translating it literally to bring out its full connection with the phenomenological notion of

Evidenz—that is, the full coming to presence of an object in its essence in phenomenological consciousness.—Trans.

18. Edmund Husserl, *Ideas Pertaining to a Pure Phenomenology and to a Phenomenological Philosophy,* trans. R. Rojcewicz and A. Schuwer (Dordrecht: Kluwer, 1989).

19. Stein, *Philosophy of Psychology,* 4–5.

20. Ibid., 22.

21. See Angela Ales Bello, introduction to the Italian translation of Edith Stein's text *Psicologia e scienze dello spirito,* trans. A. M. Pezzella (Rome: Città Nuova, 1999), 23.

22. Ibid., 30.

23. Henri Bergson (1859–1941) was a French philosopher and Nobel Laureate. He had a huge impact on consciousness studies and studies of temporality. Phenomenology and Bergson's philosophy simultaneously examined the life of human consciousness with some varying results. Bergson was a prolific author, and some of his more remarkable works included *L'évolution créatrice* and *Durée et simultaneité.*

24. Ales Bello, introduction to *Psicologia e scienze,* 31.

25. Stein, *Endliches und ewiges Sein,* 46.

26. Ibid.

27. Ibid.

28. Ibid., chap. 2, § 2.

29. Ibid., chap. 2, § 3.

30. Ibid., 47.

31. Ibid., 52.

What Makes You You?

Individuality in Edith Stein

SARAH BORDEN

For a number of years during high school and college, I worked in the-ater, and as a college student, I wanted to be a director. I spent many hours watching rehearsals and found that one can tell—surprisingly quickly—when an actor has rightly understood her character. There is a kind of "logic" or consistency to the character. One can say, "Ah, that is exactly what Helen would have done here" or "No, no, I don't believe you. Anne wouldn't have reacted that way." Similarly, I have often found myself saying of friends, "That is just the sort of crazy plan Cathy would have come up with" or "No? Are you sure it was her?" These kinds of hypothetical statements and judgments about what someone would or would not do make sense, just as we can have rather long discussions—which cannot be reduced simply to our "opinions"—about fictional characters. Individuality and our individual personalities are not something random. What makes Cathy, for example, unusual need not be a quirky deviation from the common human pattern: rather, it appears to be something quite intelligible and rooted in some kind of structure. Our choices are not completely free in the sense that they are utterly unpredictable and without patterns that can be, once someone knows us, more and less anticipated.

In the following I would like, first, to present Edith Stein's theory of individual uniqueness, which she developed, in part, out of these types of concerns. Stein was intrigued with the ways in which our personalities are intelligible. Her autobiographical writings are filled with descriptions of people that attempt to capture something essential characterizing each person. For example, she reports that her relatives called her a *Streberin*, a go-getter, and the description points to traits of energy, drive, and a certain kind of determination to finish various tasks.[1] Her descriptions of Max Scheler invoke the image of an "absent-minded professor"—brilliant (she says that in him she met the "phenomenon of genius"), with new ideas nearly bursting out of him, but unable to remember what his own hat looked like. In contrast, Edmund Husserl was methodical and thorough.[2] Her short little descriptions are filled out perhaps with an incident or two, and through these characterizations we can imagine how Scheler might write an essay in contrast to Husserl, or how Stein herself might respond to some problem.

Thus I would like, first, to present Stein's theory of individual uniqueness, which arises, in part, from such experiences of the intelligibility of individual personalities. But, second, after presenting Stein's claims, I would like to raise two questions about a central aspect of her theory. In Stein's early writings, she accounts for our intelligibility and predictability[3] as individuals by insisting that each of us has a *personal core,* and in her more metaphysical writings, Stein posits an *individual form* for each human being. While I find these claims to be beautiful and her concerns regarding individuality to be worthwhile, I am, nonetheless, worried about two possible problems with the claim that each of us has such an individual structure. Thus, after presenting Stein's position, I would like to begin evaluating it by raising two queries about her account of individuality.

Stein on Individual Uniqueness

Throughout her philosophical writings, Stein insists that each human being has a unique personal core or individual form.[4] In her dissertation, for example, she says:

> [W]e find not only that the categorical structure of the soul as soul must be retained, but also within its individual form we strike an unchangeable kernel, the personal structure. I can think of Caesar in a village instead of in Rome and can think of him transferred into the twentieth century. Certainly, his historically settled individuality would then go through some changes, but just as surely he would remain Caesar. The personal structure marks off

a range of possibilities of variation within which the person's real distinctiveness can be developed "ever according to the circumstances."[5]

She claims that regardless of where Caesar lived, even if time travel were possible, he would retain the same personality structure. While the circumstances in which he lived made an impact upon his "historically settled individuality," his fundamental possibilities would not have changed, regardless of the circumstances. In the same way, Stein insists that each of us can more or less completely realize ourselves. Perhaps our material or historical circumstances are such that certain talents cannot be developed or certain traits must remain hidden, but there is, nonetheless, something to be realized, some personal structure that exists, regardless of whether it is in fact realized.

In her first two *Jahrbuch*[6] essays, written just a few years after her dissertation, Stein makes a similar claim, describing a personal core central to each person. This core cannot be developed, nor can it deteriorate; it can only be exposed (or not).[7] The personal core appears to be loosely analogous to a physical object and has parts and characteristics in much the same way that a car has a radiator, tires, and door locks or a squirrel has a tail, fur, intestines, and teeth. Someone might have in her soul the trait of generosity or a talent for sensing ghosts *whether she was generous or not, and whether she at any point in her life sensed ghosts.* Developing some trait or virtue is, according to Stein's early texts, more like finding something than creating something new. And the personal core will remain the same wherever it is found, although the historical and material conditions of a life will affect how that structure is realized.

In the second *Jahrbuch* essay, Stein adds the claim that the only way the core can be transformed is if a change enters the person via "a transformation through an 'otherworldly' power—that is, a power situated outside of the person and outside of all of the natural connections in which she is entangled."[8] Our personal core characterizes us in such a way that we ourselves cannot change that fundamental structure. We may be able to suppress or deny our personal core, but change of the core itself occurs only through some external transforming power.

Several years later, after her conversion and entrance into the Catholic Church, Stein made the even stronger claim that we cannot even realize or unfold this core fully without divine assistance. In her comments at the end of an essay on St. Elizabeth of Hungary ("The Spirit of St. Elizabeth as It Informed Her Life"), she says that there is in each of us a form that longs for self-expression. Merely importing an image or model from someone else (perhaps a mentor or revered saint) and attempting to imitate it, however, will be insufficient. While such imitation may be important in many ways (and perhaps even necessary), it runs the risk of deforming our own structure.[9] If, however, we attempt to develop our individual structure on our own, we are likely to fail. We have neither the knowledge nor the power within ourselves to unfold freely and naturally our own form. This form is deeply hidden, and to realize it we need divine help. Thus Stein once again insists that each of us has a unique individual structure that is already present within us, even if it is not yet realized. And she further claims that God alone can help us fully unfold that form.[10]

We should make clear that what is gained in understanding or having insight into someone's personal core differs from simply understanding the possible motives in a given situation. Stein describes motives as intelligible, but not necessary, connections between acts. For example, I may be motivated to complete a chord in a certain way, or motivated by the logic of an argument to accept a certain conclusion. While such motives are intelligible (and the tones do motivate certain kinds of completion and the argument the acceptance of a specific conclusion), they do not *cause* these outcomes. The song may be left unfinished, and I may become stubborn, refusing to accept the conclusion of the argument. Motives, in contrast to causes, are intelligible but do not necessitate the next step.

Stein insists that the intelligibility of personalities does not consist simply in understanding human motives. I may have insight into certain kinds of motivational chains, but that does not thereby mean that I have insight into your personality. Rather, understanding the core personality of an individual is necessary in order to have insight into "what is a plausible motive for this individual."[11] I may, for example, talk with a friend about the man she has decided to marry. She tells me stories about their times together, the projects they do, and interests they share. This information, however, is not sufficient for knowing why she chose to marry this man. Rather, what gives me such insight is an understanding of what she values and why she finds these particular shared interests compelling reasons to marry. All our decisions are motivated, but there can be competing motivations. To understand or have insight into how any particular person will act, one must understand more than simply motives. One must also understand or have some grasp of that person's core. Thus, in an essay delimiting the elements affecting and conditioning human actions, Stein reiterates the claim that all of us have our own personal core or core personality that colors all that we do and all decisions that we make. (Neither complete nor direct insight into the core of another is possible, but partial insight is, and that insight allows us to grasp another's individual structure and thus discuss the hypothetical acts of another.)

Finally, in chapter 4 of *Finite and Eternal Being*, a work completed twenty years after her dissertation, Stein says, "'Socrates,' as the name of the final determination of the essence, means something different from the human being Socrates himself, and the being-Socrates of this human being must be something different from his spatio-temporal existence [*Dasein*]."[12] Here she points to *being-Socrates*, not *being-human*, as the essence, and she insists that this individual form differs from Socrates' real being. As such, the being-Socrates, the individual form of Socrates, is independent of his historical and material conditions. The historical and material conditions may affect the degree to which the form is unfolded, but they do not shape the essential possibilities. Our individual form, therefore, is not the result of our experiences but instead prescribes the possibilities available to experience.

In the same work, Stein clearly distinguishes her position from Thomas Aquinas's. For Aquinas, if there were an "individual form," it would be the species-form individuated; it would be an individual instance of the universal (the human form or human nature). In contrast, Stein insists that "[i]t has already become clear that we cannot agree with this conception: we see the essence of Socrates in his being-Socrates (in which the being-human is enclosed), and we observe it as not merely numerically different but, rather, different from the essence of every other human being through a special particularity."[13] It is clear that Stein intends her position to go beyond Aristotle[14] and Aquinas, both of whom see the species-form (in our case, the human form) as the final determination of form. Whatever the individual form is, it is, according to Stein, distinct from and more fundamental than the species-form.

Stein expresses dissatisfaction with the Aristotelian-Thomistic position, and she insists that the individual uniqueness of each person is not merely a contingency of her history dependent upon the degree to which the human form is realized, as if our essence were "a *kind* that was *individuated* into a multitude of the same structure."[15] Our individual uniqueness is something valuable—not a matter of a greater or lesser realization of what is common (i.e., the human form). Further, if one wants to claim, as Aquinas certainly did, that each human being has an immortal soul, then it is at least intelligible to say that each individual "should reproduce the divine image in a 'wholly personal way.'"[16] Why would God need to create many that are identical in form? Would it not be better to say that each soul reflects the glory of God in a unique way? Thus Stein insists that, while we all share the common human form, each of us also has his or her own unique individual form.

In positing a formal element to individuality Stein insists that there is something intellectually accessible (although not directly accessible) and predictable about each truly unique person. Thus she insists that all Socrates' actions come from one root,[17] and she looks at our regular attempts to find the key to someone's behavior. It is precisely these aspects that make a story or drama, for example, convincing. We can talk intelligibly yet also hypothetically about the *kinds of* things so-and-so would or would not do. Such hypothetical actions fit a pattern that characterizes the person. If there were no structure characterizing each person, such hypothetical talk would be non-sensical.

Further, Stein seems to think that it is our individual form or this individual structure that we come to appreciate in understanding both ourselves and others in their unique personalities. Thus Stein repeatedly insists on a personal core or individual form that is the final determination of the soul and that, in the schema of *Finite and Eternal Being,* contains the species-form but is more fundamental than that. Finally, a recognition of the significance of our individuality and individual uniqueness is necessary to appreciate the relation between human beings and the divine.[18]

Before turning to a critique of Stein's position, I would like to make a brief detour. Stein does *not* claim that our personal core or individual form makes us unique in the sense of unrepeatable. Forms are, by their nature, repeatable. A form or structure is precisely what can be in more than one instance. Individual uniqueness—if what we mean by that is unrepeatability—must lie in something else. For Stein, that something else is our experience—our choices, habits, situations, and histories.[19] Our individual forms may happen to be unique insofar as my personal structure differs from Caesar's or my friend Cathy's, but it need not be unique in the sense of unrepeatable. Unrepeatability may only be due to nonformal elements.

In *Finite and Eternal Being,* Stein describes human beings as a unity of body, soul, and spirit, and she distinguishes these three elements: the soul makes the material body alive and fashions the matter (this is soul in the Aristotelian tradition). The body is that which is shaped by the soul. And spirit is noncorporeal, rational, and free. (Stein insists that we should not, with this division, understand three regions existing independently of each other.)[20] We cannot be identified simply with our individual form insofar as we are more than our soul and even more than a soul forming a body. We are also spirit. If we understand the soul as that which includes our individual form,[21] then the spirit is our freedom in relation to that. Stein says, "*[S]elf-formation* is not only the formation of a body but also and even properly formation of one's own soul. The human being is a spiritual person because he stands freely against not only his body but also his soul, and only so far as he has power over his soul does he also have it over his body."[22] Our individual form—that is, our soul—dictates neither our actions nor our personalities. We may choose how to act, and, in choosing how to act, we also choose how and to what degree our own individual form is realized.[23]

Thus full individuality must be attributed to more than our personal core or individual form. It also—and even primarily—involves our ability to transcend ourselves. In both her *Jahrbuch* essays and her later writings, Stein insists that we always retain the power to choose among various options, including options regarding our own self-development. Our individual forms do not dictate our actions. They do, however, prescribe which possibilities are available and thus the options among which we may choose.[24] The individual form will affect all that I do, as I can only do what is possible for me. But I may choose—to a lesser or greater degree—which possibilities to unfold and the degree to which they are unfolded. (Stein certainly seems to think that our individuality will also, at least in certain ways, "stream out" involuntarily.) Thus Stein insists that, although we have an individual form, that alone is not constitutive of our personality. Our choices, habits, beliefs, wishes, and fears influence how and to what degree that unique form is unfolded.

Spirit, understood as the power over our soul, is expressive only through the soul, just as our willful actions have only the body as their physical "tool." Yet insofar as and to the degree that the spirit is distinct from and controls our soul, we are free. And in that freedom, in that transcendence of our own structure, lies our true individuality.

Two Questions Concerning Individual Forms

Stein's conception is beautiful and deeply attractive to me, and her focus on individuality is extremely valuable. There is certainly an emphasis (and a right and good one) in our culture, both philosophical and social, on individual uniqueness. There is something convincing about the idea that there is a predictable structure to our personalities, and I have certainly seen willful strivings both to develop and to repress personal traits—in both good and bad ways. These descriptions strike me as right.

Nonetheless, I worry about two possible problems with Stein's account. First, it is not clear to me that individual form or a personal core is explanatorily necessary, and, second, I fear that such individual structures may undermine our fundamental commonality. These are two rather large objections to raise, and I will only briefly articulate the reasons for my hesitation.

Before turning to these questions, however, I would like to make clear where the possible problems lie. There is an ambiguity in some of Stein's descriptions of our individual uniqueness. At times, she describes the personal core as something coloring all that we do and functioning more like an adverb than a noun. For example, she says that, although two people do the same thing, it is not the same.[25] The action of each person has a different style or "personal note." There is, thus, no fundamental difference in possibilities, only one in the *way* in which the possibilities are actualized. I am not objecting to this understanding of personal core or individual form. On other occasions, however, especially in *Finite and Eternal Being*, the personal structure sounds more like a noun, an a priori structure prescribing the capacities and predispositions of the person. As such, there are not simply differences in style between two people but also differences in a priori possibilities. This seems to be the most plausible way to read her claim, for example, that "the being-human as such is the essence of all individual human beings, common, always and everywhere remaining the same; beside that, however, each has something that differentiates him through content from others."[26] Here Stein points to a common human form and to something (the individual form) differentiating each human being through content. Presumably, this difference in content is a priori—that is, prior to any of our experiences or choices—and prescribes the possibilities available to an individual in a way analogous to the human form in Aristotle or Aquinas. Likewise, she says, "[A]n individual human being is not capable of unfolding within his life all possibilities that are grounded in his essence (understood as individual essence). His power is so limited that he must purchase his accomplishments in one area with gaps in another."[27] Stein makes a point here of saying that the possibilities in question are not the human ones per se but the possibilities of our individual essence. I take it that her distinction here points to a real difference in content—that is, a difference in the possibilities in each essence, among human beings. My worry is that individual forms so understood will lead us to conclusions that Stein herself would not have endorsed. Thus my questions are applicable only to one interpretation of Stein's claims, and, while this interpretation fits with many, if not most, of her claims, she does state her position slightly differently at times. (It is likely that Stein herself was struggling with these questions and attempting to figure out how to articulate her philosophical intuitions when she ceased writing philosophical works.)

My first question regarding individual forms thus understood is whether they are necessary. If we have freedom as well as conditioning through our matter and our social, cultural, and historical conditions, do we also need individual forms? I worry that individual forms—understood as a priori—may be an overdetermination. What Stein attempts to account for through individual forms can, it appears, be accounted for (for the most part) through other means.[28] We can think of the "class clown," the funny guy in a classroom or office. For example, my cousin, a man quick with a joke, explains his own personality as, in part, the result

WHAT MAKES YOU YOU?   291

of choices made at a young age. He wanted others to laugh with him rather than at him. Thus one of the primary traits of his personality can be accounted for through a series of choices he made as a child. Or I think of my own case. My older sister, who set out to forge a path in the world, as all older siblings must, was a bit nervous, self-conscious, and scared in the undertaking. As I came along two years behind her, I saw her nervousness and insecurities and thought—as many middle children do—how undignified! And I determined to present a face to the world that had a bit more poise, a little less fear. Likewise, when we are getting to know someone—a friend or potential spouse, for example—we often tell stories about our childhood, the things that we did, the events that happened, and the culture of our family. These stories are intended, in part, to explain who we are. Given these kinds of examples, it is not clear to me that our personalities need to be accounted for through an a priori individual form; rather, they may be partially chosen and partially an "accident" of our histories. In suggesting the role of accident, I do not mean to devalue individuality—as Stein is careful to avoid doing—but I do want to place the value in our choices amid the conditions we face, not in a priori possibilities.[29]

In his struggle with God in the garden outside Milan, Augustine describes his weakness as one of habit, a weakness of will but not of nature.[30] He says: "I was held back not by fetters put on me by someone else, but by the iron bondage of my own will."[31] He had acquiesced in his desire, which "became a habit, and the habit, being constantly yielded to, became a necessity."[32] With perhaps not such a negative tone, personality could be seen in much the same way. Our personalities are in part characterized by our choices (from among the human possibilities) and, being consistently chosen, become abiding traits of our nature. (Personalities would then also be alterable, to a greater and lesser degree, in a way analogous to habits.) Thus it could be our factual conditions, our matter, experiences, and real choices that determine who we are as individuals, not an essential a priori individual nature.

Likewise, if Stein is attributing traits and personal capacities to the individual form or personal core, it is not clear to me that she needs to do so. Aristotle and Aquinas both insist that all human beings have the same kind of structure, the human structure. It is clear, however, that different human beings differ. Some are musical, whereas others are tone-deaf. One person may be quick with a joke, whereas another lacks wit. Such differences need some kind of explanation. We could, however, claim with Aristotle and Aquinas that the possibilities of each human essence are identical—that is, our structure is the same—but our diverse talents and skills are due to various a posteriori conditions. For example, perhaps one person, because of material conditions (and therefore a posteriori), has a weak connection between her ear and brain. While she can hear voices, music, and most noises, she finds it difficult to catch subtle nuances in tones or other sounds. Thus she claims that she is "unmusical" and turns her attention instead to visual stimuli. The possibilities within her essence are identical with those for any other human being, but due to material circumstances she is inclined toward some avenues of communication and expression rather than others.[33] Thus we could claim that all human possibilities are identical and thereby justify the assumption of sameness, while attributing difference to the way the essence unfolds in real situations—including physical, psychological, and spiritual factors. And if such explanations are plausible, it is not clear to me that an a priori individual form is necessary to account for the differences we experience among diverse human beings.

Given these alternate explanations of our differences and unique personalities, individual forms appear to be unnecessary at a descriptive level. Further, I worry that such individual structures may lead us into a small quagmire. Stein's position is comparable with John Duns Scotus's, and there are traditionally two problems raised with Scotus's attempt to posit an individual form or *haecceitas*.[34] The first is the formal distinction: that is, his attempt to explain unity in difference. (This is, incidentally, a problem with which I believe Stein can deal adequately.)[35] The second is the tendency to compromise our fundamental human commonality. If we are *at base* different, as, it seems to me, we must be, given individual forms (even if we all share a human nature that is distinct from our individual nature), how then do we affirm human commonality and, among other things, equality? If our differences turn out to be more fundamental than our similarities—that is, if our individual form is more basic than our human one—then it is not clear that we are genuinely similar in such a way that a democracy, for example, or genuine empathy could be adequately grounded. Thus I fear that Stein's notion of individual form undercuts other things that she may very much want to affirm.

Stein compares her position on individual forms in human beings with Aquinas's claim regarding the angels.[36] Aquinas claims both that matter is the principle of individuation in composite physical substances and that angels do not have matter.[37] He accounts for the individuality of angels by claiming that each angel is the sole member of its species: "[S]ince the essence of simple substances is not received in matter, no such multiplication is possible."[38] Thus there cannot be many members of the same angelic species; rather, for angels, the individual *is* the species. The multitude of angels is due to the multitude of species of angels, and all are considered angels, of the genus "angel," insofar as they are incorporeal, finite intelligences. Stein's claim regarding human beings is similar. Each individual human being is, analogously, her own "species" and the only member of this "species." No one shares any other person's individual form. Therefore, while all human beings share in the human form, so too do we differ formally just as angels, according to Aquinas, differ formally.

Stein insists, however, that we are all truly alike; we have a common nature. There are, thus, traits characterizing all human life. She claims, for example, that each human spirit is united to a body and must develop out of a matter-bound soul. All human life is alike in a fundamental sense—it is bound to corporeal matter—and differs in that respect from angelic life. But despite this difference, angels and humans are alike for Stein insofar as each is its own "species": that is, the most fundamental form in each human being is not repeated in any other. Thus, for all the similarities among human beings, we are—at base—different from one another. Since all angels can truly be classified as "angels" because they have certain characteristics in common (as noncorporeal, finite intelligences), so all human beings can be classified as "human" (as corporeal, matter-bound, finite, intelligent beings). But for neither angels nor human beings is this commonality due to a commonality of the most basic form (although the commonality is, nonetheless, formal according to Stein).

Stein herself suggests this analogy, and I think that it is a fair analogy. It is limited, however, insofar as Stein insists that all human beings do have a common form. Our individual forms do not provide different *categories* for each of us but, rather, provide specifications of these categories.[39] Nonetheless, it seems to me that the similarity between Stein's claim regarding human beings and Aquinas's regarding angels is troubling. Stein claims that each human being is an embodiment of the universal human nature and a member of the whole, humanity, as each angel is an embodiment of the universal angelic nature. But she goes on to qualify this comparison by saying that the relation between the individual and community differs for human beings and for angels. In the angelic world, each individual angel presents a particular step in a hierarchy, and together they build a harmony and great chain.[40] In contrast, for human beings, Stein insists that there is no such hierarchy.[41] The reason for this difference is that angels are independent of each other in a way that human beings are not. She says, "No angel, however, owes its nature to another; none needs the others for the unfolding of its nature—they build a unity as the 'heavenly court' that surrounds the throne of the Almighty."[42] Angels have a hierarchy while humans do not because humans need each other in order to *become* themselves in a way that angels do not. Human beings experience enrichment and completion through each other; they "owe" their possession of their own nature to other human beings.

Stein's claim here draws from her dissertation on empathy and her theory of human development. In *On the Problem of Empathy*, she presents a series of arguments for the thesis that we need other human beings in order to under-stand ourselves fully as human individuals. Among her arguments is, first, the claim that empathy with another is the condition for constituting the world as real, including myself as a real object in the world. I see the other perceiving, un-derstanding, and evaluating me, and in comprehending the other doing so, I am able to do the same for myself.[43] In doing this to another and recognizing that another may so see me, I begin to evaluate my own actions and to discover my character. Thus we all recognize tendencies in ourselves—persistent traits, tal-ents, and capacities; we begin to discover a character (which we ourselves are) that reveals itself in our actions.

Second, the actions of the other inform me of what I may do and of what I may become. Neither our possibilities nor our potentialities are self-evident. Rather, they are what can be but are not yet. For example, if I see someone else jump a fence or act kindly when taunted, I may then recognize my own po-tential to jump fences or to act kindly despite unkind circumstances. Thus the other person's actions are the catalyst for my understanding of my own possi-bilities. Thus when Stein says that the human being *owes* his or her nature to another in a way that angels do not, I take her to mean that because our nature is partially hidden and must be revealed gradually in time, often through a diffi-cult process, we cannot without help "claim" our own nature. Because this pro-cess is not instantaneous and because our knowledge of ourselves and our poten-tialities is incomplete, we need other people even to be ourselves.

Stein's claim in *Finite and Eternal Being* that we experience enrichment and completion through other human beings, understood in light of the theory of empathy, is the basis for her argument that, although the fundamental unique-ness of angels may open the door for hierarchical relations among the angels, it does not do so in human beings. While angels have different fundamental forms (although, presumably, sharing an angelic form) and stand in hierarchical arrangements, human beings—despite their differences in individual forms—do not. The equality of human beings (in contrast to that of angels) lies in our interdependence.

It is not clear, however, that Stein's argument can defend real equality. Stein herself argues in her dissertation that enrichment—understood in the sense briefly described above—occurs only in the context of commonality. In *On the Problem of Empathy,* she says: "Inasmuch as I now interpret it [another living body] as 'like mine,' I come to consider myself as an object like it."[44] It is seeing the other as *like* me that allows me to so objectify myself and thus be enriched in the meeting of the other. I see the other as an object to be considered, under-stood, and evaluated, and *recognizing that I am like the other* I can also consider, understand, and evaluate myself. Thus the basic commonality between us allows the other to enrich and complete me. If, however, I did not consider the other as like me—if I considered her a "saint," for example, and far beyond my meager spiritual powers[45]—I would also not feel the pull to become like the other and thereby enriched by her. It is precisely in recognizing the similarities, and thus an unrealized but real possibility, that I gain, in the sense Stein claims, understanding of myself and enrichment from my experiences with another. (Saying that we need others like ourselves in order to develop fully need not imply that we need others who act and think as we now act and think, but, rather, others with the same possibilities. In a very real sense, it is the other who does *not* act as we do or think as we do who is most helpful in revealing to each of us our not-yet-realized potentialities and encouraging us to further development.) Thus it seems that, if the individual form adds traits to the common form, we can experience enrichment only in the traits we have in common.

In *Finite and Eternal Being*, Stein states that we need other human beings in order to develop our humanity, and the contrast is made between the angel, who does not "owe its nature to another," and the human being, who does owe its nature to another. Our debt to other human beings creates the equality among all human beings. But it seems to me that we owe our nature to another *only insofar as* we are similar. Where we are different, the other may offer help for self-understanding and development only in the weak sense of telling us what we are not.

If I am correct that, although we need others in order to develop ourselves, another may do so only insofar as we are similar, then Stein's argument does little to show that all humans are equal. Thus there is no reason to think that human beings, each with a unique individual form, are not by nature arranged hierarchically as angels are. The need for other human beings, which Stein points to, does not, thereby, show that all humans are equal. I may learn quite a bit about myself through an empathetic relation with a dog. For example, I recognize in my dog the ability to make someone feel loved, a talent for careful watchfulness, and abounding joy. I can then recognize such traits in myself—to greater and lesser degrees—and desire more fully to unfold them. Thus my dog has been helpful in my own self-knowledge and self-development. But we need not thereby conclude that my dog deserves the same treatment I deserve or that ethical injunctions apply equally to me and to my dog.

Thus if the individual form adds traits to the universal form in such a way that there are a priori possibilities present in the individual nature that are not in the universal human nature (or vice versa), then the notion of a personal core or individual form compromises the commonality and equality among all human beings achieved through the notion of a common form. While I do not think that Stein would want either to compromise the commonality or the equality of all human beings or to accept the ethical, political, religious, and social results to which such a compromise would lead, they nonetheless appear to be an implication of her claim.

Thus I think that an a priori principle of individual uniqueness may not be necessary to account for our unique personalities and, further, that such individual structures may lead to a compromise of our fundamental commonality. And thus claims regarding a personal core or an a priori individual form may be deeply problematic. If, however, individual forms are either adverbs of our actions, providing a unique way in which we do each action, or a posteriori—that is, intelligible patterns of actions based upon choices we have repeatedly made or material or historical conditions—they may avoid the problems I have raised.

Stein's position on individuality is deeply challenging. She clearly recognizes the great value and worth of our individuality and individual uniqueness, and she insists that all philosophical thinking be mindful of this. She is also concerned to preserve the real commonality of all human beings. All her thinking about the person attempts to reconcile and to gain an ever deeper understanding of both these insights. And it is the task of those of us who wish to follow her to evaluate whether, and how, her own account has preserved these insights.

NOTES

1. See Edith Stein, *Life in a Jewish Family: Her Unfinished Autobiographical Account*, ed. Lucy Gelber and Romaeus Leuven, OCD, trans. Josephine Koeppel, OCD (Washington, DC: ICS Publications, 1986), 141.

2. See ibid., esp. chap. 7.

3. Here and throughout the essay, I do not mean *predictable* in any strict sense. I do not mean to imply or suggest that we could ever predict someone's behavior in the way that one can predict the results of an experiment or other causal processes. Stein strongly insists on this in "Sentient Causality," in *Philosophy of Psychology and the Humanities*, ed. Marianne Sawicki, trans. Mary Catharine Baseheart and Marianne Sawicki (Washington, DC: ICS Publications, 2000), 1–128.

4. Stein will not, however, say whether nonhuman entities have a personal core or individual form (although she does attributes such unique individuality to angels in her later writings). See, e.g., Edith Stein, *Finite and Eternal Being*, trans. Kurt Reinhardt (Washington, DC: ICS Publications, 2002), chap. 4, § 3, 1 and 2.

5. Edith Stein, *On the Problem of Empathy*, trans. Waltraut Stein (Washington, DC: ICS Publications, 1989), 110. ("Nicht nur, daß die kategoriale Struktur der Seele als Seele erhalten bleiben muß, auch innerhalb ihrer individuellen Gestalt treffen wir auf einen unwandelbaren Kern: die personale Struktur. Ich kann mir Caesar statt in Rom in einem Dorf und kann ihn mir ins zwanzigste Jahrhundert versetzt denken; sicherlich würde

seine historisch feststehende Individualität dann manche Änderungen erfahren, aber ebenso sicher wird er Caesar bleiben. Die personale Struktur grenzt einen Bereich von Variationsmöglichkeiten ab, innerhalb dessen sich ihre reale Ausprägung 'je nach den Umständen' entwickeln kann." *Zum Problem der Einfühlung* (Halle: Buchdruckerei des Waisenhauses, 1917), 123.

6. *Jahrbuch für Philosophie und phänomenologische Forschung* (Yearbook for Philosophy and Phenomenological Research) was a journal started in 1912 by Edmund Husserl, Max Scheler, Alexander Pfänder, Adolf Reinach, and Moritz Geiger as a forum for phenomenological research. It quickly became the preeminent source for phenomenological publications. (Husserl published *Ideas I* in the first volume [1913], and Heidegger's *Being and Time* appeared in the 1927 *Jahrbuch*.)

7. See, e.g., Stein, *On the Problem of Empathy*, chap. 4, § 5, and "Individual and Community," chap. 2, § 3c, in *Philosophy of Psychology*.

8. Stein, *Philosophy of Psychology*, 233.

9. Stein also discusses the ways in which we may deform our personal core in "Individual and Community." See Stein, *Philosophy of Psychology*, chap. 2, § 3c.

10. See Edith Stein, *The Hidden Life: Hagiographic Essays, Meditations, Spiritual Texts*, trans. Waltraut Stein (Washington, DC: ICS Publications, 1992), 27–28. Stein's comments here are brief, and thus another interpretation may be possible. But in light of her comments in both earlier and later works, this strikes me as the best reading.

11. Stein, *Philosophy of Psychology*, 95.

12. "'Sokrates' als Bezeichnung der letzten Wesensbestimmtheit meint etwas anderes als den Menschen Sokrates selbst, und das Sokratessein dieses Menschen muß etwas anderes sein als sein Dasein." Edith Stein, *Endliches und ewiges Sein: Versuch eines Aufstiegs zum Sinn des Seins* (Louvain: E. Nauwelaerts, 1950), 149. All translations from this text are my own. An English translation of the text, *Finite and Eternal Being*, vol. 9 of *The Collected Works of Edith Stein*, ed. Lucy Gelber and Romaeus Leuven, trans. Kurt F. Reinhardt (Washington, DC: ICS Publications, 2002), came out after I finished this essay; the previous passage appears on page 155 of the English version.

13. "Es ist früher schon deutlich geworden, daß wir uns dieser Auffassung nicht anschließen können: wir sehen das Wesen des Sokrates in seinem Sokratessein (in dem das Menschsein eingeschlossen ist) und betrachten es als nicht nur zahlenmäßig, sondern durch eine besondere Eigentümlichkeit vom Wesen jedes anderen Menschen verschieden." Stein, *Endliches und ewiges Sein*, 439. See Stein, *Finite and Eternal Being*, 478.

14. She says, "If we want to take the essence as τὸ τί h\ν ει\ναι, then there is, in contrast to Aristotle, the distinction that we interpret it as individual determination, not as species determination." ("Wenn wir das Wesen als τὸ τί h\ν ει\ναι in Anspruch nehmen wollen, so besteht gegenüber *Aristoteles* der Unterschied, daß wir es als individuelle Bestimmtheit, nicht als artmäßige Bestimmtheit auffassen.") Stein, *Endliches und ewiges Sein*, 159. See Stein, *Finite and Eternal Being*, 166.

15. "Weil nun die einzelne Seele an dem für sie bereiteten Ort erblüht—vorbereitet durch den geschichtlichen Werdegang ihres Volkes, ihrer engeren Heimat, ihrer Familie— und weil sie nach ihrer reinen und vollen Entfaltung an der für sie bestimmten Stelle einem ewig-unverwelklichen Kranz eingereiht werden soll, darum ist es nicht angemessen, ihr Wesen als eine *Art* zu fassen, die sich in einer Vielheit gleicher Gebilde *vereinzeln* könnte." Stein, *Endliches und ewiges Sein*, 464. See Stein, *Finite and Eternal Being*, 508.

16. "So ist die einzelne Seele mit ihrer 'einmaligen' Eigenart nicht ein Vergängliches, das nur bestimmt wäre, die Arteigentümlichkeit für eine vorübergehende Zeitdauer in sich auszuprägen und während dieser Zeitdauer an 'Nachkommen' weiterzugeben, damit sie über das Einzelleben hinaus erhalten bleibe: sie ist zu ewigem Sein bestimmt, und das läßt es verständlich erscheinen, daß sie Gottes Bild auf eine 'ganz persönliche Weise' wiedergeben soll." Stein, *Endliches und ewiges Sein*, 461. See Stein, *Finite and Eternal Being*, 504.

17. She says, "All free spiritual actions also strongly carry the stamp of the personal characteristic that is at home in the interior of the soul." ("Um so stärker trägt aber auch alles freie geistige Verhalten den Stempel der persönlichen Eigenart, die im Innersten der Seele beheimatet ist.") Stein, *Endliches und ewiges Sein*, 405. See Stein, *Finite and Eternal Being*, 441. See also Stein, *Endliches und ewiges Sein*, 150–51, and *Finite and Eternal Being*, 153–55.

18. Stein opens the final chapter of *Finite and Eternal Being* with the claim that "[i]n the treatment of the being of the human person, another question is often encountered that we have touched upon in other contexts and that now must be clarified if the nature of human beings, their place in the order of the created world, and their relation to divine being is to be understood: the question of the *being individual* (of the individuality) of human beings, which can be treated only in the context of a discussion of being individual in general." ("Bei der Behandlung des menschlichen Personseins ist öfters an eine andere Frage gerührt worden, auf die wir auch in anderen Zusammenhängen schon gestoßen sind und die jetzt geklärt werden muß, wenn das Wesen des Menschen, seine Stellung in der Ordnung der geschaffenen Welt und sein Verhältnis zum göttlichen Sein verständlich werden soll: die Frage des *Einzelseins* (der Individualität) des Menschen, die sich nur im Zusammenhang einer Erörterung des Einzelseins überhaupt behandeln läßt.") Stein, *Endliches und ewiges Sein*, 431. See Stein, *Finite and Eternal Being*, 469.

19. Stein claims that uniqueness is a "product" of many factors. By this, I take her to mean that uniqueness in the sense of unrepeatability is the result of our experiences and historical and material conditions. See Stein, *Endliches und ewiges Sein*, 406, 458, and *Finite and Eternal Being*, 442, 500–501.

20. See Stein, *Endliches und ewiges Sein*, 342, and *Finite and Eternal Being*, 371.

21. See Stein, *Endliches und ewiges Sein*, 344–45, 396, and *Finite and Eternal Being*, 373–74, 430.

22. "Aus dem Gesagten ist schon klar geworden, daß *freie Formung* oder *Selbstgestaltung* nicht nur Gestaltung des Leibes, sondern auch und sogar vornehmlich Gestaltung der eigenen Seele ist. Der Mensch ist geistige Person, weil er nicht nur seinem Leib, sondern auch seiner Seele frei gegenübersteht, und nur soweit er über seine Seele Macht hat, hat er sie auch über den Leib." Stein, *Endliches und ewiges Sein*, 394. See Stein, *Finite and Eternal Being*, 429.

23. Stein makes a similar claim in "Individual and Community," insisting that we may suppress or deny our own personal core.

24. Here I intend to claim that the individual form prescribes our *possibilities*, not our *potentialities*. In *Endliches und ewiges Sein*, Stein consistently speaks of *Möglichkeit* (possibility) rather than *Potentialität* (potentiality or potency). (See, e.g., Stein, *Endliches und ewiges Sein*, 34 and 38, where she claims the language of *Möglichkeit* for her project.) I take her choice of terms to be significant. Briefly, *potentiality* refers to the possibilities

of already existing entities; there can be no potentialities for nonexistent or not yet existing entities. Possibility, however, is not directly connected to real existence but, rather, analogous to a logical possibility. Part of Stein's interest in possibilities, in contrast to potentialities, arises from her claims regarding the different kinds of being. See Stein's discussion in chap. 3 of *Endliches und ewiges Sein*.

25. For example, she says: "The soul is something in itself. . . . And this has its characteristic quality that imprints a particular stamp on the whole life in which it is unfolded: it makes that—if two do the same—still not the same. The soul in its interior feels *what* and *how* it is in that dark and inexpressible way that indicates to it the mystery of its being *as* mystery without revealing it." ("Die Seele ist etwas in sich: das, als was sie Gott in die Welt gesetzt hat. Und dieses hat seine eigentümliche Beschaffenheit, die dem ganzen Leben, in dem es sich entfaltet, einen eigenen Stempel aufprägt: sie macht es, daß—wenn zwei dasselbe tun—es doch nicht desselbe ist. *Was* und *wie* sie ist, das spürt die Seele in ihrem Inneren, in jener dunklen und unsagbaren Weise, die ihr das Geheimnis ihres Seins *als* Geheimnis zeigt, ohne es zu enthüllen.") Stein, *Endliches und ewiges Sein*, 406. See Stein, *Finite and Eternal Being*, 442. See also Stein, *Endliches und ewiges Sein*, 150–51, and *Finite and Eternal Being*, 156–57.

26. She says, "[D]as Menschsein als solches ist das gemeinsame, immer und überall gleichbleibende Wesen aller einzelnen Menschen, daneben aber hat jeder etwas, was ihn von andern inhaltlich unterscheidet." Stein, *Endliches und ewiges Sein*, 458. See Stein, *Finite and Eternal Being*, 500.

27. "Schon der einzelne Mensch ist nicht imstande, in seinem Leben alle Möglichkeiten zu entfalten, die in seinem Wesen (als Einzelwesen verstanden) begründet sind. Seine Kraft ist so begrenzt, daß er Höchstleistungen auf einem Gebiet mit Mängeln auf einem andern erkaufen muß." Stein, *Endliches und ewiges Sein*, 463. See Stein, *Finite and Eternal Being*, 507.

28. I add the qualification "for the most part" because I suspect that we will need to give up something of what Stein insists on if I am correct (we may, e.g., need to rearticulate how we understand the relation between created beings and their Creator).

29. If, on the other hand, Stein places such things as mathematical talents or a musical ear in the individual form, it is not clear to me, first, that these talents are central to our personalities as such (Stein herself suggests this in "Individual and Community," chap. 2, § 3c) or, second, that these are genuinely formal and not also or even primarily material. See the discussion in the following paragraphs.

30. By *nature* here, I am referring to human nature per se, not our fallen nature. Human nature in its essential structure or original state cannot be fallen; otherwise, Jesus could not have become genuinely human yet without sin. See Augustine's argument in *De spiritu et littera* [On the Spirit and the Letter].

31. *The Confessions of St. Augustine*, trans. Rex Warner (New York: Penguin, 1963), 168 [bk. 8, chap. 5]. ("Velle meum tenebat inimicus et inde mihi catenam fecerat et constrinxerat me.") Augustine, *Confessiones*, ed. Lucas Verheijen, Sancti Augustini Opera, Corpus Christianorum, Series Latina 27 (Turnholt: Brepols, 1981).

32. Ibid. ("Quippe ex uoluntate peruersa facta est libido, et dum seruitur libidini, facta est consuetudo, et dum consuetudini non resistitur, facta est necessitas.")

33. We could also argue that due to material circumstances (among others) certain possibilities contained in the human essence never become real potentialities for a

person. If the girl were deaf, for example, she would not even have the potential for certain kinds of self-expression and communication.

34. John Duns Scotus (ca. 1266–1308), a medieval Christian thinker often called the Subtle Doctor, is famous for, among other things, his criticisms of Thomas Aquinas's understanding of individuality.

35. For a more thorough defense of this claim, see Sarah Borden, "An Issue in Edith Stein's Philosophy of the Person: The Relation of Individual and Universal Form in Endliches und ewiges Sein," (PhD diss., Fordham University, 2001), chap. 5.

36. See Stein, *Finite and Eternal Being*, chap. 8, § 3, 2.

37. See Thomas Aquinas, *De ente et essentia*, in *Opera omnia*, vol. 43, ed. H. F. Dondaine, OP (Rome: Editori di San Tommaso, 1976), chap. 4.

38. Thomas Aquinas, "On Being and Essence," in *Selected Writings of St. Thomas Aquinas*, trans. Robert P. Goodwin (New York: Bobbs-Merrill, 1965), 54. ("Sed cum essentia simplicis non sit recepta in materia, non potest ibi esse talis multiplicatio.") Aquinas, *De ente et essentia*, p. 376b.

39. Stein also gives an analogy with colors, suggesting that our common human form and our individual form are related as *color* in general is related to a *specific color*. See Stein, *Finite and Eternal Being* chap. 8, § 3, 2. Among the things that are red are cardinals, sunsets, the hair of Red Skelton, and the dusty-red sands of the Painted Desert. Each is truly red, yet none is the same color of red. Likewise, in each individual human being, the individual form would be most foundational, but it is an instance of and specification of the common human form, which makes all of us human beings.

40. See Stein, *Finite and Eternal Being*, chap. 7, § 5, 2, and Stein's 1941 article, "Ways to Know God: The 'Symbolic Theology' of Dionysius the Areopagite and Its Factual Presuppositions," trans. Rudolf Allers, in *The Thomist* 9 (July 1946), 379–420, for a discussion of angels and their hierarchical relations.

41. Thus, even while insisting that the individual forms of human beings are of the same kind—that is, within the general human category—Stein still recognizes the potential danger of the ranking of the forms. I take it that as soon as a formal difference in content (and particularly an a priori one) is posited, this possibility is opened.

42. "Aber kein Engel verdankt dem andern seine Natur, keiner bedarf zur Entfaltung seiner Natur der andern—eine Einheit bilden sie als der 'himmlische Hof,' der den Thron der Allerhöchsten umgibt." Stein, *Endliches und ewiges Sein*, 466. See Stein, *Finite and Eternal Being*, 509.

43. She says, "To consider ourselves in inner perception, i.e., to consider our psychic 'I' and its attributes, means to see ourselves as we see another and as he sees us." Stein, *On the Problem of Empathy*, 88. ("Uns in innerer Wahrnehmung betrachten, d.h. unser seelisches Ich und seine Eigenschaften betrachten, heißt uns so sehen, wie wir einen anderen und ein anderer uns sieht.") Stein, *Zum Problem der Einfühlung*, 99.

44. Stein, *On the Problem of Empathy*, 88. ("Indem ich es nun als 'meinesgleichen' auffasse, komme ich dazu, mich selbst als ein Objekt ihm zu betrachten.") Stein, *Zum Problem der Einfühlung*, 100.

45. This is, it seems to me, one of the dangers of overly hagiographical styles of writing about saints. If saints are souls of a different nature than the "rest of us," they can be neither examples nor encouragements for us.

Chapter 16

Religious-Philosophical Reflections on the Relationship of Freedom and Commitment in Edith Stein and Simone Weil

BEATE BECKMANN-ZÖLLER

translated by Stephen Lake

Two Philosophers on the Theme of "Freedom"

Two female philosophers should enter into an imaginary dialogue: Edith Stein (1891–1942) and Simone Weil (1909–43). During the decades under National Socialism, which witnessed such a great lack of freedom, they were both thinking about freedom and relating to God. They are bound not only by their gender and the passion with which they philosophized but also by their being Jews (the one from Silesia, the other a Parisian with roots in Alsace). They were declared atheists in their youth and early student years; later, however, both reflected on the possibility of experiencing God. Both are fascinating for the keenness and rigor with which they lived and thought—and died. Simone Weil requested the permission of the French government (in exile in London) to undertake a dangerous mission

for her homeland, a request that was ultimately denied. Then, despite physical exhaustion and persistent illness, she, while in exile, refused to take more nourish-
ment than what was rationed for a healthy French citizen—and she died of mal-
nutrition on August 24, 1943.[1] Edith Stein offered herself up in prayer that she
might take up the cross under which the Jews were suffering. Her prayer appears
to have been heard: on August 2, 1942, she was taken by the SS from her convent in
the Dutch city of Echt, and on August 9 she was gassed in Auschwitz.[2]

At a superficial first glance, the course of these two lives suggests certain
common trajectories; but it is otherwise in the intellectual realm. A closer study
of their writings makes clear how very different Simone Weil's explosive mode
of thought—her barely restrained passion and her impatience with the injustices of life and with errors of thought—is from Edith Stein's sober, dry mode
of thought, which can be traced unmistakably to her rigorous methodological
schooling in the phenomenological approach of her teachers Adolf Reinach
(1883–1917) and Edmund Husserl (1859–1938). Erich Przywara distinguishes
the "pure essentialism" of Edith Stein from the "pure existentialism" of Simone
Weil.[3] As different as their methodological approaches may be, the similarities
between the two women resurface in the direction of their thought toward the
eternal. Rightly, then, Elisabeth Goessmann speaks of an "opposite pair of siblings."[4] From their open gaze into the infinite these two seekers after God draw
different conclusions, which will here be investigated in light of their understanding of "freedom in the face of the absolute."

Encountering God and Freedom

An essential difference lies in the reflections and reactions of the two philosophers to when "God comes to mind."[5] Both admitted that in the first place they
had not intentionally sought after God.[6] Edith Stein was intellectually interested
in religion, especially by way of Max Scheler's early writings in religious philosophy.[7] In the "Göttingen Phenomenological Society" she studied Scheler's theses with peers and teachers, although at that time her studies did not yet lead her
to an existential interest in religion. Life lacked nothing for many intellectual
German-Jewish atheists of the 1910s, for whom German customs were sacred,
the ethic of the humanist bourgeoisie was morally binding, and the university
was church, as witnessed by Edith Stein's teacher Husserl.[8] From her childhood
on, Simone Weil also showed herself morally bound in a rigorous way to the
principles of goodness, justice, and truth—in an emphatically matter-of-fact
sense. Both Jewish women can serve as examples of how the separation of religion

and morality in the aftermath of Kant marked the humanist bourgeoisie in its various ways of life, whether Protestant or Jewish.

Both Edith Stein and Simone Weil discovered in the Catholic Church a good way to connect in their own lives—existentially and epistemologically—on the one hand, a moral impetus with religious feeling and, on the other, their encounter with their neighbor with their encounter with God on high.[9] In the first instance the church was perceived as the "Agora," the marketplace where the truth clarified and declared itself in thought. But neither philosopher remained exclusively here in the marketplace of dogmatics and religious philosophy; rather, their path led them even further toward the mystical "nuptial chamber,"[10] the place where the resurrected Christ encounters the human person in an intimate, personal way.

Edith Stein was confronted with the living Christ through the mediation of Reinach's widow, as she—comforted in such a supernatural way—bore the death of her husband in the war. A while later, after a deep inner crisis and emptiness, Edith Stein was gripped by her reading of the biography of the mystic Teresa of Avila. The very next day, she requested reception into the Catholic Church—a request that, despite all her impetuousness, did not prevent her in the process from taking account of the feelings of her Jewish mother.

Things were otherwise with Simone Weil. She experienced in the midst of her own misfortune, in the deepest state of helplessness as a result of chronic headaches, the closeness of a personal God. She would not have sought out the encounter with him on her own, and yet she was prepared for it through her feeling of ethical duty and her devotion to all things true and beautiful. But for a lifetime she refused to let herself follow the movement from her mystical and spiritual contact with the resurrected Christ toward his body, the church: "I have always remained at this exact point, on the threshold of the Church, without moving, quite."[11] Only shortly before her death did she request baptism, which a friend, Simone Deitz, administered, as we know from her testimony.[12] Unfortunately, we do not have any text written by Weil herself during her last days, marked by absolute exhaustion, before she fell into a coma and soon thereafter died.[13]

Simone Weil's way to the church may be described as an orbiting: she wandered around the church, questioned, and tested it from without. And even then she never sensed the call to enter the embrace of the church strongly enough to have been able to give herself over to it. Put in other words, she felt no compulsion, no current that overcame her, that robbed, or even attacked, her senses. Was she perhaps waiting on something to which the church of Christ in some substantial respect did not correspond?

The questions of religious philosophy that lie behind both of these lives are the following: How is the relationship of human freedom to the irresistible force of grace to be understood? If the compulsion to commit to the church is not felt irresistibly, then is it God's will that a person not enter into the church? Is a freely willed commitment to the church possible? Edith Stein's reflection on the "realm of freedom" in her essay "Nature, Freedom and Grace"[14] is well suited to attempt an analysis of and answer to these questions.

The Realm of Freedom: Between Nature and Grace (Edith Stein)

Edith Stein begins her investigation of freedom with the natural-naive life of the human soul. It consists in impressions and reactions—that is, it is prompted from without or from within by stimuli, and it responds to them. Already in this automatic interaction Edith Stein discovers a specific human activity of willing and acting: a possibility of freedom. It is, however, always experienced as limited, as "passive activity." There appears, therefore, to be a still more foundational principle of freedom in humans. This fundamental principle of freedom is restricted by the laws of natural reason and morals but also because the soul needs something foreign in order to be able to react at all. For that reason one cannot speak at this point of any absolutely free action or of any self-originating freedom. To react means to be unfree, unsettled, restless, out of bounds. What is accordingly sought is an inner center, the act-center of the person, from which "active activity," freedom in the full sense, would be possible.

The relationship of the human act-center to the "realm of nature" is characterized in a manner similar to the relationship of that center to the "realm of grace." From the realm of grace, or "on high," or simply "from above," the choice and reaction of the human person are influenced through divine commands, through religious experiences. Here again one can speak only of a kind of passive activity with regard to human action. Even if the center of the person finds itself in the state of grace—a state that Stein calls "being freed"—it is still not centered "above." It does not have its middle point, it is not at rest in itself, in the realm of grace proper; rather, it is only anchored there.

Thus the center of the person receives impulses from above, from the realm of grace, just as it does from below, from the realm of nature. In this way, the human being is positioned between animals and angels. It reacts to natural as well as to supernatural impressions, it makes choices, and enjoys thereby its own autonomy *(Eigenstand)*. Stein does not envision merely a dialectical fluctuation between the two types of passive activity, between the spiritual and the bodily.

Rather, she posits in addition a free center of action in humans. This place of "active activity," the realm of freedom, is, however, only a point, possessing no extension.

In the first instance, freedom presents itself as being freed from the bonds of nature. The human being experiences itself as a being with an open, not a fixed, world. At this point it would be possible to dwell in an absolute, autonomous freedom. Freedom with respect to nature, or the world, could theoretically find expression in an absolute unmooring from nature or the world. In the living, concrete reality of the world one must, on the contrary, always choose between various possibilities. The center of the person (or the soul) attaches itself to one concrete possibility, which excludes many other potentialities; thereby, the person simultaneously gives up absolute freedom. So for a human being, only in turning away from the concrete choice is it possible not to lose the point of freedom upon which infinite potency rests and simultaneously swirls as active activity. Here the human being has "all" possibilities: she leaves all possible paths open, without consciously deciding on any one possibility. In such an instance, however, "merely" all paths are open, for she cannot decide on any concrete path, since this fixation would tear her away from the point of absolute potency.

If one thought through the further implications of Edith Stein's thought on this point, one would be condemned to absolute motionlessness and paralysis and hence to unfruitfulness. It is a matter, then, of using the point of absolute freedom, the moment of active activity, in order to let freedom be fruitful, to root it in an existentially embodied form and, thus, to enter a new realm: "The person who situates herself in the realm of nature has the possibility of shutting herself off from that which presses in on her from outside. But so long as she has no other bulwark than *her freedom,* she can do that only to the extent that she frees herself completely and completely gives her all. Only in a *new realm* can her soul gain a new fullness and thereby at last become her own home."[15] At this theoretical level, according to Stein, the soul is challenged "to give up" part of its freedom in order to be able "to begin" to do anything at all with it. Simone Weil does not join Edith Stein in taking this step.

"Divine Compulsion" and Dissolution (Simone Weil)

To enter a new realm, Simone Weil would first have had to have been prepared to be overcome herself, as happened upon her first encounter with God in the Romanesque Chapel of Santa Maria degli Angeli in Assisi, "an incomparable marvel of purity." There, as she wrote, "something stronger than I was compelled me for the first time in my life to go down on my knees."[16] Simone Weil would recognize this overpowering by God as God's will and was able to respond to it.[17]

When Simone Weil spoke on the topic of God's will, it ultimately concerned "divine compulsion": "In this domain we experience the compulsion of God's pressure, on condition that we deserve to experience it and exactly to the extent that we deserve to do so. God rewards the soul that thinks of him with attention and love, and he rewards it by exercising a compulsion upon it strictly and mathematically proportionate to this attention and this love."[18] This compulsion of God over the human will exercises power over the soul: it is "impelled ever further and becom[es] the object of a pressure that possesses itself of an ever-growing proportion of the whole soul. When the pressure has taken possession of the whole soul, we have attained the state of perfection."[19] In her fourth letter to Father Perrin, Simone Weil wrote that she did not have the feeling that God wanted her in the church; he was not compelling her.[20]

Weil did not want to follow a free calling on the grounds that she could not completely rule out self-deception. For she felt she could not defend herself with absolute certainty against her own selfishness, which, so she claimed, longed for nothing more than self-dissolution among the masses. The stark individualistic character of her life would not lead one to suspect that Weil harbored this wish. Nonetheless, she admitted herself susceptible even to National Socialist ways of thinking,[21] perhaps even to conforming to them in a general way.[22]

Here Simone Weil did not succeed in holding difference and closeness in a positive tension: to avoid the danger of "Church patriotism," she did not make herself at home in the community of the followers of Christ. It was her fear, she wrote, "to find I am 'at home' in any human *milieu* whatever it may be. . . . I feel that it is necessary and ordained that I should be alone, a stranger and an exile in relation to every human circle without exception."[23]

Objectification and Denial

It was out of intellectual responsibility that Simone Weil derived the duty to let "my thought . . . be indifferent to all ideas without exception, including for instance materialism and atheism; it must be equally welcoming and equally reserved with regard to everyone of them. Water is indifferent in this way to the objects that fall into it. It does not weigh them; they weigh themselves, after a certain time of oscillation. . . . and I could never be like this if I were in the Church."[24] Simone Weil describes here her tendency to turn her own person into an object of thought, a tendency toward depersonalization. Time and again one finds images or indications of the fact that she wanted to be transparent and inconspicuous before God and humankind—in this case watery and in another earthy, like an inlaid cobblestone.[25] Her refusal to confront God face to face is expressed more forcibly in the following reflection: "If one could imagine any possibility of error in God, I should think that it had all happened to me by mistake. But perhaps God likes to use castaway objects, waste, rejects."[26] The obedience of the material becomes her highest principle and guiding ideal.[27]

Only if her spirit were to fail—the spirit that she distanced from the body, from the affirmation of her own embodiment as well as of the body of Christ—would she give up her resistance. The consequence of her denial was the restless immobility with which Simone Weil remained before the door of the church. Nonetheless, she experienced there too union with the impersonal God[28]—beyond all reason: "I have always remained at this exact point, on the threshold of the Church, without moving, quite still, ἐν ὑπομένῃ (it is so much more beautiful a word than *patientia!*); only now my heart has been transported, forever, I hope, into the Blessed Sacrament exposed on the altar."[29]

Gravity from Below and Above

Simone Weil distinguishes theoretically between three realms of reality. That upon which a human has not the slightest influence, the realm of things, may be compared with Edith Stein's realm of nature. This first realm is completely subservient to the will of God. The second realm is subject to the rule of the human will—humanity's openness to the world with respect to nature—in which the impetus of the soul is guided by natural reason. Weil recommends, "in this domain we have to carry out, without faltering or delay, everything that appears clearly to be a duty."[30] Edith Stein always includes the realm of the laws of natural reason and morals in the natural realm, not yet in the realm of grace.

As for the third realm, Simone Weil calls it the realm of those things, "which, without being under the empire of will, without being related to natural duties, are yet not entirely independent of us."[31] This is the realm in which the will of God rules over the will of human beings. Here it is a matter of, in a way, receiving orders; one's own initiative or activity is not required.

If one looks more closely, there are actually only two levels in Weil's reconstruction of freedom that together appear to influence her theory: "The most beautiful life possible has always seemed to me to be one where everything is determined, either by the pressure of circumstances or by impulses . . . and where there is never any room for choice."[32]

Ultimately, Weil here limits life to two dimensions in which no true liberty, and concomitantly no liberation in Stein's sense, is possible: There is on the one hand the compulsion of nature and on the other the unmediated compulsion of grace. Simone Weil permits the ability to say "I" to count as the one free act to which a human being, with respect to her "I," might still be capable. However, this is not given over to God but rather given up in self-annihilation, in an ultimately Buddhist form of the dissolution of the "I": "We possess nothing in the world—a mere chance can strip us of everything—except the power to say 'I.' This is what we have to give God—in other words, to destroy. There is absolutely no other free act which it is given us to accomplish—only the destruction of the 'I.'"[33]

At the point where, for Edith Stein, there lies commitment, for Simone Weil there is only detachment: "Two ways of killing ourselves: suicide or detachment. To kill by our thought everything we love: the only way to die. Only what we love, however. ('He that hateth not his father and mother . . .' but 'Love your enemies . . .') Not to desire that what we love should be immortal. We should neither desire the immortality nor the death of any human being, whoever he may be, with whom we have to do."[34] This position appears extraordinarily difficult, though it becomes understandable in light of Weil's own experience of slavery in the factory: "What I went through there marked me in so lasting a manner that still today when any human being, whoever he may be and in whatever circumstances, speaks to me without brutality, I cannot help having the impression that there must be a mistake and that unfortunately the mistake will in all probability disappear. There I received forever the mark of a slave, like the branding of the red-hot iron the Romans put on the foreheads of their most despised slaves."[35] Ultimately, divine compulsion remains, therefore, a compulsion that requires from humans something close to a "passive passivity." Since there is no actual third element, no mediating center of action, Simone Weil exhausts herself in this dialectical dualism of the compulsion of nature and the compulsion of grace.

Overcoming Paralysis According to Edith Stein
(Personally Structured Spiritual Freedom)

Only through an active step of realizing one possibility, and thus through foregoing all other possibilities, is paralysis overcome at the point of absolute freedom: The person commits herself; she opens herself to another spiritual realm and attains something new; she escapes from emptiness into the bounds of fullness. She is not receptive to nature; it is experienced only in her resistance to jolts and impressions, pleasure and ecstasy. Human freedom is receptive to the element of difference in the spiritual, which can separate and differentiate, and which brings with it crisis. In this freedom of being, in contrast to the previously mentioned freedom of choice, critique becomes possible—that is, space and distance from that which seeks to assail.

In the freedom of being, then, freedom of choice is abdicated. The free person who remains at the point of noncommitment, of absolute freedom, wanders in a circle as if wandering around the perimeter of a magnificent garden. She may perceive her way as a corridor with many doors through which she may, time and again, catch a glimpse of the garden. Perhaps she fears that the garden could prove to be an illusion, boring, or threatening. She therefore retains her freedom of choice and remains, as if on the run, on a fruitless path as a voyeur and eternal wanderer. The freed person, by contrast, steps in the freedom of being into the garden of commitment and fruitfulness. She thereby loses many possibilities and therefore the power of absolute freedom of choice in the face of every decision. But through her decision and commitment she gains herself and fullness.[36]

There are accordingly three levels of freedom for Edith Stein. Being unfree means that the soul experiences her bondage to the world. At the point of decision—the moment of (1) *active activity*—the soul realizes that its bonds are loosed but that it is not yet free to do what it wishes. Only when the soul is in the state of grace does it experience its liberation, its being freed, loved, and loving at the same time and therefore connected to the person of God, who is its liberator. At the point of freedom, the free center of action is attentive to impulses that come from the realm of grace and responds in (2) *active passivity*. At the same time the free center of action is detached from the realm of nature and reacts to it in liberated, (3) *passive activity*.

According to Edith Stein the spiritual is to be conceived not as an impersonal but as a personal force, as something that issues from a person, not from mere matter.[37] This presupposes a decision of faith, upon which everything else hangs. Edith Stein precludes every sort of objectification and functionalization of the person, and therefore the abuse of the person both by others and by itself. Edith Stein overcomes the temptation of objectification by uncovering a Trinitarian structure in her conceptual scheme (the realms of nature, freedom, and grace).

Simone Weil, however, succumbs to the temptation of devaluation, detachment, and dissolution to a monstrous degree. One could call it "the Buddhist temptation," which preys especially upon the most moralistic Christians: "The extinction of desire (Buddhism)—or resignation—or *amor fati*—or desire for the absolute good—these all amount to the same: to empty desire, finality of all content, to desire in the void, to desire without any wishes. To detach our desire from all good things and to wait. Experience proves that this waiting is satisfied. It is then we touch the absolute good."[38] Freedom is won; but when the capacity to commit oneself anew is not included in this freedom, it remains empty and destructive, implosive.

How does Edith Stein distinguish the spiritual spheres to which a human being can be receptive? In short, the good spirit—that is, God—is concerned about human beings, whereas evil spirits are concerned only about themselves: they misuse human souls, ultimately to the detriment of human peace and salvation. God, on the other hand, makes the soul authentic whenever it lets go of itself and throws itself upon him. To put this in metaphorical terms, the soul does not remain "clinging," as when a fly gives up its own sting and self-defenses; it remains with God as long as he holds onto it. And God determines the moment when he throws the soul again back upon itself, in order that it learn to stand for itself and independently come back to him. First the soul "flies" to him and "clings" to him; then it "hobbles" and "grasps"; later still it learns to "walk upright toward God" and to "embrace" him.

The Location of Freedom and the Path to Commitment

According to Edith Stein (who here thinks in keeping with the scholastic tradition), within the soul as the principle of life, interactions occur between the aspect of the spiritual soul—our cognitive powers (what she calls *spirit*)—and the aspect of the sensorial soul—our powers of striving (what she calls *soul*). These interactions are important for the fact that there can indeed be connections, commitment between the realm of nature and the realm of grace, and that the absolute can penetrate the relative without destroying it. On the one hand, spirit guarantees the soul's openness to the world. The soul is, however, receptive only to impressions that it receives from outside. The awakened, freed spirit, by contrast, sorts out which impressions actually and effectively are impressed upon the soul and which thereby form it, whether they are renewing and empowering or injurious and weakening.

Spirit is the knowing element that perceives and receives the world as well as the supernatural world of God. Spirit can esteem, prize, and find value in something unknown. And yet the soul (more precisely, the heart as the center of the person) can reject for itself the recognition of this good and can refuse devotion to this spiritual sphere—or, to be more precise, to the person who stands behind it. Spirit alone cannot arrive at devotion, as Stein and Weil agree: "The belief is verbal and does not penetrate the soul" (Weil).[39] "Spirit can see while the soul remains empty" (Stein).[40]

If at this point one thinks further with Edith Stein, the following images come to mind: it is the task of spirit "to calculate" the risk of the leap and the distance to the other shore, to weigh the danger and the chances of crossing; spirit gropes around and sees. The soul, by contrast, lets itself be filled by a new spiritual sphere, makes the decision to leap, and does so, if need be, with its entire existential power, by making itself subject and obedient to its living aspect, the sensorial soul. When this new location in the world becomes visible for others—and sooner or later it will for an attentive observer—then the leap is truly, existentially complete.

The human heart, as the inalienable core of the person, stands as the "in-between organ" between the spiritual and sensorial soul and is therefore not directly categorized in either of the realms of nature or grace. That is to say, the heart can be courted and corrupted or won over by either side. Nonetheless, from the very beginning, it does not belong to either of these two sides completely, rather to neither, although it contains a seed of both within it. It can restore recognition to the soul after a completed leap, the permission now to think in new ways and move the world. The heart as a free center of human action no longer perceives the world immediately, face to face—and thus no longer perceives it to be threatening. (Of course, the "I" could be devoured or consumed by that which is foreign, by the world, by others, impressions, and ecstasies.) Instead, it perceives from the perspective of God, via the roundabout path *(Umweg)* of a distanced, critical view from above.

So the soul is no longer restlessly driven back and forth by impressions that it receives from the world. It must not seal itself off and protect itself against the siege that chains the senses. There is no longer any dulled sadness, and the soul is no longer defenseless against surging impressions and the emotions set loose by them. It is spiritually awakened; it is "so opened as to be able to receive something within itself. The soul can be truly embedded only in spiritual spheres, not in nature."[41]

In the spiritual life, mediated by the heart, the sensorial soul comes to rest. Here it has the free space out of which it will be able to act freely. The heart's command to the sensorial soul is to perceive nature now with greater distance;

and no longer to react to it out of fear as something dangerous and threatening but rather to place it lovingly in its place and to give all impressions their true place in life. This is not a one-time activity but rather an ongoing engagement.

Threats to the Human Spirit

Edith Stein conceives the relationship of the human person to the realm on high as one of being "led from above," which is different in an important way from "leading from above." Here Stein again carefully indicates only a passive activity. It might be just as conceivable for the human being to fix the center of her person in the realm of her own spirit and from there to "lead from above"; but in doing so, the "core of the person" would be reduced to an actively constituting organ of knowledge. Herein may lie the main temptation of all reductionist types of thinking. Only an all-encompassing philosophy rooted in the natural life of the soul, like the philosophy of Edith Stein, will reject this temptation and recognize the spiritual spearhead of the *anima intellectiva* as being not only actively expressive but passively receptive as well.

The religious thinker, like Simone Weil, might be tempted at this point to fix the center of the human person in the "realm on high": in an almost passive passivity, the saint would still find herself determined by foreign influences. She would no longer be actively determining but rather would be "lived" by "divine compulsion" from above and would thereby be lost for the task of shaping the world in the here and now. Edith Stein avoids both possibilities in that she holds opens the mediating point of the "realm of freedom," which serves as a hinge between nature and grace.

If one misunderstands this being "led from above," it becomes destructive to the world at the moment in which the human being fails to recognize itself as integrated below with its fellow creatures. If one were to allow oneself and one's reason to be the only valid "above," then everything else would seem irrational, counterrational, and therefore less worthy of respect. Henceforth, one's gaze would be locked in a single direction, staring down from above on the world below.

One's perspective can be freed from this rigidity and one-sidedness only when one encounters a person. Edith Stein formulates it this way: "His [the human being's] freedom reaches so far that it can get a glimpse into unknown spheres or can close them off—but only to the extent that these spheres present themselves to him. He [the free human being] cannot conquer what does not give itself to him. A human being can only grasp grace insofar as grace grasps him."[42]

The Committed Freedom of the Saints
(Freedom of Being—Freedom of Choice)

The "logic of the heart" (Pascal) is a free, active, and loving activity. And yet it appears that the saint, such as Mary, the immaculately conceived, can act only in a way that is holy, pure, correct, just, and full of love before God. It appears as if the freed, holy person has no choice, as if she must follow a "compulsion to goodness." Can that be freedom?

According to Edith Stein, this is freedom *(Befreitheit)* and freedom of being *(Wesensfreiheit);* this is the true state of being freed *(Befreitsein).* This freedom allows human beings to be fully themselves, content in themselves, and at rest. From this state of rest, which implies neither apathy nor paralysis, a free movement toward the other person is possible. In this freedom, one aspect of the freedom of choice is no longer actively realized, or phrased another way, the freedom to choose evil or a lesser good. However, the freed human being still has the potentiality to do evil, for he has advanced in the respective gifts of differentiation and knowing. The structure of freedom is not split; but for the freed person there is a qualitative leap that unmasks the possibility of evil as so much less worthy of being wished and desired that it no longer obtains as a reality, although it is always present as an idea: "At the place of freedom no use is made of freedom."[43] But it is still, therefore, freedom, not divine compulsion.

According to Edith Stein, freedom must always be presupposed already so that one can choose the free act, so that one can commit oneself to the "realm on high" and thereby want to give up an aspect of the freedom of choice. The fall was, accordingly, a "free fall." Indeed, prelapsarian human beings made no actual use of their freedom of choice. Nonetheless, it was still structurally present and did not obtain as a *deus ex machina,* or more to the point, *ex diabolo.* The devil could only apply his bow to strings that had already been tightened, albeit not yet played upon. The abdication of freedom and of many possibilities for the sake of one, can take place only in freedom. "One must be free in order to be able to be freed. One must have oneself in hand in order to be able to let oneself go."[44]

The Covenant of Freedom: Being Set Free to Lead
a New Life in the Church

Is human individuality destroyed through the dominion and fullness of grace? asks Edith Stein. Put differently, must not the absolute annihilate the relative when the two are brought into contact with each other? Is not the relative either elevated, transported into the fullness of the absolute or banished into the depths of absolute nothingness? That would be the case only if there were absolutely no kinship between the divine and the human, no analogy in Splett's sense of a correspondence *(Ent-Sprechung)*. But God as the Not-Other (Cusa) knows his others, and we others can come to recognize ourselves in him as the Not-Other. An inexpungable seed in us influences all our reactions, including our reaction on the entrance of the absolute into our relative thinking. Since this entrance happens in the realm of freedom, it will not be destructive; rather, on the one hand, God will both leave the person to act out of freedom and actively set the person free. The essence of the absolute is at the same time passive in an active way: it lets the person act freely in a discreet, reservedly passive way, namely, in setting the person free.

At this point, Edith Stein's thought may, I believe, be taken up and extended in the following way. Only the absolutely free person—God himself—or a freed mediator [45] can set another free. He allows himself to enter into a relationship with another, into a covenant; he lets himself commit. This commitment entitles him to set the other free in a passive, relaxed manner and action. The other may be bound up by his natural incapacities, by his mediocrity,[46] and in fulfilling different expectations. He is so re-active that he must be granted rest, freedom from natural impulses, by the one who sets him free.

The one driven by impulses is placed within an enclosed *(umfrieden)* setting, in a garden, where the soul comes to rest in God's spirit. The wild undergrowth of the soul is cut down, one's weak shoots are identified, and the free one now sets free and liberates that which is one's own—the not-yet-free self that perhaps remains hidden unto oneself. This happens either through being transferred to a new setting, where the wild undergrowth of unnecessary activities has no chance to take root and proliferate, or through active gardening, by "freeing" the garden of weeds and by constantly being attentive to the uniqueness of the other. This will require a strong commitment and also the gifts of differentiation and selflessness. Many of the so-called free—who are better called the "commitmentless"—have talked the unfree into their own wishes and dreams instead of waiting actively to listen until the actual uniqueness of the other manifests itself.

What happens when the person who up to now has been unfree recognizes the possibility of freedom? One has perhaps felt oneself being let free through the call of the commitmentless and has allowed oneself to be led toward this point of freedom. But what the commitmentless shows to the one who is bound is only a minimal point, not a space for living. How shall the one who is unfree come to be at peace in the state of abandonment to boundlessness and commitmentlessness when that person is in a state of unrest and unfreedom? The sign pointing the way to peace—the bounded place of rest—is not to be found in the mere freedom that allows the unfree to do anything but commits him to almost nothing. This freedom would paralyze the person and throw him into an even deeper emptiness and tighter ensnaring than ever before. There is no peace *(Befriedung)*, no contentment *(Zufriedenheit)* that comes via progress, no growth without enclosed *(umfrieden)* boundaries. Where there is no enclosure *(Umfriedung)*, one experiences an emptying of that which was in existence. The inability to commit oneself to something new, to something demanding a tough sacrifice, wanes. Thus the impulses of one's soul become even more strongly unleashed. The spirit hastily rushing about cannot put to rest those impulses, since it is not bound to anything but rather is itself without a resting place. If out of necessity it must be bound to a thing, a task, or a person, then it feels unfree and resigned because it had to give up so many other possibilities and activities for the sake of this commitment. Here there is no fruit, only fruitlessness.

A possibility for freedom lies in following the call of freedom into association and commitment *(Verbindung)*—into the covenant *(Bund)*—the call of God through those who have been more or less freed, through the church. In the church is found the solution, the point of contact between God and human beings. "In my arguments about the insolubility of the problem of God," wrote Simone Weil, "I had never foreseen the possibility of that, of a real contact, person to person, here below, between a human being and God."[47]

Conclusion: Freedom, Friendship, Fruitfulness

Edith Stein's theory of freedom illuminates how the path can unfold from freedom to being freed, from possibility to reality, from the sowing of seeds to the bearing of fruit. For Simone Weil, the lack of peace certainly sorted itself out mercifully in her mystical experiences, in which God greeted her before the door of the church. In her theory, however, the third element that establishes peace is ultimately lacking, the element through which she, with one free step, could have entered the church.

In the foregoing investigation it has been shown that the theme of freedom remains essential, whether one is "outside" or "inside" the church, whether one is considering joining the church or remaining in it. The offer to live freely in friendship between the absolute and the relative, between God and humanity, i.e., no longer as "slaves,"[48] contains the possibility of fruitfulness through committed friendship.[49] In this context Simone Weil saw a portrait of herself in the parable of the barren fig tree.[50] Affording oneself the "luxury" of unfruitfulness may arise out of the pride of wanting to remain pure and untouched. Fruitfulness means, ultimately, allowing oneself to be inseminated and to bear, as opposed to produce, fruit. That bearing fruit is possible and desirable here and now, in each and every moment, is shown by the scene of the thief on the cross. In the immediacy of the verdict on his life he did not remain content with an intellectual insight; rather, spiritual devotion sprang up in his heart so that the fruit of his life would, in his very last minute on the cross, be recognized and accepted.[51] Wherever decisions of this kind fail to be made, we find ourselves living under the "rule of the cowards" (Chesterton).[52]

NOTES

This essay was first published in German with the title "'An der Schwelle der Kirche': Freiheit und Bindung bei Edith Stein and Simone Weil," *Edith Stein Jahrbuch* 4 (1998): 531–47.

1. Dorothée Beyer, *Simone Weil: Philosophin-Gewerkschafterin-Mystikerin* (Mainz: Gruenewald, 1994), 156; Simone Pètrement, *La vie de Simone Weil, avec des lettres et d'autres textes inédits,* vol. 2 (Paris: Fayard, 1973), 517 (trans. Raymond Rosenthal as *Simone Weil: A Life* [New York: Pantheon, 1976]).

2. Hanna-Barbara Gerl, *Unerbittliches Licht: Edith Stein. Philosophie, Mystik, Leben,* 2nd ed. (Mainz: Gruenewald, 1998), 28 ff.

3. Erich Przywara, "Edith Stein und Simone Weil: Zwei philosophische Grundmotive," in *Edith Stein: Eine grosse Glaubenszeugin. Leben, Neue Dokumente, Philosophie,* ed. Waltraud Herbstrith (Annweiler: Thomas Plöger, 1986), 235. Originally published in French in *Études philosophiques* 11 (1956): 458–72.

4. Elisabeth Goessmann, "Simone Weil und Edith Stein: Die Einheit von tätigem und betrachtendem Leben," in *Die Frau und ihr Auftrag: Gestalten und Lebensformen* (Freiburg: Herder, 1964), 171.

5. See Emmanuel Lévinas, *Of God Who Comes to Mind,* trans. Bettina Bergo (Stanford, CA: Stanford University Press, 1998).

6. See Simone Weil to Father Perrin, May 15, 1942, in *Waiting for God,* trans. Emma Craufurd (New York: G. P. Putnam's Sons, 1951), p. 62: "As soon as I reached adolescence, I saw the problem of God as a problem the data of which could not be obtained here below, and I decided that the only way of being sure not to reach a wrong solution, which seemed to me the greatest possible evil, was to leave it alone. So I left it alone." See also Edith Stein, *Aus dem Leben einer jüdischen Familie und weitere autobiographische Beiträge,* vol. 1 of *Edith Stein Gesamtausgabe* (Freiburg: Herder, 2002), 91. "Here [in Hamburg at her sister Else's, when she was fifteen years old], completely consciously and of my own free will, I broke myself of the habit of praying" (English translation from Edith Stein, *Life in a Jewish Family, 1891–1916: Her Unfinished Autobiographical Account,* ed. Lucy Gelber and Romaeus Leuven, OCD, trans. Josephine Koeppel, OCD, vol. 1 of *The Collected Works of Edith Stein* [Washington, DC: ICS Publications, 1986]), 109.

7. Max Scheler lived from 1874 to 1928. His main work of religious philosophy, "Probleme der Religion (zur religiösen Erneuerung)," in *Vom Ewigen im Menschen* (Leipzig: Der neue Geist, 1921; trans. Bernard Noble as *On the Eternal in Man* [1960; reprint, Hamden, CT: Archon Books, 1972]), appeared during his "Catholic phase" (from the years of World War I through 1921). From 1922–23 until his death in 1928, he spoke out against his former Catholic convictions.

8. In a conversation with Sr. Adelgundis Jaegerschmid on April 28, 1931, Husserl stated: "True science is honest and pure; it has the advantage of real modesty and yet possesses at the same time the capacity for criticism and differentiation. The world today does not know true science anymore; it has fallen into the narrowest of specializations. It was otherwise during our time. The lecture hall was for us the church, and the professors were preachers." "Gespräche von Sr. Adelgundis Jaegerschmid OSB mit Edmund Husserl," in *Edith Stein: Wege zur inneren Stille*, ed. Waltraud Herbstrith (Aschaffenburg: Kaffke, 1987), 206. A more intense intellectual confrontation with the Jewish religion can be found in the circle surrounding Martin Buber and Franz Rozensweig. On the other hand, there were several religious conversions among Husserl's students. See Jacques Vidal, "Phénoménologie et conversion," *Archives de philosophie* 35 (1972): 209–43.

9. Intellectually, Edith Stein also considered Protestantism. The fullness of the Catholic Church's liturgy, as it was before the Second Vatican Council was, however, decisive in determining her preference. Therefore, when she (and also Simone Weil) speak of "the church," it is always the "Catholic Church." Simone Weil had studied, among other groups, the Huguenots, but for her Christianity was and always remained Catholic, although she differentiated between being "Catholic de jure" (as she referred to herself) and "Catholic de facto." See Weil to Perrin, May 15, 1942, in *Waiting for God*, 61 ff.

10. "When genuine friends of God—such as was Eckhart to my way of thinking—repeat words they have heard in secret amidst the silence of the union of love, and these words are in disagreement with the teaching of the Church, it is simply that the language of the market place is not that of the nuptial chamber." Weil to Perrin, May 15, 1942, in *Waiting for God*, 79.

11. "ἐν ὑπομένῃ (it is so much more beautiful a word than *patientia!*); only now my heart has been transported, forever, I hope, into the Blessed Sacrament exposed on the altar." Weil to Perrin, May 15, 1942, in *Waiting for God*, 76.

12. Georges Hourdin, *Simone Weil* (Paris: La Découverte, 1989), 230.

13. According to Beyer, it is a matter of speculation to what degree Simone Weil herself considered this emergency baptism to be valid, since she neither received communion nor requested it. See Beyer, *Simone Weil*, 153.

14. Edith Stein, "Natur, Freiheit und Gnade" [Nature, Freedom, and Grace], in *Phänomenologie und Ontologie*, vol. 9 of *Edith Stein Gesamtausgabe* (Freiburg: Herder, 2006). As Claudia Wulf discovered, the title was mistakenly attached to the wrong manuscript in the archive in Cologne. See Claudia M. Wulf, "Rekonstruktion und Neudatierung einiger früher Werke Edith Steins," in *Edith Stein: Themen, Bezüge, Dokumente*, ed. Beate Beckmann and Hanna-Barbara Gerl-Falkovitz (Würzburg: Königshausen & Neumann, 2003), 249 ff. Below, quotations from this work are taken from Edith Stein, *Welt und Person: Beitrag zum christlichen Wahrheitsstreben*, vol. 6 of *Edith Steins Werke* (Freiburg: Herder, 1962).

15. Edith Stein, *Welt und Person*, 143.

16. Weil to Perrin, May 15, 1942, in *Waiting for God*, 67–68.

17. She states, however, that "[i]t may well be that my life will come to an end before I have ever felt this impulse." Weil to Perrin, January 19, 1942, in *Waiting for God*, 50.

18. Weil to Perrin, January 19, 1942, in *Waiting for God*, 44–45.

19. Ibid., 45.

20. Weil to Perrin, May 15, 1942, in *Waiting for God*, 74: "I have never once had, even for a moment, the feeling that God wants me to be in the Church. I have never even once had a feeling of uncertainty. I think that at the present moment we can conclude finally that he does not want me in the Church."

21. "I am aware of very strong gregarious tendencies in myself. My natural disposition is to be very easily influenced, too much influenced, and above all by anything collective. I know that if at this moment I had before me a group of twenty young Germans singing Nazi songs in chorus, a part of my soul would instantly become Nazi. That is a very great weakness, but that is how I am." Weil to Perrin, n.d. ("Letter II"), in *Waiting for God*, 52–53.

22. "*Temptation of resignation.* Subsume external things and human beings under everything that is subjective, but never the subject—i.e., the power of judgment. Never promise more, never give more to the other than you would require of yourself if you were him. (?)" Simone Weil, *Cahiers [Aufzeichnungen]*, ed. and trans. Elisabeth Edl and Wolfgang Matz (Munich: Carl Hanser, 1991), 1:58 ff; English translation taken from *The Notebooks of Simone Weil*, trans. Arthur Wills (New York: G. P. Putnam's Sons, 1956).

23. Weil to Perrin, n.d. ("Letter II"), in *Waiting for God*, 53, 54.

24. Weil to Perrin, n.d. ("Letter V"), in *Waiting for God*, 85.

25. In her final works on politics and mysticism, Weil concludes that the core of human beings is the *longing* for the good and is therefore something impersonal. Cf. Beyer, *Simone Weil*, 147.

26. Weil to Perrin, May 15, 1942, in *Waiting for God*, 72.

27. Goessmann, "Simone Weil," 177.

28. Cf. Dorothée Fragemann, "Simone Weil et Edith Stein: Une comparaison," *Cahiers Simone Weil* 11, no. 4 (1988): 320–23, esp. 323. Fragemann compares the two thinkers' approach to mysticism, which meant an encounter with, for Stein, a personal God and, for Weil, a both personal and impersonal God.

29. Weil to Perrin, May 15, 1942, in *Waiting for God*, 76.

30. Weil to Perrin, January 19, 1942, in *Waiting for God*, 44.

31. Ibid.

32. Weil to Perrin, May 15, 1942, in *Waiting for God*, 63: "I saw that the carrying out of a vocation differed from the actions dictated by reason or inclination in that it was due to an impulse of an essentially and manifestly different order." See also: "It is for the service of Christ as the Truth that I deprive myself of sharing in his flesh in the way he has instituted. He deprives me of it, to be more exact, for never up till now have I had even for a second the impression of there being any choice." Weil to Perrin, n.d. ("Letter V"), in *Waiting for God*, 86.

33. Simone Weil, *Gravity and Grace*, trans. Emma Craufurd (London: Routledge and Kegan Paul, 1952), 23; originally published as *La pesanteur et la grâce* (Paris: Plon, 1947).

34. Ibid., 15.

35. Weil to Perrin, May 15, 1942, in *Waiting for God*, 67.

36. "Whoever loses his life for my sake will find it." A paraphrase of Matthew 10:39.

37. Stein, *Welt und Person*, 144.

38. Weil, *Gravity and Grace*, 12–13.

39. Weil, "Implicit and Explicit Love," in *Waiting for God*, 211.

40. Stein, *Welt und Person*, 147 f.

41. Ibid., 148.

42. Ibid., 147.

43. Ibid., 138.

44. Ibid., 139.

45. Ibid., 160 ff.

46. "At fourteen I fell into one of those fits of bottomless despair that come with adolescence, and I seriously thought of dying because of the mediocrity of my natural faculties." Weil to Perrin, May 15, 1942, in *Waiting for God*, 64.

47. Weil to Perrin, May 15, 1942, in *Waiting for God*, 69.

48. John 15:15.

49. The parable of the barren fig tree (Luke 13:6–9).

50. Weil to Perrin, May 26, 1942, in *Waiting for God*, 100.

51. Luke 23:40–43.

52. "All around us is the city of small sins, abounding in backways and retreats, but surely, sooner or later, the towering flame will rise from the harbour announcing that the reign of the cowards is over and a man is burning his ships." Gilbert Keith Chesterton, "A Defense of a Rash Vow," in *The Defendant* (London: M.M. Dent and Sons, 1914), p. 26.

Review of Literature in English on Edith Stein

SARAH BORDEN

Since her 1987 beatification there have been an increasing number of works about Edith Stein's life and thought. While the majority of these have been largely biographical, interest in her scholarly writings is growing. In the following, I have attempted to provide information and brief critical comments on a few key texts in each major area of Stein studies, focusing primarily (although not exclusively) on books and articles in English. My goal is to help others sort more easily through the material available—to provide a kind of road map (although certainly not a complete one) or quick sketch for research purposes. I have divided the sections as follows: first, more general topics (biographies, bibliographies, and overviews); second, topics arranged chronologically as Stein developed interest in each of these areas; and, finally, studies on Catholic-Jewish relations in light of Stein's beatification and canonization and miscellaneous information, including works that do not fit into the other categories and addresses that may be useful. Bibliographical information for the texts mentioned in this review is collected at the end.

The German editions of Stein's work appear in the *Edith Steins Werke* (eighteen volumes), published by Herder in Freiburg, Germany. The Archivum Carmelitanum Edith Stein, in conjunction with the Edith Stein International Institute, has begun a critical edition of Stein's works, *Edith Stein Gesamtausgabe,* which will include twenty-four volumes and present material unavailable in the older *Werke.* The order for the *Edith Stein Gesamtausgabe* will be: biographical writings (vols. 1–4), philosophical writings (vols. 5–12), anthropological and pedagogical writings (vols. 13–16), spiritual writings (vols. 17–19), and translations (vols. 20–24).[1]

The Institute for Carmelite Studies (ICS) in Washington, D.C., began publishing English translations in 1986 in the series *The Collected Works of Edith Stein.* ICS owns the right of first refusal for all English translations of Edith Stein's collected works. Thus far (as of Fall 2004), nine volumes have been published: *Life in a Jewish Family,* translated by Josephine Koeppel; *Essays on Woman,* translated by Freda Mary Oben; *On the Problem of Empathy* and *The Hidden Life,* both translated by Waltraut Stein; *Self-Portrait in Letters,* translated by Josephine Koeppel, *Knowledge and Faith,* translated by Walter Redmond; *Philosophy of Psychology and the Humanities,* translated by Mary Catharine Baseheart and Marianne Sawicki; *Finite and Eternal Being,* translated by Kurt Reinhardt; and, most recently, *The Science of the Cross,* translated by Josephine Koeppel. Marianne Sawicki's translation of *An Investigation Concerning the State* is expected soon.

Perhaps in part because of the lack of translations (with an exception of her dissertation, Stein's major philosophical writings were not available in the ICS series prior to 2000), scholarship on Stein in English is significantly behind that in several other languages. Most notable is the work done in Germany and Italy. The *Edith Stein Jahrbuch,*[2] published annually by Echter in Würzburg, Germany, regularly has articles appraising the state of Stein scholarship in different languages and providing an extensive bibliography. Thus far, there are contributions on Stein studies in Spanish (1995), German (1996), Polish (1997), Italian (1999), English (2000), Japanese (2001), and French (2002).

Biography

The first in the series *The Collected Works of Edith Stein* is *Life in a Jewish Family: Her Unfinished Autobiographical Account.*[3] This is a rather long text covering the years 1891 to 1916. Stein began writing it in 1933, just before her entrance into the Carmelite order. In the foreword, she says, "Recent months have catapulted the German Jews out of the peaceful existence they had come to take for granted," and in these events Stein saw an obligation to give her testimony, affirming the humanity of Jews for those who knew only a caricature. Her work does not discuss her conversion to Catholicism or events in the years following (with the exception of a few interspersed stories), most likely because she did not want to compromise her original intention in writing (that is, to write about a Jewish life, not a Christian one).[4] The book is a wealth of information, however, about Stein's early years, including many interesting stories about the Phenomenological Circle in Göttingen just prior to World War I. Of interest are also Stein's descriptions of her work in a hospital for infectious diseases during the war. Sr. Josephine's extensive notes at the end are extremely helpful both in explaining German culture and habits of the time and in giving factual data about Stein and her family.[5]

A second, shorter autobiographical work is Stein's "How I Came to the Cologne Carmel," published in *Edith Stein: Selected Writings*. This piece, as the title suggests, tells of Stein's decision to enter the Carmelite order, from the loss of her job at Münster (due to anti-Semitic sentiments and state policies) through her arrival at the cloister on the day of her entrance in 1933.

There are numerous biographical books, essays, Web sites, and plays, with varying degrees of historical accuracy.[6] The classic text on Stein, by Teresia Renata Posselt (Sr. Teresia de Spiritu Sancto), is *Edith Stein*, the first book about Stein's life. Posselt was Stein's mistress of novices in Cologne and later prioress of the Cologne Carmel, and the book is particularly beautiful when it turns to descriptions of Stein's life in the Carmelite monastery. Posselt originally put together a little pamphlet in response to the overwhelming number of inquiries from friends, relations, and admirers regarding Stein's life and fate. This was expanded with the addition of documents and testimonies from Stein's various friends and acquaintances, and by 1950 a fifth edition was being prepared and the book had been translated into four languages.

Among the other classic biographies is Hilda Graef's *The Scholar and the Cross: The Life and Works of Edith Stein*. Graef interviewed many of Stein's former acquaintances and friends, giving an interesting variety of perspectives on Stein's life. (Graef has also edited a collection of excerpts from Stein's work in *Writings of Edith Stein*. Unfortunately, most of the excerpts are too short to be very useful for research.) Probably the best-known biography still in print is *Edith Stein: A Biography*, the translation of Waltraud Herbstrith's[7] *Die wahre Gesicht Edith Steins*. This includes considerable material on Stein's life in the Carmelite order and, although somewhat hagiographical in style, is clear, careful, and quite reliable.[8]

The biography *Aunt Edith: The Jewish Heritage of a Catholic Saint*, by Susanne Batzdorff (Stein's niece), is a valuable addition to the biographies available. It is compassionate and maintains a very clear Jewish perspective. In addition to correcting several erroneous claims about Stein's childhood, it provides background information about the Stein family and the Germany of Stein's youth. It also contains a fairly long chapter on the family's reactions to Edith Stein's "autobiography" that is helpful in evaluating Stein's comments on her own life.

Bibliography

The most comprehensive bibliography I know of is on the Baltimore Carmel's Web site: www.baltimorecarmel.org (follow the links to Carmelite Saints on the Net). This source is over 150 pages and growing, but, unfortunately, it only lists works about Stein (including books, articles, cassettes, and musical pieces) without giving any critical comments or dividing the sources by topic or language. More useful in this respect is Sr. Mary Anne Brennan's bibliography published at the end of *Arthur Giron's Edith Stein: A Dramaturgical Sourcebook*, edited by Donald Marinelli. Brennan lists English texts, articles, and dissertations on Stein, giving a short paragraph summary of each.

Included on the Baltimore Carmel Web site are links to a chronology of Stein's life, various articles on Stein and Catholic-Jewish relations, and a time line, put together by Marianne Sawicki, of Stein's various works (see also www.marianne sawicki.com). Also of interest is chapter 5 of Sawicki's book on Stein, *Body, Text, and Science*, where she traces various readings of Stein, including both pre- and posthumous interpretations, and gives an overview of trends in Stein research.

Finally, in *Edith Stein: Von der Phänomenologie zur Mystik. Eine Biographie der Gnade*, Andrés Bejás gives an extensive bibliography as well as a listing of the manuscripts available at the various archives. (The latter is, unfortunately, now rather outdated—both because some of the texts have subsequently been published and because of the 1999 move of the Archivum Carmelitanum Edith Stein from the Netherlands to Würzburg, Germany.)

General Overviews of Stein's Thought and Writings

One of the most significant overviews of Stein's thought in English[9] is Mary Catharine Baseheart's *Person in the World: Introduction to the Philosophy of Edith Stein*.[10] Baseheart organizes the work around "the question of person," moving from a discussion of Stein's life and philosophical development to more detailed presentations of her work on the individual, community, woman, education, essence and existence, and finally, infinite Being. The first, more biographical part of this work is very readable and accessible. Unfortunately, the rest of it is much less so. The latter chapters are most useful as resources for serious researchers, citing places where Stein makes various arguments; however, they are not as helpful for theoretical guidance in finding one's way through Stein's texts.

Freda Mary Oben's *The Life and Thought of St. Edith Stein*, though containing a noteworthy final section dedicated to the debates surrounding Stein's beatification and canonization, is not a thorough study of Stein's theoretical works. A better overview of Stein's thought can be found in Graef's *The Scholar and the Cross*. Although largely biographical, this book includes a number of chapters on Stein's writings on women, spirituality, and education, and it succeeds in providing a useful overview of Stein's works. In 2003, Continuum Publishers published a general overview (*Edith Stein*, by Sarah Borden) of Stein's thought in their series "Outstanding Christian Thinkers." This book is intended to cover the major areas of Stein's thought, as well as introducing readers to the philosophical context of Stein's writings.

Several edited volumes may also be helpful in getting a sense of Stein's thought. In German, some books comparable to the present volume are *Studien zur Philosophie von Edith Stein* (edited by R. L. Fetz et al., from the Internationales Edith-Stein-Symposion, Eichstätt 1991) and lectures from a conference in Rome the year of her canonization, Symposium Internationale Edith Stein, presented in *Teresianum* 50, parts 1 and 2 (1999). See also the articles on Stein in *Internationale Katholische Zeitschrift Communio* 27 (November–December 1998), and *Edith Stein: Testimone di oggi profeta per domani*, ed. J. Sleiman and L. Borriello (Vatican City: Libreria Editrice Vaticana, 1999).

Stein's Phenomenology

Stein's doctoral dissertation was translated by Waltraut Stein (Edith Stein's niece) as *On the Problem of Empathy*.[11] The translation is clear, and, in the introduction, W. Stein points to several ideas in the text that deserve further analysis, including Stein's use of the *mode of nonactuality*, which could be compared with Freud's *subconscious*, and the body as a *zero point of orientation*. The main body of the text, E. Stein's dissertation, focuses on a technical problem in phenomenology— how we are given foreign experiences—and, for the genre, is clear, short, and accessible. I recommend checking W. Stein's translation against English translations of Husserl (and others in the phenomenological school) to compare the phenomenological terminology used.[12] In 2002, Michael Andrews completed his dissertation on Stein's theory of empathy, "Contributions to the Phenomenology of Empathy: Edmund Husserl, Edith Stein and Emmanuel Levinas," under John Caputo, focusing on the connection between epistemology and ethics and situating Stein's work more fully in the discussions of continental philosophy. (Of particular interest are also Andrews's analyses of the influence of Max Scheler on Stein's thought.)

Stein's second significant phenomenological work is her 1922 contribution to Husserl's *Jahrbuch,* translated by Marianne Sawicki and Mary Catharine Baseheart as *Philosophy of Psychology and the Humanities.* The introduction by Sawicki is especially useful for placing Stein's work in a historical and intellectual context, and the editor's notes are a fascinating addition (providing, among other things, notes regarding the German words and examples of Stein's points from her own life). I expect the publication of this text to increase substantially the English resources available for research on Stein's phenomenological thought.

The earliest article in English discussing Stein's philosophy is James Collins's article "Edith Stein and the Advance of Phenomenology," published in 1942 in *Thought.* Collins also dedicates twenty pages to Stein in his 1962 book *Three Paths in Philosophy,* covering much of the same material as in his article, although not exclusively so. The best book to date giving a critical analysis and evaluation of Stein's phenomenological work is Marianne Sawicki's *Body, Text, and Science: The Literacy of Investigative Practices and the Phenomenology of Edith Stein* (1997).[13] Sawicki presents Stein's model of *constitution* from her early phenomenological works (primarily her dissertation on empathy [*Einfühlung*] and her contributions to Husserl's *Jahrbuch*), contrasting Stein's and Husserl's understandings of constitution. Sawicki puts forward the challenging thesis that Stein and Husserl fundamentally disagree about how to understand constitution and that areas of apparent agreement (for example, in *Ideas II*) must be explained in terms of Stein's own work editing Husserl's papers.[14] Sawicki proceeds to clearly articulate Stein's theory of the person and a hermeneutic developed from that. Responses to Sawicki's thesis have been mixed, but this book is clearly the central English text on Stein's phenomenological work. It can be supplemented by several other papers by Sawicki; I especially recommend "Personal Connections: The Pre-Baptismal Philosophy of Edith Stein" (also on the Baltimore Carmel Web site, www. baltimorecarmel.org) and Sawicki's introduction to Stein's *Philosophy of Psychology and the Humanities.*

I have found Philibert Secretan's work on Stein to be dense but extremely insightful.[15] See, for example, his essay "The Self and the Other in the Thought of Edith Stein" in Analecta Husserliana 6, where he distinguishes Stein's use of the terms *psyche* (soul) and *spirit* in her *Jahrbuch* contributions and offers a critique of egological phenomenology.

SARAH BORDEN

Very little work has been done on Stein's *Eine Untersuchung über den Staat* (*An Investigation on the State*), written just after World War I; it is in the process of being translated by Sawicki and is expected from ICS soon. Mary Catharine Baseheart has a useful article, "Edith Stein's Phenomenology of the State," summarizing Stein's essay (focusing particularly on her distinctions among *mass, society,* and *community,* and her analogy between the state and personhood) in Lenore Langsdorf's *Reinterpreting the Political.* More analysis is included in Antonio Calcagno's article "*Persona Politica*: Unity and Difference in Edith Stein's Political Philosophy," but none of the preceding provide a comprehensive analysis or evaluation. Marianne Sawicki is now preparing such a study for Rowman and Littlefield's series on twentieth-century political thinkers. I hope that Sawicki's study, in addition to the translation, will help in this area.

Stein's Writings on Women

Some of Stein's lectures on women are collected in the second volume of *The Collected Works of Edith Stein* (*Essays on Woman,* trans. Freda Mary Oben). It is always a good idea to read a translated text in conjunction with the original, if at all possible, and this is especially true in the case of this translation. The translator, Freda Mary Oben, has written a good general text on Stein (*Edith Stein: Scholar, Feminist, Saint*),[16] but her translation of the essays on woman is a bit loose and, at times, imports connotations not present in the original.[17] Translation is a difficult process, and Oben was clearly attempting to retain a readable style. This seems to me to have occurred, on occasion, at the expense of accuracy and tone.[18] It should also be noted that the final essay in the 1987 edition of *Essays on Woman,* "Challenges Facing Swiss Catholic Academic Women," is not by Stein but, rather, by Dr. Hilda Vérène Borsinger. The 1996 revised edition corrects this problem.

Freda Mary Oben has translated several additional essays that do not appear in the English edition of the text on women, among them "Mission of the Catholic Educator," "Woman's Vocation," and "Maternal Pedagogy." See Oben's 1979 dissertation, "An Annotated Edition of Edith Stein's Papers on Woman," from the Catholic University of America.

Among the noteworthy articles on Stein's theory of woman are Jane Kelley Rodeheffer's "On Spiritual Maternity: Edith Stein, Aristotle, and the Nature of Woman" and, especially, Linda Lopez McAlister's article "Edith Stein: Essential Differences" (included in this book). McAlister argues that Stein mutes her essentialist claims regarding the nature of men and women through not only her theory of type but also her theory of individuality. Thus Stein turns out to be a rather unusual essentialist with very "unessentialist" conclusions.

Mary Catharine Baseheart's article "On Educating Women: The Relevance of Stein" presents a clear summary of Stein's views on the education of women. In "Sex and Gender Differentiation in Hildegard of Bingen and Edith Stein," Prudence Allen analyzes Stein's position on women and compares it with papal teaching.[19] Finally, I found Rachel Feldhay Brenner's article "Edith Stein: A Reading of Her Feminist Thought," in *Studies in Religion/Sciences religieuses* (and included in this book), to be useful. Brenner provides a good summary and analysis of Stein's views on women, pointing to tensions in Stein's thought and offering helpful interpretations of how we should understand and, to some degree, resolve those tensions.

Stein's Writings on Education

While teaching at St. Magdalena's in Speyer, Stein became interested in pedagogical questions, looking particularly at the education of women, and in the 1920s and early 1930s she gave several lectures on the education of women (some of these appear in *Essays on Woman*). In 1932 Stein began teaching at Deutsche Institut für wissenschaftliche Pädagogik (German Institute for Scientific Pedagogy) in Münster. Her lectures, both those given in the winter semester of 1932–33 and those planned for the spring semester (which were never given because Stein was prevented from lecturing due to the non-Aryan laws) were published as volumes 16 and 17 of *Edith Steins Werke, Der Aufbau der menschlichen Person* and *Was ist der Mensch? Eine theologische Anthropologie*. These can be supplemented by volume 12, *Ganzheitliches Leben: Schriften zur religiösen Bildung*; this volume is a collection of works written between 1926 and 1938 covering topics such as the calling of the teacher, the life of women, and the art of education. (None of these are yet available in English.) It should be emphasized that Stein's work on education is only preliminary and tentative. She lost her job in Münster while in the midst of developing a proposal for the reform of higher education. Thus these writings should be read as incomplete and still in a formative stage, not as a complete proposal in itself.

Several studies of Stein's educational theories have been written (interestingly enough, most of them in English), most notably, June M. Verbillion's dissertation, "A Critical Analysis of the Educational Theories of Edith Stein" (Loyola

University, 1960), and Anselm Mary Madden's dissertation, "Edith Stein and the Education of Women: Augustinian Themes" (St. Louis University, 1962). Verbillion spends the first third of the text presenting Stein's personal and philosophical biography, and in the latter four chapters she argues for six theses or principles of a Steinian theory of education.[20] In contrast, Madden traces Augustinian themes—particularly, a focus on affectivity, interiority, solidarity, and Christian culture—in Stein's educational theory. Both of these analyses are quite positive toward Stein's work and provide an introduction to her pedagogical thought; neither, however, is rigorously systematic. Bruno Reifenrath's *Erziehung im Licht des Ewigen: Die Pädagogik Edith Steins* is, in contrast, more thorough, drawing extensively from Stein's various philosophical writings and comparing Stein's theory of education with other contemporary pedagogical theories.

Stein's Translation Work

One area of interest is Stein's various translations, including John Cardinal Newman's letters and papers, Thomas Aquinas's *De veritate* (On Truth), and Henri Bremond's *Heiligkeit und Theologie: Vom Carmel zu Kardinal Bérulles Lehre*. The reviews of Stein's translation of Aquinas by her peers (see especially, T. A. Graf's, J. de Vries's, and Rudolf Allers's) provide a mixed picture of her work—some are highly positive while others are quite critical of Stein's understanding of Aquinas—and her own index for choice of terms in translating *De veritate* is an interesting study in itself.[21] Copies of the index are available at the end of volume 4 of *Edith Steins Werke* (the second volume of Stein's translation of Aquinas's *De veritate*).

Stein's Later Philosophical Writings

Stein wrote an article, published in the 1929 Festschrift in honor of Husserl's seventieth birthday, comparing Thomas Aquinas and Husserl. This short essay has been translated as "Husserl and Aquinas: A Comparison" by Walter Redmond and appears in *Knowledge and Faith*.[22] A partial (and, I think, smoother) translation of the essay also appears as an appendix in Baseheart's *Person in the World*, 129–44. Baseheart dedicates much of her 1960 dissertation to an analysis of the comparisons between Husserl and Thomas mentioned in Stein's Festschrift essay, presenting evidence for these similarities, first in the texts of Husserl and Thomas and then in Stein's works (primarily the Festschrift article and *Finite and Eternal*

Being). She attempts to show how Stein is similar to and different from her two "masters." Baseheart's dissertation limits itself to the topics raised in Stein's very brief essay (philosophy as science, natural and supernatural reason, consciousness and Eternal Being, essence and existence, and intuition and abstraction), which offers only a preliminary study of the impact of both thinkers on Stein's work. Baseheart's dissertation is extremely useful, but it only begins the analysis of Stein's "synthesis." Hilda Gosebrink has a more critical analysis of the Festschrift essay in "Meister Thomas und sein Schüler Husserl: Gedanken zu einem fiktiven Dialog zwischen Thomas von Aquin und Edmund Husserl von Edith Stein,"[23] in *Erbe und Auftrag* (a condensed version of her thesis on the same topic), where she argues that Stein inadequately understood Aquinas and confused theology and philosophy. (Stein presents her theory regarding their relation in chapter 1 of *Finite and Eternal Being*.)[24]

The main philosophical works in Stein's more "Thomistic phase" are *Finite and Eternal Being*[25] and *Potenz und Akt* (volume 18 of *Edith Steins Werke*). Both works are rather technical and are in need of extensive commentaries. Augusta Gooch begins some of that work in her dissertation, "Metaphysical Ordination: Reflections on Edith Stein's 'Endliches und Ewiges Sein.'" Gooch focuses on *being* (*Seiende*) *as such* and the ordering of particular types of being and distinct ways of being, picking up significant themes in Stein's text. Her discussions are at times very helpful and informative, but, unfortunately, much of the time, while she makes exhaustive distinctions, it is not clear why these are significant, nor do Stein's metaphysical claims become evident.[26] Overall, Gooch's dissertation did less than I hoped in making clear precisely how we should understand the structure of being in Stein's work or what is original in Stein's text. One of the best, most straightforward, albeit short, summaries of *Finite and Eternal Being* is Käthe Granderath's master's thesis from Loyola University (March 1961), "From Finite to Eternal Being: Edith Stein's Philosophical Approach to God."[27] Granderath points out many of the places where Stein relies on other thinkers and provides several helpful connections and schemas.[28]

A frequently quoted secondary text discussing *Finite and Eternal Being* is Höfliger's dissertation on Stein and the problem of universals, "Das Universalienproblem in Edith Steins Werk 'Endliches und Ewiges Sein,'" which situates Stein's position within the scholastic debate on this topic. He has an invaluable glossary in the first chapter explaining the key terms and providing extensive citations of Stein's use of these in *Finite and Eternal Being*.

Antonio Calcagno's essay on Heidegger and Stein ("*Die Fülle oder das Nichts?* Edith Stein and Martin Heidegger on the Question of Being"), which focuses on her appendix on Heidegger,[29] approaches *Finite and Eternal Being* from a different and illuminating angle. It would be very fruitful and, I suspect, necessary for fully understanding *Finite and Eternal Being* to have a fuller comparison of Stein's text and Heidegger's *Being and Time*.

Philibert Secretan presents a nuanced interpretation explicating a central theme in *Finite and Eternal Being*, the meaning of being as the unfolding of meaning, in "Edith Stein on the 'Order and Chain of Being.'" And in "*Actio, Passio et Creatio* in the *Endliche und Ewige Philosophie* of Edith Stein," Antonio Calcagno argues that "[p]ostmodernity, in emphasizing difference, has rendered difference a universal logical category which has eclipsed the ground narrative of the being of the human person." He then uses Stein's later works both to reveal affinity between Stein and postmodern thought and to present challenges to postmodernity in its focus on difference.

For an analysis with a more negative conclusion regarding Stein's later writings, see Karl-Heinz Lembeck's "Zwischen Wissenschaft und Glauben: Die Philosophie Edith Steins," in *Zeitschrift für katholische Theologie,* and "Die Phänomenologie Husserls und Edith Steins," in *Theologie und Philosophie.*

It is common to claim that Stein moved from phenomenology to Thomism and then finally to mystical thought (see, for example, Guilead's *De la phénoménologie à la science de la croix: L'itinéraire d'Edith Stein* and Dubois's "L'itinéraire philosophique et spirituel d'Edith Stein"). Insofar as the claim suggests that she "moved beyond" her previous work, this seems to me deeply mistaken.[30] While it is true that Stein no longer used a strictly phenomenological method in her later work, there is a tremendous amount of phenomenological reflection in her later writings, and I think a study critically comparing her 1922 and 1925 *Jahrbuch* essays (*Philosophy of Psychology and the Humanities* and *On the State*), for example, and *Finite and Eternal Being* would reveal that fully to make sense of Stein's later work, inquiry into her early work is necessary.

Stein's Spiritual Writings

The Hidden Life: Hagiographic Essays, Meditations, Spiritual Texts collects several of Stein's spiritual writings, most of which were intended for nonacademic audiences, and John Sullivan (the editor of the ICS series) has edited a volume of short religious texts from Stein *(Edith Stein: Essential Writings).*[31] Similarly, *The Science of the Cross* (translated by Hilda Graef and more recently by Josephine Koeppel) was most likely written to introduce St. John of the Cross to Stein's religious sisters who could not read him in Spanish. In contrast, Stein's "Ways to Know God: The 'Symbolic Theology' of Dionysius the Areopagite and Its Objective Presuppositions" is a more scholarly piece. It was originally written for the journal *Philosophy and Phenomenological Research,* although it was finally published in *The Thomist* in 1946.[32] Stein examines the corpus of Pseudo-Dionysius's texts, elucidating the claim that God is the first theologian. Among the interesting aspects of this article is Stein's use of the Husserlian notions of *intention* and *fulfillment* in her discussions of theological knowledge.

The most extensive secondary writing on Stein's theology available in English is Anthony Kavunguvalappil's dissertation, "Theology of Suffering and Cross in the Life and Works of Blessed Edith Stein." Kavunguvalappil focuses on Stein's theology of suffering (particularly in *The Science of the Cross*) as a kind of expiation and way to become united with God. The book is largely expository, quoting extensively (too extensively at times) from her texts and letters. There are few scholarly works in English on Stein's theological writings,[33] and Kavunguvalappil's text helps fill this lacuna, but it could certainly be supplemented with other more systematic and critical studies.

Jewish-Catholic Relations and Stein's Canonization

In 1987, Pope John Paul II beatified Edith Stein,[34] and on October 12, 1998, the church canonized her Saint Edith Stein (or Saint Teresa Benedicta of the Cross).[35] Kenneth Woodward traces the history of her beatification in *Making Saints: How the Catholic Church Determines Who Becomes a Saint.*[36] Her beatification and subsequent canonization sparked both controversy and discussion. Among the significant questions raised are how martyrdom should be understood and the significance of the canonization of a prominent Jewish convert. Harry Cargas edited a volume of papers with essays by Freda Mary Oben, Daniel Polish, Eugene Fisher, Emanuel Tanay, Susanne Batzdorff, Judith Hershcopf Banki, Nechama Tec, Zev Garber, and Rachel Feldhay Brenner several years after the beatification (*The Unnecessary Problem of Edith Stein*), discussing the major controversies.

Helpful additions to this book include Nancy Fuchs-Kreimer's essay in *Lilith,* comparing Stein's conversion and Franz Rosenzweig's near-conversion ("Sister Edith Stein: A Rabbi Reacts"). The difference between the two, Fuchs-Kreimer contends, is that Stein, as a woman, would not have had the resources of the Jewish tradition open to her in the way that they were to Rosenzweig—a point the Jewish community should take seriously in any self-evaluation. Fuchs-Kreimer's essay is reprinted in *Never Forget: Christian and Jewish Perspectives on Edith Stein* (ed. Waltraud Herbstrith), which is a wealth of information on reactions to Stein and her beatification. David Novak, in his essay "Edith Stein, Apostate Saint"

in *First Things,* points to fundamental differences between the attitude devout Jews and devout Catholics must take to Edith Stein—a point that cannot be overlooked in the attempt to use Stein as a bridge between Catholics
and Jews. (See also his lecture *The Significance of Edith Stein for the Jews* in the
Edith Stein Center Lecture series at Spalding University.) And Raphael James
Baaden offers six suggestions for how we can understand Stein's beatification
in a positive light for Jewish-Catholic relations in "Jewish Scholar Allowed Input
for Stein Beatification."

Other Works

Every once in a while, one finds a book that not only presents useful and interesting information but also inspires one on how to live—regardless of one's
interest in Stein or Holocaust studies. In my opinion, one of the best books on
Stein, as well as a wonderful book on the art of living, is Rachel Feldhay Brenner's[37] *Writing as Resistance: Four Women Confronting the Holocaust: Edith Stein,
Simone Weil, Anne Frank, Etty Hillesum.* Brenner looks at these four women as
examples of different but related models of resistance to the Holocaust.[38] She
focuses on the ways each continued to affirm her humanity and that of others
amid a pogrom intended to annihilate their humanity; she says, "This study's intent is to represent the four women neither as saints nor as emblems of ideological controversies, but rather as individuals who opposed the terror by insisting on their own humanity" (178). In the process of presenting the differing
models of resistance, Brenner uses several elements of Stein's philosophy (specifically her writings on women and her early phenomenology) to develop a theoretical framework. She is quite successful in giving clear and concise presentations of different aspects of Stein's (and Weil's) thought, although her contrast of
reciprocity and *receptivity* (chapter 3) would have benefited from better acquain-
tance with Stein's later works.[39]

In the introduction to Henry Bordeaux's *Edith Stein: Thoughts on Her Life
and Times,* the translators, Donald and Idella Gallagher, clearly state that this
book is neither a biography nor a testimony on Stein's life. Rather, it is "a series
of meditations upon a life singularly poignant and deeply moving" (viii). Bordeaux writes well and gives us a series of images from Stein's life, his own experiences, and various and sundry other literary and spiritual figures, tied together by the theme of each chapter.[40] Events in Stein's life are used primarily to
give Bordeaux a chance to talk on topics he cares about and present several sig-

nificant events and experiences in his life. It is well worth reading, but less for what it tells us about Edith Stein or her thoughts about a subject, and more for Bordeaux's ability to weave inspiring ideas and tales together.

There are several plays and films about Stein's life. The most famous of these is Arthur Giron's *Edith Stein*. It first opened in 1969 at the Arena Stage in Washington, D.C., and a significantly revised version opened in the winter of 1988 at Pittsburgh Public Theater. This play is intended "to dramatize the conflicts" Stein faced—not to provide a documentary of her life (which it certainly does not)[41]— and it presents a rather symbolic depiction of her life, couching the whole narrative (perhaps unwisely) in the 1987 controversy regarding a Carmelite convent at Auschwitz.[42]

Addresses

The Würzburg monastery houses the Archivum Carmelitanum Edith Stein and the Edith Stein International Institut, as well as an excellent library of Carmelite texts. The address is:

Karmelitenkloster
Sanderstr. 12
D-97070 Würzburg
Germany

Mary Catharine Baseheart started the Edith Stein Center for Study and Research in 1991, and Dr. John Wilcox continues her work. The center is a useful resource for research and has a friendly working environment; it also welcomes contributions—copies of dissertations, articles, and so forth—on Stein. The address is:

Dr. John Wilcox
Edith Stein Center for Study and Research
Spalding University
851 S. Fourth St.
Louisville, KY 40203

Numerous German texts on and about Stein can be ordered from the Edith-Stein-Archiv at the Karmel "Maria vom Frieden," Vor den Siebenburgen 6, 50676 Köln, Germany, or through the Edith-Stein-Karmel, Neckarhalde 64–66, D-72070, Tübingen, Germany.

I have also ordered German texts through Schoenhof's Foreign Books in Cambridge, MA. The address is: 76A Mount Auburn Street, Cambridge, MA 02138; tel. 617-547-8855; fax 617-547-8565; e-mail: info@schoenhofs.com; www. schoenhofs.com.

NOTES

1. See the announcement at www.geocities.com/baltimorecarmel/stein/crited.html.
2. The *Edith Stein Jahrbuch* was started in 1995, and each volume has a general theme (*Das Weibliche, Das Christentum*, etc.). A large number of the articles are not about Stein, and the quality of the articles varies greatly. While some are wonderful reference tools, I have been, on the whole, disappointed in the amount of genuinely scholarly work on Stein published there.
3. The subtitle was added by the publishers, and there is some debate both about whether it is appropriate to call the work "unfinished" and whether it is truly an autobiography. Regarding the latter question, see Marianne Sawicki's *Body, Text, and Science*, esp. 175–83.
4. Information about her later years can be gleaned from her letters and various biographies.
5. Sr. Josephine Koeppel has also written an interesting biography, in the series "The Way of the Christian Mystics," entitled *Edith Stein: Philosopher and Mystic* (Collegeville, MN: Liturgical Press, 1990).
6. Susanne Batzdorff has said, "The tremendous proliferation of 'legendary material' and the liberties taken with historical fact are mindboggling. Stories that are either wholly or partially untrue have been stated as fact and then repeated. To correct such a factual error is almost impossible, for it attains a stubborn life of its own and drives out the true fact. . . . I counteract this tendency by providing corrective information, but it seems at times futile—like putting one's finger in the dike to stem the mighty tide. Even if errata are subsequently corrected, these corrections are not always seen by those who read the original story." "Catholics and Jews: Can We Bridge the Abyss?" *America* (March 11, 1989), 223, reprinted in *Edith Stein: Selected Writings*, 115–16.
7. Sr. Waltraud's religious name is Teresia a Matre Dei. She has written extensively on Stein (primarily biographical works and essays about her spirituality and Jewish-Catholic relations), and several earlier pieces are under her religious name.
8. There are a number of other biographies, including Florent Gaboriau's *The Conversion of Edith Stein*, which looks at Stein's life as a series of conversions, and María Ruiz Scaperlanda's *Edith Stein: St. Teresa Benedicta of the Cross*. Much less hagiographical in tone is Ulrika Lindblad's "Rereading Edith Stein: What Happened?" which may offer a counterpoint to the biographies listed here.
9. There are, however, several in other languages, most notably Philibert Secretan's *Erkenntnis und Aufstieg: Einführung in die Philosophie von Edith Stein* (Innsbruck: Tyrolie-Verlag, 1992); Hanna-Barbara Gerl's *Unerbittliches Licht: Edith Stein: Philosophie, Mystik, Leben* (Mainz: Matthias-Grünewald, 1991); Luciana Vigone's rather short text *Introduzione al pensiero filosofico di Edith Stein* (Rome: Città Nuova, 1991); Florent Gaboriau's *Lorsque*

Edith Stein se convertit (Geneva: Ad Solem, 1997); and Reiner Matzker's *Einfühlung: Edith Stein und Phänomenologie* (Frankfurt: Peter Lang, 1991). These go into varying levels of scholarly discussion of Stein's writings and thought. A short English substitute is an article, "Edith Stein," put together by Mary Catharine Baseheart, Linda Lopez McAlister, and Waltraut Stein summarizing Stein's life and thought in *A History of Women Philosophers*, vol. 4, ed. Mary Ellen Waithe (Dordrecht: Kluwer Academic Publishers, 1995).

10. Unfortunately, this book, like most Kluwer texts, is expensive, approximately $100.

11. The first chapter was not published with the dissertation in 1917 and is, as far as I know, lost.

12. A useful place to start might be Dorian Cairns's *Guide for Translating Husserl* (The Hague: Martinus Nijhoff, 1973).

13. This book is approximately $137. The nearly identical text can be ordered as Sawicki's dissertation (under the title *Body, Text and Science in the Phenomenology of Edith Stein*) through UMI (Bell & Howell) for about $100 less. The number there is 1-800-521-0600, and the Web site is www.bellhowell.inforlearning.com.

14. Sawicki's claim rests, in part, on a reconstruction of Stein's work on Husserl's *Ideas II* (which she puts forward in chap. 4).

15. I would like to see his *Erkenntnis und Aufstieg* (cited in n. 9) translated into English.

16. Oben divides this short book (approximately eighty pages) into three chapters. The first is biographical, giving a short paragraph apiece to Stein's major writings and providing an engaging account of Stein's life and death. The last two chapters give an extended discussion of two aspects of Stein's thought—her understanding of women and her theology of suffering. This book is highly readable, although hagiographical in tone, and offers a helpful introduction, albeit short (too short in several discussions), to two areas of Stein's thought.

17. For example, in just the first few pages, she translates "und zwar eines, das ihm nicht nur von außen her aufgenötigt ist—durch die Gesetzlichkeit, die in der Arbeit selbst liegt, oder durch äußere Vorschriften—, sondern das sichtlich von innen her kommt" (which I would translate roughly as "and certainly one that is not only forced from the outside—through the lawfulness that lies in the work itself or through outer prescriptions—but also one that becomes evident from within") as "[i]ndeed, this character emerges as a moral force from within; it is not imposed upon the professional life from without either by the authenticity of the work itself or other regulations"—the introduction of the phrase "moral force" is, to my mind, much more loaded than Stein's original. Soon thereafter she changes Stein's "Gefährtin des Mannes" (companion of man) to "wife."

18. On several occasions, in the service of simplicity, she drops brief arguments made by Stein; for example, changing "[s]ie ist eine Pflege- und Erziehungsfunktion, also eine echt mütterliche" ("[i]t is a function of care and formation, therefore, a genuinely maternal [one]") to "[i]t is a concerned, formative and truly maternal function."

19. Allen's substantial two-volume text entitled *The Concept of Woman* (Grand Rapids, MI: William B. Eerdmans, 1985, 2002) (discussing the history of views on women) is a significant contribution to feminist philosophy, and she employs a number of the categories in another, shorter article on Stein entitled "Metaphysics of Form, Matter, and Gender" in *Lonergan Workshop*, vol. 12, ed. Fred Lawrence (Boston: Boston College, 1996), 1–25.

20. These are: (1) "All true education is based on a thorough study of the nature of the educand; such a study of the education of young women is yet to be written" (89); (2) "The

goal of education for each young woman should be in the formation of a person who is what she is meant to be" (92); (3) "Preparation for both marriage and celibacy should be given to all young women in high school" (95); (4) "The curricula in girls' schools should follow from the premise that the entire human person is to be developed in a feminine way and such curricula should take great cognizance of the psychological attitude of women" (98); (5) "The teaching of religion to young women should stress imitation of Mary, the *Virgo Mater*, as the prototype of pure femininity" (100); and (6) "The school should aim at cultivating in the young woman an awareness of the feminine ethos so that she may find womanly satisfactions in life and at the same time provide society with the comforts of this feminine ethos" (102).

21. Marianne Sawicki has put forward the hypothesis (conversation, October 1997), which has not, to my knowledge, been tested, that Stein's translation influenced transcendental Thomism insofar as she made it easier to read Thomas through more Kantian language and categories.

22. Stein originally wrote this essay as a fictitious dialogue between the two figures. At Martin Heidegger's request, she rewrote the essay in a more traditional form. Redmond translates both essays, placing them side by side for an easy comparison.

23. Gosebrink focuses on the earlier edition of the essay as it was in dialogue form, not as published in the Festschrift.

24. Karl Schudt's dissertation addresses this topic in a great deal of depth. See "Faith and Reason in the Philosophy of Edith Stein" (PhD diss., Marquette University, 2001).

25. Kurt F. Reinhardt's translation was published in 2002. For an alternative translation, see Augusta Gooch's first-draft translation of *Finite and Eternal Being,* available for photocopy at the Edith Stein Center for Study and Research, Spalding University, Louisville, Kentucky. Be warned that copies of the German edition of *Endliches und ewiges Sein* are difficult to find and that it will probably not be reprinted prior to the completion of the critical edition.

26. This is a weakness that is better addressed as Gooch proceeds.

27. This text has not been, as far as I know, published. The copy I read is at the Carmelite monastery in Würzburg.

28. I have also tried to lay out Stein's understanding of being and essence, comparing Stein's position with Thomas Aquinas's, John Duns Scotus's, and Husserl's, in Sarah Borden, "An Issue in Edith Stein's Philosophy of the Person: The Relation of Individual and Universal Form in 'Endliches und ewiges Sein'" (PhD diss., Fordham University, 2001).

29. Stein wrote two appendices for *Finite and Infinite Being,* one on Martin Heidegger and the other on St. Teresa of Avila. They were not published with the German edition but appear rather in *Welt und Person,* vol. 6 of *Edith Steins Werke* (Freiburg: Herder, 1962), 39–68 and 69–135. In both of these appendices (as in other writings), Stein spends the first and largest portion of the text with exposition and only at the end (or end of a section) offers her own critical comments and evaluation.

30. John Nota, in "Misunderstanding and Insight about Edith Stein's Philosophy," *Human Studies* 10 (1987): 205–12, denies that *Finite and Eternal Being* can even be read as a Thomistic work. I am sympathetic to Nota's claim.

31. It is worth mentioning Patricia Marks's devotional text entitled *A Retreat with Edith Stein: Trusting God's Purpose* (Cincinnati, OH: St. Anthony Messenger Press, 2001).

32. It was translated by Rudolf Allers, appearing in *The Thomist* 9, no. 3 (1946): 379–420. The Edith Stein Guild of New York has also published a pamphlet containing this essay. The German version of the text appears in *Erkenntnis und Glaube,* vol. 15 of *Edith Steins Werke* (Freiburg: Herder, 1993).

33. Kavunguvalappil cites Herbert Hecker's dissertation, *Phänomenologie des Christlichen bei Edith Stein* (Würzburg: Echter, 1995), as another text with similar themes. (In the German system, unlike that of the United States, dissertations must be published.)

34. Pope John Paul II's address at the beatification can be found in *L'osservatore romano* 20 (May 18, 1987): 19–20; *The Living Word* 93 (1987): 353–62; *Edith Stein Symposium: Teresian Culture,* ed. John Sullivan, OCD, Carmelite Studies 4 (Washington, DC: ICS Publications, 1987), 295–309; *Origins* 17 (June 4, 1987): 48–50; and Sullivan's *Holiness Befits Your House: Canonization of Edith Stein—A Documentation,* 21–29.

35. Pope John Paul II's address at the canonization can be found in *Carmelite Digest,* 14, no. 1 (Winter 1999): 4–13; *L'osservatore romano* 41 (October 14, 1998): 1, 10; and Sullivan, *Holiness Befits Your House,* 7–11.

36. See also Ambrose Eszer's article in Sullivan, *Edith Stein Symposium.* Eszer, who was postulator for Stein's beatification, describes Stein's beatification process and defends the declaration of her as a martyr.

37. I have seen this book listed under both Feldhay and Brenner. The World Catalog lists her works under Brenner. This difficulty also arises with Angela Ales Bello, Francisco Javier Sancho Fermín, and others.

38. There are numerous essays comparing Stein and Weil: see, for example, Cecilia McGowan's "Simone Weil and Edith Stein: Two Great Women of Our Century," in *Desert Call* 24 (Summer 1989): 4–5; 24 (Fall 1989): 16–19; and 24 (Winter 1989): 16–18, and Neville Braybrooke's articles, including "The Called and the Chosen: A Comparative Study of Edith Stein and Simone Weil," *Religion in Life* 28, no. 1 (1958): 98–103; "Edith Stein and Simone Weil," *Hibbert Journal Quarterly for Religion, Philosophy and Theology,* 253 (1965–66): 75–80; "Edith Stein and Simone Weil," *Vox Theologica: Interacademiaal Theologisch Tijdschrift* 29, no. 3 (1959): 65–69; "Edith Stein and Simone Weil: Spiritual Heroes of Our Times," *American Ecclesiastical Review* 163 (November 1970): 327–33; "Edith Stein and Simone Weil: A Study in Belief," *Spiritual Life* 14 (Winter 1968): 241–47; and "Simone Weil and Edith Stein: Modern Mystic-Martyrs," in *Christian Century* 81 (November 25, 1964): 1461–63.

39. In general this text is clear, with extremely helpful comparisons between the four women as well as other significant thinkers of this century. The one disappointing exception to the general clarity is the conclusion, which plays with too many philosophical and theological concepts, leaving a rather imprecise and unclear conclusion to an otherwise well-written book.

40. There are a few points in Bordeaux's biographical sections about which I am hesitant. For example, in chap. 3, he claims, on the authority of Pauline Reinach, that Stein's reading of St. Teresa's autobiography occurred at the Reinach home. I have discussed this point with Waltraud Herbstrith (November 1999), who questions the accuracy of this account. Most biographers put the reading of St. Teresa's autobiography at Hedwig Conrad-Martius's home several years later. I tend to lean toward the Conrad-Martius version—this story is much more widespread and fits better with the timing of other events—but

it is worth noting that there are two accounts of Stein's conversion, and there may be another story incorporating both versions.

41. Robert Neal Black's *Edith Stein: A Ceremony of Remembrance* (Boston: Baker's Plays, 1998) is more accurate historically, although it has taken certain artistic liberties as well.

42. There are various critical reviews and evaluations of the play. See, for example, J. B. Miller's "Jewish Victims and German Indifference," in *The Christian Century* 105 (December 14, 1988): 1144–45, and Edward R. Isser's "Theatrical Exploitation: The *Perdition* Affair and *Edith Stein*." It seems to me that the latter text is somewhat unfortunate insofar as Isser's analysis suffers from many of the same problems of which he accuses Giron. For example, Isser claims that "Giron glosses over and ignores the actual circumstances of Stein's arrest and deportation" and then proceeds to tell us what those circumstances are, glossing over and ignoring the nuances of the negotiations for transfer to Switzerland and failing to mention the role of the bishops' letter in Edith's and Rosa's arrest. Thus his conclusion that her sacrifice "was not a case of religious martyrdom" is a bit premature (147).

BIBLIOGRAPHY FOR THIS REVIEW

Adamska, Janina, and Zdzislaw Florek. "Das Werk Edith Steins in Polen." *Edith Stein Jahrbuch* 3 (1997): 403–6.

Allen, Prudence. "Sex and Gender Differentiation in Hildegard of Bingen and Edith Stein." *Communio* 20 (Summer 1993): 389–414.

Allers, Rudolf. Review of Stein's translation of Aquinas's *De veritate*. *Das Neue Reich* 13 (1931): 911.

Andrews, Michael. "Contributions to the Phenomenology of Empathy: Edmund Husserl, Edith Stein and Emmanuel Levinas." PhD diss., Villanova University, 2002.

Baaden, Raphael James. "Jewish Scholar Allowed Input for Stein Beatification." *National Catholic Reporter*, May 8, 1987, 8.

Baseheart, Mary Catharine. "Edith Stein's Phenomenology of the State." In *Reinterpreting the Political: Continental Philosophy and Political Theory*, ed. Lenore Langsdorf. Albany, NY: SUNY Press, 1998.

———. "Edith Stein's Philosophy of Woman and of Women's Education." *Hypatia* 4, no. 1 (1989): 267–79.

———. "The Encounter of Husserl's Phenomenology and the Philosophy of St. Thomas in Selected Writings of Edith Stein." PhD diss., University of Notre Dame, 1960.

———. "On Educating Women: The Relevance of Stein." *Continuum* 4 (Summer 1966): 197–207. Also in *Response* 1 (1967): 4–8, 32–34, and *Search*, 9, no. 9 (1967): 344–50.

———. *Person in the World: Introduction to the Philosophy of Edith Stein*. Boston: Kluwer, 1997.

Baseheart, M. C., Linda Lopez McAlister, and Waltraut Stein. "Edith Stein." In *A History of Women Philosophers*, vol. 4, ed. Ellen Waithe, 157–87. The Hague: Martinus Nijhoff, 1990. Boston: Kluwer, 1995.

Batzdorff, Susanne. *Aunt Edith: The Jewish Heritage of a Catholic Saint*. Springfield, IL: Templegate Publishers, 1998.

Bejás, Andrés. *Edith Stein: Von der Phänomenologie zur Mystik. Eine Biographie der Gnade.* Disputationes Theologicae 17. Frankfurt: Peter Lang, 1987.

Bergman, Susan, ed. *Martyrs.* San Francisco: Harper, 1996.

Berkman, Joyce Avrech. "'I Am Myself It': Comparative National Identity Formation in The Lives of Vera Brittain and Edith Stein." *Women's History Review* 6, no. 1 (1986): 47–73.

Bordeaux, Henry. *Edith Stein: Thoughts on Her Life and Times.* Trans. Donald Gallagher and Idella Gallagher. Milwaukee: Bruce Publishing, 1959.

Borden, Sarah. "Bibliography of Secondary Sources on Edith Stein." Retrieved from www.geocities.com/ baltimorecarmel/stein/borden.html.

———. *Edith Stein.* Outstanding Christian Thinkers. London: Continuum Publishers, 2003.

Brennan, Mary Anne. "Bibliography." In *Arthur Giron's Edith Stein: A Dramaturgical Sourcebook,* ed. Donald Marinelli, 179–210. Pittsburgh, PA: Carnegie Mellon University Press, 1994.

Brenner, Rachel Feldhay. "Edith Stein: A Reading of Her Feminist Thought." *Studies in Religion/Sciences religieuses* 23, no. 1 (1994): 43–56.

———. *Writing as Resistance: Four Women Confronting the Holocaust: Edith Stein, Simone Weil, Anne Frank, Etty Hillesum.* University Park: Pennsylvania State University Press, 1997).

Calcagno, Antonio. "*Actio, Passio et Creatio* in the *Endliche und Ewige Philosophie* of Edith Stein." In *Phenomenology of Life and the Human Creative Condition,* book 1, Analecta Husserliana 52, 369–86. Boston: Kluwer, 1998.

———. "*Die Fülle oder das Nichts?* Edith Stein and Martin Heidegger on the Question of Being." *American Catholic Philosophical Quarterly* 74, no. 2 (2000): 269–85.

———. "*Persona Politica*: Unity and Difference in Edith Stein's Political Philosophy." *International Philosophical Quarterly,* 37, no. 2 (1997): 203–15.

Cargas, Harry, ed. *The Unnecessary Problem of Edith Stein.* Lanham, MD: University Press of America, 1994.

Coleman, John A. "After Sainthood." In *Saints and Virtues,* ed. J.S. Hawley. Berkeley: University of California Press, 1987.

Collins, James. "Edith Stein and the Advance of Phenomenology." *Thought* 17 (December 1942): 685–708.

———. "Edith Stein as a Phenomenologist." In *Three Paths in Philosophy,* 85–105. Chicago: Henry Regnery, 1962. Reprinted and expanded in 1969 as *Crossroads in Philosophy.*

Conn, Joann Wolski. "Edith Stein and Authentic Feminism." Review of *Essays on Woman. Cross Currents* 28 (1988): 223–26.

de Vries, J. Review of Stein's translation of Aquinas's *De veritate. Scholastik* 7 (1932): 451 and 8 (1933): 131.

Dubois, Marcel-Jacques. "L'itineraire philosophique et spirituel d'Edith Stein." *Revue Thomiste* 73 (1973): 181–210.

Eszer, Ambrose. "Edith Stein, Jewish Catholic Martyr." In *Edith Stein Symposium: Teresian Culture,* ed. John Sullivan, 310–27. Washington, DC: ICS Publications, 1988.

Fetz, Reto Luzius, Matthias Rath, and Peter Schulz, eds. *Studien zur Philosophie von Edith Stein: Internationales Edith-Stein-Symposion Eichstätt 1991.* Phänomenologische Forschungen 26–27. Freiburg: Alber, 1993.

Fuchs-Kreimer, Nancy. "Sister Edith Stein: A Rabbi Reacts." *Lilith* 16, no. 1 (1991): 6–7, 28.

Gaboriau, Florent. *The Conversion of Edith Stein*. Trans. Ralph McInerny. South Bend, IN: St. Augustine's Press, 2002.

Giron, Arthur. *Edith Stein* [a play]. New York: Samuel French, 1991. See also *Arthur Giron's Edith Stein: A Dramaturgical Sourcebook*, ed. Donald Marinelli, 37–131. Pittsburgh, PA: Carnegie Mellon University Press, 1994.

Golay, Didier-Marie. "Edith Stein in Frankreich." *Edith Stein Jahrbuch* 8 (2002): 376–92.

Gooch, Augusta. "Metaphysical Ordination: Reflections on Edith Stein's 'Endliches und Ewiges Sein.'" PhD diss., University of Dallas, 1982.

Gosebrink, Hilda. "Meister Thomas und sein Schüler Husserl: Gedanken zu einem fiktiven Dialog zwischen Thomas von Aquin und Edmund Husserl von Edith Stein." *Erbe und Auftrag* 71, no. 6 (1995): 463–85.

Graef, Hilda. *The Scholar and the Cross: The Life and Works of Edith Stein*. Westminster, MD: Newman Press, 1955. New York: Longmans, Green, 1955.

————, ed. *Writings of Edith Stein*. Westminster, MD: Newman Press, 1956.

Graf, T. A. Review of Stein's translation of Aquinas's *De veritate*. *Divus Thomas* 47 (1933): 100.

Guilead, Reuben. *De la phénoménologie à la science de la croix: L'itinéraire d'Edith Stein*. Louvain: Nauwelaerts, 1974.

Hawley, John Stratton. Introduction to *Saints and Virtues*. Berkeley: University of California Press, 1987.

Herbstrith, Waltraud. *Edith Stein: A Biography*. New York: Harper and Row, 1985. San Francisco: Ignatius Press, 1992.

————, ed. *Never Forget: Christian and Jewish Perspectives on Edith Stein*. Washington, DC: ICS Publications, 1998.

Höfliger, Anton. *Das Universalienproblem in Edith Steins Werk "Endliches und Ewiges Sein."* Freiburg, Switzerland: Universitätsverlag, 1968.

Ingarden, Roman. "Edith Stein on Her Activity as an Assistant of Edmund Husserl." Trans. Janina Makota. *Philosophy and Phenomenological Research* 23 (1962): 155–75.

Isser, Edward R. "Theatrical Exploitation: The *Perdition* Affair and *Edith Stein*." In *Stages of Annihilation: Theatrical Representations of the Holocaust*, 134–49. London: Associated University Presses, 1997.

John Paul II. "Homily at the Beatification of Edith Stein." In *Edith Stein Symposium: Teresian Culture*, ed. John Sullivan, OCD. Washington, DC: ICS Publications, 1987.

Kavunguvalappil, Anthony. *Theology of Suffering and Cross in the Life and Works of Blessed Edith Stein*. New York: Peter Lang, 1998.

Lembeck, Karl-Heinz. "Die Phänomenologie Husserls und Edith Steins." *Theologie und Philosophie* 63 (1988): 182–202.

————. "Zwischen Wissenschaft und Glauben: Die Philosophie Edith Steins." *Zeitschrift für katholische Theologie* 112, no. 3 (1990): 271–87.

Lindblad, Ulrika. "Rereading Edith Stein. What Happened?" *Theology* 99 (July–August 1996): 269–76.

Madden, Anselm Mary. "Edith Stein and the Education of Women: Augustinian Themes." PhD diss., St. Louis University, 1962.

McAlister, Linda Lopez. "Edith Stein: Essential Differences." *Philosophy Today* 37 (Spring 1993): 70–77.

McInerny, Ralph. "Edith Stein and Thomism." In *Edith Stein Symposium: Teresian Culture*, ed. John Sullivan. Washington, DC: ICS Publications, 1988.

Mooney, Catherine M. *Philippine Duchesne: A Woman with the Poor*. New York: Paulist Press, 1990.

Müller, Andreas Uwe. "Das Steinische Werk in Deutschland." *Edith Stein Jahrbuch* 2 (1996): 375–91.

Nota, Jan N. "Edith Stein and Martin Heidegger." In *Edith Stein Symposium: Teresian Culture*, ed. John Sullivan. Washington, DC: ICS Publications, 1988.

Novak, David. "Edith Stein, Apostate Saint." *First Things*, October 1999, 15–17.

———. *The Significance of Edith Stein for the Jews* [cassettes]. Edith Stein Center Lecture series, 1999. Available from the Edith Stein Center for Study and Research, Spalding University, 851 S. Fourth St., Louisville, KY 40203.

Oben, Freda Mary. *Edith Stein: Scholar, Feminist, Saint*. Staten Island: Alba House, 1988.

———. "An Annotated Edition of Edith Stein's Papers on Woman." PhD diss., Catholic University of America, 1979.

———. *The Life and Thought of St. Edith Stein*. New York: Alba House, 2001.

Payne, Stephen. "Edith Stein: A Fragmented Life." *America* 179, no. 10 (1998): 11–14.

Pezzella, Anna Maria. "Edith Stein in Italien: Übersetzungen, Studien, Bibliographie." *Edith Stein Jahrbuch* 5 (1999): 423–37.

Posselt, Teresia Renata. *Edith Stein*. Trans. Cecily Hastings and Donald Nicholl. New York: Sheed and Ward, 1952.

Reifenrath, Bruno. *Erziehung im Licht des Ewigen: Die Pädagogik Edith Steins*. Berlin: Moritz Diesterweg, 1985.

Rodeheffer, Jane Kelley. "On Spiritual Maternity: Edith Stein, Aristotle, and the Nature of Woman." *American Catholic Philosophical Quarterly* 72 (suppl.) (1998): 285–303.

Sancho Fermín, Francisco Javier. "Das Steinische Werk in Spanien." *Edith Stein Jahrbuch* 1 (1995): 344–50.

Sawicki, Marianne. *Body, Text, and Science: The Literacy of Investigative Practices and the Phenomenology of Edith Stein*. Boston: Kluwer, 1997.

Scaperlanda, María Ruiz. *Edith Stein: St. Teresa Benedicta of the Cross*. Huntington, IN: Our Sunday Visitor Publishing, 2001.

Secretan, Philibert. "Edith Stein on the 'Order and Chain of Being.'" Trans. E. M. Swiderski. In *The Great Chain of Being and Italian Phenomenology*, Analecta Husserliana 11, 113–23. Dordrecht: D. Reidel, 1981.

———. *Erkenntnis und Aufstieg: Einführung in die Philosophie von Edith Stein*. Innsbruck: Tyrolie-Verlag, 1992.

———. "The Self and the Other in the Thought of Edith Stein." In *The Self and the Other: The Irreducible Element in Man, I*, Analecta Husserliana 6, 87–98. Dordrecht: D. Reidel, 1977.

Stein, Edith. *Der Aufbau der menschlichen Person*. Freiburg: Herder, 1994.

———. *Edith Stein: Essential Writings*. Ed. John Sullivan. Maryknoll, NY: Orbis Books, 2002.

———. *Edith Stein: Selected Writings*. Trans. Susanne Batzdorff. Springfield, IL: Templegate Publishers, 1990.

———. *Essays on Woman*. 2nd, rev. ed. Trans. Freda Mary Oben. Washington, DC: ICS Publications, 1996.

———. *Finite and Eternal Being: An Attempt at an Ascent to the Meaning of Being.* Trans. Kurt F. Reinhardt. Washington, DC: ICS Publications, 2002.

———. *Ganzheitliches Leben: Schriften zur religiösen Bildung.* Freiburg: Herder, 1990.

———. *The Hidden Life: Essays, Meditations, Spiritual Texts.* Trans. Waltraut Stein. Washington, DC: ICS Publications, 1992.

———. "Husserls Phänomenologie und die Philosophie des hl. Thomas v. Aquino: Versuch einer Gegenüberstellung." In *Husserl,* ed. H. Noack, 61–86. Darmstadt: Wissenschaftliche Buchgesellschaft, 1973. Reprint of article for Husserl's *Festschrift* in *Jahrbuch für Philosophie und phänomenologische Forschung,* supplement vol. (Halle: Max Niemeyer, 1929), 315–38.

———. *Knowledge and Faith.* Trans. Walter Redmond. Washington, DC: ICS Publications, 2000.

———. *Life in a Jewish Family: Her Unfinished Autobiographical Account.* Trans. Josephine Koeppel. Washington, DC: ICS Publications, 1986.

———. *On the Problem of Empathy.* Trans. Waltraut Stein. Washington, DC: ICS Publications, 1989.

———. *Philosophy of Psychology and the Humanities.* Ed. Marianne Sawicki. Trans. Marianne Sawicki and Mary Catharine Baseheart. Washington, DC: ICS Publications, 2000.

———. *Potenz und Akt: Studien zu einer Philosophie des Seins.* Ed. Hans Rainer Sepp. Freiburg: Herder, 1998.

———. *The Science of the Cross.* Trans. Hilda Graef. Chicago: Henry Regnery, 1960.

———. *The Science of the Cross.* Trans. Josephine Koeppel. Washington, DC: ICS Publications, 2002.

———. *Self-Portrait in Letters.* Trans. Josephine Koeppel. Washington, DC: ICS Publications, 1993.

———. *Was ist der Mensch? Eine theologische Anthropologie.* Freiburg: Herder, 1994.

———. "Ways to Know God: The 'Symbolic Theology' of Dionysius the Areopagite and Its Objective Presuppositions." Trans. Rudolf Allers. *The Thomist* 9, no. 3 (1946): 379–420.

Sullivan, John. "Englishsprachige Bibliographie von und über Edith Stein." *Edith Stein Jahrbuch* 6 (2000): 437–46.

———, ed. *Holiness Befits Your House: Canonization of Edith Stein—A Documentation.* Washington, DC: ICS Publications, 1999.

Suzawa, Kaori. "Edith Stein in Japan." *Edith Stein Jahrbuch* 7 (2001): 338–42.

Verbillion, June M. "A Critical Analysis of the Educational Theories of Edith Stein." PhD diss., Loyola University, 1960.

Woodward, Kenneth. *Making Saints: How the Catholic Church Determines Who Becomes a Saint.* New York: Simon and Schuster, 1990. See also "Making Saints," *Newsweek,* November 12, 1990, 80–84.

Chronology of Key Dates in the Life of Edith Stein

1891, October 12 (Yom Kippur)
Born in Breslau, Germany (now Wroclaw, Poland)

1893
Father, Siegfried Stein, dies; mother, Auguste née Courant, takes over family lumber firm

1897
Enters Victoria School (Breslau)

1911
Completes *Abitur* (comprehensive final examination required for university admission) with distinction

1911–1913
Studies at the University of Breslau: German literature, European history, psychology, and philosophy

1913, April 17
Arrives in Göttingen

1913–1915
Studies philosophy at the University of Göttingen with Edmund Husserl, the founder of phenomenology; also studies psychology, history, German literature

1915
Completes state examination with highest honors in philosophy, European history, German literature

1915, April 7
Serves as volunteer nurse with German Red Cross at the Military Hospital for Contagious Diseases in Mährisch-Weisskirchen (eastern Czechoslovakia), later awarded Medal of Bravery

1915, November–December
Substitute teacher in Latin, history, and geography in Breslau school system

1916, July
Moves to University of Freiburg to continue her doctoral work with Husserl

1916–1918
Works as teaching assistant to Husserl, and as privatdocent introduces students to the basic elements of phenomenology

1917
Completes doctoral dissertation, *On the Problem of Empathy* (published in 1917), and earns highest honors in doctoral exam at University of Freiburg

1916–1918
Serves as research assistant and editor for Edmund Husserl

1918–1933
Unable to secure *Habilitation* and a university lectureship

1921–1922
Completes essay *On the State* (published in the *Yearbook for Philosophy and Phenomenological Research* in 1925). Publication of her *Contributions to the Philosophical Grounding of Psychology and the Humanities* in the *Yearbook for Philosophy and Phenomenological Research*

1917–1921
Growing interest in religious questions, turns toward Christianity

1921, Summer
Reads autobiography of St. Teresa of Avila and decides to convert to Catholicism

1922, January 1
Baptism, first Holy Communion

1923–1932
Teaches in Speyer at St. Magdalene's (Dominican high school for girls and teacher preparation institute); completes translations and essays and lectures at various domestic and foreign educational congresses and forums

1932–1933
Lecturer at the German Institute for Scientific Pedagogy in Münster

1933, April
Loses position by government decree (Nazi Aryan Laws)

1933, April
Returns to Breslau and begins her autobiography, *Life in a Jewish Family.*

1933, October 14
Enters Carmel in Cologne

1934, April 15
Receives religious habit and adopts name Teresa Benedicta a Cruce

1935, April 21
First vows

1938, April 21
Perpetual vows

1934–1939
Authors *Finite and Eternal Being* and *Science of the Cross* and diverse works on theology, spiritual practice, and saints' lives, as well as poetry and plays

1938
Emigrates to Carmel in Echt/Holland, continues to write

1942, August 2
Gestapo arrest and transportation to Amersfoort; subsequently interned at Camp Westerbork

1942, August 9
Arrives in Auschwitz, gassed in Birkenau

1987, May 1
Beatified by Pope John Paul II in Cologne

1998, October 11
Canonized by Pope John Paul II at St. Peter's in Rome

Contributors

Angela Ales Bello, Professor of History of Contemporary Philosophy at Lateran University in Rome and former Dean of the Faculty of Philosophy, is General Secretary of the Italian Center of Phenomenological Researches. Author of many studies on Stein and female philosophers of her era, she also serves as editor of the Italian translation of Edith Stein's works.

Beate Beckmann-Zöller completed her dissertation thesis on "Phenomenology of the Religious Experience: Edith Stein and Adolf Reinach's Reflections in Philosophy of Religion" (Würzburg University, 2003). In addition to publishing various essays on Stein, Beckmann-Zöller assists Hanna-Barbara Gerl-Falkovitz in editing critical editions of the complete works of Stein, the *Edith Stein Gesamtausgabe* (*ESGA*; Freiburg, 2000–) and recently prepared and edited the critical edition of Stein's works on pedagogy.

Joyce Avrech Berkman, editor of this volume, is Professor of History at the University of Massachusetts, Amherst, where she teaches U.S. and European women's history and co-directs the Valley Women's History Collaborative. Among her many publications is *The Healing Imagination of Olive Schreiner: Beyond South African Colonialism.* Currently, she is writing a book-length comparative biography and critical study of the lives and work of Edith Stein, Gertrude Stein, and Vera Brittain.

Sarah Borden, Assistant Professor of Philosophy at Wheaton College, Illinois, holds her Ph.D. from Fordham University. Her study of the philosophy of Edith Stein appeared in 2003 as a volume in the Fordham series "Outstanding Christian Thinkers." Borden has also published and continues to update an extensive list of secondary works on Stein at Baltimore Carmel's Web site: www.baltimorecarmel.com.

Rachel Feldhay Brenner, Professor of Modern Hebrew Literature in the Department of Hebrew and Semitic Studies at the University of Wisconsin-Madison, has written extensively on literary responses to the Holocaust. She is author of *Assimilation and Assertion: The Response to the Holocaust in Mordecai Richler's Writing, A. M. Klein: The Father of Canadian Jewish Literature,* and *Writing as Resistance: Four Women Confronting the Holocaust: Edith Stein, Simone Weil, Anne Frank, and Etty Hillesum.* Her most recent book is *Inextricably Bonded: Israeli Arab and Jewish Writers Re-Visioning Culture.*

Antonio Calcagno completed his dissertation on the relationship between time and politics in the philosophies of Jacques Derrida, Sylvain Lazarus, and Alain Badiou at the University of Guelph, where he holds a Social Sciences and Humanities Research Council Postdoctoral Fellowship and teaches courses in the Philosophy Department. His current research on Edith Stein, Gerda Walther, and Hedwig Conrad-Martius focuses particularly on their social and political thought. Calcagno is currently guest editor for the *American Catholic Philosophical Quarterly*'s special issue on Edith Stein.

Lisa M. Dolling, currently Associate Professor of Philosophy and Coordinator of the Department of Philosophy at Stevens Institute of Technology, specializes in hermeneutics and philosophy of science. Dolling was previously Associate Professor of Philosophy at St. John's University, where she directed the Science and Religion Project, the Women's Studies Minor, and the Honors Program. Among her many publications is the edited volume *Tests of Time: Readings in the Development of Physical Theory*. Dolling is at work on a reader of twentieth-century women philosophers.

Hanna-Barbara Gerl-Falkovitz is Chair of Philosophy of Religion and Comparative Religious Studies at the Technical University of Dresden. An editorial consultant for a number of the critical editions of Stein's works, *Edith Stein Gesamtausgabe* (*ESGA*; Freiburg, 2000–). Gerl-Falkovitz has published widely, including monographs on Ida Friederike Görres (1901–71), Romano Guardini (1885–1968), and Christian philosophy of religion.

Dana K. Greene, Dean of Faculty and CEO of Oxford College, Emory University, has authored two biographies, published by Notre Dame University Press: *Evelyn Underhill: Artist of the Infinite Life* and *The Living of Maisie Ward*.

Patricia Hampl, recipient of many honors including a MacArthur, two NEA, and a Guggenheim Fellowships, is Regents' Professor of English at the University of Minnesota. Her books include, most recently, *I Could Tell You Stories* and the memoirs *A Romantic Education* and *Virgin Time*, as well as other works of prose and poetry.

Linda Lopez McAlister, Professor Emerita of Philosophy and Women's Studies at the University of South Florida, organized the first meeting of German and American women philosophers in 1974, out of which emerged the International Association of Women Philosophers. From 1990 to 1998, she was editor of *Hypatia: A Journal of the History of Feminist Philosophy*. She has lectured and published widely on Edith Stein, including the biographical essay that appears in *A History of Women Philosophers IV*, edited by Mary Ellen Waithe. Lopez McAlister's keynote speech heralded the opening of the Edith Stein Study Center at Spalding University.

Scott Spector, Associate Professor in the Departments of History and Germanic Languages and Literatures at the University of Michigan, Ann Arbor, is author of *Prague Territories, National Conflict and Cultural Innovation in Franz Kafka's Fin de Siècle*. He is a cultural historian specializing in modern central Europe, German-Jewish writers, and the relationships among ideology, identity, and cultural production. His current work focuses on sexuality and gender.

John Sullivan, OCD, is publisher for ICS publications in Washington, D.C., and the main force behind the Edith Stein's collected works translated into English. Sullivan is recipient of the Edith Stein Guild's 1995 Edith Stein Award for his many published essays on Stein in numerous countries and for his continued signal contribution to Stein studies, including the relatively recently published *Edith Stein: Essential Texts,* appearing in the series "Modern Spiritual Masters."

Angelika von Renteln, Special Projects Director of the Cultural Affairs Office of Dortmund, Germany, leads intercultural dialogues. She also teaches Zen meditation and works for a hospice service.

Theresa Wobbe, Professor of Political Sciences at the University of Erfurt, Germany, has published extensively on gender and the social sciences in twentieth-century Germany, including essays on theorists of sociology, on women and sociology, and on Edith Stein and her religious development.

TRANSLATORS

Antonio Calcagno (see above listing)

Stephen Lake, Assistant Professor of Philosophy at Trinity Christian College

Jonathan Knutzen, Graduate Student in Theological Studies Program at Yale University Divinity School

Index

In the index, the abbreviation "ES" refers to Edith Stein. Also, individual works by Stein and Husserl are indexed under their English language titles unless no translation appears in the text.

National Socialism, 39, 60, 96–97, 125, 170,
172, 212–13
Natorp, Paul, 273
"Nature, Freedom and Grace" (Stein), 304
nature/natural world, 31, 253–58, 272,
304–5, 307–8
neo-Kantianism, 25, 160, 273
Newman, John Henry, 7–8, 37, 49–50, 129,
149–63, 177
Neyer, Maria Amata, 4–5, 16
Nietzsche, Friedrich, 160
Noddings, Nel, 9, 207, 218, 227, 230, 235–36
Nota, Jan, 63
Novak, David, 181
Nussbaum, Martha, 9, 227, 236–37

*On the Phenomenology of the Consciousness
of Internal Time* (Husserl), 31–32, 41,
243, 248
On the Problem of Empathy (Stein), 30–31,
84, 95, 98, 102–3, 114, 218, 245, 247, 261,
275, 293–94, 324
On the State (Stein), 34, 248, 251, 326
Orth, Ernst-Wolfgang, 127

Paul, Saint, 214–16
Payne, Steven, 55
personhood, 32–33, 76, 254; body and, 26,
31, 102, 188, 205–6, 217, 255–56, 258–62,
275–76, 288–89; character and, 230–31,
233, 260–62, 294; compassion and, 6, 62,
84–90; consciousness and, 25, 41, 142,
253–55, 258, 276–78, 280; ego and, 253–59,
273, 277; empathy and, 27, 29–31, 61–62,
84, 95, 98–103, 114, 218–20, 222, 255,
259, 294; humor and, 6; individuality/
individualization and, 10, 33, 123–24, 221,
228, 235, 260, 283–96; life/living and, 10,
275–80; psyche and, 32, 255, 276–78; self
and, 6, 41, 60, 95, 102, 114, 218; soul and,
33, 142, 206, 217, 231–32, 258–59, 261–62,
275–76, 288–89, 293, 310–11
Pfänder, Alexander, 253
phenomenology, 25–27, 159, 161, 249–50,
264; impact on ES of, 25, 52–53, 179,
271–72; review of literature on,
324–26
*Phenomenology of Inner Time-
Consciousness, The* (Husserl).
*See On the Phenomenology of the
Consciousness of Internal Time*

Philosophical/Phenomenology Society
(Göttingen), 24–27, 35, 177, 184, 253
Philosophy as Rigorous Science (Husserl), 161
*Philosophy of Psychology and the
Humanities* (Stein). *See Contributions
to the Philosophical Grounding of
Psychology and the Humanities*
Pius XI, Pope, 39, 69, 160, 184, 238n.28
Plato, 274
Plotinus, 9, 231
Potency and Act (Stein), 38, 130, 329
"Problems of Women's Education, The"
(Stein), 205–6, 228
Przywara, Erich, 7, 37, 46n.73, 149–62,
177, 302
psyche, 32, 255, 276–78
psychologism, 160–61, 260

Rahden, Till van, 195n.18
Rathenau, Walter, 190
Rauch, Theodor, 130
Reinach, Adolf, 24, 27–29, 60, 127, 135,
178, 184, 245; ES's conversion and,
7, 35–36, 137–39
Reinach, Anna, 35–36, 52, 137, 303
Reinach, Pauline, 137
Renteln, Angelika von, 7, 134–48
Rich, Adrienne, 40
Rilke, Rainer Maria, 156–57
Riviere, Joan, 104
Rosenzweig, Franz, 189–90
Ruddick, Sara, 207, 219–20
Rugg, Linda Haverty, 107

Saiving, Valerie, 220–21
Sawicki, Marianne, 263
Scheler, Max, 26–27, 117n.19, 127, 157–58,
177, 184, 245–46, 253, 261, 284, 302
Schopenhauer, Arthur, 28, 59, 160
Schwind, Joseph, 150, 155
Science of the Cross, The (Stein), 2, 4, 42, 72,
130, 177, 179, 330–31
self, 6, 41, 60, 95, 102, 114, 218
self-development, 230–32, 289, 295
self-knowledge, 221–22, 230, 233
Self-Portrait in Letters (Stein), 111
"Sentient Causality" (Stein), 32, 138–40, 142
sexual equality. *See* women, equality of
Shakespeare, William, 77, 176
Simmel, Georg, 123–24
Simon, Paul, 154